AND
RACHEL
STOLE
THE
IDOLS

AND
RACHEL
STOLE
THE
IDOLS

The Emergence of
Modern Hebrew Women's Writing

WENDY   I.   ZIERLER

 WAYNE STATE UNIVERSITY PRESS
DETROIT

Library of Congress Cataloging-in-Publication Data

Zierler, Wendy.
    And Rachel stole the idols : the emergence of modern Hebrew women's
writing / Wendy Zierler.
        p. cm.
        Includes bibliographical references and index.
        ISBN 0-8143-3147-5 (cloth)
        1. Hebrew poetry, modern—Women authors—History and criticism.
2. Hebrew poetry, Modern—20th century—History and criticism. 3. Women
and literature—History. 4. Women in literature. 5. Hebrew literature—
Translations into English. I. Title.
        PJ5024.Z54 2004
        892.4'099287'0904—dc22
2004000530

∞ The paper used in this publication meets the minimum requirements
of the American National Standard for Information Sciences—
Permanence of Paper for Printed Library Materials, ANSI Z39.48–1984.

CONTENTS

CONTENTS

ACKNOWLEDGMENTS

The Rabbis instruct each of us to designate a teacher and acquire a friend. Over the course of writing this book, I have been privileged to work with teachers and colleagues all over the world who have proven exceptional role models and friends. At Princeton University, where this book was initially conceived as a doctoral dissertation on immigrant Jewish women writers in Israel and the U.S., I benefited from the guidance and knowledge of many exceptional mentors. Since my first days as a Princeton graduate student, Nitza Ben-Dov embraced me as a student, a peer, and a friend. Maria DiBattista provided sensitive and incisive comments on dissertation drafts as well as other equally important life matters. Ilana Pardes, whose polished and succinct interpretive prose has become my model for feminist critical excellence, enthusiastically supported this project and has been a great source of help along the way. Robert Alter went well beyond the call of professorial study in agreeing to serve as one of my dissertation readers. After I defended the dissertation, Professor Alter recommended that I focus my book exclusively on Hebrew women writers, and for his sage advice and substantive suggestions, I remain extremely grateful. At the University of Hong Kong, Staci Ford and Gordon Slethaug were unflagging sources of wisdom, insight, and sanity. Back in New York, the intellectual and personal generosity of my new colleagues at Hebrew Union College-Jewish Institute of Religion made it possible for me to complete this project. From Israel to Hong Kong to New York, my longtime *hevrutah,* Marcie Lenk, has accompanied me on this personal and intellectual journey. The discussion in chapter 3 of this book owes a great deal to that ongoing friendship and conversation. Rochelle Rubinstein illustrated my first attempt at a book, written when I was ten years old; it is very moving indeed to see her magnificent woodcut on the cover of this volume.

I am grateful to Yaffa Berlovitz, Naomi Caruso, Tova Cohen, Sidra Ezrahi, Yael Feldman, Deborah Greniman, Jody Hirsch, Joel Hoffman, Ruth Kartun-Blum, Alan Mintz, Dan Miron, Morris Rosenthal, David

Roskies, Raymond Scheindlin, and Chava Weissler for their assistance and good ideas. For their comments on portions of this manuscript, thanks go out to Robert Alter, William Cutter, Peter Cole, Anne Golomb Hoffman, Chana Kronfeld, and Stanley Nash, as well as to several anonymous reviewers from *Nashim, Prooftexts,* and Wayne State University Press. Carole B. Balin took precious time from her maternity leave to read the entire manuscript and make many valuable comments and suggestions; I feel blessed to have such a generous and engaged colleague. Thanks also are due to Larry Hoffman for his guidance and moral support as this book went out in search of a publisher. I am similarly grateful to President David Ellenson, Provost Norman Cohen, and Dean Aaron Panken for welcoming me so warmly into the HUC-JIR community. To Sharon Koren and Leah Silberstein, I cannot thank you enough for your intellectual and emotional support during my first years back in New York. Lastly, to the rabbinical students in my HUC-JIR seminar on the Bible and Modern Hebrew Women writers, Stephanie Alexander, Annie Belford, Karen Deitsch, Rachel Goldenberg, Rebecca Gutterman, Shoshana Nyer, Jennifer Solomon, and Taron Tachman: many thanks for your fantastic interpretations and for showing me how great literature can always yield new insights.

Nehama Edinger, John Franken, Adina Frydman, Debra Griboff, Fern Siegel, and Sara Yellen provided invaluable research and editing assistance. Without their help, I would have been unable to bring this project to its long awaited conclusion. Phil Miller at HUC-JIR Klau Library in New York and Eleanor Yadin of the New York Public Library, Dorot Division, helped me locate much needed research materials. Moshe Shalvi, publisher of *Jewish Women: A Comprehensive Historical Encyclopedia* provided additional help in tracking down illustrations and other information. Lina Barness, Dmitry Gutin, and Ruth Friedman supplied much appreciated technical assistance. Belen M. Lungcay enabled me to go to work each day knowing that my children were well taken care of. Special thanks go out to my editors at Wayne State University Press for their support of this project and their expertise: Arthur B. Evans, Adela Garcia, Jane Hoehner, Kathy Wildfong, and Sandra Williamson.

For financial assistance, I am indebted to Princeton University, the United States Israel Foundation, the Social Sciences and Humanities Research Council of Canada, the Association of Princeton Graduate Alumni, the Memorial Foundation for Jewish Culture, the Mrs. Giles Whiting Foundation, the National Foundation for Jewish Culture, the

Hong Kong University Committee on Research and Conference Grants, and the HUC-JIR Faculty Research fund. The Lucius N. Littauer Foundation provided me with a publication grant, for which I am also very grateful.

My four parents, Marion and David Zierler and Dvora and Ephraim Haimson, have been an endless source of support and encouragement, even as I cluttered their houses with books on supposed "vacation" visits from Hong Kong. The superhuman patience, wisdom, endless humor, and love of my husband, Daniel Feit has sustained me through the ten-year gestation of this book. Our beautiful children, Shara, Yona, and Amichai—who came into the world alongside these chapters—have shown a loving admiration for my work as a "doctor of books." I do not measure up to the task of thanking them, as well as the rest of my family, for what they have given me. In the words of the poet Leah Goldberg, "אֵיכָה אֶשָּׂא וְלֹא אֶשָּׁבֹר / שִׂמְחָה כָּזֹאת בְּרָכָה כָּזֹאת?" "How can I bear and not break under / such happiness, such blessing?"

W. Z.
Sivan, 5763
June 2003

ACKNOWLEDGMENTS

Ehud Ben Ezer for permission to translate poems and prose extracts and to publish photos of Esther Raab.

Ibis Editions for permission to reprint Harold Schimmel's translation of Esther Raab's "La'av."

Zipor Carmi for permission to reprint and translate poems by Anda Pinkerfeld-Amir.

The Institute for the Translation of Hebrew Literature for permission to reprint quotations from the stories "What Has Been" and "Trifles" from *The Thorny Path and Other Stories* by Devorah Baron, English translation by Joseph Schachter, © 1969, The Institute for the Translation of Hebrew Literature.

The Jewish Publication Society for permission to quote from *The Torah* © 1962, *The Prophets* © 1978, *The Writings* © 1982.

JTS Press and Ilana Pardes for permission to reprint Ilana Pardes's partial translation of Yokheved Bat-Miriam's "Kifsukim hayamim" and to print a slightly revised version of her translation of "Miriam," both originally published in her article "The Poetic Strength of a Matronym," in *Gender and Text in Modern Hebrew and Yiddish Literature*, ed. Naomi B. Sokoloff, Anne Lapidus Lerner, and Anita Norich, © 1992, The Jewish Theological Seminary of America.

Photos of Anda Pinkerfeld-Amir, Devorah Baron, Yokheved Bat-Miriam, Rachel Bluwstein, Shulamit Kalugai, Nehama Puhachevsky, and Zelda are reprinted courtesy of Machon Genazim (Israel Writers' Archives, Tel Aviv). Leah Goldberg's photo comes courtesy of Hebrew University, Photo Gruber, 1958.

Professor Mariassa Bat-Miriam Katzenelson for permission to reprint and translate poems by Yokheved Bat-Miriam.

The Montreal Jewish Public Library for permission to publish a photo of Hava Shapiro.

Morris Rosenthal, for permission to quote from his translation of Sarah Foner's *Love of the Righteous, The Treachery of Traitors,* and "A Girl Can't Become a Gaon?" in *A Woman's Voice,* © 2001 Morris Rosenthal.

Schocken Books, a division of Random House Inc., for permission to quote from *Twenty-One Stories by S. Y. Agnon,* edited by Nahum Glatzer, © 1970 by Schocken Books, a division of Random House, Inc.

Sifriyat Po'alim/Hakibbutz Hameuchad for permission to reprint and translate Leah Goldberg's "Ya'akov veRachel" and portions of "Ahavatah shel Teresa de Meun," from Leah Goldberg *Shirim,* © 1973, Sifriyat Po'alim.

Sifriyat Po'alim/Hakibbutz Hameuchad for permission to reprint and translate Zelda's "Hedra shel ima hu'ar, from *Shirei Zelda,* © Hakibbutz Hameuchad, 1985.

University of California Press for permission to quote passages from "Family," in Devorah Baron, *"The First Day" and Other Stories,* translated by Chana Kronfeld and Naomi Seidman, © 2001, The Regents of the University of California.

Sue Ann Wasserman for permission to incorporate sections of her translation of Anda Pinkerfeld-Amir's "Havah" in my own translation.

Yavneh Publishers for permission to reprint poems by Shulamit Kalugai, *Nashim* © 1942, Yavneh Publishers.

"La'av" (To the father) by Esther Raab, translated by Harold Schimmel, © Translation Institute, and appeared in *Thistles: Selected Poems of Esther Raab,* Jerusalem: Ibis Editions, 2003.

A NOTE ON TRANSLATION
AND TRANSLITERATION

English translations of Hebrew poetry and prose passages cited in this work are by me unless otherwise noted in endnotes. I was able to preserve the rhyme scheme of some poems, but in most cases rhyme was sacrificed for the sake of accuracy.

Translations from the Bible are from *The Torah, The Prophets,* and *The Writings,* published by the Jewish Publication Society (1962, 1978, and 1982, respectively), unless otherwise noted.

The transliteration of Hebrew is based on the transliteration style for Hebrew of the *Encyclopedia Judaica* with some minor modifications. Proper names and other well-known terms are spelled according to common English usage.

INTRODUCTION

וְלָבָן הָלַךְ לִגְזֹז אֶת צֹאנוֹ וַתִּגְנֹב רָחֵל אֶת הַתְּרָפִים אֲשֶׁר לְאָבִיהָ:

And Laban had gone off to shear his sheep, and Rachel stole the
idols that belonged to her father.

Genesis 31:19

Stealing the Idols of Hebrew Literary Culture

This book is a study of the emergence of modern Hebrew women's writing. It tells the story of three generations of women poets and prose writers who claimed a voice in a Hebrew literary culture in which women's voices were hitherto conspicuously absent. Like these poets and writers who obsessed over the narratives of biblical women, I begin theirs with a rereading of a biblical episode—an odd, subversive, countertraditional tale about a matriarch who steals a patriarchal, religious legacy.

In Genesis 31, Jacob the Patriarch, having detected a souring in his relationship with Laban (his father-in-law), calls his wives Rachel and Leah "to the field to his flock" (Gen. 31:4) and expresses a desire to return to the land of his "fathers." *Vata'an Rachel veLeah*: Rachel and Leah respond uncharacteristically—in one voice, as indicated by the use of the singular verb form, *vata'an*—expressing a shared anger against their father for disinheriting them and an immediate willingness to follow Jacob to Canaan. Jacob then rises up, places his wives and sons on camels, carries off his cattle and other property, and readies to depart for Canaan.

At first, Jacob is the central actor in this narrative. Everything is said and done in relation to him, and stated in masculine possessive terms: Jacob and *his* wives gather around *his* flock to discuss *his* plans to depart Padan Aram; Jacob plans and directs the transport of all of *his* property, including *his* wives and children. Their destination is *his* birthplace, the land of *his* fathers (Gen. 31:3).

1

In 31:19, however, Rachel the matriarch suddenly becomes an active player, seizing the opportunity afforded by Laban's going off to shear *his* sheep (again a masculine possessive form), to steal her father's *teraphim* (household gods, insignias). Up to this point, Rachel and Leah have followed a course initiated by Jacob and his concerns. Here, however, Rachel initiates and plots her own destiny. As the writer Allegra Goodman puts it, Rachel becomes "the author of a separate script."[1] In the next verse Jacob begins to follow Rachel's lead, with Rachel stealing the *teraphim* (verse 19) and Jacob echoing Rachel's original theft (verse 20) in "stealing the heart/mind of Laban the Aramean" *(vayignov et lev Lavan ha'arami)* and not telling him about his planned departure.[2]

Jacob reassumes center stage in the narrative when Laban overtakes him on his journey and the two men begin to air their respective grievances. But from the moment Rachel steals the *teraphim,* Jacob ceases to control the action or know all the facts. In the same way that Jacob keeps Laban in the dark about his plan to escape, Rachel keeps Jacob in the dark about her theft of the *teraphim.* In this condition of ignorance, Jacob makes his rash, Jephthah-like pronouncement: "But anyone with whom you find your gods shall not remain alive" (31:32).

Several midrashic sources contend that Jacob's sentence of death for the theft of Laban's *teraphim* is borne out in Rachel's tragic demise after giving birth to Benjamin.[3] According to a plain reading of Genesis 31, however, Rachel emerges from the episode victorious and unscathed. After all, Jacob's curse is conditioned upon Laban actually finding the *teraphim* in the possession of someone in Jacob's camp, something that Laban never accomplishes. Laban conducts a thorough search of Jacob's camp: first Jacob's tent, then Leah's, the two maidservants', and then Rachel's, *velo matsa*—and he found nothing, a verb construction repeated three times, in verses 33, 34, and 35, underscoring the increasing futility of Laban's quest. What does Rachel do to protect herself from Laban's campaign of search and seizure? She takes the *teraphim,* places them in a camel's saddle (recalling Jacob's placement of his wives and sons on camels in Genesis 31:17) and conceals them by sitting on the saddle. As her father searches her tent, she shrewdly apologizes to him for not obeying usual custom and rising "before him." "The way of women is upon me" (31:35), Rachel claims, cunningly manipulating the [male] menstruation taboo to her advantage.[4]

What are these *teraphim* that Rachel risks so much to steal? What did they stand for in Rachel's time, and how can they be used as a controlling metaphor for a study of the emergence of modern Hebrew women's writing?

The exact meaning of the word *teraphim* is disputed. According to the classic commentary of Rashi (Rabbi Solomon bar Isaac of Troyes, 1040–1105), the *teraphim* were household idols that Rachel stole from her father for pious, monotheistic reasons—"in order to distance him from the practice of idol worship."[5] This interpretation clearly stems from rabbinic discomfort with the idea of Rachel the matriarch as idol worshiper, carrying her father's household gods with her for protection or worship.[6] But if Rachel was so angry with her father that she was willing to leave his house forever without so much as a goodbye, would she really have cared about his spiritual fate?

On the basis of other instances in the Bible where the word appears, other traditional exegetes—including the Rashbam (Rabbi Samuel Ben Meir, 1085–1174)—identify the *teraphim* with the practice of divination. Thus, Rachel stole the *teraphim*, which were used by ancient magicians as a means of telling the future, in order to prevent them from speaking the truth to Laban about Jacob's planned escape.[7] If that was the case, however, Rachel should have simply broken the *teraphim* or rendered them technically ineffective. Why did she go to the trouble of stealing them, hiding them in a saddle, and tricking her father?

Citing findings from the Nuzi documents, several contemporary biblical scholars have argued that possession of the "household gods" was related to issues of clan leadership or inheritance.[8] According to Mieke Bal, the *teraphim* were symbolic tokens that indicated Rachel's right to take her children and possessions away from her father and hand them over to her husband. If Laban tricked Jacob into staying in his household for Rachel's sake, Bal argues, "Rachel completes Jacob's emancipation by adding to the material possessions he took over from her father's estate the symbolic tokens of this transition."[9] Yet Rachel's decision not to inform Jacob of her theft of the *teraphim* suggests she acts for her own sake, not his.[10]

Along these lines, feminist biblical scholar J. E. Lapsley traces the various biblical uses of the expression *lakum lifnei* (to rise before) and discovers a strong connotation of confrontation. Lapsley thus argues that Rachel steals the *teraphim* because her status as a woman in a patriarchal household prevents her from "rising before" her father with her own grievances about her rightful inheritance. "Therefore, she goes about getting justice from her father through devious and extra-legal means."[11]

3

According to Lapsley, in telling her father that she cannot "rise before" him because the "way of women is upon [her]," Rachel is "speaking two languages simultaneously": "one that is the male-dominated language that sees the 'way of women' as a sexually 'other way' of being, and the second is her own language, created from her female perspective, which understands the way of women as an unsanctioned, subversive way of attaining justice. Her subversive action in stealing the *teraphim* is matched by her equally subversive undermining of male definitions of women and her creation of new meanings out of male-generated language."[12] In Lapsley's view, Rachel steals not only the *teraphim*—the icons or symbols of patriarchal authority—but also the *language* this patriarchy has used to define her as woman and limit her access to culture and law.

"A major theme in feminist theory on both sides of the Atlantic," writes poet and feminist critic Alicia Ostriker,

> has been the demand that women writers be, in Claudine Herrmann's phrase, *voleuses de langue,* thieves of language, female Prometheuses. Though the language we speak and write has been an encoding of male privilege, what Adrienne Rich calls an "oppressor's language" inadequate to describe or express women's experience, a "Law of the Father" which transforms the daughter to "the invisible woman in the asylum corridor" or "the silent woman" without access to authoritative expression, we must also have it in our power to "seize speech" and make it say what we mean. More: there is a desire to make female speech prevail, to penetrate male discourse, to cause the ear of man to listen.[13]

I quote Ostriker here in order to advance the view of Rachel as a kind of biblical *voleuses de langue,* an archetypal feminist writer, who dares to steal across the borders of masculine culture, seize control of her cultural inheritance, and make it her own. With this idea in mind, throughout this book I follow the literary trail of several "daughters of Rachel"—Hebrew women writers who crossed traditional gender borders and entered into the predominantly masculine realm of Hebrew literature. Unlike other recent English and Hebrew-language anthologies or studies of Hebrew women's writing that focus either on poetry or prose, or on one narrowly defined period, this book looks analytically and comparatively at a range of works by the first three generations of Hebrew women writers and poets and attempts to account for the thematic and stylistic distinctiveness of their work in terms of the overarching image of stealing (into) masculine literary language and tradition.

The Emergence of Feminist Hebrew Literary Studies

This work is the outgrowth of my twin sense of amazement, first with the story of the rejuvenation of modern Hebrew as a literary and spoken language, and second with the story of women's participation in it. If, as Benjamin Harshav has written, the "unprecedented revival of the ancient Hebrew language and the creation of a new society on its base was perceived as a miraculous event,"[14] the entry of women writers into the Hebrew literary tradition after centuries of almost complete literary silence is similarly wondrous. As a child in Toronto, studying Hebrew from Israeli educators at a Jewish day school, I was frequently compelled into the literary awkwardness of writing from right to left, of expressing my deepest, most poetic feelings in an ancient language I was just learning to conjugate and separate into its grammatically feminine and masculine components. I loved learning Hebrew. I loved digging into the archaeology of it all: uncovering the allusions in modern Hebrew literary texts to passages I knew from the Bible and the *Siddur,* words I could sing from synagogue worship and the Shabbat table. But reading is one thing, writing another. It was often with a great sense of relief when morning veered into afternoon. I tucked my Hebrew notebooks back into my desk and gave literary vent to more cogent English thoughts. What, then, of those early Hebrew women writers, whose first languages were Russian, Yiddish, German, Polish, and/or French, who committed themselves to a lifetime of writing in Hebrew—in some cases, their third or fourth language? Few of them enjoyed the benefits of a systematic Jewish day school education, let alone the rigorous exposure to Hebrew and Aramaic literary texts that was part and parcel of the male *heder* or yeshiva system of education.[15] How can one begin to gauge the immensity of their achievement?

To be sure, a number of the Hebrew women writers examined in this book were granted exceptional educational opportunities that enabled them to enter into the realm of Hebrew letters. Rachel Luzzatto Morpurgo (1790–1871), a descendant of the famed Luzzatto family of Trieste, grew up in an environment steeped in Hebrew poetry and Jewish scholarship. Born into a family of Hebrew printers, Hava Shapiro (1878–1943) was educated in classical Hebrew as a teenager.[16] From age ten, Nehamah Feinstein Puhachevsky (1869–1934) received home tutoring in Hebrew language and culture.[17] The daughter of a rabbi, Devorah Baron studied sacred Hebrew texts from the women's section of her father's *beit midrash*. Yokheved Bat-Miriam's father gave her a volume of the poems of Bialik in reward for her study of Hebrew.[18] Many of these writers were encouraged in their Hebrew literary endeavors by male literary mentors or peers. At the same time, they remained highly aware of the various issues attending their female literary "firstness." What does it mean to enter so belatedly into a longstanding Hebrew literary tradition, one in which women were frequently spoken about but hardly ever spoke in their own voices?

This question takes on greater meaning in comparison to the history of Anglo-American literature by women. Virginia Woolf, perhaps the mother of contemporary feminist literary criticism and a contemporary of some of the Hebrew women writers treated in this study,[19] wrote her classic essay *A Room of One's Own* in the 1920s long after poets Anne Bradstreet (1612–1672), Margaret Cavendish (1623–1674), Aphra Behn (1640–1689), Anne Finch (1661–1720), pioneering prose writers Anne Radcliffe (1764–1823), Mary Wollstonecraft (1759–1797), Mary Shelley (1797–1851), Jane Austen (1775–1817), and later nineteenth-century luminaries such as the Brontë sisters, George Eliot, and Emily Dickinson. This list of literary predecessors notwithstanding, Woolf fretted over the absence of great women writers in the English literary tradition, what she refers to as "the perennial puzzle why no woman wrote a word of that extraordinary literature when every other man, it seemed, was capable of song and sonnet."[20] In actuality, by Woolf's time quite a few women had written several extraordinary works in English. Recast as an early twentieth-century Hebrew woman writer's lament over the absence of literary precursors, however, Woolf's comments seem particularly apt. What were the effects of the modern Hebrew woman writer's acute lack of precursors? Feminist critics Sandra Gilbert and Susan Gubar famously argued that the traditional association in Judaeo-Christian culture of authorship with masculinity afflicted nineteenth-century Anglo-American writers with an "'anxiety of authorship'—a radical fear" of being unable to create.[21] Accordingly, these writers developed various literary swerves or strategies of legitimization, as well as a poetics of duplicity that allowed them to create "submerged meanings, meanings hidden within or behind the more accessible public content of their works, so that their literature could be read and appreciated even when its vital concern with female dispossession and disease was ignored."[22] What about the earliest modern Hebrew women writers and their "anxieties of authorship"? What special strategies and techniques did they adopt to steal (into) the literary language of their forefathers and/or conjure up a literary tradition of their own?

When I first began to consider these issues, an element of the feminist critical community in the United States and elsewhere was already rejecting woman-writer-centered approaches as naïve and "totalizing." This was the beginning of the postmodernist or "postfeminist" phase, when scholars questioned the universality of women's experience under patriarchy and shifted focus away from women's history and women's writing toward more theoretical questions about the construction of gender and the subject.[23] Whereas practitioners of what Elaine Showalter termed "gynocritics" believed that women might be constituted as a distinct literary group and that there was a "difference to women's writing,"[24] postfeminist scholars questioned the very concept of "woman." In 1990, Judith Butler published her influential book, *Gender Trouble: Feminism and the Subversion of Identity*, in which she reflects that in the past, "feminist theory had assumed that there is some existing identity, understood through categories of women, who not only initiates feminist interests and goals within discourse but constitutes the subject for whom political representation is assumed." As Butler explains, however, "this prevailing conception has come under challenge. The very subject of women is no longer understood in stable or abiding terms."[25] I have both embraced and lamented these developments. To be sure, the transition from feminism to "feminisms" and "postfeminism" has engendered considerable theoretical sophistication and pluralism in feminist literary studies. Indeed, in recognition of the fact that there is no longer a single feminist approach or a universally accepted definition of gender, I have tried to incorporate a broad sampling of feminist reading strategies in this study. Fundamentally, I accept the argument that by attempting to "define women, characterize women, or speak for women,"[26] we duplicate the strategies that have always defined misogynist cultures and their assumption of woman as Other. At the same time, I remain committed to feminism as a means of transforming women's lives. Having grown up in an Orthodox Jewish community where women continue to be marginalized both in ritual and law, I cannot entirely accept the idea of "woman" as fictional construct nor relinquish the project of women's (literary) history, especially given the context of Jewish literary studies, where feminist criticism has experienced a belated awakening.

Indeed, while American feminism was moving toward what some might call its own postfeminist depletion, resulting in a body of arcane theory that was further and further removed from the experiences of women, the impact of feminist theory on Jewish studies, in general, and Hebrew literary studies, in particular, was only beginning. As in Anglo-American feminist theory, some of the first efforts to bring feminism to the study of Hebrew literature were in the area of "images of woman criticism." Nechama Aschkenasy's *Eve's Journey: Feminine Images in Hebraic Literary Tradition* (University of Pennsylvania Press, 1986) examined negative images of women as seen in a broad range of ancient and modern Hebrew literary texts. Similarly, Esther Fuchs's *Israeli Mythogynies: Women in Contemporary Fiction* (State University of New York Press, 1987) analyzed the representation of women in contemporary Israeli novels by male authors such as A. B. Yehoshua and Amos Oz, offering a woman's counterresponse through a final chapter devoted to the fiction of Amalia Kahana-Carmon.[27] Following this came greater critical interest in Hebrew women's literary history, as evidenced by the work of scholars such as Yaffa Berlovitz, Tova Cohen, Nurit Govrin, Avner Holtzman, and Lily Rattok in uncovering the life-stories and literary work of celebrated as well as neglected Hebrew women writers.[28]

Perhaps the most important work in this regard is Dan Miron's *Imahot meyasdot, ahayot horgot* (Founding mothers, step sisters, 1991), a book that offers a thought-provoking analysis of the literary politics surrounding the emergence in the 1920s of Hebrew woman poets such as Rachel (Bluwstein), Esther Raab, Elisheva (Bihovski), and Yokheved Bat-Miriam. Before 1920, Miron argues, virtually no Hebrew poetry by women was published because women poets were not able to meet the aesthetic criteria established by the reigning "Bialikite" school of poetics, which required a richly allusive and learned Hebrew diction, and in which personal materials were used only if they conveyed a broader universal message. Only when the poetics of the Bialik school were superseded by a poetics of "poverty" that championed simple language and more personal content were women poets able to publish and gain an audience. Miron contends that this "poor" women's poetry was applauded in part because it conformed to certain prevailing expectations of female modesty, intimacy, and emotionalism.[29] In his view, however, only the most conservative, nonintellectual, nonexperimental forms of women's poetry, as represented by Rachel and Elisheva, were accepted by the critical establishment. Other more overtly audacious and confrontational poets, such as Esther Raab and Yokheved Bat-Miriam, were forced to adapt these norms or be silent.[30]

Miron's theory of development and reception of early Hebrew women's poetry has garnered its share of criticism. Some have disputed his explanation for the delayed emergence of Hebrew women's poetry; others have challenged his emphasis on the politics of literary reception as the chief factor in determining literary motives;[31] still others have opposed his negative assessments of particular woman poets, calling attention to intellectual or formal features that Miron seemingly either ignored or misunderstood.[32] While I also respond to Miron's readings (as will be evident in the following chapters), my major concern with his approach derives from his general disregard for feminist theory.[33] Throughout his essay Miron considers the ways in which individual women poets negotiate between their desire to be revolutionary and bold and the opposing expectation that they conform to conventional norms of female modesty and decorum. What he does not acknowledge, however, with the exception of one reference in his essay to Virginia Woolf's *A Room of One's Own*, is the origin of this mode of critical inquiry in feminist literary criticism.[34] Like Miron, feminist literary historians, beginning with Woolf, have repeatedly tried to account for the absence of women's voices in mainstream literary traditions. Moreover, they have attempted to describe how the lack of a tradition affected women who wanted to write, mapping out various strategies early women writers developed for legitimating their position in a patriarchal literary milieu. Miron addresses some of these same issues, but in doing so he ignores the vast body of theory and criticism that precedes his inquiry. His decision to bypass feminist theory seems to derive from his disdain for the entire enterprise. "There is no place to suggest," he writes, "that the absence of women's poetry in the generation of Bialik is due to a cultural misogyny or a male chauvinism of the kind that feminist criticism searches for, both in places where it does and does not exist."[35]

I began writing this book with the aim of picking up where Miron left off, using a variety of feminist theoretical strategies to critically examine the poetic and prose works of modern Hebrew women writers. Since embarking on this project, there has been a rise in feminist Hebrew literary studies. Happily, what began as a response to Miron's founding essay has culminated in an engagement with the work of many other scholars in a flourishing field. Over the past decade, several important publications have helped bolster feminist Hebrew literary studies. In June 1990, a conference entitled "Gender and Text: Feminist Criticism and Modern Jewish Literature" took place at the Jewish

Theological Seminary of America, resulting in an important volume of feminist essays on Yiddish and Hebrew literature, the first of its kind in English or Hebrew.[36] *Women of the Word: Jewish Women and Jewish Writing* (Wayne State University Press, 1994), edited by Judith Baskin, brought additional feminist insight to the study of Hebrew women writers. Important publications by Chana Kronfeld and Michael Gluzman helped revise the longstanding map of Hebrew literary history so as to incorporate the voice of "minor" women writers such as Rachel (Bluwstein) and Esther Raab.[37] Through her analysis of the sexual politics of Yiddish and English, Naomi Seidman brought a crucial comparative aspect to the field, something equally evident in Yael Feldman's recently published *No Room of Their Own: Gender and Nation in Israeli Women's Fiction* (Columbia University Press, 1999) a pioneering study that examines the rise of Israeli women novelists in light of modernist as well as postmodernist feminist theory.[38] Carole Balin's *To Reveal Our Hearts: Jewish Women Writers in Tsarist Russia* (Hebrew Union College Press, 2000) brings a comparative perspective to Jewish women's cultural history, offering biographical framed portraits in historical context of several forgotten Jewish women writers from Tsarist Russia who wrote in Hebrew, Yiddish, and Russian. Journals such as *Prooftexts* and *Shofar* (in the U.S.) and *Sadan* and *Teoria uvikkoret* (in Israel) have pushed scholarly inquiry into questions of feminism and gender in new directions, while the recent publication of two excellent anthologies of Hebrew women's writing in English translation, *The Defiant Muse: Hebrew Feminist Poems* and *Dreaming the Actual: Contemporary Fiction and Poetry by Israeli Women Writers,* have made the corpus of Hebrew women's writing more accessible to students and general readers alike.[39] Yaffa Berlovitz's recently published anthology of pre-state women's writing, *She'ani adamah ve'adam: sippurei nashim 'ad kom haMedinah* (Hakibbutz Hameuchad, 2003), has brought new and deserved attention to Hebrew women's writing before 1948 including many voices not represented in this book. Only Lubin's recently published *Ishah Koreit ishah* (University of Haifa/Zemorah Bitan, 2003) is a similarly important contribution to the discussion. This book adds to these contributions by offering a comparative thematic framework for the study of Hebrew women's writing, including many neglected works of poetry and fiction. It also extends the canon of Hebrew women's writing by including discussions of works by Diaspora writers alongside works by authors typically mentioned in more Israel-centered accounts of Hebrew literary history.

10

One of the most important contributors to the growing field of feminist Hebrew literary scholarship, in general, and the Israel-centered version of Hebrew literary history, in particular, is Lily Rattok. Her essays on Hebrew women's poetry and prose in the Israeli press, together with her 1994 anthology of women's prose writings, *Hakol ha'aher: sipporet nashim 'Ivrit* (The other voice: women's fiction in Hebrew, 1994[40]), with its comprehensive afterword essay, have advanced the idea of a female Hebrew literary tradition with its own distinctive themes and issues.[41] One cannot overstate the importance of Rattok's contribution to this field, both as feminist interpreter and anthologizer. It is worth noting, though, where my book diverges from the assumptions she outlines in the afterword to *Hakol ha'aher* as well in other essays. According to Rattok, "Women writers of Hebrew fiction did not aim to capture the literary territory of men, nor did they seek to revolutionize the production of literature. Instead, women writers sought only to join with their compatriots in the literary arena, and they emphasized the modesty of their demands."[42] Rattok makes a similar assertion in the area of women's poetry:

> The "poetic I" in a great deal of women's poetry in Hebrew is the very opposite of the strong, confident image of the poet who struggles with the span of history and with deep theological questions. The female poetic I is very private, speaking her heart, but with virtually no communal or public aspect. She expresses no cultural, religious, or metaphysical message. She has no connection to the shining or dark worlds of the imagination, rather only with the day-to-day world, common and recognizable to all. As a result, her poetry lacks the element of loftiness that characterizes mainstream [masculine] poetry.[43]

Contrary to Rattok's contentions, which are based primarily on a study of works by Hebrew women writers and poets who ultimately immigrated to Palestine, I argue that early Hebrew women writers of prose fiction *and* poetry aimed in a real, self-conscious sense "to capture the literary territory of men"—to steal the language of the fathers as well as to create works of literature that represent their unique, women's perspective on many time-honored themes and communal issues. As Tova Cohen observes in a pathbreaking essay on the ways in which Hebrew women writers appropriated the canonical "father-tongue" of Hebrew, "those women writers who wished to express themselves through the use of the 'father tongue' but at the same time, wished to communicate as women, needed to find ways to adapt this 'father tongue' to the needs

11

of an autonomous feminine 'I.'"[44] Indeed, early Hebrew women writers and poets often engaged longstanding masculine conventions and themes, even while they pioneered innovative, women-centered approaches. These writers and poets sought "[not] only to join with their compatriots in the literary arena," but also to retell traditional, male-authored stories in new ways, often against the grain of dominant masculine modes of representation. As a rule of conduct for women, modesty may have been enforced throughout Jewish history, but while some of the works of poetry and prose examined in this book display an outer veneer of self-diminution as well as a concern with the personal realm, deeper literary analysis reveals the extent of their literary boldness, even their metaphysical strivings. Rattok claims that Israeli prose fiction by women lacks a well-developed image of the woman as storyteller. An examination of works by late nineteenth- and early twentieth-century Hebrew women prose writers—such as Hava Shapiro (1878–1943), who wrote a collection of sketches filled with images of female artists/storytellers, and Devorah Baron (1887–1956), whose stories often feature a rabbi's-daughter-narrator who reflects meta-fictively on the process of writing—reveals that from the beginning, Hebrew women writers attempted to imagine and depict a new creature: the Hebrew woman writer. According to Rattok, Israeli women writers (with Baron as foremother), unlike male writers and poets, did not attempt to assume the public role and authority "of tribal witch doctor."[45] Instead they complied with male expectations and retreated to a more personal feminine space. In opposition to Rattok, I maintain that in adopting women-centered strategies, early Hebrew women poets and writers consciously refused the patriarchal script. As early as Rachel Morpurgo in nineteenth-century Italy, women poets and prose writers were staking a claim to public/prophetic Hebrew discourse. When they seized upon the personal as a vehicle of expression, they often did so as a subversive means of gaining access to the public and national language of Hebrew representation so long denied women.

Thus, one of the basic images that informs this book is *border-crossing,* a concept that evokes a geographical as well as a social landscape. Like the biblical Rachel, all the women writers treated in this book were immigrants, either in a literal or a literary sense. Remember that Rachel's theft of the *teraphim* comes just as she prepares to leave home and transgress the boundaries of her former life in the house of Laban. In her study of the themes of exile and homecoming in modern

Jewish literature, Sidra DeKoven Ezrahi refers to the story of Rachel stealing the *teraphim* as emblematic of a Jewish desire to carry along in their wanderings tangible signs of former homelands and holiness. According to Ezrahi, "Rachel carried her *teraphim,* her household gods, from place to place, even when admonished that holiness could not be confined in local icons and lowercase homelands."[46] If the story of Rachel's theft of the *teraphim* provides an apt metaphor for the study of modern Hebrew women's writing it is precisely because it brings together the idea of border-crossing with a concern for tradition, legitimacy, and homeland.

To be sure, border-crossing entails a measure of anxiety as well as exhilaration. When you cross a border for the first time, you suddenly become international and traveled; you find yourself visiting new and exciting places, both geographically and culturally. But border-crossings are always restricted forms of movement. They usually require the approval of border officials. Documents must be presented that authorize movement, that prove citizenship and legitimacy. To a degree, the women writers who crossed borders into Hebrew literary culture were all required to orchestrate their entry. For some, the preferred strategy was to steal across the borders, to bury and smuggle in the subversive, iconoclastic feminist message; for others, the strategy involved an open declaration of new literary custom and intent. This book attempts to sketch a broad thematic and stylistic map of these myriad literary border-crossings, to tell the story of first steps.

The organization of the following chapters is by and large thematic, with the exception of chapter 1, which provides a history of Jewish women's writing leading up to and including the period(s) under question as a way of elucidating my argument about the distinctiveness and novelty of modern Hebrew women's writing.[47] As part of this history, I include readings of particular texts that shed light on it or provide insight into the particular issues confronting early Hebrew women writers. The remaining chapters explore how different early modern Hebrew women poets and/or prose writers stole into a particular thematic space or wrested away an icon of representation. Chapter 2 investigates the ways in which a diverse group of early Hebrew women poets cleared a place for themselves in Hebrew literary culture by reclaiming and re-visioning the stories of biblical women; here I focus exclusively on poetry. The same focus on poetry persists in chapter 3, where I consider the biblical and rabbinic convention of female personifications of the Land, examining how three

13

women poets seized this tradition away from their fathers and male contemporaries and made it their own. Chapter 4 includes discussion of both
poetry and prose and takes up the equally longstanding theme of female
barrenness and the efforts undertaken by early Hebrew women poets and
prose writers to de-allegorize and personalize it. The last two chapters of
the book deal with issues of exile and community. Chapter 5 concentrates
on the prose writings of Sarah Feige Meinkin Foner, Hava Shapiro, and
Devorah Baron, and their depictions of women who dare to enter new
geographical, intellectual, social, and religious spaces; significantly, most
of these early fictions of transgressed boundaries culminate in exile and
alienation rather than homecoming. In Baron's later fiction, however,
female community becomes an antidote to this condition of exile, an idea
taken up again in chapter 6, "The Rabbi's Daughter in and out of the
Kitchen." This chapter, which examines a poem by Rachel Morpurgo, a
novella by Baron, and a poem by the later poet Zelda Mishkovsky, identifies the kitchen as a symbol of the social limitations traditionally placed
on female creativity, as well as a potential site for female community,
communion, and creative reflection.

A History of Jewish
Women's Writing

> Every literary movement has its roots in a past, which it at once
> perpetuates, repudiates and transforms. For women, the past is
> doubled. We have a shared and canonized literary heritage written
> overwhelmingly by men. . . . *We also have a long line of uncanon-*
> *ized poetic ancestresses* who have contrived to articulate, often in
> highly coded form, images of woman—and of reality—which are
> in quite crucial aspects different from men's.
>
> ALICIA SUSKIN OSTRIKER [emphasis added]

If, as feminist critic Alicia Suskin Ostriker proposes, women "have a
long line of uncanonized poetic ancestresses," who are the ancient foremothers of Hebrew literature? Where in biblical and post-biblical literature can we find the uncanonized contributions of women?[1]

In a landmark essay entitled "Women as Creators of Biblical
Genres," S. D. Goitein argues that in the ancient world, women were
the primary creators or practitioners of several (oral) genres, many of
which were preserved in written form in biblical literature. In the
ancient Near East, women composed victory songs, songs mocking the
enemy, female wisdom poetry, the "female rebuke," the *shiluah* or send-
off song, as well as other cultic forms.[2] In Goitein's words, "anyone who
makes even a quick survey of women's poetry in the Bible, will be surprised to see how plentiful is the material that has been preserved."[3]

Goitein's argument does not speak to the question of whether
women authored the written texts attributed to them in the Bible, such as
Deborah's song or Hannah's song. Moreover, the traces of female oral
forms in the Bible in no way indicate that women played a major role in
shaping the biblical worldview. Quite the contrary. The rich and varie-
gated body of feminist biblical criticism, beginning with Elizabeth Cady
Stanton's *Woman's Bible* (1895, 1898), attests to the largely patriarchal sensibilities of the biblical authors, as well as the effect of the Bible in pro-
mulgating various negative attitudes toward women.[4] That said, Goitein's

15

observation about the significant roles played by women in the public ritual life of the ancient Near East remains important. Biblical women, Goitein writes, "took part in public life as bearer of the word and expresser of the feelings of the people as a whole."[5] In contrast, the post-biblical record of women's verbal/literary creativity in Hebrew is extremely sparse. Following the biblical period, barely a handful of Jewish women wrote in Hebrew. That was the case until the middle of the nineteenth century.

To be sure, the general exclusion of women from the realms of sacred study and public worship where Hebrew was the principal language of discourse did not conduce toward the development of female Hebrew literary activity.[6] For centuries, Jewish communities throughout the world upheld a segregated educational system that required all Jewish males to engage in the study of the Bible, Talmud, and law codes, but exempted—or, in some cases, explicitly forbade—women from intellectual engagement with sacred texts.

The prohibition against women studying Torah can, in large part, be traced to a debate between Rabbi Eliezer ben Hyrcanus and Ben Azzai in Mishnah Sotah 3:4. The context of the mishnah is the laws concerning an errant wife whose husband suspects her of having had an extramarital affair and compels her to drink the "bitter waters" (Num. 5:11–31). The mishnah states that if the errant wife "had merit, her merit will mitigate [the punishment] for her." Following this, Ben Azzai pronounces that from this we learn that "a man should teach his daughter Torah so that if she drinks, she will know that merit mitigates." Rabbi Eliezer counters this statement and pronounces that "he who teaches his daughter Torah teaches her licentiousness." In the discussions about this mishnah in B. T. Sotah 21a, the rabbis attempt to understand exactly what sort of merit is being invoked here. They dismiss outright the possibility that it is the merit of Torah study itself, since women are not commanded to study. (Ravina suggests that it is the merit of "taking her sons to study Torah and Mishnah and waiting for her husband to come home from the study house.") According to Daniel Boyarin's reading of this passage, Ben Azzai's dissenting opinion is never directly addressed in this Talmudic discussion and is, therefore, "effectively nullified."[7] Instead, the Talmud promotes Rabbi Eliezer's opinion, which views the study of Torah by women as directly linked to licentious behavior. As Boyarin explains, "The historical effect of the Babylonian text . . . which was hegemonic for later European culture, was to suppress quite thoroughly the possibilities for women to study Torah until modern times."[8]

A long legal tradition has followed this initial debate between Ben Azzai and R. Eliezer. Over the generations, various rabbis took up the matter again and attempted to qualify or limit the prohibition against Torah study that stems from R. Eliezer's statement. Maimonides (1135–1204), for example, bases his understanding of R. Eliezer's prohibition on what he sees as the general intellectual incompetence of women, an offensive interpretation, to be sure, but one that might also be understood as sanctioning Torah study for intellectually gifted women who disprove the rule.[9]

Indeed, despite the general prejudice against broad education for women—often the rabbis supported a practical education for women that involved teaching the laws that pertained to them so they might live a pious life, but limited the act of study for its own sake[10]—there were always exceptional Jewish women from wealthy and/or scholarly families who received rich educations and contributed in noteworthy ways to the development of Jewish religious, intellectual, and literary life. The Talmud repeatedly quotes the insights and opinions of Beruriah (second century C.E.), the daughter of R. Haninah ben Teradiyon and wife of R. Meir; of Yalta (first century C.E.), wife of R. Nahman Bar Ya'akov; and of Imma Shalom (fourth century C.E.), wife of R. Eliezer and sister of Rabban Gamliel.[11] In the twelfth century, Rachel, one of the daughters of the illustrious Rashi, is reputed to have helped her father respond to a legal question, indicating an advanced knowledge of Hebrew and rabbinic sources, while Dolce, the wife of R. Ele'azar of Worms helped lead prayers for the women of the synagogue.[12] The daughters and wives of eighteenth- and nineteenth-century Hassidic rabbis frequently served as spiritual figures, the most famous being Hannah Rachel Werbermacher, commonly referred to as the Maid of Ludomir.[13] My decision to devote the last chapter of this book to the representation of the rabbi's daughter in works by twentieth-century Hebrew women writers reflects an awareness of the extraordinary position occupied by the daughters and wives of rabbis over the ages. It is important to emphasize, however, that while several medieval and Renaissance rabbis were prolific poets, virtually none of these rabbis' daughters or wives became Hebrew writers.[14]

Membership in a scholarly or wealthy family enabled certain women to make important contributions to the literature of their native countries. Kasmunah, the daughter of medieval Spanish statesman, military commander, and Hebrew poet Shmuel Hanagid (993–1056), wrote and published poetry in Arabic.[15] Devorah Ascarelli (sixteenth century) of Rome published a book of Italian translations of Hebrew liturgical poetry, in addition to translating the works of Moses de Rieti and composing her own Italian poetry on Jewish themes.[16] Sara Copia Sullam (1592–1641), a prominent participant in the cultural life of Renaissance Venice, read Hebrew but wrote poetry and prose in Italian, defending her faith in polemical essays against the poet Ansaldo Ceba and Baldassar Bonifaccio, Bishop of Capodistria.[17] In Berlin, between 1780 and 1806, wealthy, enlightened Jewish women such as Henriette Herz, Rachel Levin, Dorothea Mendelssohn Veit, Sarah Levy, Amalie Beer, Sara and Marianne Meyer, Philippine Cohen, and Rebecca Friedländer presided over literary salons and exerted a great deal of influence on German literary and intellectual culture. As Deborah Hertz notes, however, the German Jewish salon women present an "ambiguous legacy" since so many of them broke entirely with the Jewish community and converted to Christianity.[18] Certainly none of these assimilated salon women wrote in Hebrew.

Arguably the greatest contributions made by women in Jewish literary history were in the area of Yiddish-language literature. In contrast to Hebrew, which was considered an almost exclusively male linguistic province, Yiddish was commonly associated with women, as indicated by its other name, *mameloshen* (mother tongue), and by the special typeface known as *vayber taytsch* (women's German) used in printing Yiddish women's books.[19] Yiddish texts such as the *tsenerene,* the popular Yiddish retelling of the Bible by R. Jacob ben Isaac Aschkenazi of Yanov (1618), were intended mainly for female readership, on the assumption that women knew Yiddish, not Hebrew. The preface to Moses Ben Henoch Altschuler's Yiddish ethical work, *Brantshpigl* (1596), explicitly announces that "this book is made in Yiddish for women and for men who are like women and cannot learn much."[20] In his famous essay, "Yiddish and the Female Reader," Yiddish literary critic Shmuel Niger notes that "Yiddish literature is perhaps the only literature in the world that until recently was sustained by the female and not the male reader."[21] Niger's statement doesn't confer special honor upon Old Yiddish literature or its women readers for their part in sustaining it. As Naomi Seidman aptly observes, "Yiddish femininity nearly always marked both Yiddish and women as inferior within a rigid patriarchal order that valorized both Hebrew and masculinity."[22]

Negative associations notwithstanding, the literary and spiritual achievements of Yiddish women writers were extremely significant, evidence of the ability of women to turn their marginal linguistic spaces into sites of resistance and growth. Occasionally, female authorship of Yiddish literary works was also accompanied by Hebrew literary output as well. One of the most impressive and least-acknowledged achievements of this sort was by Rebekah bas Meir Tiktiner, a sixteenth-century figure who wrote a Yiddish ethical tract called *Menekes Rivka,* first published in Prague in 1609. Surprised to discover such an erudite woman, the male printer prefaced the book with the following publisher's statement: "This book is called *Menekes Rivka* (Genesis 35:8) in order to remember the name of the authoress and in honor of all women to prove that a woman can also compose a work of ethics and offer good interpretations, as well as many a man."[23] Perhaps even more remarkable than this printer's preface is Rebekah Tiktiner's own preface, written in rhymed Hebrew, in which she self-consciously declares her authorial ambitions in writing this book and trumpets her achievements in language evocative of Jacob's rolling the stone from the well in Genesis 29:

ראה ראיתי. בלבי הגיתי. קול הרימותי וקראתי. הנה עתה באתי.
והיום יצאתי. ובאר מים מצאתי. והאבן הגדולה מן הבאר גלותי.
וממנו שתיתי. ועוד צמיתי. ואמרתי בלבבי. אלכה ואביא. לקרובי וקרובתי
ותגלני עצמותי. שישתו לימים אורך ...

> Indeed I have seen. In my heart, I considered. I raised my voice and called out. Behold now I have come. And today I go out. A well of water I have discovered. And have rolled the great stone off the rock. And drunk from it. And still I was thirsty. And I said in my heart. I shall go and bring. For those men and women near to me. And my bones shall rejoice. That they will drink throughout their days. . . .[24]

Tiktiner's prefatory Hebrew poem imitates a masculine literary convention, in which a work of sacred commentary or religious instruction is introduced by a rhymed poem that confesses the author's goals or misgivings about his work.[25] In conforming to this convention, Tiktiner announces a desire to claim a space not just in Yiddish letters but also in the (Hebrew) scholarly tradition. Remarkably, this poem has garnered little scholarly attention.[26] More commonly noted, along with other works of early modern Yiddish women's poetry, is Tiktiner's Yiddish liturgical poem in honor of the holiday of Simhat Torah ("A simhas toyrah lied").[27]

Another fascinating, better known piece of Yiddish women's writing is the autobiography of Glikl bas Judah Leib (seventeenth century), commonly referred to as Glückel of Hameln.[28] Glikl began writing her

19

memoirs in 1689 after the death of her husband Haim and continued working on the narrative for several years, finally composing a seven-book work that combines personal reflection and self-examination with Jewish morality tales. As Natalie Zemon Davis writes, "[t]hrough this unusual literary structure, Glikl bas Judah Leib wrote a book of morals, spiritual inquiry, and religious reflection which, in rabbinical eyes, she had neither the learning nor the standing to do."[29]

Women also made significant contributions to the Yiddish devotional literature of the *tkhines,* a body of writing that pioneering scholar Chava Weissler has described as revealing "an intensely lived religious life and a richly imagined spiritual world."[30] According to Weissler, while most of the *tkhines* from Western Europe were probably written or compiled by men for the use of women, some of the *tkhines* that originated in Eastern Europe in the seventeenth, eighteenth and early nineteenth centuries were written or reworked by women.[31] Sarah Bas Tovim (eighteenth century), perhaps the best known author of *tkhines,* wrote *Tkhine sha'ar hayikhed al 'oylemes* (Tkhine of the gate of unification concerning the aeons) as well as *Shloyshe she'orim* (Three gates), a work combining both eschatological and domestic concerns. Serl, daughter of Yankev Segal of Dubno (the Dubno Maggid, 1741–1804), authored the *Tkhine imohes fun Rosh Hodesh Elul.*[32] Shifrah, the daughter of Joseph and wife of Ephraim Segal, judge in the rabbinical court of Brody, is credited with the authorship of *Imrei shifre* (The sayings of Shifra, 1770), a text that makes extensive use of mystical material from the Zohar.[33] Leah Dreyzel, who came from a noted Hassidic family, composed *Tkhine 'es rotsn* and *Tkhine sha'arei tshuve.* Sarah Rivka Rachel Horowitz, another eighteenth-century figure, wrote *Tkhine imohes* (*Tkhine* of the matriarchs), a truly exceptional work in that it includes a Hebrew introduction, an Aramaic poem, and a Yiddish paraphrase of the liturgical poem, all of which address the spiritual powers of women.[34] Weissler notes that this is the only premodern text she has seen "in which an Ashkenazic woman discusses such issues as the significance of women's prayer, the proper way for women to pray, and circumstances under which women should and should not submit to their husband's authority."[35] Because she wrote in Hebrew and Aramaic for women, Leah Horowitz was so anomalous she had no audience; consequently, later editions of her *tkhine* dropped the Hebrew and Aramaic portions.[36]

The keyword here is anomalous, for while scholars have managed to gather together a handful of medieval and early modern Hebrew poems by women—literary gems that have recently been collected in *The Defiant Muse,* a breakthrough bilingual anthology of Hebrew feminist poems[37]—these examples are the exceptions that prove the rule of female Hebrew literary silence. One of the most fascinating items included in *The Defiant Muse* is a poem from the Cairo Genizah entitled "Hayizkor ya'alat hahen,"[38] (Will her love remember), attributed to the wife of Dunash ben Labrat, the tenth-century Spanish Hebrew linguist and poet. "Hayizkor" is an expertly metered and rhymed poem, spoken in the worried voice of a woman whose husband is about to depart on a long trip. "There is no need to emphasize the wonderful nature of this discovery," writes scholar Ezra Fleischer. "*If the title is correct,* then we're looking at the first woman poet after Deborah the Prophetess, and she reveals herself not as a *humble woman rhymester,* rather as a true poet, trained in the craft of poetry, one who approaches her work, both from a formal and a thematic point of view, with absolute confidence"[39] (emphasis added). Fleischer's speculation about the correctness of the title of this poem is significant; to date, "Hayizkor" is the only poem we know of attributed to Dunash's wife—a fact that casts some doubt on whether she actually wrote it or whether Dunash himself wrote it as if from his wife's mouth, along with the companion poem that answers the wife's concerns. Fleischer chooses to conclude that Dunash's wife indeed authored the poem, and he pays considerable tribute to her skills, which, in his estimation, surpass what scholars have come to expect from tenth-century Hebrew poets. His repeated use of the term "humble woman rhymester," however, demonstrates his limited expectations of women's poetry. By persistently contrasting the achievements of these lesser women poets with those of Dunash's wife as seen in "Hayizkor," Fleischer makes abundantly clear exactly how unusual a figure Dunash's wife must have been in her time.

The three or four examples of Jewish women in Europe or North Africa who wrote Hebrew poetry in the centuries thereafter and whose poems are also represented in *The Defiant Muse* anthology were unusual. In the early 1970s, Avraham Habermann brought to light a religious poem entitled "Mi barukh nora ve'adir" by a woman named Merecina, a *rabbanit* (rabbi's wife) from Gerona (fifteenth century).[40] Scholars of Jewish life and lore in Kurdistan brought similar attention to the story of Asenath, daughter of Rabbi Samuel Adoni Barzani and wife of Rabbi Judah Jacob Mizrahi from sixteenth-century Kurdistan, who, when widowed and financially imperiled, wrote a long rhymed Hebrew poem appealing for the right and the financial backing to assume her husband's scholarly position until her young son grew up.[41] According to folklorist Yona Sabar, Rabbi Asenath, as some referred to her, was an extremely learned woman, well-versed in Torah and in Jewish mystical literature. She was also known for performing miracles. According to one fascinating story recorded by Sabar, "after [Asenath] had borne one son and one daughter to her husband"—thus enabling her husband to fulfill his halakhic obligation to procreate—"she prayed to God to terminate her menses, so that she might devote herself to Torah in sanctity and purity, and God fulfilled her request."[42] This story is suggestive for two reasons: it emphasizes the exceptional, even magical nature of Asenath's scholarly and literary achievements, and it alludes to a conflict between maternal obligation and scholarly vocation. One possible reading of the story is that it endorses planned parenthood; Asenath already has two children and recognizes that she cannot have more and at the same time devote herself to scholarship. In praying for a miraculous end to her menses, however, Asenath seems to demonstrate a desire not only to control the size of her family but also to do away with her femininity. In order to be a rabbi/poet and inhabit the masculine realm of Hebrew letters, Asenath wants to cease being a woman in an active, biological sense.[43]

The recently uncovered story of Freyha Bat-Yosef, a Moroccan Jewish woman scholar and Hebrew poet also included in the *Defiant Muse* anthology, is another case in point. About twenty-five years ago in Strasbourg, scholar Joseph Chetrit discovered a poem attributed to Freyha among some manuscripts of Moroccan Hebrew and Judaeo-Arabic poetry. This discovery was extremely significant because until then, scholars of the Jewish literature of North Africa believed it to be an exclusively male-authored literature. Freyha's poem displays a level of erudition and literary training comparable to the male poets of that time and region. As in the case of Asenath, who became a folk heroine, Freyha's scholarly and literary expertise—along with the tragic story of her death—rendered her larger-than-life. During the conquest of Tunis by the Algerians (1756), Freyha became separated from other family members and was never seen again. In the aftermath of her disappearance, Freyha's rabbinic father converted their home into a memorial to his lost daughter: the *mikvah* was placed where Freyha's bed used to be; the *aron kodesh* (Holy Ark) was placed in the site of her former library. The women of the community turned to Freyha as an inspirational figure and invoked her name in times of distress.[44] Once again we have an example of a scholarly and literary Jewish woman whose extraordinary attainments lifted her above the level of regular humanity, who was transformed in death into something of a saint.

These examples of premodern Hebrew poetry by women—our precious few poetic ancestresses—prove that the Hebrew woman writer was not created ex nihilo in the nineteenth and twentieth centuries. As the editors of the *Defiant Muse* note, "[w]hereas the hidden treasures of medieval Hebrew poetry have yielded only two clear women's voices [the wife of Dunash and Merecina], the early modern Hebrew texts . . . although still few in number, testify to women's creative production before the modern era."[45] That said, the number of works in Hebrew written by women before the nineteenth century is excruciatingly small. The point emphasized by scholars who have researched the stories of women such as Dunash's wife and Freyha is their sense of wonderment that these women poets even existed. It is not until the nineteenth century that this picture begins to change.

The Haskalah Poetry of Rachel Morpurgo

The nineteenth-century *Haskalah* (enlightenment) and *Hibat Tsiyyon* (Love of Zion) movements brought about a regeneration of Hebrew and with it a rise in women's involvement in Hebrew writing.

First and most prolific among these women readers and writers of Hebrew was Rachel Luzzatto Morpurgo (1790–1871), a member of the famous and learned Luzzatto family of Trieste, Italy—her cousin was the Haskalah scholar and writer Solomon David Luzzatto commonly known as SHaDaL (1800–1865). Morpurgo received an exceptionally rich education in Jewish sources, including the study of the Talmud and the Zohar.[46] Like many members of her extended literary family—which included rabbis, doctors, merchants, poets, and scholars of the Hebrew Haskalah—Morpurgo wrote occasional verse in Hebrew: rhyming riddles and lyric poems inspired by engagements, weddings, births, and deaths. In addition to this occasional poetry, Morpurgo also wrote about religious faith, contemporary political events—such as the Rebellions of 1848— and perhaps even more significantly, about her personal literary aspirations and frustrations. Her poetic achievements were especially remarkable given the conditions under which she worked. Unlike many of the great British and American women writers of the nineteenth century who remained unmarried and were thus left relatively free to pursue a curriculum of writing and study, Morpurgo was often inhibited by domestic duties and responsibilities. As the Italian rabbi and poet Vittorio (Yitzchak Haim) Castiglioni writes, while Morpurgo was blessed with a rich education from her parents and broader family, she had little leisure in her adult married life to study and write. With no domestic help, she raised three sons and one daughter, who remained unmarried until the end of their days. In contrast to her life before marriage, when she had ready access to her parent's vast library, there were few books in the house she lived in with her husband, and because of her various domestic responsibilities she found little time to read. Only on nights when she could not sleep, and on Rosh Hodesh (the New Moon), when it was customary for women to refrain from needlework, did she have the opportunity to read and compose poetry. Her husband, Jacob Morpurgo, whom she loved so ardently as a young woman that when her parents opposed the match she vowed to marry no other man,[47] was less than encouraging to Rachel the poet; only when he witnessed the praise she was receiving for her poetry, did he countenance her literary activities.[48] Despite these obstacles, Morpurgo continued to write poetry throughout her life. Publishing some fifty poems in the journal *Kokhavei Yitshak* (The Stars of Isaac)—the poems appeared after her death in collected form under the title *Ugav Rachel* (Rachel's flute, 1890)—Morpurgo gained much acclaim among readers in Germany and Italy. Readers were astonished to encounter a woman capable of composing erudite, rhymed, and metered poetry in Hebrew, and contemporary praise was considerable. Disconcerted by this gender-based praise, Morpurgo set about composing poetry in response, beginning with this 1847 sonnet, a reaction to the critical reception of her poetry[49]:

ואלה דברי רחל בבוא לאזניה כי שמה נזכר לתהלה במכתבי עתים

אוֹי לִי תֹאמַר נַפְשִׁי, כִּי מַר לִי מָר,
סָפַח רוּחִי עָלַי וָאֶתְיַמָּר,
שָׁמַעְתִּי קוֹל אוֹמֵר: שִׁירֵךְ נִשְׁמָר,
מִי כְמוֹתֵךְ רָחֵל לוֹמֶדֶת שִׁיר?

רוּחִי יָשִׁיב אֵלַי: רֵיחִי נָמַר,
גּוֹלָה אַחַר גּוֹלָה, עוֹרִי סָמַר,
טַעְמִי לֹא עָמַד בִּי, כַּרְמִי זֵמָר,
מִכְּלִמּוֹת אֶפְחָד, לֹא עוֹד אָשִׁיר.

24

אֶפְנֶה צָפוֹן דָּרוֹם קֵדְמָה וָיָמָה.

דַּעַת נָשִׁים קַלָּה, לָזֹאת הוּרְמָה.

אַחַר כַּמֶּה שָׁנִים, הֵן עַתָּה לָמָה

יִזָּכֵר מִכֶּלֶב מֵת כָּל-עִיר כָּל-פֶּלֶךְ?

הִנֵּה הָעֵד יָעִיד תּוֹשָׁב וָהֵלֶךְ:

אֵין חָכְמָה לְאִשָּׁה כִּי אִם בַּפֶּלֶךְ.

And These Are Rachel's Words on Hearing She Has Been Praised in the Journals

Woe unto me, my soul says, bitterly pained,
    My spirit became exalted,* and I grew vain.
    A voice said: your poem will remain
    Who other than you, Rachel, has learned to sing?

My spirit returns to me: my scent has turned ill [lit has changed]
    Exile after exile has stiffened my skin,
    My taste is spent, my vineyard cut thin,
    I dread shame, and will not sing on.

North, south, east, west.
    Women are light-headed, above these I am best.
    Remembered in city and province just a few years or less,

No more than a dog fallen dead?
    And every citizen and traveler will say instead
    "There is no wisdom to woman but in needle and thread."[50]

*stillborn wife of Jacob Morpurgo

(*Jerusalem Talmud Yevamot,* chapter 12, halakha 6)

At first glance, Morpurgo's sonnet reads as a profession of female modesty, a poetic protest against all the praise and attention that has been lavished upon her. In the octet, Morpurgo explains that the male Hebrew reading public has singled her out for special praise because she is a woman, but while they trumpet her singular achievements, she fears that she cannot live up to the test of real fame and has already exhausted her talent.

As Tova Cohen has brilliantly illustrated, however, Morpurgo presents this seeming denigration of her achievements and abilities through a complex network of allusions to Hebrew literary and legal sources—from the Bible, the Palestinian Talmud, the poems of Solomon Ibn Gabirol—thus demonstrating a poetic high seriousness, a complete mastery of the Hebrew literary "father tongue," and an ability to appropriate the "language of the father" and make it her own.[51] Indeed, Morpurgo's deft and canny usage of canonical masculine Hebrew literary sources indicates that rather than abrogating her newly awarded place in the realm of Hebrew writing, she wishes to stake a lasting claim. According to Cohen, Morpurgo marshals many of the techniques typical of [male] Haskalah poetry. The key, of course, is that she explicitly adapts these features of the "father tongue" literature to the purpose of countertraditional feminine expression.[52]

Morpurgo's use in line two of the expression *tafah ruhi 'alai,* an explicit allusion to the discussions of levirate marriage in Jerusalem Talmud Yevamot 12:6—Morpurgo herself inserts a note in the text pointing her reader in the direction of this classical source—is an excellent case in point. The Talmudic discussion here concerns an incident where Levi bar Sisi is being considered by the people of Simonia for the position of district Rabbi. In order to interview him, they seat him upon a great stage and begin to ask him questions about points of Jewish law, beginning with, "a woman without arms—with what does she remove the shoe [in the levirate ceremony]?" Levi bar Sisi does not answer this question or any of the others that follow, and so the people of Simonia appeal to Rabbi Judah the Prince who had originally recommended him for the post. Rabbi Judah summons Levi bar Sisi and asks him all the same questions ("If a woman spit blood, what is the law? . . . A woman without arms—how does she remove the shoe?"), which he proceeds to answer correctly. Rabbi Judah proceeds to ask him why he didn't answer these questions when posed by the people of Simonia. Levi bar Sisi replies that "they made a great stage and seated me on it, *and my spirit became exalted*" (emphasis added).[53] In speaking about her own misgivings about being "exalted" by her male literary peers through the language of this Talmudic passage, Morpurgo manages to accomplish several things simultaneously. First, she displays a high level of erudition and therefore proves herself praiseworthy. Second, she cites an occasion of male scholarly arrogance. Third, for those

Rachel Morpurgo, from the frontis-
piece to *Ugav Rachel,* 1943.

who know the context of the Talmudic discussion, she hints at the demeaning nature of the interchange, which raises the tragic subject of a
woman without arms or a woman who spits blood merely as a pretext for
testing a scholar's knowledge of the law. Morpurgo's invocation of the
Talmudic source shows her desire to be incorporated into the Hebrew tradition of sacred and belle-lettres but also indicates the ways in which this
tradition must be reconfigured to empower or "arm" women and to clear
a space for women's voices.

    The spatial and geographical references found in the second stanza
of the poem underline this desire to create an imaginative space for
women's writing within the landscape of Hebrew poetry. Here, too,
Morpurgo employs traditional Hebrew literary tropes, albeit in untradi-
tional ways. As Yaffa Berlovitz observes, in the second stanza Morpurgo
expresses her sense of "failure" as a poet in the same language used to
describe the people of Israel who wander from exile to exile and who are
compared in the prophetic writings to a ruined vineyard. "There is a sense
of identification here," Berlovitz writes, "between woman, as the persecuted minority on the margins of the male mainstream, and the Jew, the

persecuted minority on the margins of the gentile society."[54] In the first line of the third stanza, Morpurgo refers to the promise of God to Jacob at Beit-El, that his descendants will multiply and spread throughout the land, "to the west, and to the east, and to the north, and to the south" (Gen. 28:14), to emphasize her feeling of exclusion from the male mainstream and the absence of a female creative space. If the biblical verse envisions a geographical ubiquity for the descendants of Jacob, Morpurgo perceives a chauvinistic belief in women's intellectual inferiority (or light-headedness) as similarly ever-present[55]; in her estimation, readers value her literary accomplishments only by imagining her as something other than a woman.[56] Spatial imagery of this sort recurs in the last stanza as well, where Morpurgo plays on the double meaning of the Hebrew word *pelekh,* as province and spindle. In this poem, Morpurgo raises a protest not against praise in general but against the specific kind of praise she has received, which, instead of guaranteeing her a place in the "province" of Hebrew letters, reinforces the general assumption that women's place is by the spinning wheel.[57]

Remarkably, this sonnet forecasts future critical attitudes toward Morpurgo's poetry. Indeed, while Morpurgo's male contemporaries heaped encomiums upon her verse because she was a woman, later Hebrew literary critics dismissed her talent as limited and her poetry as minor. Critic and publisher Y. Zemorah begins his preface to the second (1943) edition of Morpurgo's collected poems with the fabulous statement that "Rachel Morpurgo never saw herself as a poet and never intended to write poetry for its own sake; she certainly never had a poetic inclination to express herself."[58] According to Zemorah, editor Castiglioni did well to characterize her poetry through the image of the *'ugav* (flute), "that intimate homely instrument." Noting her religiosity and her domestic obligations, he says rather condescendingly that in the religious community, poetry serves the purpose only of prayer or of secular amusement. In Zemorah's opinion, "Rachel Morpurgo's poetry oscillates between these two poles. Too bad that she wasn't able to tip the balance favorably in either direction." All her poetry, he argues, is the product of external impulse; she never aspired toward the inner "joy of creativity."[59] In light of the sonnet quoted above, which expresses an ambition to create works that attract an enduring, unbiased readership, Zemorah's remarks seem puzzling, at best. How could Morpurgo have written poetry over the course of more than forty years without a "poetic inclination"? And how does one decide whether a poet's impulse is external or internal? Don't all poets, to some extent, respond to external stimuli? True, Morpurgo often signed her poems with such diminishing epithets as "the lowly and young," "the tiniest of the tiny," and *RiMaH* (the Hebrew word for "worm" and an acronym for her name, *Rachel Morpurgo Haketanah* [Rachel Morpurgo the Small]), but these signatures can hardly be seen as a negation of her poetic aspirations; these persisted until the end of her days, as did her publications. Instead, like the dubious professions of modesty in "V'eleh divrei Rachel," they can be read as part of a complex poetics of duplicity—an attempt to satisfy male expectations of female demureness while subtly undermining this humble stance with statements of poetic ambition.

Zemorah's underestimation of Morpurgo's achievement, as well as his failure to notice the subversive quality of her poetry, is echoed by Dan Miron in *Imahot meyasdot, ahayot horgot*. At the beginning of his book, Miron places Morpurgo within the category of the "rhymesters of the Hebrew Enlightenment," arguing that Morpurgo's poetry "should be distinguished from the few serious poets of the period, who truly struggled spiritually and poetically with their optimistic rational worldview, on the one hand, and the social, cultural and spiritual state of the people, on the other."[60] But as Michael Gluzman has argued, Miron's contentions are based on a very specific aesthetic, which privileges broad sociopolitical themes over more personal ones.[61] In reality, Morpurgo's poetry *did* deal with highly "poetic" themes: love, death, faith, community survival, and the particular challenges faced by the woman poet in stealing the language of and claiming a place in the male Hebrew literary tradition.

Hebrew Women Writers of the Russian Haskalah: Sarah Feige Meinkin Foner and Hava Shapiro

Female Hebrew literary activity continued apace in Morpurgo's wake. The leaders of the Hebrew Haskalah movement, Yehudah Leib Gordon and David Frischmann, were particularly eager to see women's voices incorporated into Hebrew literature. In the minds of Frischmann and Gordon, "[w]omen were considered more in communion with nature, graced from birth with feeling and aesthetic refinement. And because of their lack of education, women's thinking had not been warped by the patterns of scholastic erudition."[62] Gordon's interest in fostering female readers and writers of Hebrew is evidenced by the correspondence he conducted with several young female Hebraists, including Rebecca Ratner and Nehamah

Feinstein (later Puhachevsky), both of whom wrote to Gordon in Hebrew professing their interest in his Hebrew poetry and in his literary protests against the subjugation of Jewish women.[63] Gordon also carried on a warm and supportive correspondence with Sara Schapira, an aspiring poet who published a short Hebrew lyric poem entitled "Zion!" in Saul Pinhas Rabonivitch's journal *Kenesset Yisrael*,[64] and with Miriam Markel-Mosessohn, to whom he dedicated "Kotso shel yud" (The tip of the yud), his famous satirical poem criticizing the position of women in Judaism.[65]

But as Carole B. Balin notes in her recent study of Jewish women writers in Tsarist Russia, *maskilim* such as Gordon and Frischmann rarely regarded

> educating women as a good in and of itself, or as a necessary means to female self-fulfillment. Instead, their seemingly progressive activities on behalf of women's emancipation were informed by the ideas of the so-called "enlightened" philosophers who idealized the nuclear family and motherhood, thereby reinforcing differences between the sexes and the appropriateness of an exclusively domestic role for women. Only the woman who had received an excellent education and who had fully developed her intellectual potential could properly fulfill her roles of wife and mother. . . . In effect, *maskilim* were upholding the gender division etched by centuries of Jewish law and custom by rationalizing it anew with ideas and vocabulary from the "modern" cult of domesticity.[66]

Even during the Haskalah, then, an intellectual movement that criticized traditional attitudes toward women and seemingly sought out women's voices, it was difficult for a Hebrew woman writer to actualize her literary potential. Balin's account of the literary career of Hebrew translator and (for a brief time) journalist Miriam Markel-Mosessohn (1839–1920), for example, resonates very distinctly with Morpurgo's earlier story. Like Morpurgo, Markel-Mosessohn received an intensive Hebrew education as a child. As in the case of Morpurgo, her uniqueness as a woman in a largely male Hebrew literary world resulted in a ready audience for her translations and essays. At the same time, the societal expectations of women, internalized by both Morpurgo and Markel-Mosessohn, were stumbling blocks on the way to major literary achievement. As Balin writes, Markel-Mosessohn failed to live up to the expectations of her fellow *maskilim*, "for her own were a constant hindrance to her progress. She failed to realize her potential as a writer because she was haunted by traditional Jewish expectations for women that she had come to accept and demand of herself. She maintained that publishing original works would shame her by exposing her efforts to transgress sacred male ground"[67]

Sarah Feige Meinkin Foner (1854–1936), another nearly forgotten literary woman from the Haskalah period, was perhaps more intrepid than Markel-Mosesohn in her persistent willingness to transgress the "male ground" of Hebrew belle-lettres. Foner published the first Hebrew novel by a woman, *Ahavat yesharim o hamishpahot hamurdafot* (A righteous love or the Persecuted families), when she was only twenty-six years old.[68] Set in nineteenth-century Italy, *Ahavat yesharim* tells the story of a beautiful and well-educated young Jewish woman named Finalia, daughter of a Jewish French dignitary who has sought refuge in Milan from the wrath of Napoleon. Finalia falls in love with a young Italian Jew named Victor, but their relationship is continually threatened by other men who try to win her heart and by threats against the lives of both Finalia's father and Victor. To be sure, *Ahavat yesharim* has its flaws; its plot is fantastic,[69] its character development sketchy. The novel also evinces errors in style and grammar, defects that riled contemporary reviewers. David Frischmann wrote a witheringly sarcastic review of the novel that likens the flaws of her novel to an act of murder perpetrated in prose. The gratuitously harsh and patronizing tone of this review is remarkably revealing, since Frischmann professed interest in seeing more women's contributions to Hebrew literature. "Behold," writes Frischmann as a preface to his sexist remarks, "young women are without strength, soft-hearted and forgiving and merciful, so if I made a polite bow and welcomed her nicely, she would relax and put aside her rage and in a soft voice whisper and peep, 'I forgive you.'"[70] Frischmann's condescending characterization of young women as weak and easily mollified by hollow gestures of gentlemanly courtesy is amplified in his concluding remarks, where, regretting that he cannot "curtsey before a young lady," he rejects Foner's Hebrew literary contribution outright. Frischmann ends by advocating a perpetuation of Jewish gender segregation, urging young Jewish women to attend to conventionally feminine issues and leave the future of Jewish culture to men like him. "Let each and every young woman learn what it is her obligation to learn and we here shall worry about our own fate, shall look after and do what we must do."[71]

Frischmann's negative review of the first volume of *Ahavat yesharim* may well have been the single greatest factor impeding the publication of volume two, which never made it to print. In more recent times, David Patterson has echoed Frischmann, referring to Foner's novel as a "pathetically weak tale of adventure and romance." Patterson's only compliment relates to Foner's treatment of a true story concerning a Jewish child who was kidnapped by the church to be brought up Catholic.[72] These criticisms notwithstanding, *Ahavat yesharim* remains a significant achievement. The novel's flaws in style, plot, and characterization are not unique in the context of Haskalah novel writing. What does set this work apart from others of the period is that it offers a female-authored image of the "New Hebrew Woman." Here is the first extended literary work written in Hebrew by a woman, one that makes liberal use of traditional Hebrew sources and provides in the character of Finalia a portrait of an enlightened and devout Jewish woman. The book insists, first and foremost, on a woman's right to pursue her own goals and marry the man she loves rather than enter into a marriage of political or economic expedience. To Foner's credit, despite the mean-spirited reviews of her first work, she continued to write. Indeed, of all the Hebrew women writers of the Haskalah, Foner was the most prolific, publishing four books. *Derekh yeladim* (The children's path, 1886) was the first Hebrew children's story published by a woman.[73] This was followed by *Beged bogdim* (The treachery of traitors, 1891),[74] a historical novel set in the Second Temple period, and *Mizikhronot yemei yalduti: o, mar'eh ha'ir Dvinsk* (Memories from my childhood, or Images of the city of Dvinsk, 1903),[75] a Hebrew memoir about the city of her youth.

Foner was exceptional as both a literary and religious figure. According to the testimony of her great-grandson Morris Rosenthal, she was known to wear a *tallit* and regularly conducted scholarly conversations with various rabbis in Pittsburgh, where she eventually settled.[76] In a 1931 article, Y. S. Weiss severely criticized Foner for reverting to orthodoxy in her later years. According to Weiss, Foner wore a *shaytel* and preached at various New York synagogues about the importance of observance and Jewish education, a transformation Weiss considered blatantly hypocritical, given her former support of the Haskalah.[77] Weiss evinces a limited knowledge of Foner's writings on the subject of religious observance, however, for as early as 1903, while still living in Europe, Foner advocated a form of enlightened traditionalism in her writing.[78] Indeed, throughout her career, Foner demonstrated a willingness to stake out uncommon positions and assume unconventional roles both for herself and her fictional heroines. Despite these exceptional achievements, however, little attention has been paid to Foner by the Hebrew literary establishment, a wrong this book hopes to redress.[79]

Another forgotten figure is Hava Shapiro (1878–1943), who used the pen-name *Eim kol hai,* alluding to the etymology of the name given to the first Hava/Eve. Shapiro made Hebrew literary history by writing the first manifesto on the need for genuine women's voices in Hebrew literature. In the preface to a book of Hebrew sketches entitled *Kovets tsiyyurim* (Collection of sketches, Warsaw, 1909), Shapiro laments the lack of women's voices in Hebrew literature. "Time and again," she writes, "when we [feminine plural] are amazed and awed by the talents of a 'wonder worker' one who 'penetrates the woman's heart,' we feel at the same time as though a strange hand has touched us. We have our world, our own pains and longings, and at the very least we should take part in describing them."[80] Shapiro set it as her task in her book of sketches to bring to the masculine Hebrew literary tradition the long-absent perspective of women.[81] Her decision to identify this historical women's literary effort with the biblical first woman suggests a desire to make a lasting contribution, one that reaches back to the beginnings both of human and Hebrew literary history. Shapiro's *Kovets tsiyyurim* is an extraordinary and, again, under-acknowledged work.[82] Most of the sketches deal either allegorically or realistically with the experiences of women. All the women or female figures attempt in one way or another to cross social borders and enter cultural or religious places typically off-limits to them.

In one allegorical sketch entitled "Hanets vehaderor" (The hawk and the sparrow), for example, Shapiro tells the story of a lost *deror* (sparrow, feminine noun), who seeks shelter and protection from an older *nets* (hawk, masculine noun), but who soon finds that her association with the overprotective, paternal hawk places limits on her desire to sing and fly and exercise her natural powers. Significant to our discussion of stealing the thematic and linguistic idols of Hebrew literature is the repetition in this story of the verb *lehitganev* (to steal away/into). One spring morning, the rays of the sun "steal" or "sneak into" the nest shared by the hawk and the sparrow, filling the *deror*—a word that means freedom as well as sparrow—with new inspiration and aspiration. Soon after this, the sparrow "sneaks away" from the nest, rising up into the air and flying off to seek new vistas. The emphasis in this sketch on the twin images of stealing (away) and singing suggest that it is an allegory about an aspiring young woman writer/intellectual who is learning how to escape the tutelage and/or protection of a man. The related images of flight and transgressed boundaries in this and other sketches bespeak Shapiro's desire to see the spaces of Jewish and intellectual life reconfigured to accommodate the entry of women writers and intellectuals.[83] As we shall see in chapter 5, Shapiro dedicated several of her sketches to the subject of Jewish women's desire to cross social borders and enter into new religious and intellectual spaces.

Many of these sketches have a distinctly autobiographical aspect. Shapiro herself led an extremely unconventional life for a woman of her time and religious background, leaving her husband and child in order to pursue a doctorate at the University of Berne and carrying on a long, tortuous affair with fellow Hebrew writer Reuven Brainin. Like many of her fictional heroines, Shapiro never achieved the literary success and acceptance she deserved. As Balin observes, whereas Shapiro began her writing career with the goal of "depicting women's experience realistically and fully," she abandoned this project soon after the publication of her first book.[84] Instead, she pursued a career in Hebrew journalism, working in extreme isolation, forever regretting thereafter her failure to "succeed in ink."[85] In a 1939 article, eminent literary critic Yosef Klausner describes Shapiro's status as a *bat-yehidah*—a solitary Hebrew literary daughter in the Diaspora—and offers her the following blessing on the occasion of the thirtieth anniversary of the publication of *Kovets tsiyyurim:* "May you be privileged to see many Hebrew women writers both in the Land of Israel and in the Diaspora, and may you cease to be a 'solitary daughter' even in the lands of dispersion."[86] Given Shapiro's deportation to Terezin in 1941 and her death in 1943, Klausner's blessing, issued on the eve of World War II, takes on an awful irony.

Border-Crossings: Hebrew Women Writers in the Promised Land

In her pathbreaking M.A. thesis on Hava Shapiro, Naomi Caruso speculates on what would have happened to Shapiro had she decided, after receiving her doctorate in 1910, to immigrate to Palestine. "In Palestine," Caruso writes, "she would have found a growing number of women writers like Hemda Ben-Yehudah, Nehama Puhachevsky or Yehudit Harari Eisenberg, who too were the product of the Russian Enlightenment but who came to Palestine imbued with an ideology and became part of the new historical process of the Return to Zion."[87] To be sure, the waves of Zionist immigration to Palestine, which brought educated and ideologically committed women to the Land of Israel, resulted in a major stage of development in Hebrew women's writing.

Now a critical mass of Jewish women began to write Hebrew prose fiction—women such as Itta Yellin (1868–1943), Nehamah (Feinstein) Puhachevsky (1869–1934), Hemda Ben-Yehudah (1873–1951), Yehudit Harari (1886–1979), and Devorah Baron (1887–1956).[88] The flowering of Hebrew poetry by women came subsequently, with poets such as Yokheved Bat-Miriam (1901–1980), Rachel (Bluwstein, 1890–1931), Esther Raab (1894–1981), Elisheva (1888–1949)[89], Shulamit Kalugai (1891–1972), Anda Pinkerfeld-Amir (1902–1981), Miri Dor (1911–1945),[90] and Leah Goldberg (1911–1970). Several of these women began writing long before their immigration to Palestine.[91] Some wrote in their native tongues, such as Rachel, Elisheva, and Pinkerfeld-Amir, who early in their careers composed in Russian or Polish. Others, such as Puhachevsky, Baron, and Bat-Miriam, began publishing in Hebrew even while they were still living in Russia. For many of these women, the experience of leaving their native homelands and crossing the literal border to the Land of Israel nurtured, shaped, and enriched their literary crossing into the realm of Hebrew writing. "Here, in Israel," writes Yaffa Berlovitz, in an afterword to her anthology of Hebrew women's prose from the First Aliyah (1882–1903), "in the midst of a narrow and poor Jewish community, in the desolate atmosphere of a faraway wilderness, removed from every cultural center . . . women arise with the desire to express themselves as publicists, belle-lettrists, and memoirists, and the stage is set for the participation of women in the literary life of the Land of Israel."[92]

To be sure, the revolutionary ideologies that began to overtake Russia at the beginning of the twentieth century strengthened the aspirations of Jewish women for greater participation in Jewish/Hebrew culture. As historian Deborah Bernstein writes in her book on the women's workers' movements in Palestine, "The Jewish women of Palestine, like their sisters throughout the world of the late nineteenth century, and the beginning of the twentieth, aspired to formal and legal equality—the right to elect and be elected, the right to enter all occupations, and the right to earn the same basic salaries that men earned. . . . They aspired to become 'full human beings' and full partners in all fields of social creation."[93] This revolutionary/egalitarian ideology, together with a Zionist nationalistic consciousness, impelled a number of women into the world of Hebrew letters. In the area of prose writing, many were encouraged to record their experiences in fictional form by lexicographer/editor Eliezer Ben-Yehudah. Like Gordon and Frischmann before him, Ben-Yehudah believed that the Jewish senses had too long been impoverished by life in the Diaspora; Jewish literature had become overly intellectual, desiccated, emotionless. In order to restore feeling to Hebrew literature, Ben-Yehudah called upon the literary participation of women.[94] "The need of the day," Ben Yehudah preached, "is for women to penetrate Hebrew literature; only they will bring feeling, softness, pliancy, fine nuance and changes into the dead, old, forgotten, hardened and dry Hebrew language—simplicity and precision, rather than grandiose rhetoric."[95]

This view, which combined a curious blend of feminism and essentialism—women are by their nature and essence soft, emotional, pliant, and capable of nuanced feeling, and for this reason they will bring simplicity and emotional precision to a literary language long desiccated and disused—compelled Ben-Yehudah to enlist any and all women to write for the various newspapers he published. His second wife, Hemdah, demonstrated no literary inclination prior to immigrating to Israel, yet under his tutelage she became a primary contributor to his publications.[96]

Anxieties of Authorship: The Example of Yokheved Bat-Miriam

What does it mean to be a poet or prose writer in a language and culture where women's contributions have been relatively absent? What does it mean to be a writer and a pioneering builder of an old/new Jewish homeland? To be sure, early Hebrew women writers both in Israel and abroad demonstrated mixed feelings about their distinct positions in Jewish social and literary history. The early poetry of Yokheved Bat-Miriam, collected under the title *Merahok,* provides an excellent example of the ambivalent responses offered by the first Hebrew women poets to their remarkable historical position. The ambitious, aspiring pose adopted by the speaker in many of her early poems, her complicated and original syntax, her striking metaphors of color and recurrent use of images of wide-open space and distance all connote a brave discovery of new geographical and literary worlds.[97] Even before her immigration to Palestine in 1929, Bat-Miriam wrote poems proclaiming the desire and ability to span continents and oceans, to explore unprecedented vistas in order to unite with the "you" of love, transcendence, and/or poetry. At the same time, she often abrogated the bold assertion after daring to utter it. Frequently, Bat-Miriam's speaker unleashes her bold thoughts but cannot escape the self-perception that in doing so, she is being witch-like and sinful; we see this in the following poem, which opens the title cycle of *Merahok* (originally published in *Hatekufah* in 1922):

אֶת-הַמֶּרְחָק, שֶׁנָּח

בֵּינִי וּבֵינֵךְ -

אֶעֱבֹר כֻּלּוֹ

וּלְפָנַיִךְ אָבוֹא.

אֶת-כֻּלּוֹ, הַכָּחֹל,

אֶכְבֹּשׁ,

כִּנְשִׁימָה אֶבְלָעֵהוּ,

וְאָבוֹא

לֵאמֹר דְּבַר-מָה לָךְ.

מָה אֹמַר?

וְאִם אֹמַר? ---

וּכְשֶׁאֹמַר

וְאֶפְנֶה לָלֶכֶת,

יִסָּגְרוּ מֶרְחָבִי, כִּכְנָפַיִם שֶׁנֶּאֱסְפוּ,

וְרַק שְׁבִיל צַר יִתְפַּתֵּל,

כְּמוֹ נֶעְלָם

שֶׁנִּגְלָה לְפָנַי,

וּלְרַגְלַי מִפַּיִס יָנוּחַ.

אֶת שְׁבִילִי זֶה

בַּעֲלֵי אֱלוּל אֲרַפֵּד,

וּבֵין שְׁדֵרוֹת לְבָנִים, עַל אֲשָׁרָם אֲבֵלִים,

חוֹטֵאת וְשָׁחָה אָשׁוּב לְבַדִּי.

I.
The distance, that lies
between you and me
I'll cross completely
and come before you.
All of its blueness   5
I'll conquer
and like a breath, swallow it,

and come
to tell you something.
What shall I say?   10
And if I say? — — —
And when I say
and turn to go,
my expanses will be shut, like gathered wings,   15
and but a thin path will thread itself
like a disappearance
revealed before me,
resting appeased at my feet.
This, my path   20
I'll drape with Elul leaves,
and amid columns of birch and their mourning bliss,
sinning and bent, I'll return alone.[98]

This poem can be divided neatly in two halves, as indicated by the triple
dash at the end of line 11. In the first half, the speaker audaciously introduces her plan to unite with the addressee, perhaps a lover, perhaps God
or some other figure of transcendence. Intrepidly, she will cross the blue
expanse dividing them (the oceans? the blue skies?), swallow it whole like
a breath, and then stand before this "you" to speak. Notice the way Bat-
Miriam mixes images of space and utterance. Indeed, at the heart of this
poem is a concern with how one commits the transgressive act of speech.
The poet-speaker aspires not only to collapse the distance between her and
the addressee but also to say something to him, to encapsulate the moment
with some momentous (poetic) declaration. Then the speaker stops short.
What shall she say to him? Will she say anything at all? Right here, at the
very moment of union and poetic utterance, the speaker falls silent, the
poem folding in on itself "like gathered wings," and the poet trembling
before the seeming omnipotence of her male addressee. What begins as a
triumphant ascension or transgression seems to culminate in a disappearance, an autumnal fall from aspiration (as signified from the fall leaves of
Elul, the Jewish month of penitence preceding the New Year), a shame-
filled repentance for daring to speak.

   According to Ruth Kartun-Blum, this and other poems in the title
cycle of *Merahok* are primarily about the conflict between a desire for

material bodily love and a spiritual desire for transcendence.[99] Kartun-Blum reads this poem as expressing the speaker's regret at violating her monastic ideal and giving worldly expression to her romantic desires; for Bat-Miriam, "the sin inheres in the desire to realize the feeling, to achieve a resolution."[100]

I'd like to suggest an alternative reading, one that concentrates more on the poet's fervent and transgressive desire to claim (or steal) a poetic voice in a formerly masculine literary culture. As noted earlier, the poem divides into two neat halves, with the second half expressing regret or undoing the bold assertions of the first. Yet what do we make of the fact that the lines in the second half are longer and far more redolent with metaphor and description? Does this increased poeticism represent a falling away from speech? Is it possible that in imagining a union with the (male) addressee, the poet-speaker has experienced a kind of artistic epiphany, allowing her to speak even more freely and poetically? Is this a poem about the speaker's regret over daring to speak or does it dramatize the poetic process that begins with an impatient spring-like burst of feeling and ambition and culminates with a contemplative emotional autumn?

Throughout the poem cycle, Bat-Miriam's speaker expresses feelings of sinfulness and regret, but unlike Kartun-Blum, who reads these expressions at face value, I see them as dubious declarations at best. Notice, for example, the celebratory description of sinful excess in the second poem of the cycle:

בַּחֲלוֹמִי

רָאִיתִי אֵשׁ יְרֻקָּה,

עוֹלָה וּמְהַבְהֶבֶת.

עוֹלָה וְנִמְשֶׁכֶת,

נוֹטָה לַצְּדָדִים,

רוֹעֶדֶת,

חֲרֵדָה וְשׁוֹאָגֶת.

בַּחֲלוֹמִי רָאִיתִי אֵשׁ יְרֻקָּה.

הִתְעוֹרַרְתִּי, קַמְתִּי מִמִּטָּתִי.

נֶגְדִּי גָּבַר אוֹר-שֶׁמֶשׁ-הַיּוֹם,

וּכְמִתְחָרָה אֶת-עֵינַי לְפָנָיו

פָּתַחְתִּי לִרְוָחָה.

עָמַדְתִּי,

אָמַרְתִּי:
רָעָה הִנֵּנִי.

אֵשׁ גְּדוֹלָה,
גְּדוֹלָה מֵאוֹר-שֶׁמֶשׁ-הַיּוֹם,
אָחֲזָה בְּצִיצִית רֹאשִׁי הַלּוֹהֵט
וַתַּעַל בְּעֵינַי,
וַתִּרְעַד עַל שְׂפָתַי,
וַתְּלַהֵט אֶת יָדַי וְרַגְלַי –
וַתִּהְיֶינָה נְשׂוּאוֹת כְּמוֹ רוּחוֹת
בְּמִדְבָּרִיּוֹת דּוֹמְמִים, צְמֵאִים.
וָתָּרֶם אוֹתִי לְמַעְלָה –
גְּלוּיָה
וּפְתוּחָה נֶגֶד אַרְבַּע רוּחוֹת הָעוֹלָם
וְלִפְנֵי שֶׁמֶשׁ צוֹעֵק וּפוֹרֵץ
הִצִּיגַתְנִי,
שִׁבְעָתַיִם בּוֹעֶרֶת מִמֶּנּוּ,
רָעָה,
בְּלַהֲבוֹת אֵשׁ אֲחוּזָה,
בְּיִלְלַת-פֶּרֶא עַל שְׂפָתַי,
נֶגֶד שֶׁמֶשׁ-הַיּוֹם.

II.
In my dream
I saw a green flame,
rise and flicker,
rise and continue,
incline to the sides,   5
tremble,
frightened and roaring.
In my dream I saw a green flame.

I awakened, rose from my bed.
The daylight sun grew strong before me   10

and as if contesting my eyes before it
I opened to the expanse,
I stood,
I said:
Here I am, wicked.   15

A huge flame,
larger than the daylight sun,
took hold of the lock *[tsitsit]* of my burning head
and rose in my eyes,
and trembled on my lips,   20
and kindled my hands and feet—
and they were carried like winds
in silent thirsty deserts.
And raised me aloft —
exposed   25
and open to all four winds of the world
and before a screaming bursting sun,
I was presented
sevenfold as bright as him,
wicked,   30
bound to fiery flame
a wild scream on my lips
against the day sun. (*Merahok*, pp. 7–8)

The first stanza of the poem circumscribes the vision, tucking the marvelous oxymoronic image of the green flame neatly into the nether world of dreams, between the repeated lines: "In my dream I saw a green flame." In the second stanza, though, it is morning. The speaker awakens from her dream and faces the daylight sun—inspired and emboldened by light—like H. N. Bialik's poetic speaker in his famous poem *Tsafririm* (Imps of the sun). In contrast to Bialik's poem, where inspiration comes to the poet in the form of mischievous, "wanton, madcaps of light" that "leap and dance and touch [his] soft skin"[101] in a form of sexual play, Bat-Miriam describes a far more aggressive and explosive encounter. In the third stanza the poetic vision overcomes all boundaries of time, space, even gender. In defiance of the daylight sun, the dream persists, exceeding its nocturnal incarnation. At this point in the poem, the speaker steals the poetic/prophetic language of Ezekiel 8:2–4 as a means of expressing her own vision of inspiration. Suddenly, the poet speaker sees a huge flame that takes hold of a lock of her hair [tsitsit roshi], sets her on fire, and carries her aloft. The poem reaches its climax as the female speaker, hovering in the heavens, proclaims herself sevenfold as bright as the (male-gendered) sun, an allusion to Isaiah 30:26, where the prophet foresees that "on the day that the Lord binds up the breach of his people, and heals the stroke of their wound," the light will be "sevenfold, as the light of seven days." As in the case of the Ezekiel reference, this biblical allusion endows Bat-Miriam's vision with a prophetic importance. More precisely, Bat-Miriam's speaker seizes upon the language of prophecy as a means of giving voice to her countertraditional poetic vision. While there are several women prophets in the Bible, no biblical/prophetic dreams are attributed to women. Bat-Miriam's speaker, who dreams in the language and imagery of Ezekiel and Isaiah, conjures up the image of the woman prophet/poet as dreamer.[102] David Jacobson reads this poem as transforming "Ezekiel's vision of a fiery God who causes the prophet to view Israel's evil into a vision of a cruel sun-god who implants an evil fiery passion within the speaker and shouts at her."[103] According to Jacobson, in these early poems Bat-Miriam "conveys her longing to discover the image of a divine being who could serve as a positive alternative to the cruel uncaring image of the shouting, bursting sun-god."[104] Contrary to Jacobson's reading, I would argue that Bat-Miriam is championing herself over the sun-god and celebrating her superior form of illumination, even as she seems to apologize for it. Yes, the poem describes an explosive daytime encounter between the speaker and the screaming sun, but the speaker bravely and proudly announces that in her inspired state she is sevenfold as bright as the sun. The speaker relishes rather than rails against this poetic confrontation.

The combination of audacity and trepidation evident in these early poems by Bat-Miriam is a widespread feature of early Hebrew women's writing both in the Diaspora and the Land of Israel. These women knew well that they were treading on territory previously off-limits to them. It was their unprecedented task to cross into these spaces, seize the language, and transform it into something new, even as it echoes or borrows from tradition. On occasion, they faltered in this task, but more often than not they triumphed.

"Hidden Flames"

Hebrew Women Poets and the Search for Foremothers

The rabbis taught: Four traits are attributed to women: they are gluttonous, prying, lazy, and jealous. Gluttonous, as it is written: "And
she took from its fruit." (Gen. 3:6) Prying: "And Sarah overheard."
(Gen. 18:10) Lazy: "Make ready quickly three measures of fine
meal." (Gen. 18:6) Jealous: "And Rachel was jealous." (Gen. 30: 1)
Rabbi Joshua added wrathful and talkative. Wrathful: "And Sarah
said to Abraham: 'My wrath is upon you.'" Talkative: "And Miriam
and Aaron spoke." Rabbi Levi added stealing and gadding about.
Stealing: "And Rachel stole the idols." (Gen. 31:19) Gadding about:
"And Dina went out."

GENESIS RABBAH 45:5

Is it possible that the whole story of canonicity, the whole story of
authority in our culture, is intimately bound up with the repressed
Mother, shimmering and struggling at the liminal threshold of consciousness against whom the Father must anxiously defend itself?

ALICIA SUSKIN OSTRIKER

In a recent article entitled "The Double Canonicity of the Bible," critic
Robert Alter explores the importance of the Hebrew Bible as a "great
compendium of cultural"[1] and literary references for the Hebrew writer.
According to Alter, the canonical status of such controversial, even subversive works as Job, Ecclesiastes, and Song of Songs indicates that books
of the Bible were canonized not simply for ideological reasons but also
for reasons of literary and/or intellectual merit.[2] The "age-old sense of the
Bible as a literary canon not just a religious one,"[3] Alter argues, is reflected
in the ways in which Hebrew writers, throughout Hebrew literary history, persistently reinvented and redirected sacred biblical language for
their own literary ends. "Even in periods when Jews had no option at all
of secular cultural activity, the evidence of what they composed in

Hebrew argues that they never ceased to respond to the literary dimensions of the Bible."[4]

Alter's essay aims, in part, to polemicize against those postmodern critics who see canon formation purely as a function of ideological rather than literary criteria. Ironically, however, his attempt to deflect or underplay the role of ideology in canon conformation points toward the need to address the political/ideological dimensions and gender biases of literary history. What Alter does not acknowledge in his essay is the masculinely gendered nature of this history of biblical "double canonicity." Throughout the essay, Alter refers to the Hebrew writer's experience of the Bible as the ideological as well as "literary repository of the culture" in universal, gender neutral terms. Yet, for obvious historical reasons, the writers he adduces to illustrate this ongoing literary interaction with the Bible—Samuel Hanagid, Judah Halevi, Solomon ibn Gabirol, Saul Tchernihowsky, Hayyim Nahman Bialik—are all men.

It is not my intention here to dispute Alter's thesis, which itself is highly persuasive, but rather to investigate its implications for the Hebrew woman writer interested in attaching herself to this tradition. What is the significance of biblical "double canonicity" for early twentieth-century Hebrew women writers? What does it mean for a woman writer to enter so belatedly into this multivalent three-thousand-year-old ideological/literary dialogue?

In a 1954 essay, critic Eli Schweid ventured to answer this question through a comparison of the treatment of the Bible in the poetry of Haim Nahman Bialik and Rachel (Bluwstein). According to Schweid, male poets such as Bialik wrote from "within" the Bible. That is to say, their language and style were thoroughly shaped by their years studying the Bible and the rabbinic commentaries. Bialik and his cohorts, whose yeshiva education immersed them in the double canonicity of the Bible, consequently steeped their poetry in complex intertextual references to sacred Jewish sources. In contrast, early Hebrew women poets such as Bluwstein, comparatively new to the Hebrew language and the sacred texts, approached the Bible as if from the outside. In Schweid's view, Rachel wrote "about" rather than from "within" the Bible, re-depicting its characters and recuperating their stories as representative of her own personal experiences.[5]

According to Schweid's delineation of the differences between Bialik's and Bluwstein's approaches to biblical materials, Rachel's use of Tanakh clearly emerges as a species of stylistic and thematic limitation. To illustrate this, Schweid offers a "parable about a thirsty wayfarer, who passing by a well, stops for a moment to take a drink. But when he rolls the stone off the mouth of the well, what reflects back at him from the depths is his own image."[6] Schweid's depiction of Bluwstein as a thirsty traveler plainly betrays his sense of her linguistic and literary limitations. The immigrant woman poet, new to the land and language of the Bible, needs to nourish her style and content by drinking deep from the wellspring of traditional sources. She manages to roll the stone off the well top—an image drawn from the story of Jacob and Rachel in Genesis 29, chosen, perhaps, because of Rachel's personal affinity for the story of her biblical namesake—but her narcissistic self-obsessions prevent her from penetrating the depths of these ancient literary sources. Instead, her poetic vision clings to the surface of things, fixing on her personal experiences as reflected or echoed in the biblical story. The result, in Schweid's estimation, constitutes a form of poetic weakness. Rachel wrote poetry of the individual, he observes, but in this individualistic poetry "there is no sense of power, like that demonstrated by a man when he fights for truth, no sense of secure faith like that of a man who has the strength in his arms to wage battle."[7]

Like Schweid, my basic premise is that early Hebrew women writers often experienced and approached the dual authority of the Bible differently than their male counterparts. I concur with him that these women writers often wrote as outsiders. But like Lori Lefkowitz, I "see Woman as outsider looking in with powers and privileges that accrue from distance."[8] In other words, contrary to Schweid, who privileges a form of poetry clearly associated with masculinist notions of poetic power,[9] I do not assume that this outsider position necessarily resulted in a lesser form of poetry. On the contrary, I maintain that Hebrew women poets discovered a particular way of reading and writing about the Bible that demonstrates originality as well as literary/ideological strength. If, as Alter contends, (male) Hebrew writers over the course of Jewish history evinced a "double responsiveness to Scripture read in the richness of the original language,"[10] early Hebrew women writers demonstrated a "double transgressiveness": a suspicious or oppositional stance with respect to the frequently patriarchal ideology of the biblical story (or that of its predominantly male interpreters), as well as marked awareness of the unprecedented and therefore subversive nature of female Hebrew literary interaction with the biblical text. This quality of "double transgressiveness," I would argue, is reflected with particular poignancy in their poems about biblical women.

45

Recall, for a moment, the midrash from Genesis Rabbah quoted as the first epigraph to this chapter. In this midrash, the rabbis propose a litany of negative attributes essential and eternal to femininity, using the stories of such biblical women as Eve, Sarah, Rachel, Dina, and Miriam as proof texts. Gluttony, eavesdropping, laziness, jealousy, wrathfulness, talkativeness, stealing, and gadding about—the list reads like the "eight deadly sins" of womankind. To be sure, rabbinic literature includes commentaries that offer more positive portrayals of women, in general, and biblical women, in particular. What is significant and representative about this midrash, however, is that it is a male-authored text, intended for male consumption, that selectively reads the stories of biblical women to comment on the nature of womankind. The net effect of the rabbi's focusing on the most derogatory aspect of each individual biblical woman's story and then combining these aspects together into one big picture is a historical continuum of feminine vice.

To be sure, early Hebrew women writers, too, attempted to draw parallels between their own contemporary experiences and those of biblical women in order to create a chain of shared female tradition. But their ends were conspicuously different from those of the rabbis cited above. "Ei-sham" (somewhere), a poem by Shulamit Kalugai (1891–1972), can be read as countercommentary on Genesis 45:5:

אֵי - שָׁם

אֵי-שָׁם נָחוֹת בְּסֵתֶר
נְשֵׁי חֵן, הָדָר, גְּבוּרָה
לְרֹאשׁ בַּת-שֶׁבַע כֶּתֶר,
מַטֶּה בְּיַד דְּבוֹרָה.

דּוּמָם עָצְמָה עֵינֶיהָ,
בְּאֵין אוֹנִים לֵאָה,
וְעַל חָרְבַּן בָּנֶיהָ
תִּשָּׂא רָחֵל קוֹלָהּ.

וְתֵאָנַח בְּלַחַשׁ,
תָּנוּד לָהֶן שָׂרָה.
בְּלִי נִיב תַּחֲלֹם, בְּלִי רַחַשׁ,
יָעֵל עַל מוֹת סִיסְרָא.

46

לֵב שׁוּלַמִּית יִפְעַם עוֹד
לְזֵכֶר אֲהָבִים.
וְרוּת תָּשִׁיר לַנֶּכֶד
שִׁירִים מוֹאָבִיִּים.

אִי-שָׁם נָחוֹת בְּסֵתֶר
נְשֵׁי חֵן, הָדָר, גְּבוּרָה
לְרֹאשׁ בַּת-שֶׁבַע כֶּתֶר,
מַטֶּה בְּיַד דְּבוֹרָה.

Somewhere

Somewhere in secret they rest,
Women of grace, splendor, bravery.
On Bathsheba's head, a crown,
In Deborah's hand, a staff.   4

Silently, helplessly,
Leah closed her eyes,
And over her sons' desolation
Rachel raises her voice.   8

And sighing softly,
Sarah nods to the others.
Without word, without murmur,
Yael dreams of Sisera's death.   12

Shulamith's heart beats again
To the memory of love.
And Ruth sings her grandson
Moabite songs.   16

Somewhere, in secret they rest,
Women of grace, splendor, and bravery.
On Bathsheba's head, a crown,
In Deborah's hand, a staff.[11]   20

Like the classical midrash in the epigraph to this chapter, Kalugai's poem gives a selective reading of several stories of biblical women, bringing them together under a single rubric. Indeed, in this poem, the melding of diverse stories of biblical women is underscored by the shifting tenses, the frequent use of compound sentences and the ambiguous syntax. Frequently, Kalugai places the subject at the end of the sentence, making it unclear where one sentence ends and the next begins. In line 5, for example, it is initially unclear who closes her eyes, Deborah or Leah. Likewise, in line 9, we are not immediately sure whether it is Rachel or Sarah who sighs; and in line 11, one gets the momentary impression that Sarah, rather than Yael, is dreaming of Sisera's death. These grammatical ambiguities suggest simultaneity of action, as though the various women of the Bible are being brought back to life, all at once, at the behest of the modern woman poet. As seen in Genesis Rabbah 45:5, this blending of individual stories is a common midrashic technique. In Kalugai's unconventional midrash, the stories of biblical women join to create a female tradition of "grace, splendor, and bravery."

It is important to note that Kalugai identifies grace and splendor precisely in those unexpected or "hidden" places left unexplored in conventional midrash. In the first line of the poem, Kalugai refers to "they"—"women of glory, splendor and bravery"—resting somewhere "in secret," suggesting the need for the woman poet or critic to uncover and reinterpret their secret stories. If Jewish tradition has always represented the splendor of monarchy in masculine terms through images of King David and King Solomon, Kalugai specifically sets a crown on the head of Bathsheba, the wife of David and mother of Solomon. If the staff, as symbol of authority and miraculous power, is typically associated with Moses, Kalugai passes the staff into the hands of the female prophet-poet Deborah.

Likewise, a great deal of attention is given in this poem to unacknowledged or unelaborated instances of female emotion and reflection. We read about Leah's quiet feelings of helplessness, a comment, perhaps, on the difficulties that face women in a society that prizes physical beauty above all other qualities. We see Sarah sighing and attempting to comfort her female descendants, bespeaking Kalugai's desire to view Sarah as founding mother of Israelite sisterhood. We see Yael dreaming quietly about the murder of Sisera, as if basking in a glow of personal triumph. All these are images not typically found in biblical or rabbinic representations. Perhaps the most iconoclastic moment in the poem

48

comes in lines 15 and 16, where Kalugai allows Ruth—purported ancestor of the Davidic dynasty, celebrated in the commentaries for her willingness to follow her mother-in-law and forsake her Moabite past—to sing Moabite songs to her grandchild. Kalugai allows a place in her brief portrait of Ruth for nostalgic reflection on her Moabite past, for a complex, textured identity.

Poets such as Kalugai and her better known peers—Yokheved Bat-Miriam, Rachel, Esther Raab, Anda Pinkerfeld-Amir, and Leah Goldberg—attempted to rediscover and/or invent a genealogy of female agency and creativity. As Sandra M. Gilbert and Susan Gubar have famously suggested, in order for the woman writer to establish her rightful place in the realm of literature, she often needs to revisit and re-imagine her past, to "redefine the terms of her socialization." Frequently, they observe, "she can begin such a struggle only by actively seeking a female precursor who, far from representing a threatening force to be denied or killed"—as in Harold Bloom's model of the strong poet who must poetically wrestle his precursor to death in order to clear space for his original poetry—"proves by example, that a revolt against patriarchal literary authority is possible."[12]

Feminist biblical critics and theologians such as Elisabeth Schüssler Fiorenza have argued that the feminist critique of biblical patriarchy requires a strategy of reading that is both "deconstructive and reconstructive."[13] This two-tiered approach encapsulates the interaction with the biblical text that is evident in many of the poems I shall discuss in this chapter. First, early Hebrew women poets adopt what I would call a *hermeneutics of displacement,* offering readings of the text that displace male figures and misogynist interpretations from their position of centrality, often consigning the forefathers to the wings while shifting the foremothers to center stage. Second, they enact what Alicia Ostriker has more generally termed a "hermeneutics of desire" (an interpretive process wherein the poet-interpreter finds in the story what she wants to find[14]), but what I would like more specifically to call a *hermeneutics of identification*—a form of biblical revision that places special emphasis on the stories of biblical women artists and poets and other liberating images with which modern women poets can personally *identify.* Frequently these poets recognize features in their biblical foremothers that a patriarchal tradition of reading and commentary had previously ignored: a poetic or creative spirit, a vocation or distinctive (literary) voice. As I have already intimated in the context of Schweid's remarks on Rachel's poetry, the "hermeneutics of identification" often assumes an explicitly personal or individualistic form, with the poet claiming an intimate, abiding personal connection with the given female biblical figure. Because many of these women poets had crossed geographical borders and immigrated to the Land of Israel from the Diaspora, they often envisioned themselves as emulating, even re-embodying their foremothers.

Of course, not every poem in Hebrew written by a woman using biblical materials will conform identically to the interpretive pattern I have described.[15] As Miriam Peskowitz cautions, "women's speech, thoughts, feelings, stances, and positions are multiple, complicated, and often contradictory and at odds with one another."[16] These poets wrote not only about the female figures in the Bible but also about biblical men.[17] By the same token, many male Hebrew poets of this era wrote about biblical women, some even with a staunchly feminist sensibility.[18] That said, early twentieth-century Hebrew women poets realized that theirs was unprecedented female/feminist foray into Hebrew literature, and their poems about biblical women bear the imprint of this transgressive move in ways not typically duplicated by male Hebrew poets writing at the same time and about the same figures.

The World According to Eve

A marked difference in approach can be observed between the ways in which male and female Hebrew poets of this period poetically represented the story of Adam and Eve. Here are two poems about Eve by men, the first by Yehudah Karni (1884–1949) the second, by poet-editor Jacob Fichman (1881–1958):

The First Envy

And so it was with Eve, immediately upon tasting
From the Tree of Knowledge — sin testified against her
And she shrieked in terror:

"The snake has tricked me into tasting
Good and evil and pushed me
Into the abyss.   6

Behold, death faces me and comes
To take my soul;
Soon I'll drown in the darkness.

God will create a second woman
For the man, and in the shadow of the mount
And to the rustle of the leaves   12

He will lie with her, and bring life to his seed with her
— And I, my flesh will rot and fester
My womb crawling with worms.

Ah, for you, Adam,
I take pity
But envy burns like fire in my bones.   18
No, no, together we'll line our resting place,
To eat and die —
In my arms, with me, rotting in the netherworld."

"And she gave also to her husband," but he too
Did not die, and began to lust for
Eve's nakedness.   24

And though there was no other woman but her — from then on
Eve tracked Adam's every footstep,
For like death was her envy.[19]

Eve

I loved Adam, he, wise like God
And strong of heart, with good blood.
But the snake whispered astounding things to me,
His whisper painful but also caressing.   4

51

When Adam fell asleep, the garden became stupefied,
Its birds silent, its grasses wet, —
And then he'd call from the thicket, and like a magic flame
His speech would catch fire in my heart: To pluck, to pluck!   8

When dawn arose, Adam's warm hand
Once again caressed my skin, and how soothing his hand
To the heart, listening to the tune of his blood.

Indeed, each daytime thought quieted in the light,   12
Bent over to the other side, and every plot
of the garden was spellbound until evening against the shadowy
   thicket.[20]

Both of these poems offer male-biased interpretations of the biblical story. Karni's "First Lament," based almost entirely on Rashi's interpretation of Genesis 3:6, suggests that in sharing the fruit with her husband, Eve was motivated chiefly by a jealous desire not to see him wed and have children with another woman. According to this interpretation, Eve is a petty, jealous wife, whose extreme possessiveness overrides her concern for her husband's well-being. As indicated by the punned usage of the words *rahmi* (my womb crawling with worms, line 15) and *rahmi* (my compassion or pity, line 17), Karni links Eve's insufficient compassion or concern for Adam to female biology, suggesting that Eve's traits are essential to womankind. Whereas Adam invokes the word *besari* (my flesh) to assert his intrinsic connectedness to the newly born *ishah* (woman) in Genesis 2:23—"this one at last / Is bone of my bone / And flesh of my flesh./ This one shall be called Woman / For from man she was taken," Eve/woman refers selfishly to *ani besari* (I, my flesh) in line 14 as a means of expressing her personal fear of death and bodily decomposition. Like many interpreters, Karni reads the end of the story, where Adam and Eve recognize their nakedness, as an etiology of human lust; in his rendering, however, male lust is stronger. For this reason, Eve's "sinful" decision to give her husband the fruit as a means of keeping him by her side results in a need for even greater vigilance on Eve's part to keep her husband's lust at bay. This is Eve's punishment.

Fichman's "Eve" presents a similarly stereotypical impression of Eve/woman as a creature hopelessly struggling between good and evil impulses. The good in her derives from Adam's wise, strong, godly, daytime influence.[21] Fichman's Adam/man is identified with the sun, symbolic of the light of reason, as opposed to Eve/woman, who is allied with the moon and emotional caprice. Under Adam's purview, Eve's thoughts bend in the direction of what is good and wise. But Eve's evil, serpentine impulses run riot at night, while the wise and godly Adam sleeps, suggesting that only under the protective aegis of a man can a woman stay on the proper path. If in Genesis 3, Adam evinces little wisdom, initiative, or strength, readily accepting the fruit from Eve despite his knowledge of the divine prohibition, Fichman insists on Adam's wisdom and godliness, over and against Eve's susceptibility to the evil serpent's ways.

In contrast to the poetic interpretations offered by Karni and Fichman, women poets such as Anda Pinkerfeld-Amir and Yokheved Bat-Miriam read the story of Eve against the grain of misogynist bias. From Elizabeth Cady Stanton to Virginia Woolf to Phyllis Trible,[22] Judaeo-Christian women writers and critics have stressed the importance of confronting the judgments traditionally passed against Eve and reclaiming the first biblical woman as a positive role model. Eve's alleged first sin often legitimated the oppression of women under various religious structures. As Cady Stanton writes in *The Woman's Bible,* "The Bible teaches that woman brought sin and death into the world, that she precipitated the fall of the race, that she was arraigned before the judgment seat of Heaven, tried, condemned and sentenced. Marriage for her was to be a condition of bondage, maternity a period of suffering, and anguish, and in silence and subjection she was to play the role of dependent on man's bounty for all her material wants."[23] A writer's decision to support Eve rather than her detractors constitutes a rejection of misogyny from its inception. Women poets writing in Hebrew were not extraordinary among Judaeo-Christian writers in their desire to offer a more favorable history of Eve.[24] Yet a fundamental uniqueness attaches to Hebrew feminist revisionist mythmaking of this kind. Because their poems are in the same language as the myths themselves, the poets can give subtle attention to the minute implications of biblical Hebrew word choices.

In "Eve," Anda Pinkerfeld-Amir employs a dual hermeneutic of displacement and identification to challenge the very idea of Eve's sin. In her poetic rendition of the story, Eve does not eat the apple; she studies it, and thus grows into an awareness of her analogous ability to bear fruit:

Pinkerfeld-Amir:

חַוָּה

יוֹם אַחַר יוֹם נֶחֱרָז,
לַיְלָה אַחַר לַיְלָה —
בְּעֶדְנָה שְׁטָפוּנִי וּבְרֹנֶן.

מִבֹּקֶר עַד עֶרֶב לְטָפַתְנִי הַשֶּׁמֶשׁ,
מִבֵּין הַפְּאֵרוֹת קַרְנֶיהָ הִגְנִיבָה,
לִנְשֹׁק תַּלְתַּלִי.
מֵעֶרֶב עַד בֹּקֶר
הָאֵזוֹב הָרַךְ הָעֵדֶן שֲנָתִי,
פִּנֵּק חֲלוֹמוֹתָי.

עַד אֶשְׂבַּע,
עַד אִיעַף,
עַד אֶלְאָא —
וְלֹא אוּכַל עוֹד.

הִבְשִׁילָה הַשֶּׁמֶשׁ גְּוִי,
הַלַּיְלָה הֵעִיר לְשַׁדִּי,
וְאֵין לָהֶם מַעַן.
יִכְבַּד עָלַי כָּל טֶפַח עוֹרִי
כְּמוֹ אָבָה פְּרֹץ,
וּמוֹצָא לוֹ אָיִן.

וְהִנֵּה רְאִיתִיךָ, עֵץ,
הִכַּרְתִּיךָ בַּתַּפּוּחַ זֶה,
חָכְמַת כָּל לְשַׁדֶּיךָ בּוֹ אָצַרְתָּ.

וָאֵדַע הַסּוֹד, לְמַעֲנוֹ גָּדַלְתָּ,
לְמַעֲנוֹ גָּבַהְתָּ, וְאַף הִסְתָּעַפְתָּ.
גַּם אֲנִי גָּדַלְתִּי,
גַּם אֲנִי גָּבַהְתִּי —
כָּמוֹךָ אֶשָּׂא אֶת פִּרְיִי.

54

אָכֵן לִמַּדְתַּנִי, עֵץ.

אֵיכָה זֶה רֵיקָה עַד עַתָּה הָלַכְתִּי
בֵּין נוֹשְׂאֵי פְּרָיִם?
וְאַךְ פָּנַי כָּבַשְׁתִּי
בְּכִלְמָה מוּזָרָה
בִּפְנֵי אֵילוֹת שֶׁתָּפַח גֻּנָּן,
הַכּוֹרְעוֹת מִכָּבְדָּן.
כָּל צִפּוֹר זְעִירָה
יוֹשְׁבָה עַל בֵּיצֵיהָ,
פְּרִי דָמָהּ וּקְרָבֶיהָ,
הִכְלִימַתְנִי.
בִּפְנֵיהָ קְטַנְתִּי,
אֲשֶׁר נוֹצַרְתִּי אַךְ לְצָהֳלָה;
אֲשֶׁר דָּלַגְתִּי מֵעַיִן אֱלֵי עַיִן,
וְרַגְלַי רָחַצְתִּי בִּגְבִישׁ זַכּוּתָם;
אֲשֶׁר קָפַצְתִּי מִמֶּגֶד אֱלֵי מֶגֶד,
לְחִכִּי עָרֵב, לְשַׂמְּחֵנִי.

וְעַתָּה אֵדָעָה,
וְאֶכְבַּד מְאֹד, אַף אֶאֱשַׁר:
אָחוֹת אֲנִי לָכֵן,
אֵילוֹת תְּפוּחוֹת,
זְאֵבוֹת כְּבֵדוֹת,
מְעַט–וְנִכְרַע מִכָּבְדֵּנוּ.
כְּמוֹכֵן–כָּמוֹנִי.

וְלֹא עוֹד אֵבוֹשׁ בִּפְנֵיכֶן–
מֵיטַב דָּמִי, כְּמֵיטַב דְּמֵיכֶן,
יִתְגַּבֵּשׁ לִפְרִי.
קַבֵּל אֲקַבְּלֶנּוּ,
נָשׂא אֶשָּׂאֶנּוּ,
אַף אִם לָאָרֶץ יַשְׁחֵנִי,
כְּמוֹכֵן.

55

הָלַךְ לֹא אֵלֵךְ עוֹד רֵיקָה בֵּינֵיכֶם,
כְּנַחַל זֶה פָּזִיז, לֹא יָדַע
אָנָה יֵלְכוּ מֵימָיו הַקַּלִּים.

תְּבָרֵךְ לִי, נַחַשׁ-לַחַשׁ שֶׁבַּלֵּב,
לַפְּרִי הַבָּא,
בּוֹ אֶגָּאֵל,
אַף אִם עֶדְנָה פּוֹחֶזֶת לֹא אֵדַע עוֹד.

Eve

Day after day was threaded together
night after night —
they washed over me in pleasure *[ednah]* and in song.

From morning until evening the sun caressed me,
smuggling its rays between the branches   5
to kiss my curls.
From evening until morning
the soft hyssop refined my sleep,
pampered my dreams.

Until I was sated,   10
until I tired,
until I wearied —
and could no longer.

The sun ripened my body,
the night awakened my juices,   15
and they had no destination.
Every inch of my skin grew heavy on me
as if wanting to burst forth
but there was no opening.

56

Then behold, I saw you, tree,   20
I recognized you in that apple,
within which you have stored the wisdom of all your juices.

And I knew the secret for which you grew,
for which you rose and spread out.
I too have grown,   25
I too have risen tall —
like you I shall bear my fruit.
This is what you have taught me, tree.

How is it that I walked empty up until now
among the fruit bearers?   30
And hid my face
in freakish shame
from the does whose bodies bulged,
who kneeled under their weight.
Every tiny bird   35
sitting upon her eggs,
fruit of her blood and entrails,
made me ashamed.
In the face of her I became small,
I, who was created only for mirth;   40
who skipped from spring to spring,
and washed my feet in their crystal clarity;
who leaped from delicacy to delicacy,
to please my palate, to gladden myself.

And now I know,   45
And I grow heavy, yet happy:
I am a sister to you,
bulging does,
heavy she-wolves,

a little longer — and we'll kneel under our weight.   50
As you are — so am I.

No more shall I be disgraced before you —
my best blood, like the best of your blood
will crystallize into fruit.
Surely I shall accept it,   55
Surely I shall bear it,
even if it bows me to the ground,
like you.

No longer shall I walk empty among you,
like a hasty stream, not knowing   60
where its swift waters run.
Blessed will you be to me, snake-whisper in my heart,
to the fruit you have brought me,
through it I shall be redeemed,
even if I know no more wanton pleasure.[25]   65

Pinkerfeld-Amir's poetic reinterpretation of the Eve story is based on a causal connection between Eve's eating the fruit in Genesis 3:6 and her subsequent pregnancy in Genesis 4:1. Contrary to the biblical verse, where Adam is described as "knowing his wife" whereupon she conceived, in Pinkerfeld-Amir's version, Adam, like God, is entirely displaced from the narrative. Eve alone, through knowledge and recognition, emerges from her languid, solipsistic life of *ednah* in Eden and joins the other fruit-bearing creatures of nature: the fruit trees, the does, and she-wolves (lines 45–51). Whereas before she walked humble and ashamed in the luxuriant and prolific garden, now she, too, will bring forth offspring.

Pinkerfeld-Amir's Eve does not sin as much as she awakens and matures. In contrast to classical biblical interpretation, which has long understood the pain suffered in pregnancy and parturition as a divinely ordained pathology—as it says in Genesis 3:16, "I will make most severe your pangs in childbearing; In pain shall you bear children. Yet your urge shall be for your husband, and he shall rule over you"—this Eve declares herself the master of her own pregnancy, which she perceives not as a painful punishment but a blissful heaviness, a happy burden. Likewise, Pinkerfeld-Amir rewrites the role of the snake in this primal myth. In contrast to the biblical tale, in which a mythical snake tricks a gullible Eve into committing her grave sin, she envisions a metaphorical snake— a *nahash-lahash* (snake-whisper), a play on the Hebrew expression *lahash-nahash,* which means spell or incantation, derivative of snake-sorcery. This metaphorical or magic snake within her heart "brings her to fruit," inspiring her to see her own fecundity. Unlike the biblical narrative, then, where God curses the snake for tempting Eve to sin, this snake-whisper is blessed and welcomed, the impulse that propels her into pregnancy.

Like traditionalists who reinforce the link between female identity and pregnancy, the poem seems to describe Eve in purely biological terms. Yet the displacement of Adam from the story detaches Eve's pregnancy from its biological/sexual origins. In so doing, the poet opens up the possibility for a more metaphorical interpretation of Eve's story. Indeed, the references throughout the poem to acts of perception and knowledge acquisition—Eve "sees," "recognizes," "knows the secret," learns from the tree and is thus redeemed—suggest that Pinkerfeld-Amir wants to reclaim Eve not just as a biological foremother but as a progenitor of other forms of creative cognition. Eve grows heavy in this poem, both literally and metaphorically. At the beginning, she is light-hearted, airy, skipping from one delight to the next, as if created only for joy. But by the end of the poem she becomes weighty with responsibility and redemptive purpose.[26]

Like Pinkerfeld-Amir, Yokheved Bat-Miriam also wrote a number of poems retelling the story of Adam and Eve. The first poem, "Ofel hatohu" (Dark emptiness, 1926), redramatizes Eve's experiences as she wanders within and beyond the primeval forests of Eden:

אֹפֶל הַתֹּהוּ וּמֶרְחָק מִתְרַקֵּם
בְּעֵינֵי הַנַּעֲרָה הַפְּתוּחוֹת.
תְּהוֹם מְרֻוַּחַת, גְּבוּלוֹת נְטוּשׁוֹת
בְּקַרְנֵי שְׂפָתֶיהָ הַנְּבוּכוֹת.

נְתִיבוֹת מְאִירִים בְּיַעֲרוֹת קְדוּמִים
מָשְׁכוּ יָדֶיהָ הָרַכּוֹת,

וּגְמִישׁוּת הַחַיָּה מַעְפִּילָה בֶּהָרִים
בְּנִדְנוּד רַגְלֶיהָ הַדַּקּוֹת.

אֵלָנִי בַשָּׂדֶה, אִילָן מִתְחַטֵּא—
גּוּפָהּ הָעוֹלֶה בְרַחַשׁ,
תְּכֵלֶת וְרוּחוֹת וְשֶׁמֶשׁ שׁוֹפַעַת
בְּרֹאשָׁהּ הִתְעַטְּרוּ בְלַחַשׁ.

וּכְמַלְכָּה אוֹבֶדָה תִּתְהַלֵּךְ וְתָנוּד
נִכְלָמָה, נְבוֹכָה וְזָרָה—
וּפִתְאֹם כְּפֶלֶא לְעוֹבֵר אָרְחוֹת
תָּגֵל בַּת-צְחוֹק מְאֻשָּׁרָה – –

Darkness of desolation and distance forms
in the girl's open eyes.
Spacious depth, abandoned borders
in the corners of her bewildered lips.   4

Illuminating paths in ancient forests
pulled her soft hands
and the agility of an animal climbing in the mountains
in the swinging of her narrow feet.   8

My tree in the field, my preening tree —
her body rising with a whisper.
Azure and winds and abundant sun
quietly crowned her head.   12

And like a queen astray she'll walk and wander
ashamed, bewildered, and strange —
and suddenly, like a miracle to the wayfarer,
she'll reveal a contented smile.[27]

60

Allusions to the biblical creation account and the story of Adam and Eve abound in this poem. The descriptions of the dark desolated landscape *(ofel hatohu)* reflected in the girl's eyes and the spacious depths *(tehom)* reflected in her lips point to the well-known description of the earth at the time of creation in Genesis 1:2: "the earth being unformed and void *(tohu vavohu),* and darkness over the surface of the deep *(tehom).*" The reference in line 3 to "abandoned borders" evokes the end of Genesis 3, where Adam and Eve, banished from Eden, are forced into a realm where the geographical, social, and ethical boundaries are no longer clearly drawn. The fluidity and flexibility of time in this poem, which moves from the present, to the past, to the future tense, suggests an encounter between the biblical past and the contemporary moment; though never explicitly named, the wandering young girl in this poem *(na'arah)* seems to merge with the biblical Eve insofar as she is likened, in line 7, to a *hayah* (animal or beast) climbing the mountains, a subtle reference to the etymology of the name *Havah* (Eve), "the Mother of all life" *(eim kol hai).* The connection between Bat-Miriam's *na'arah* and the biblical Eve strengthens further in line 9, where the girl makes an apostrophe to "my tree in the field, my preening tree," evoking the image of the biblical Tree of Knowledge as sensuous and alluring. The description of the tree here as an *ilan mithateh* (preening tree) is especially interesting given that it visually evokes the Hebrew word for sin *(het)* and yet means something totally different. Bat-Miriam thus recalls, and at the same time, subverts the conventional reading of this biblical episode as the story of how the first woman brought sin and punishment into the world. Notice that there is no indication here of divine punishment or banishment; borders have been transgressed and/or abandoned, possibilities have opened up. Wandering about in this newly expansive, unlimited territory, the girl is "ashamed, bewildered, and strange" to these new surroundings, but she is not reproved or cast out. The poem ends miraculously with the girl suddenly discovering a sense of contentment as she continues along her uncharted path. She likes the leeway afforded by this boundless territory, the freedom of a world without limiting borders.

In two later poems entitled "Adam" and "Eve," Bat-Miriam returns to similar themes, but this time she includes Adam. In contrast to the biblical account in Genesis 3, where Adam is created from the dust of the earth and then Eve is created from his rib—symbolic of her secondary, derivative, lesser status—here Adam and Eve stand alone in

the world and then discover each other. Whereas in the biblical narrative, Eve, in giving Adam the fruit, precipitates Adam's moral downfall,
here she stands together with Adam as a cosmically heroic figure:

אָדָם

הִבְהִיקוּ הַיּוֹם וְהַלַּיְל
בֵּין אֶבֶן, שָׂדֶה וּמֶרְחָב,
כְּאֵזוֹב יְרַקְרַק שֶׁל הַמַּיִם,
כִּצְדָפִים בֵּין חוֹל וְכוֹכָב.

לְבַדּוֹ, עַל פָּנָיו, כַּעֲנֶנֶת,
בְּחֵרוּת צְלוּלָה רְחָפָה
חִידַת דְּבָרִים וָרֶנֶן
מַחְשְׁבֹתָם הַכְּבוּשָׁה כְּסוּפָה.

שָׁלֵם מוּל שְׁלֵמוּתוֹ שֶׁל הַחֶסֶד,
וּזְרוֹעוֹתָיו, כִּיאוֹרוֹת מְשַׂחֲקִים,
עִמְעֲמוּ דִּמְעָתוֹ הָרוֹסֶסֶת,
שָׁלְווּ אֶת חוֹפָיו הָרְחוֹקִים.

לְבַדּוֹ, וּמִמּוּל וּלְפֶתַע,
כְּאוֹר הַנֶּאֱחָז בְּאוֹר,
נִצְּבָה חַוָּה בַּפֶּתַח
וַיִּגַּע בְּיָדָהּ וַיִּזְכֹּר:

שֵׁם וְכִנּוּי לְרֶמֶשׂ,
עֵץ-פְּרִי וְחַיַּת-הַשָּׂדֶה,
לְעִצְּבוֹנוֹ, לִתְשׁוּקָתָהּ הָאִלֶּמֶת
וּלְרַהַב לִבּוֹ הַמְּפֻתֶּה, –
הָעוֹבְרִים בַּסַּף, וַיַּעַל
רֵיחַ חַיִּים לְפָנָיו.
שָׂעִיר וְצוֹנֵן כְּסַעַר,
כְּנְתִיב אֱלֹהִים מִשַּׁלְהָב.

62

חַ וָּ ה

נוֹשְׁמָה עֲלָטַת פָּנֶיהָ
כְּלֶהָבָה נִפְרַחַת מֵרָחוֹק,
זָעָה בְּזָוִיּוֹת שְׂפָתֶיהָ
וְנוֹשְׁבָה וְנוֹשְׁבָה בְּבַת-צְחוֹק.

נוֹגְעָה בְּשׁוּלֵי הַיֶּרֶק,
בְּעֵץ-פְּרִי וְחַיַּת-הַשָּׂדֶה,
בְּמוֹעֲדֵי שַׁחַר וָעֶרֶב,
בְּחָזוּת, עָנָן וּמַרְאֶה.

שָׁתְקָה. וּכְאֵד וּכְהֶבֶל,
כְּעַיִן בְּרִסִיסֵי הַדִּמְעָה,
תַּעֲתָה שְׁתִיקָתָהּ מוּל מַחְשֶׁבֶת
דְּבָרִים וְחֵרוּתָם הַגֵּאָה.

מֵחֶסֶד צְלוּלָה וּמֵרֶגֶשׁ
בְּכִי-זֶמֶר פָּעֲתָה הַיָּד,
אוֹסְפָה וּמְלַטְּפָה כָּל רֶגַע-
גָּמוּל, מִתְחַטֵּא וְנִמְלָט.

מִנֶּגֶד כְּמַיִם מוּל סַהַר,
הִצְטַיֵּר אָדָם וְצָעַד.
וַתִּנְהַר מֵאֵימָה וּמִדַּעַת
וַתִּגְאֶה הַגְּוִיָּה לָעַד,—

פּוֹרֶשֶׂת מֵעֵבֶר לָעֵדֶן,
עַל קוֹץ וְדַרְדַּר, שַׁבָּתוֹן
מִתְהַדֵּד מְחַיִּים וּמֵהֵדֵר
מָוֶת סוֹד וְדִמְיוֹן.

63

CHAPTER 2

Adam

The day and the night flashed
between stone, field, and expanse,
like greenish hyssop of the water
like shells between sand and star.   4

Alone. Upon his face, like a cloud,
hovering in pure freedom like a gale
the riddle of things and the song
of their suppressed thought like a storm.   8

Complete before the completeness of grace,
and his arms, like rivers from heaven,
dimmed his sprinkling tear,
calmed his distant shores.   12

Alone, and in front of, and suddenly,
like light caught in light
there stood Eve in the opening
and he touched her hand and remembered: 16

the name and title of each crawling thing,
tree and beast of the field,
of his sorrow, of her mute desire,
and the haughtiness of his tempting heart, —   20
all passing in the procession, and
before him rose life's scent.
Showering and chilly like a storm,
like God's path ablaze.   24

Eve

The darkness of her face breathes
like a flame flown up [bloomimg] from afar

64

trembling in the corners of her lips
and blowing and blowing with a smile. 4

She touches the edges of the greenery,
the fruit trees and the animals of the field,
mornings and evenings
of revelation, cloud and vision. 8

She was silent. And like mist and vapor,
like an eye with tears dropping,
her silence wandered before a thought
of things and their proud freedom. 12

Out of pure grace and feeling
her hands bleated a sob-song
gathering and caressing each moment —
weaned, preening, and fleeting. 16

From afar, like water against the crescent moon
Adam was drawn and stepped forth.
And she brightened with fear and knowledge
and she rose up proudly, forever thoughtful, — 20

Spreading out beyond Eden,
over thorn and thistle, a Sabbath
resounding with life and glory
death, mystery, and imagination.[28] 24

As critic David Jacobson observes, Bat-Miriam repeats a number of elements in both poems, thereby stressing the shared experiences of the first man and woman:

> She experiences the same divine grace *(hesed)* that he does. At the same time, she shares much of his tearful longing and the realization that the world is free and independent of him. Adam dreams of "distant shores" *(hofav hare-*

hokim), and Eve's face seems to reflect a "kind of flame blooming from afar" *(kelehavah nifrahat merahok)*. Adam's tears are described as "sprinkling," and Eve's silence is "like an eye with drops of tears" *(ke'ayin birsisei hadim'ah)*. Adam stands perplexed before the riddle of the world which hovers in pure freedom *(beherut tselulah)* and Eve's silence wanders before the things of the world "and their proud freedom" *(devarim veherutam hage'eh)*.[29]

Indeed, Bat-Miriam casts Adam and Eve in equally grand roles; their behavior, appearance, and personality are seen in terms of weather patterns (clouds, storms, winds) or such cosmic elements as darkness, flashing light, the crescent moon, and so on. Adam's predominant feature, at least in the first few stanzas of "Adam," is his sense of individuality and completeness. Yet a storm brews beneath the surface of this perceived, peaceful wholeness, echoing God's statement in Genesis 2:18, *lo tov heyot adam levado*—"it is not good for man to be alone." In fact, only when Eve appears *bapetah* (in the opening or entrance) does Adam recall all the names and categories that he had previously formulated as a way of processing his experiences. The presence of Eve as Other and partner allows Adam to specify and label his relation to other beings and experiences. Now he knows how to name not just the animals but also "his sorrow" and "her mute desire," allusions to the divine punishments meted out to Eve for eating the fruit in Genesis 3:16. But whereas the word *itsavon* (sorrow) is used in Genesis 3:16 to refer to the pain of childbirth, here it is Adam's pain *(itsvono)*. And while the biblical Eve is punished with a desire for Adam even as he rules over her, in Bat-Miriam's version Eve's "mute desire" for Adam is detached from the punitive context of male domination. As Eve appears, a scent of life rises before Adam, again recalling the etymology of Eve's name, as the mother of all life. With a sense of life's varied possibilities, Adam looks out at the fiery path that leads away from Eden.

In "Eve," Bat-Miriam offers a closer look at the figure of Eve, resurrecting her, as in the case of Pinkerfeld-Amir's depiction, not only as the mother of all life but also as the progenitor of poetic perception. Bat-Miriam's first woman is magnificently sensual, spending her days in the Garden of Eden touching the edges of the greenery and caressing the animals of the field. But the Eve of this poem is much more than a creature of the senses; her experience of the Garden of Eden is simultaneously spiritual and physical. Building on Eve's words to the snake in Genesis 3:3, Bat-Miriam adds a prohibition against even touching the fruit of the Tree of Knowledge, suggesting that Eve's experience of touching Eden's life forms yields a revelatory knowledge and a poetic voice. As in Pinkerfeld-Amir's "Eve," no snake dupes this Eve into eating the fruit of the Tree of Knowledge. In fact, no eating takes place at all. Eve's interactions with her surroundings are so intense that all her senses blend into one mystical whole; her hands speak, sing, hear, and experience time, and there is something exquisitely, religiously sinful about this. Note, of course, that in this poem, as in "Ofel hatohu," Bat-Miriam uses the verb *mithateh* (preening, luxuriating, line 16). Eve's interaction with the tree thus entails not sin but sensual/poetic indulgence.

The verb used here to refer to Adam's appearance on the scene is *mitstayer,* evocative of *vayitser,* the verb used to connote God's formation of Adam from the dust of the earth. Is Adam being created at this moment? Or is he being sketched out in Eve's mind, an anxious, imaginary embodiment of her sense of transgressive, newfound knowledge? In contrast to the Adam poem, where Adam and Eve physically interact, it is not clear in "Eve" whether Adam is there with her or if she is inferring what Adam might think of her if he were there. Her response to Adam's appearance combines fear, knowledge, pride, and a sense of impending exile. The mixed nature of Eve's emotions in the wake of her newfound knowledge and the necessity of revealing this knowledge to Adam are evident in the alliterative play of the words *vatig'eh haguyah,* which can be translated either as "she rose up proudly, forever thoughtful" or as "she rose up proudly, forever banished."[30] Stretching her gaze beyond Eden, Eve sees the thorns and thistles, which offer her, like Pinkerfeld-Amir's Eve, an alternative to a life of undifferentiated splendor and pleasure. Along with this palpably non-Edenic landscape, Eve espies "death, mystery, and imagination." Bat-Miriam's invocation of "death" as part of Eve's discovery relates to the divine prohibition to Adam against eating the fruit in Genesis 2:17: "for on the day that you eat it you shall surely die." In Bat-Miriam's version of the biblical story death is not a punishment but a source of "mystery, and imagination"; no retributive God appears to chastise Eve for her knowledge or banish the primeval couple from the Garden of Eden. Eve's poetic contemplation of nature yields knowledge and the discovery of alternate vistas of the imagination. According to the logic of this poem, were it not for Eve's sensual excesses in Eden and Adam and Eve's consequent departure from the garden, there would be no "death, mystery, or imagination"—indeed no source of poetry—in the world. In this sense, the biblical Eve emerges as the primary foremother, not only for Hebrew women poets but for women poets in general.

Anda Pinkerfeld-Amir, courtesy of
Machon Genazim.

Yokheved Bat-Miriam, courtesy of
Machon Genazim.

Shulamit Kalugai, courtesy of
Machon Genazim.

Rachel (Bluwstein), courtesy of
Machon Genazim.

Leah Goldberg, courtesy of *Jewish Women: An Historical Encyclopedia.*

Esther Raab, courtesy of Ehud Ben Ezer.

In contrast to the Eve poems analyzed thus far, Shulamit Kalugai adopts a different approach, choosing to accept a more conventional view of Eve while championing the legendary figure of Lilith. In Kalugai's "Eve,"[31] Adam chastises Eve for eating the fruit, but Eve responds (after being coached by the wily serpent) with tears and kisses, thereby mollifying him and urging him to eat along with her.[32] In Kalugai's rendition of the story, the serpent not only encourages Eve to eat the fruit but also teaches her to adopt these manipulative strategies. Kalugai's poem accepts the notion of an Eve whom God has condemned to be dominated by her husband, but it mitigates the punishment by suggesting that Eve has learned to wield power by implementing the feminine "wisdom of tears, of tears and kisses." (*Nashim* 20) This poem hardly presents a strong resistant reading of the Eve story.[33]

Kalugai reserves this strong reading for her poem on Lilith, the legendary "First Eve." The main source for the myth of Lilith comes from the Alphabet of Ben Sira (eighth century), which tells of a woman created from the earth at the same time as Adam, who insisted on equality in sexual matters and was thus sent away, only to live on as a succubus. The second, more compliant Eve is identified with the biblical woman created from Adam's rib. In this poem, Kalugai's speaker builds on the Lilith tradition, ultimately endorsing the wild aggressiveness of Lilith over more compliant forms of femininity:

ל י ל י ת

סֵפֶר כָּל אוֹת בּוֹ הִצְהִיבָה,
סֵפֶר נוֹשָׁן אֲדַפְדֵּף.
טוּרֵי הַשּׁוּרוֹת שֶׁהֶחֱוִירוּ,
דַּפִּים שֶׁדָּהוּ אֲלַטֵּף.

סֵפֶר סְתָרִים מִימֵי קֶדֶם,
סֵפֶר רָזִים עַל לִילִית.
אִשָּׁה אוֹ שֵׁדָה — לֹא יָדַעְתִּי,
אֵלֶּה — מִי יוּכַל לְהַגִּיד?

"טְמֵאָה", יְנַדְּפֶנָּה הַסֵּפֶר,
"טְמֵאָה, רְשָׁעָה, קַטְלָנִית,
פְּרוּעַת הַשֵּׂעָר תְּהַלֵּכִי,
נִּנְעָץ מַבָּטֵךְ כַּחֲנִית.

71

אוֹיָה לַנִּכְסָף אַחֲרֶיךָ,
לְעֵלֶם חוֹלֵם וּבוֹדֵד,
אוֹיָה לְאִשָּׁה וּלְגֶבֶר,
אוֹיָה לַפָּרוּשׁ, לַנּוֹדֵד".

"סוּרִי, — מַשְׁבִּיעַ הַסֵּפֶר, —
סוּרִי, פּוּקִי, מִרְשַׁעַת, מִזֶּה!
אָרוּרָה כָל תְּנוּעַת אֲבָרַיִךְ,
צְחוֹק שְׂפָתַיִךְ, נְשִׁימַת הֶחָזֶה.

בְּשֵׁם מָרָן שְׁמַיָּא וְאַרְעָא
וּבְשֵׁם שְׁכִינָתוֹ הַקְּדוֹשָׁה,
הֵעָלְמִי, הִסְתַּלְּקִי, צְאִי, הַגּוֹזִי
רוּחָא בִישְׁתָּא, שֵׁדָה אוֹ אִשָּׁה!

בְּמַטֵּה בֶן-עַמְרָם, בְּאֵפוֹד אַהֲרֹן,
בְּחוֹתֶמֶת שְׁלֹמֹה הַטְּמִירָה,
נְעוּלוֹת בְּפָנַיִךְ דַּלְתֵי בַּיִת זֶה,
אֲסוּרָה כָל זָוִית, כָּל קוֹרָה.

בַּאֲשֶׁר תַּעֲמְדִי, בַּאֲשֶׁר תִּסְתַּתְּרִי,
בְּהָקִיץ אוֹ בְּנוּמַת הַחֲלוֹם,
לַיְלָה זֶה, שָׁעָה זוֹ אַשְׁבִּיעֵךְ, הַלֵּילִית,
אַשְׁבִּיעֵךְ, אַל תָּבוֹאִי הֲלוֹם!"

אֲדַפְדֵּף אֶת הַסֵּפֶר, צְהַב-הֶעָלִים,
וְהִנֵּה, תּוֹךְ הַכְּתָב הַדֵּהֶה,
מִתְפַּתֵּל שְׂעָרָה הָאָרֹךְ שֶׁל לֵילִית,
מִשְׁתַּפֵּךְ זֶרֶם חַי, גַּל כֵּהֶה.

רֵיחַ בֹּשֶׂם שְׁמָנִים לְקֻוְצּוֹת שְׂעָרָה,
רֵיחַ בֹּשֶׂם כְּרָמִים וְשָׂדוֹת.
מְלַטֵּף וּמַסְעִיר חֵד קוֹלָהּ הַקָּרֵב,
נִשְׁמָתָהּ עַל כָּל דַּף, בְּכָל אוֹת.

72

וָאֶלְחַשׁ גַּם אָנִי: "לַיְלָה זֶה, שָׁעָה זוֹ,
בְּהָקִיץ אוֹ בְנוּמַת הַחֲלוֹם,
אַשְׁבִּיעֵךְ, הַלִּילִית, אֲבִיטָר, אֲבִיקָר,
אַשְׁבִּיעֵךְ, בּוֹאִי בּוֹאִי הֲלוֹם !"

חָתוּם וְנָעוּל, נָח הַסֵּפֶר,
סֵפֶר נוֹשָׁן עַל לִילִית.
אִשָּׁה אוֹ שֵׁדָה — לֹא יָדַעְתִּי,
אֵלָה — מִי יוּכַל לְהַגִּיד?

Lilith

I leaf through an ancient book
a book with each letter yellowed.
I caress faded pages,
columned lines grown pale.   4

A book of secrets from ancient times,
a book of mysteries about Lilith.
Woman, demon — Who knows?
Goddess — Who can say?   8

"Defiled," the book reviles her,
"Defiled, evil, murderer,
With rumpled hair, you go about,
your piercing glance like a spear.   12

Woe for him who pines for you,
the dreaming and lonely lad,
woe for woman and man,
woe for the recluse, the wanderer."   16

"Turn away and be gone," the book adjures, —
turn away and be gone, you shrew!

73

Cursed be every movement of your limbs,
your laughter, the breath of your breast.   20

In the name of the Master of heaven and earth,
in the name of His holy presence,
take off, disappear, be gone, and fly away
you spirit of shame, demon woman!   24

By the staff of Amram's son and the vest of Aaron,
and by the hidden seal of Solomon,
the doors of this house are sealed before you
each corner, each beam, forbidden.   28

Wherever you stand, and wherever you hide
whether awake or in dreamy sleep,
tonight, this hour, I adjure you, Lilith,
I adjure you, do not come in here!"   32

I leaf through the book, its yellowed pages,
and there, amid the faded script,
Lilith's long hair uncoils,
a live stream flows out, a dark wave.   36

The smell of perfumed oil on the locks of her hair,
the perfumed smell of vineyards and fields.
The approaching echo of her voice caresses and storms,
her breath on each page, each jot.   40

And I whisper as well: "Tonight, this hour,
whether awake or in dreamy slumber,
I adjure you, the Lilith, Avitar, Avikar,
I adjure, come, do come in here!"   44

Sealed and locked, the book rests,
The ancient book about Lilith.

Woman, demon — Who knows?
Or goddess — Who can say? (*Nashim*, pp. 28–30)   48

The first half of the poem responds to the various legends about Lilith as a succubus who preys on women and children, who seduces men at night and begets demon children with them. Like so many women in Jewish history, Kalugai's speaker initially internalizes the fear of female sexuality represented by the demonic Lilith.[34] As the poem progresses, Kalugai's Lilith becomes more alluring and attractive, her wild, sensuous hair streaming like a dark wave before the eyes of the poet. Suddenly the ugly, unkempt, and dangerous Lilith becomes associated with perfumed fields and vineyards, like the Shulamite in the Song of Songs or Eve in the Garden of Eden. The she-demon is recast as a lover, one whose ancient voice storms with passion and also caresses the listener. Like many contemporary feminists who have sought to recover the stories of female witches and demons, arguing that these legends are evidence of patriarchal efforts to suppress female sexuality and power, Kalugai endeavors in this poem to resurrect Lilith from the pages of Jewish literary history, to summon her forth personally as a positive, generative role model.

Matriarchal Voices: Rachel as Biblical Namesake

The intimate connection between biblical women and the artistic aspirations of early Hebrew women poets becomes even stronger in poems that dramatize stories of the biblical matriarchs and prophets-poets. Rachel Morpurgo (1790–1871), the first modern Hebrew woman poet, drew a strong connection between her poetic activity and the story of her biblical namesake, the matriarch Rachel. The invocation of Rachel in Hebrew poetry of the nineteenth century was hardly original or unconventional. Allusions to Rachel abound in the poetry of the nineteenth-century *Hibat Tsiyyon* period. A popular choice was Jeremiah 31:15–17, where the voice of the biblical Rachel is heard in Ramah, as she weeps for her exiled children; the Lord answers Rachel and tells her to cease weeping: eventually her children will return to their former borders. For early Zionists, Rachel became a patron saint of sorts: the mother waiting for her exiled sons to return to her bosom and rebuild the Land of Israel.[35] There is something crucially different, however, about Morpurgo's poetic (re)presentations of the biblical matriarch. Unlike her male contemporaries, she adopts the voice of Rachel as a source of personal identification and inspiration.

Morpurgo's earliest poem referring to Rachel is "Kol beramah nishma" (A voice is heard in Ramah), which refers directly (in line 7) to the passage from Jeremiah 31:

קול ברמה נשמע

אֵלִי אֵלִי צוּר גֹּאֲלִי
הַבֵּט וּרְאֵה וּשְׁמַע קוֹלִי,
אֶבְכֶּה אֶזְעַק וְאֶתְחַנָּן
חוּס נָא חֲמוֹל עַל עַם נִפְּעָם.

הוֹאֵל הָקֵם אֶת אָהֳלִי
כִּי אֵין דּוֹרֵשׁ אֵין עוֹזֵר לִי.
בָּנִים יָשׁוּבוּ לִגְבוּלָם
עֲלֵי רֹאשָׁם שִׂמְחַת עוֹלָם.

אָנָּא שָׂא נָא כֹּבֶד פִּשְׁעָם
חִישׁ נָא הָרֵם בְּחִיר הָעָם.
לֹא עוֹד תִּבְכִּי, כִּי אֵל חָנַן:

אִס יִתְמַהְמַהּ לוֹ אֲיַחֵל
בֵּיתוֹ יִבְנֶה חוֹמוֹת וָחֵל
וּבְשִׁיר חָדָשׁ תָּשִׁישׂ רָחֵל.

A Voice is Heard in Ramah

My Lord, my Lord, rock and redeemer
Look and see and hear my voice.
I cry and wail in supplication
Take pity and spare a troubled nation.   4

Set up my tent, consent to my plea
For there is none to beg, none to aid me.
Sons will return to their frontiers [borders]
In boundless joy for endless years.   8

Lift the weight, O Lord, of what they've transgressed
Hasten, raise up the nation's best.
Weep no longer for the Lord has been gracious.

If he tarries I shall wait.   12
His house shall be rebuilt, wall and barricade
And in new song **Rachel** shall celebrate.[36]

"Kol beramah" was first published in 1855, the same year Morpurgo published "Shir tehilah" (Song of praise), a poem written in response to Sir Moses Montefiore's settlement in Jerusalem.[37] On the most basic level, "Kol beramah" is a poetic acknowledgment of the return of European Jews to the land of Rachel, the biblical matriarch. But Morpurgo identifies Rachel not simply as the mother of the Zionists but as a poetic foremother. In this verse, the poet herself becomes Rachel weeping in Ramah, pleading the cause of her exiled sons. In line 11, however, Morpurgo's speaker steps out of this role and addresses her predecessor in the second person, assuring her that the day will come when she will cease her weeping. The net result is an imagined intergenerational collaboration, wherein the younger poet draws strength from the predecessor figure and vice versa. Morpurgo's poem ends with the line "uveshir hadash tasis Rachel" (and in new song Rachel shall celebrate), a line that deliberately conflates the biblical Rachel with Rachel Morpurgo the poet, thereby turning a woman's lament into a woman's poem.[38] If the biblical Rachel has been traditionally summoned forth in Hebrew literature as a means of lamenting and protesting the exile, Morpurgo has audaciously designated herself Rachel's successor, and her poetry as a new, post-biblical message of redemption.[39]

Later in her career, Morpurgo made even more complex usage of the story of the biblical Rachel in her poem "Ad lo zakanti" (Before I grew old, 1861), which portrays her struggle to find the time and proper context to write poetry.

עַד לֹא זָקַנְתִּי, עֵת לֹא יָשַׁנְתִּי
הַסְכֵּן הִסְכַּנְתִּי, לֵאמֹר שִׁירָה.
עִם לָבָן גַּרְתִּי, לָכֵן אֵחַרְתִּי
אָמֹור אָמַרְתִּי, תִּכְלֶה צָרָה.

בָּחוֹן בָּחַנְתִּי, סִפְרִי טָמַנְתִּי
הָעֵט צָפַנְתִּי, לֵאמֹר סוּרָה.

אָמְנָם רָאִיתִי, לַשָּׁוְא צִפִּיתִי
עֵת כִּי חָזִיתִי, דּוֹבֵר סָרָה.
גַּם כִּי עָנִיתִי, יוֹם יוֹם אִוִּיתִי
קַוֹּה קִוִּיתִי, מֵאֵל עֶזְרָה:

Before I grew old, when I wasn't asleep
I habitually lent my voice in song.
With Laban I lived, and therefore was late
Telling myself, this pain shall end.   4

like
Rachel's
teraphim

I deliberated, hid my book,
Concealed my pen, and said, "Turn away."

I realized, in fact, it was futile to expect,
Seeing the one who urges disloyalty.   8

Even as I suffered, day by day I yearned
And hoped for help from the Lord.[40]   10

"Ad lo zakanti" is built upon several "thefts" of biblical language. The
first appears in line 2 of the poem, where Morpurgo's speaker recalls her
former habit of writing: *hasken hiskanti leimor shirah*. The construction
hasken hiskanti appears only once in the Bible, in the context of Balaam
the prophet's abortive effort to curse the Israelites on behalf of Balak, the
king of Moab (Num. 22). En route to carry out Balak's mission, Balaam's
she-ass (who is carrying Balaam and his belongings) sees an angel of God
three times and consequently strays three times from the proper path.
In response, Balaam beats the she-ass mercilessly, until God opens her
mouth and allows the animal to speak her mind. Balaam says that if he
had a sword, he would happily slay her for her mockery. And what does
the talking she-ass say in response? "Look, I am the ass that you have
been riding on all along. Have I been in the habit *[hahasken hiskanti]* of

78

doing thus to you?" (Num. 22:30) Morpurgo's decision to convey her own literary frustrations by way of this subtle allusion to the miraculous speech of Balaam's she-ass is ingenious. In juxtaposing the idea of female poetic aspiration with the story of Balaam's devoted but abused she-ass, Morpurgo highlights the many obstacles that face the woman poet writing in Hebrew—including her domestic role as a female beast of burden and the cultural assumption that she cannot speak publicly or prophetically. Marvelously, the Bible allows this female donkey, who demonstrates greater loyalty and spiritual/moral insight than her purported prophet master, to protest her situation. In borrowing the words of the she-ass, Morpurgo decries the limitations placed on female creativity and intellectualism, but she also memorializes an extraordinary incident where the Bible allows a female donkey to upstage a male prophet.

The more obvious theft of language in this poem is in line 3, where Morpurgo seizes upon the words said by the biblical Jacob in his message to his brother Esau, whom he is preparing to meet after leaving Laban's household: "Thus shall you say, 'To my Lord Esau, thus says your servant Jacob: I stayed with Laban [im Lavan garti] and remained until now [va'ehar ad 'atah]" (Gen. 32:5). Morpurgo revises and reinvents this biblical phrase by using the voice of Jacob to speak for the biblical Rachel and for Rachel Morpurgo, the poet. The matriarch Rachel lives in Laban's household even longer than Jacob does. Laban is directly responsible for the deferral or repression of Rachel's personal goals: delaying her marriage to Jacob and controlling her economic future. But while the Bible gives Jacob ample opportunity to express and resolve his anger with Laban (see Gen. 32), Rachel is compelled to express her anger inaudibly and indirectly through the theft of the *teraphim;* she conceals, hides, and defers self-expression. In using the words of the biblical Jacob to speak for herself—a modern-day Rachel—Morpurgo ironically casts her husband Jacob Morpurgo in the role of the villainous Laban, blaming him for the repeated deferral of her literary aspirations. The biblical Rachel feels compelled to steal the *teraphim* and conceal them in her saddle in order to make the accusing Laban "go away." Likewise, Morpurgo is constantly forced, because of her domestic responsibilities, to hide the transgressive evidence of her literary inclinations, to denigrate her achievements and put away her book and pen.

In line 8, the words *dover sarah,* evocative of the prohibition in Deuteronomy 13:6 against false prophecy—"As for the prophet or dream-diviner, he shall be put to death; for he urged disloyalty to the Lord your God"—add yet another layer of meaning. If earlier, Morpurgo places the man she lives with in the role of Laban the Aramaean, here she indicates that she has been the victim of slanderous or disloyal [masculine] speech, by her husband, perhaps, or by a person of religious authority, or a literary critic. Morpurgo thus takes us back to the beginning of the poem and her prior allusion to the story of the heedless prophet Balaam and his visionary she-ass. In referring to the speaker's realization about the *dover sarah,* Morpurgo uses the verb *haziti,* a verb that not only can refer to sight or visual perception but also to prophecy. Through this verb choice, the speaker designates herself the true visionary in contrast to her treacherous male counterparts. The reference at the end of the poem to her sufferings and her continued yearning for help from God again calls to mind the image from Jeremiah 31 of Rachel as the weeping mother, waiting for the return of her exiled sons (Jer. 31). But the sufferings of this latter-day Rachel are personal rather than national in nature, having more to do with artistic than maternal aspiration, with a condition of individual rather than collective exile.[41]

Morpurgo, who was familiar with medieval Hebrew poetry and influenced by its forms, also seems to have incorporated into "Ad lo zakanti," elements from "Afales ma'agali," a non-liturgical poem by the great medieval Hebrew poet Solomon Ibn Gabirol.[42] Ibn Gabirol's poem deals with a poet's struggle to rein in his evil impulses and direct his energies toward sacred, spiritual pursuits. In addition, the poem treats the ways in which a negative environment inhibits spirituality and creativity. Here are lines 15 and 16 from "Afales ma'agalai" (I will make plain my paths):

וְהִסְכַּנְתָּ הַסְכֵּן / לַחֲשֹׁב רָע מִכֵּן / וְהִנֵּה אַךְ עַל־כֵּן / סְבִבוֹתַי פַּחִי

לָךְ יָשֵׁן עוּרָה / מְשַׁדַּי גוּרָה / וּמִתֵּבֵל סוּרָה / וְאִם תָּמוּת תֶּחִי

And you became accustomed / to valuing evil over right, / and nonetheless you say/"snares are all around me."

From your sleep awaken, / and go in fear of God, / and from the world remove yourself / and [even] if you die, you'll live.

Not only does Morpurgo imitate Ibn Gabirol's rhyme scheme, she echoes his evocation of Numbers 22:30. First there is the expression *hiskantah hasken* to connote a habitual behavior or struggle, which Morpurgo uses to depict her ongoing literary habits and subsequent frustrations. Ibn Gabirol accuses himself of spiritual slumber *(lekha yashen)* and issues himself a wake-up call, which Morpurgo links to her habit of writing poetry late at night when she wasn't sleeping *('eit lo yashanti)* and her desire to return to her literary activities. Ibn Gabirol orders himself to fear God and turn away from worldly temptation *(umiteivel surah)*, bringing to mind Morpurgo's decision to hide her book and pen and turn away *(surah)*—to disengage either from the world and/or from poetic activity. Ibn Gabirol's poem continues with an extensive diatribe against people in his community who make his superior spiritual/poetic goals difficult to attain, likening his situation to that of Moses in Egypt and Abraham in Ur Kasdim—a theme Morpurgo also expresses in her poem by likening her life to that of Jacob in the house of Laban. Here we have a woman poet audaciously casting her poetic ambitions against the background of the great religious/artistic struggles of one of the most important Hebrew poets in Jewish history! By integrating elements from biblical sources as well as from Ibn Gabirol's poem, Morpurgo indicates a desire to claim a lasting place within the tradition of Hebrew literature as well as to make over this tradition to reflect her own aesthetic and social concerns.

Like Rachel Morpurgo, the twentieth-century poet Rachel (Bluwstein) merges her voice with her biblical namesake. To be sure, Bluwstein also wrote poems about a number of male personages in the Bible: Elijah the prophet ("Eliyahu," 1928), Jonathan ("Yonatan," 1928), Moses ("Minneged," 1930), and Job ("Tanakhi patuah besefer Iyov," 1931). In all these poems, she draws a personal connection between herself and the biblical male characters. Suffering from tuberculosis and unable to carry out her dream of agricultural work on the land, she identified so strongly with the thwarted hopes of the biblical Moses that she gave her last book of poems the title *Nevo,* after the mountain where Moses climbed to catch a glimpse of the Canaan he would never inhabit. Often in her poems about male figures, Rachel's speaker differentiates between herself and the biblical character. In the Elijah poem, for example, Rachel's speaker compares her attic room to that of Elijah the prophet in Kings 17:8–24, but she laments that, unlike Elijah, she cannot bring the dead back to life.[43] Likewise, she empathizes with Job but regrets that in her modern-day situation, she has no Job-like forum to

81

speak her mind before God and seek divine solace.[44] While these poems about men offer a personal perspective on biblical stories, they hardly evince the sense of spiritual kinship notable in her poems about Rachel the matriarch.

In "Rachel," the modern poet envisions herself as a spiritual, even biological descendant of her biblical foremother:

ר ח ל

הֵן דָּמָהּ בְּדָמִי זוֹרֵם,
הֵן קוֹלָהּ בִּי רָן–
רָחֵל הָרוֹעָה צֹאן לָבָן,
רָחֵל–אֵם הָאֵם.

וְעַל כֵּן הַבַּיִת לִי צַר
וְהָעִיר–זָרָה,
כִּי הָיָה מִתְנוֹפֵף סוּדָרָהּ
לְרוּחוֹת הַמִּדְבָּר;

וְעַל כֵּן אֶת דַּרְכִּי אֹחַז
בִּבְטְחָה כָּזֹאת,
כִּי שְׁמוּרִים בְּרַגְלַי זִכְרוֹנוֹת
מִנִּי אָז, מִנִּי אָז!

(Handwritten annotations: "— she stresses Rachel the shepherd — not the wife — her earlier existence & action"; "of her later rebellious actions by allusion to blood, voice, a way"; "flows"; "a) — missing her life in the fields"; "b) — but also women shouldn't be confined to home/house — should be able to follow the wind"; "to me"; "So, thus"; "forever"; "her scarf"; "flutter"; "for"; "will grasp firm to my way"; "so, so in this certainty"; "that in my feet are preserved memories"; "since then")

Rachel

Surely, her blood flows in my blood,
Surely, her voice sings in mine —
Rachel who grazed Laban's flock,
Rachel — Mother of mothers.   4

Therefore, the house is narrow to me,
and the city — strange,
for her scarf once waved
to the winds of the desert;   8

and therefore, I shall hold firm to my way
with assurance such as this,
for safeguarded in my feet are the memories,
of back then, of back then! (*Rachel,* p. 157)   12

Eli Schweid has observed correctly that the Rachel who emerges from
this poem differs substantially from the Rachel who rises out of the pages
of Tanakh.[45] Notice the narrow band of details that Bluwstein's speaker
chooses for her poetic evocation of the biblical matriarch. Genesis 29:9
tells us that Rachel was a shepherdess but then quickly moves on to the
famous story of Jacob's love for the beautiful Rachel, his willingness to
work seven years for her hand in marriage, Laban's scheme to replace
Rachel with Leah, and so on.[46] As the biblical story progresses Jacob
completely takes over Rachel's shepherding function, as indicated in
Genesis 31, where Jacob calls together *his* wives to *his* field where he pas-
tures *his* sheep. Rachel Bluwstein's revision of the biblical story displaces
Jacob from his textual centrality and focuses exclusively on Rachel, particularly on those details with which the poet can identify. Like her biblical foremother, this modern Rachel has performed agricultural work in
the Land of Israel. Longing in her illness to return to her work on the
land, she (wishfully) imagines herself re-embodying the matriarch's
blood and walking in her footsteps.

At first blush, Bluwstein's utilization of blood and voice imagery
seems straightforward enough, even cliché. But what do these references
to Rachel's blood and voice really signify? What do we know from the
Bible about Rachel's blood and her voice? Rachel begins to speak in
Genesis in the context of her aspiration for sons, that is to say, in service
of the patriarchal plot.[47] Later, with the instance of the stolen *teraphim,*
Rachel speaks a coded subversive language. Is it possible that in using
the imagery of blood and voice, Bluwstein is evoking this very episode,
specifically Rachel's statement to her father Laban that she cannot rise
before him because "the [menstrual bloody] way of women is upon me"?
Is the modern poet's adoption of the biblical foremother's cunning linguistic manipulation of the masculine blood taboo representative of a
strategy of linguistic/poetic duplicity? Rachel's speaker's resolution in
the last lines to hold firm to *darki* (*derekh sheli,* my way or path) directly
recalls the biblical Rachel's use of the expression *derekh nashim li* (a
woman's way is upon me). The penultimate line, in which she attests

that the memories are safeguarded in her feet, also points to this incident, specifically Rachel's act of sitting upon the camel's saddle and guarding/hiding the *teraphim* with her lower body.[48] Insofar as the word *raglai* (feet) can also connote a unit of prosody (poetic feet), Bluwstein declares an enduring connection to the biblical Rachel that is not only biological or physical but also linguistic and poetic in nature. Her poetic feet and stanzas will guard the buried memories and reincarnate the biblical matriarch.

In Rachel's second poem about the biblical matriarch, "Zemer nugeh" (Sorrow song), the emphasis on voice is even more pronounced, with the poetic speaker comparing her quest for communication with an unnamed "distant one" to the story of the biblical Rachel:

זֶמֶר נוּגֶה

הֲתִשְׁמַע קוֹלִי, רְחוֹקִי שֶׁלִּי,
הֲתִשְׁמַע קוֹלִי, בַּאֲשֶׁר הִנְּךָ —
קוֹל קוֹרֵא בְּעֹז, קוֹל בּוֹכֶה בִּדְמִי
וּמֵעַל לַזְּמַן מְצַוֶּה בְּרָכָה?

תֵּבֵל זוֹ רַבָּה וּדְרָכִים בָּהּ רָב.
נִפְגָּשׁוֹת לְדַק, נִפְרָדוֹת לָעַד.
מְבַקֵּשׁ אָדָם, אַךְ כּוֹשְׁלוֹת רַגְלָיו.
לֹא יוּכַל לִמְצֹא אֵת אֲשֶׁר אָבַד.

אַחֲרוֹן יָמַי כְּבָר קָרוֹב אוּלַי,
כְּבָר קָרוֹב הַיּוֹם שֶׁל דִּמְעוֹת פְּרִידָה.
אֲחַכֶּה לְךָ עַד יִכְבּוּ חַיַּי,
כְּחַכּוֹת רָחֵל לְדוֹדָהּ.

Sorrow Song

Will you hear my voice, my distant one,
will you hear my voice, wherever you are —
a voice calling strong, a voice crying silently
and above time, commanding blessing?   4

This world is wide with many paths.
They meet narrowly, part forever.
A man seeks, but his feet fail,
he cannot find what he has lost.   8

.

Maybe my last day is already near,
already near, the day of tearful parting,
I shall wait for you until my life dims,
as Rachel awaited her lover.[49]   12

The matriarch Rachel's name appears only at the very end of the poem, although in the first stanza there are several hints that her story is relevant to an understanding of the poem. These hints are all associated with the idea of voice. The speaker calls out strongly, cries silently, transcends time, and commands blessing, elements that evoke the matriarch Rachel as she appears in Jeremiah 31:15. In a midrash based on this verse that comes from the introduction to Lamentations Rabbah,[50] Rabbi Samuel bar Nahman imagines a string of biblical figures, including Abraham, Isaac, Jacob, Moses, Jeremiah, and Rachel, who stand before God and protest the exilic condition of the People of Israel. God ignores all the pleadings of the patriarchs but ultimately listens to Rachel. Is Rachel the poet calling forth these images of the biblical Rachel as a vocal, protective foremother who bests her male counterparts for the attentions of God and commands divine blessing? Is the modern Hebrew poet Rachel attempting to cast her poetic voice in the mold of a strong, vocally effective foremother?

Of course, if Rachel's speaker designates the biblical Rachel as poetic role model it is not only to legitimize her literary authority but also to express her sense of their shared tragic destiny: women fated to die young. Throughout the poem, Rachel's speaker vacillates between a tenacious desire to speak to and be heard by her distant one and a resignation to the futility of her efforts, culminating in the naming of the biblical Rachel and her story of continually thwarted dreams.[51] In the first stanza, this thematic oscillation is represented through a pattern of statement and counterstatement, wherein the second half of each line undermines the first. The repeated question, "Will you hear my voice," a double call to be heard, is immediately undercut by the epithet, "my distant one," and by the indeterminate geographical designation, "wherever you are"; the strength of the (poetic) voice in line 3 is muffled by the silent weeping in the second half of the line. A similar effect occurs in line 4 in which the speaker describes her voice as transcending time and "commanding blessing," a bold description bespeaking miraculous strength and resolve, a kind of poetic injunction or moral imperative recalling the biblical commandments and God's assurance that an observance of these commandments will yield divine blessing. At the same time, there is something unsettling about this yoking together of command and blessing. Should blessing not issue naturally and munificently from its source? Must it be commanded—desperately willed—into existence?

The next two stanzas reinforce this tone of desperation as the poet reflects upon the failures and missed opportunities of life. Then comes the explicit reference to the biblical Rachel, as the poetic speaker resolves to wait for her beloved "as Rachel waited for her lover." Jacob, the main character in the biblical account, is left unnamed, thereby allowing Rachel to assume center stage. At the same time, the fact that the addressee in this poem remains anonymous suggests that the gap between the speaker and the "distant one" will remain forever. The interruption of the consistent poetic meter of the poem (anapest, iamb, anapest, iamb) in this last line of the poem reinforces this notion of endlessly deferred union; this last line is shorter than the rest, containing eight metrical feet (anapest, iamb, anapest) as opposed to the regular ten feet, thereby mirroring the truncated life of the biblical Rachel, her tragic death in childbirth, and her thwarted, unrequited hopes.[52]

In Leah Goldberg's 1935 poem "Ya'akov veRachel" (Jacob and Rachel), the voice of the female speaker also fuses with that of the biblical Rachel, albeit with cynical, modern-day overtones:

יַעֲקֹב וְרָחֵל

בַּלַּיְלָה סְפִינוֹת מְזַמְּרוֹת לַסַּעַר
וְגוּפוֹת מֻפְלָגִים אֵלַי גְּבוּל הַחַמְסִין
וַאֲנִי יוֹשֶׁבֶת בְּבֵית-הַקָּפֶה
וּמוֹנָה אֶת תְּנוּדוֹת הַפָּנָסִים

עֶשְׂרִים וָתֵשַׁע. שְׁלוֹשִׁים וּשְׁתַּיִם...
מְלַקֶּקֶת שַׁלְהֶבֶת אֶת שְׁחוֹר הַזְּכוּכִית.

- רִבּוֹנוֹ שֶׁל עוֹלָם! פָּרַשְׂתָּ שָׁמַיִם
עַל אַדְמַת אַגָּדָה מִזְרָחִית.

פֹּה הָיְתָה עֲרָבָה וְהַצֹּאן רָעֲתָה בָּהּ,
הַשֵּׂיוֹת נִרְדְּמוּ בֵּין זְרוֹעוֹת הַנָּשִׁים.
וּבַלַּיְלָה הִשְׁחִירוּ חוֹלוֹת, כְּמוֹ קַעֲבָה
מְנַשִּׁיקוֹת שְׂפָתוֹתַי הַפּוֹשְׁעִים.

וּבֶן הָרוֹעֶה הָלַךְ אֶל הַחוֹף
לִדְלוֹת מִן הַיָּם כּוֹכָב צוֹלֵל,
וַיִּשְׁמַע קוֹל: יַעֲקֹב, יַעֲקֹב,
מַלְאָכִים בּוֹנִים סֻלָּמוֹת בְּבֵית-אֵל.

אֲבָל פֹּה בָּנוּ בֵּית-קָפֶה קָטָן
(אַרְבָּעָה שֻׁלְחָנוֹת בַּחוּץ וְשִׁשָּׁה בִּפְנִים),
אָז אָמַר יַעֲקֹב לְבִתּוֹ שֶׁל לָבָן:
חַכִּי לִי, רָחֵל, שֶׁבַע שָׁנִים.

וְהִיא יָשְׁבָה וְעִשְּׁנָה. עֵיפוּת. קִפָּאוֹן —
הַמִּטַּטֶּלֶת גּוֹזֶרֶת: לַחְכּוֹת לַחְכּוֹת...
מַרְדִּיפָה אַחֲרֵי מְחוֹג הַשָּׁעוֹן...
גַּם עֵינֵי רָחֵל רֵכוֹת...

"יַעֲקֹב, יַעֲקֹב, אֲרַשְׂתִּיךָ לָעַד,
אֲבוֹי לִמְחַדֵּשׁ הַזְּמַנִּים.
כִּי בְּאַהֲבָתִי אוֹתָךְ — לַיְלָה אֶחָד
הָיָה לִי כְּשֶׁבַע שָׁנִים!"

Jacob and Rachel

At night the boats sing to the storm
and bodies sail toward the border of the *hamsin*
and I sit in a café
and count the movements of the lanterns —   4

Twenty-nine. Thirty-two.. . .
A flame licks the darkness of the glass.
Master of the Universe! You have spread heavens
over a legendary eastern land. ֍

Here was a wilderness where sheep grazed,
the she-lambs slumbered in the arms of women.
And the night sands blackened, like the *ka'abah* stone
Kissed by the lips of sinners.   12

And the shepherd's son went to the shore
to draw from the sea a diving star
and he heard a voice: Jacob, Jacob,
angels are building ladders in Beit-El.   16

But here they've built a small café
(four tables outside and six inside),
Then Jacob said to the daughter of Laban
Wait for me, Rachel, for seven years.   20

And she sat and smoked. Fatigue. Frigidity —
The pendulum decrees: wait wait. . . .
From chasing the hand of the clock
even Rachel's eyes have become tender.   24

"Jacob, Jacob, I have betrothed you forever,
Woe for the Renewer of time.
For in loving you — one night
Was to me like seven years!"[53]   28

In this poem the biblical story of Jacob and Rachel is set in modern-day
Tel Aviv, where the speaker identified as Rachel sits bored and frustrated
in a café, forever involved in acts of counting: lanterns, tables, minutes,
years.[54] While attention is paid to the ancient, God-endorsed exploits of

Jacob, the Rachel of this poem is all modern and sardonic—the product of a myth debunked. If Jacob naïvely goes to the shore to pull a fallen star from the water (symbolic of God's promises to the forefathers), Rachel stares at the much less lofty lights of the street lamps as they play against the windowpanes and is bored. This Rachel is neither inspirational nor heroic: she is cynical and unfulfilled. And yet she is the focal point of the poem, providing a model for the ironic, cosmopolitan viewpoint of a modern Hebrew woman poet.

Throughout the poem, Goldberg ironically juxtaposes the heroic biblical past, as well as the sacred Arab/Muslim context as indicated by the reference in line 11 to the ka'aba stone in Mecca, with the antiheroic twentieth-century present. The references in line 5 to the numbers twenty-nine and thirty-two directly allude to the Genesis narrative: Jacob arrives in Padan Aram and meets Rachel in Genesis 29; Jacob, Rachel, and Leah finally part with Laban in Genesis 32; and Rachel dies in Genesis 35, a seven-chapter span equivalent to the seven years of waiting referred to in the last line of Goldberg's poem. At the same time, these numbers also point to Goldberg's own day—1929, 1932, and ultimately 1935, the date of the poem's publication.

Line 24 of the poem explicitly alludes to the physical descriptions of Laban's two daughters, Leah and Rachel, as provided in Genesis 29:16–17. The biblical text describes Leah as having "tender eyes" and depicts Rachel as "comely in features and comely to look at."[55] Goldberg's poem creates an ironic distance between the biblical text and the contemporary revision of the story; this Rachel also has "tender," jaded eyes, suggesting the poet's desire to depict a different kind of female heroine, one who is noteworthy for what she thinks and feels rather than for what she looks like. The biblical story, told primarily from Jacob's point of view, romanticizes the seven years during which Jacob worked for Rachel, implying that these years were "but a few days" for Jacob, given his love for Rachel (Gen. 29:20). Goldberg's poem subverts this expression and notes that one jubilant night of lovemaking has given rise to a lengthy period (as if seven years) of romantic disappointment and boredom. Goldberg's woeful invocation in line 26 of the *mehadesh zemanim,* the unnamed "Renewer of time," plays on the holiday liturgy that blesses God for being a *mekadesh Yisra'el vehazemanim,* a sanctifier of Israel and its time/holidays. But time here has lost its meaningful, sacred quality. Instead it plays out endlessly and repetitively like a broken record. The reference in line 25 to an eternal betrothal

89

alludes to Hosea 2 and the liturgy recited when one puts on phylacteries during morning prayers and pledges eternal devotion to God. But Goldberg's speaker assumes the biblical/liturgical voice not to pledge devotion but to protest the position of the unloved woman in the male-centered love plot. Goldberg has turned the Bible and its characters on their heads, thereby creating a countertradition with a feminist voice.

Deborah: Political and Poetic Precursor

In her classic feminist essay *A Room of One's Own,* Virginia Woolf, anxious about the paucity of great women writers from the past, composes a fictional biography of Shakespeare's sister. She dubs her Judith, fashions her a poet and adventurer, and tells a tragic story of failed literary ambition, unwanted pregnancy, and eventual suicide.[56] Unlike Woolf, Hebrew women poets looking for female precursor poets did not need to draw their images purely from their imaginations. They could turn to the stories of such biblical women poets as Miriam, Deborah, and Hannah, using their stories to construct some notion of a shared female literary tradition.[57]

Once again, Rachel Morpurgo took the lead, with her sonnet "Re'eh zeh hadash hu" (Look, this one is new, 1859), a poem that evokes the leadership of the prophet-poet Deborah while addressing the novelty and acceptability of women assuming such roles. This is not an immediately accessible poem; it is filled with allusions that do not translate easily. When one teases out these various allusions, however, what emerges is a poem that brings together statement and counterstatement, common utterances and uncommon meanings:

רְאֵה זֶה חָדָשׁ הוּא

אִם בָּאֲרָזִים נָפְלָה שַׁלְהֶבֶת
מִבְחַר נְשֵׁי תֵבֵל לְאוֹת תִּהְיֶינָה
אִם תְּהִלָּה הוּשַׂם וְשָׁל בָּהֵנָה
מִי זֹאת לְעֻמָּתָן תְּהִי נִצֶּבֶת?

לֹא יֵשׁ לָאֵל יָדִי לְחַזֵּק בֶּדֶק
כִּי אִם דְּרֹשׁ שָׁלוֹם וְלִשְׁפֹּט צֶדֶק

90

הִנֵּה דְּבוֹרָה שׁוֹפְטָה הָיְתָה
לֹא אֶעֱשֶׂה עוֹלָה וְלָהּ יָאֲתָה.

שֶׁבַח תְּהִלָּה עִם יְקַר תִּפְאֶרֶת
אַף הִיא בְּכָל שָׁנָה בְּשֵׁם נִזְכֶּרֶת (הפטרת בשלח)
לָכֵן לְרֹאשׁ נָשִׁים תְּהִי כּוֹתֶרֶת. –

שָׁאוֹל יִשְׁאֲלוּ בְּאֵבֶל לָמָּה?
כִּי אֶשְׁבָה דוּמָם כְּמוֹ אֲחֲלָמָה – (מלשון חלום)
מַה-תַּעֲשֶׂה רָ מָ ה ! כְּרָחֵל נֶאֱלָמָה!

Look, This One Is New

If a flame fell upon the cedars,
The elect women of the world would remain as a sign.
If these were charged with error and folly
Who else would stand in their place?   4

I don't have it in my hands to repair the breach
Only to seek peace and judge fairly.
Behold, Deborah was a judge.
I shall not give an offering; for that is her due.   8

Adoration, praise, precious glory
Every year, she is remembered by name.
Therefore she is a crown on the heads of all women.

You may ask, why so mournful?   12
For I sit silent as a stone [as if in a dream].
What can woR.M. do? Rachel like a ewe struck dumb![58]

The title of this poem originates with Ecclesiastes 1:10: "Sometimes there is a phenomenon of which they say, "Look, this one is new!—it occurred long since, in ages that went before us."[59] Seemingly rejecting

91

the very idea of novelty or discovery, this verse has given rise to a common expression frequently used in rabbinic sources. In midrashic literature, it serves as a proof text for the idea that in Torah study, there is no such thing as innovation, for all new knowledge is contained within the old, having been told to Moses at Sinai.[60] In the Responsa literature, the phrase "Look this is a new one!" is used rhetorically to oppose any new and seemingly preposterous reading of the law.[61] In using this phrase, which favors the old over the new, Morpurgo makes an argument in support of updated roles for women specifically by suggesting that these roles are not novel at all and that tradition offers ample precedent for women's involvement in leadership and literature. For those who might oppose the seeming innovation of female Jewish leadership, Morpurgo's implied retort is, "It has already occurred, in ages that went by before us—"specifically in the person of Deborah the prophet, whose name is invoked every year in synagogue when we read the Haftarah (the prophetic portion) for the weekly Torah portion of *Beshalah* (Exod. 13:17–17:16)

Like the title, the opening line of the poem also alludes to and revises a longstanding Hebrew expression. In B. T. Moed Katan 25b, we are given a sampling of funeral speeches over the death of great sages, including the line, "If flame has fallen upon the cedars, what will the moss on the wall do?" In short, if the great scholars, the mighty, have been felled by death, what will be the fate of the weak and common man? Morpurgo begins her poem with a borrowing from the first part of this expression, "If a flame fell upon the cedars," but instead of the common usage of the phrase, which implies the inability of the weak to survive in the absence of the strong, Morpurgo states that if tragedy should strike the great (male) leaders or sages, the elect of the "weaker sex" would be capable of competent leadership.

In the second stanza, Morpurgo envisions herself judging wisely and seeking peace, after the manner of Deborah the prophet. In line 8, she elevates Deborah to the level of a quasi-deity, when she pledges not to make an offering. Compare Kings 5:17, where Na'aman, the leprous military leader of Aram, who is cured by a prophet of Israel, subsequently pledges not to sacrifice to any other gods but the God of Israel. Morpurgo's piecemeal insertion of this phrase *(lo e'eseh 'olah)* is followed by the words *velah ya'atah* (for that is her due), yet another scriptural allusion, this time to Jeremiah 10:7: "Who would not revere You, O King of nations, for that is Your due." Instead of God, however,

"Deborah," illustration of the prophet Deborah from *Shaharut* (The Youth) IV: 9 (December 1919), p. 136

Morpurgo invokes Deborah as deserving of reverence and emulation. This worshipful depiction of Deborah is underscored by Morpurgo's attribution of the terms *tif'eret* (beauty or glory) and *koteret* (crown), qualities reminiscent of the kabbalistic *sefirot* or emanations of God.[62]

In the same way the title implies an idea and its refutation, this poem both presents and undermines its assertion of feminine power. In the first stanza, Morpurgo trumpets the ability of the elect women of the world to take the place of the male "cedars." In the last line of this same stanza, she expresses concern over who would take the place of these few elect women, if they were somehow rendered incompetent.[63] Is this poem a lament over the seeming paucity of women who can actually take up a role as intellectual or social leaders? In the second stanza she casts herself in the role of Deborah's successor, but she also admits her inability to fix all that needs repairing. After her tribute to Deborah, she moves abruptly to a statement of mournful self-denigration. Unlike the powerful and eloquent Deborah, she has been sitting silent like *ahlamah,* the biblical word for an amethyst stone (see Exod. 28: 19) that also calls to mind the word for dream *(halom).* What can she, *Rachel Morpurgo Haketanah,* a tiny worm-like dreamer, do in this world of action? Invoking the literal meaning of the name Rachel as ewe, she refers to herself as a *Rachel ne'elamah,* an expression originating in Isaiah 53:7, alluding to a ewe standing mutely before those who shear her wool.[64]

This is an erudite poem. It demonstrates an extraordinary mastery of literary sources, speaks about female leadership, and offers audible praise for a female predecessor poet. But it ends with literary frustration. How are we meant to interpret the self-denigrating conclusion of the poem? Does Morpurgo feel guilty for being so intelligent and literary and thus uses feminine modesty as a cover? Or does she marshal the convention of feminine modesty and self-diminution—the "way of women," as in the biblical Rachel's speech to her father in Genesis 31— as a means of expressing genuine frustration and anger over women's limited opportunities for literary involvement and creative expression?

Esther Raab, the first modern Hebrew woman poet born in the Land of Israel, invoked the figure of Deborah the prophet in ways that similarly reflect both confidence and apprehension. In a 1952 prose piece entitled "Shetei yeladot bepardes pore'ah" (Two girls in a blooming orchard), Raab dramatizes a debate between two girls working in the field. The first girl dreams of being a bride, while the second declares that she wants to emulate Deborah: "I want another great king to rule in Israel like Saul or David, and I want to fight the Arabs. Haki will help me. He'll go into the Turkish army and learn how to fight and we'll win! And afterwards, I want to compose a beautiful poem like Deborah the prophet; I've already written it. . . . Do you hear how Deborah sings, 'Until I, Deborah, wrote, until I arose, Mother in Israel,' I want to be the mother of Israel, I want to be important, I am important."[65] In this passage, the young female speaker expresses admiration for the political/military strength of David and Saul, but she singles out Deborah as a personal role model. She chants and repeats her "wants" in a way that bespeaks self-assurance as well as anxiety; this monologue is her way of convincing not just her companion but also herself of the feasibility of her heroic imaginings. Like Deborah who exhorts Barak to undertake battle against the Canaanites, she imagines spurring her (boy)friend Haki on to battle and fantasizes about composing a poem in the victorious aftermath. She asks her girlfriend whether she hears how Deborah *sings*, in the present tense, as if to conjure up the biblical prophet-poet in the present moment, in the guise of herself.

This imaginative fusion of the modern poet with the biblical foremother poet figures even more prominently in Raab's well-known early poem, "Savtot kedoshot biY'rushalayim" (Holy grandmothers of Jerusalem, 1930), where Raab traces a spiritual lineage from her pious grandmothers in Jerusalem to the biblical Deborah:

סַבְתּוֹת קְדוֹשׁוֹת בִּירוּשָׁלַיִם,
זְכוּתְכֶן תָּגֵן עָלַי:
רֵיחַ סְמָדַר וּפַרְדֵּסִים פּוֹרְחִים
עִם חֲלַב אֵם הֵשְׁקִיתִי;
כַּפּוֹת רַגְלַיִם
רַכּוֹת כְּיָדַיִם
בְּחוֹל לוֹהֵט מְמַשְׁשׁוֹת;
וְאֵקָלִיפְּטִים פְּרוּעִים
טְעוּנֵי צְרָעוֹת וּדְבוֹרִים
שִׁיר עֶרֶשׂ לִי דוֹבְבוּ;
שֶׁבַע אֶטָּבֵל בְּיָם תִּיכוֹן
לִקְרַאת דָּוִד אַלוּפֵי הַמֶּלֶךְ
וְאַעַל אֵלָיו בְּהַרְרֵי-יְרוּשָׁלַיִם
אֵימָה-הֲדוּרָה.
וְעִם דְּבוֹרָה תַּחַת הַתֹּמֶר
אִשְׁתְּ קָהֳוָה וַאֲשׂוֹחֵחַ
עַל הֲגָנָה וּמִלְחָמָה
סַבְתּוֹת קְדוֹשׁוֹת בִּירוּשָׁלַיִם,
זְכוּתְכֶן תָּגֵן עָלַי.
עָלָה רֵיחַ בִּגְדֵיכֶן בְּאַפִּי,
רֵיחַ נֵרוֹת-שַׁבָּת וְנַפְטָלִין.

Holy grandmothers of Jerusalem,
may your merit protect me:
fragrance of blossoms and orchards blooming
I was given to drink with mother's milk;
soles of feet   5
soft like hands
grope in blazing sands;
and wild eucalyptus
laden with wasps and bees
whisper me a lullaby;   10
Seven times I'll immerse in the Mediterranean
for the coming of David my beloved the King
and to greet him, I'll climb the mountains of Jerusalem,
awesome glorious.
And with Deborah under the palm tree,   15
I'll drink coffee and chat
about defense and war.
Holy grandmothers of Jerusalem,
may your merit protect me.
The smell of your clothing has risen in my nose,   20
smell of Sabbath candles and naphthalene.[66]

According to Anne Lapidus Lerner, this is a poem about a poet-speaker's "search for self-definition," as expressed through her "veiling and revealing of herself through possessives, verbs, prepositions, but never appearing as a freestanding word 'I' *[ani].*"[67] According to my reading, this poem is also about the speaker's desire to guard and legitimize a "Deboraic" identity and vocation, as "Poet/Mother in Israel." Reminiscent of the liturgical appeal to *zekhut avot*, the merit of the forefathers, as reason for the forgiveness of one's present-day sins, Raab, aware of the transgressive nature of female creative activity, invokes her worthy predecessors to protect her poetic exploits. Significantly, Raab's speaker appeals to the worthiness not of her (grand)fathers but her righteous grandmothers from Jerusalem.[68] Both Anne Lerner and Reuven Shoham have argued that there is an unbridgeable gap in this poem between the pious world of the holy grandmothers in Jerusalem and the rural world of hot sands and wild eucalyptus in Petah Tikvah, as described in lines 3–10. According to Shoham, Raab's speaker glances back nostalgically but without lament at these old grandmothers, a world from which she has departed forever, opting instead to forge her connection with the Jewish past through the Bible. But note that Raab bookends her poem with references to the holy grandmothers, suggesting their role is more integral to the aims of the speaker. Instead of seeing the grandmothers of Jerusalem and the biblical references as opposing alternatives, one can read this poem as an attempt to bring these realms together. Like the Shulamite in the Song of Songs who repeatedly calls out to the daughters of Jerusalem as she searches for her beloved, Raab's speaker invokes the holy grandmothers to fortify or join her heroic, poetic quest. In the case of the Shulamite, the appeal to the daughters reveals a combination of confidence and anxiety. "I am dark but comely, O daughters of Jerusalem," says the Shulamite, only to undermine this declaration of beauty in the next verse, where she says, "Don't stare at me because I am swarthy / Because the sun has gazed upon me" (Song of Songs 1:5–6). The Shulamite's indecision about her sun-scorched dark skin speaks to a sense of uncertainty about the proper place of a woman. Does she belong inside, where she is protected by the sun, or outside, where she is free to experience nature and love?

In Raab's poem, the grandmothers offer the shelter and protection of inside spaces and religious tradition. Indeed, Raab tells us in several prose pieces that as a child, whenever she became delirious with malaria-induced fever, she would be sent to Jerusalem to be cared for by her grandmother.[69] Raab's references to the grandmothers, then, are part of an effort to construct a lineage that supports the poet's evolving poetic and heroic personality, one that offers comfort and the preservation of the past, as symbolized by the reference in line 21 to napthalene, as well as inspiration. This protective lineage, together with a rich exposure to the natural beauty of the Land of Israel nurtures her poetic development like "mother's milk" and fortifies her move into the masculine world of writing and politics, symbolized by her declared intention to purify herself ritually and go up to Jerusalem to greet the great poet-warrior King David. Lily Rattok notes that this immersion, evoking the Jewish laws requiring women to immerse in a *mikvah* (ritual bath) before marriage and after menstruation, "increases the feminine strength of the speaker, endowing her with a regal splendor. . . . Whether we are speaking here about an erotic encounter or a meeting for the sake of receiving inspiration from King David, the woman standing before him is no longer the pampered child she once was."[70] The grammatical ambiguity of line 14, where it is unclear whether the royal city of Jerusalem or the speaker is being portrayed as "awesome glorious," supports this idea that the speaker has joined David's regal and poetic ranks. Similarly, the dual meaning of the word "alufi" (*David alufi hamelekh*) as my lord and my beloved or my intimate friend, indicates the poet's desire to combine images of loftiness and intimacy, to bring the poet into David's inner circle.

The tone of the poem shifts in lines 15–17, when Raab's speaker imagines a coffee date with the biblical Deborah. (This encounter has already been foreshadowed by the reference in line 9 to wasps and bees [*devorim*].) In contrast to her awesome ascent to David's palace, Raab's meeting with the prophet Deborah is presented as congenial and comfortable. Together, the biblical and modern poets sip coffee and chat about *haganah umilhamah* (defense and war). The word *haganah* (protection) recalls the holy grandmothers of Jerusalem (*zekhutkhen tagen alai*—may your merit protect me) and links various elements of the creative genealogy: the hot sun and sands of the motherland, the poetic and military exploits of Deborah the foremother poet, and the protective light and warmth of the grandmother's Sabbath candles.[71]

Resurrecting Miriam

In *Imahot meyasdot, ahayot horgot,* Dan Miron attempts to explain the significance of Raab's designation of Deborah as a biblical role model. In Miron's view, Deborah, the political leader and poet, comrade to army commander Barak, represents a powerfully subversive model for the early Hebrew women poet. She symbolizes independence, authority, and strength—the very traits that Eli Schweid suggested were missing in the poetry of Rachel. Miron underscores the boldness of Raab's choice by offering a close reading of the eulogy given by Haim Nahman Bialik upon the death of Rachel (Bluwstein), in which he designates a different kind of biblical role model for the modern Hebrew woman poet:

> A great loss has been incurred by Hebrew literature and by Hebrew poetry here in our land, the Land of Israel, by the death of one of the new choir, Miriam's choir, as I would call it, or Miriam's daughters—the Hebrew poetesses, who have arisen over the past few years. A new vision has been revealed with great beauty by the small choir of Miriam's daughters who have inserted their melodies into the chorus of Hebrew poets and added new tones. I am speaking here about the poet Rachel, who died at the very height of her

poetic powers. There was something of an echo in her poetry of those destined for sacrifice, of the poetry of Jephthah's daughter who went to mourn
with her friends on the mountains. The flower-beds of her poetry with their
white blossoms will whiten forever, together with the flowerings of other like
poets who died in the prime of their lives.[72]

Miron contends that Bialik's eulogy mixes compliment with insult, since
it places Rachel, somewhat dismissively, among the minor women poets,
whom he identifies with Jephthah's martyred daughter, but, more
importantly, with the prophet-poet Miriam.[73] Bialik's choice of Miriam
rather than Deborah as role model for this group of woman poets is
strategic for it serves to minimize their achievements. In contrast to
Deborah, Miron argues, Miriam was no originator. Unlike her brother,
she did not lead the children of Israel out of Egypt. She did not bring
the tablets down from Mount Sinai, nor did she compose her own song
of the sea. She merely added a female refrain to an already extant male
(Moses') song. Miron claims Bialik saw the newly emergent Hebrew
women poets as true descendants of Miriam in their limited roles; these
poets might add new melodies and tones to the male chorus of Hebrew
literature, but they ought not endeavor to replace the male chorus nor
disturb its harmony.[74]

Miron's analysis of Bialik's eulogy is significant, for it exemplifies
just how differently "Miriam's daughters" themselves read her story.
Rachel's friend and contemporary, the poet Yokheved Bat-Miriam, designated herself rather literally the daughter of Miriam, by adopting the
matronym "Bat-Miriam" as her family name. According to her daughter, Dr. Mariassa Bat-Miriam Katzenelson, Yokheved Bat-Miriam intentionally changed her last name from a patronym (Zhelezniak) to the
matronym Bat-Miriam "because she saw herself as the daughter of that
same Miriam, the sister of Moses, the first woman poet in Israel."[75] She
also wrote poems that clearly demonstrated her desire to claim Miriam
as her spiritual/aesthetic precursor. In contrast to Miron's negative
assessment of Miriam's importance, Bat-Miriam designates her as a
brave and influential political leader as well as a poetic originator.

Feminist biblical critics often discuss the story of Miriam because
she plays a crucial role in the first part of the Exodus narrative—she
watches over the baby Moses in the basket, arranges for her mother to
serve as a wet nurse for Pharaoh's daughter, and sings with Moses by the
sea—yet our knowledge of her, as transmitted through the biblical text,
remains extremely fragmentary, perhaps even repressed.[76] Alicia Ostriker,

Alicia Ostriker

for example, sees the prominence of Miriam at the beginning of the Exodus story and her disappearance in the end as indicative of a general trend in the Bible wherein the "women must be rejected in order for the story of male maturity, male leadership, male heroism, to take place."[77] Biblical scholar Alice Bach similarly asks, "Is Miriam's Song a female echo to the song of Moses? Or is Miriam's finale all that remains of her story after the patriarchal redactors inserted their man Moses in their text?"[78] With this idea in mind, feminist biblical critics have gone in search of missing fragments, opposing the notion of Miriam's derivative, secondary position. Perhaps most momentous have been the discovery and publication of a Dead Sea Scroll fragment suggesting that, according to one tradition, Miriam indeed had "her own song, which was different from the Song of the Sea."[79]

Well before the flowering of feminist biblical criticism, Yokheved Bat-Miriam was asking these same critical questions through her revisionist poetry about Miriam. Bat-Miriam's first book of poetry bears the imprint of the Miriam story. The title *Merahok* (1932) and the numerous repetitions of this word throughout the book allude to the biblical account of Miriam standing "from afar" as baby Moses is set adrift in a basket upon the Nile (Exod. 2:4). Throughout the title cycle, the poet-speaker stands, yearns, calls out, and reaches out *merahok*, suggesting a melding of the speaker's aspirations with those of the biblical Miriam.

The epic stature and aspirations represented by the figure of Miriam are seen most vividly in the two poems in which Bat-Miriam resurrects the biblical prophet-poet, identifying her as a precursor poet and a personal source of inspiration. The first poem, "Kifsukim hayamim" (The days are like verses,), presents a view of life and experience in the Land of Israel as bearing a mythical, biblical quality or moment.[80] Like a feminist biblical scholar searching for the missing fragments of Miriam's "Song of the Sea," Bat-Miriam uses her poem to uncover the "concealed hymns" of the biblical female past and bring them to life in a modern-day context:

concealed

Geniza –
time as buried text

כִּפְסוּקִים הַיָּמִים, מִזְמוֹרִים נִגְנְזוּ,
הַלֵּילוֹת כְּ"סֶלָה" סוֹגֵר הַשִּׁיר.
writing
בְּמִזְמוֹר לַמִּזְרָח הֵם יַחַד מִתְלַכְּדִים
וְנִטְוִים וּמוּשְׁכִים כְּשַׁעֲוָה וָקִיר.

P. 11

כְּאׇהֳלֵי רוֹעִים יְרִיעוֹת הַשַּׁחַק,
וּמֹשֶׁה שֶׁנּוֹפַל עַל פָּנָיו – הַצֵּל,
כְּכַדֵּי בְּנוֹת כְּנַעַן – עַרְבֵי הַכְּחוֹלִים,
כְּסַהֲרוֹן זָהָב – הַסַּהַר בַּלֵּיל.

וְנִשְׁמַע לִי : עוֹלֶה וְחוֹזֵר וְנִשְׁנֶה
שְׁמִי שֶׁעוֹד רָעַד עַל גַּלֵּי מֵי שָׁחוֹר,
שְׁחוֹרִים הֵם פָּנַי, בְּבוּאָה רְחוֹקָה
נִשְׁתַּיְרָה מִדּוֹרוֹת חֲרֵרָה בַּיְאוֹר

וְנִדְמֶה: הִנֵּה אַשְׁלִיכָה אֶת יָדִי –
וְאֶקְשֹׁר הַמָּחוֹל בְּעוּגָב וְגִיל,
תִּתְעוֹרֵר, תִּתְלַקַּח וְתַעַן לִקְרָאתִי
שִׁירַת-יָם-קְדוּמִים שֶׁנִּגְנְזוּ בַּגְּוִיל...

The days are like verses; hymns concealed,
the nights like *selah* sealing the song.
In a hymn to the East they unite,
weave and pull, like wax and wall.[81]   4

Like shepherds' tents are the curtains of the sky,
and Moses falling prostrate — the shadow,
like the vases of Canaan's daughters — the blue evenings,
like a golden crescent, the night moon.   8

And it hearkens to me: rising time and again
my name still trembling on the waves of black water.
Black is my face, a distant reflection
a remnant of generations, tremulous in the Nile.   12

And it seems: here I'll cast my hands
and launch the dance with pipe and joy,
she will awaken, flare up and answer me
in an ancient sea song hidden in parchment.[82] (*Merahok* 77)   16

101

At the beginning of the poem, the scene is cast in terms of textual metaphors, suggesting that a picture of the biblical past is being spun or pulled out from fragments of text. The days are compared to biblical verses or concealed hymns; the nights which end her days are likened to the word *selah* that traditionally closes a Hebrew liturgical poem. By the second stanza, the process of transforming text into life is well under-way. Thus the poet moves from textual metaphors to more visual, panoramic images: the clouds lining the sky are likened to shepherds' tents; the blue evenings in their indigenous beauty are compared to the clay vases of Canaan's daughters. Bat-Miriam's hermeneutics of dis-placement is evident in line 6, where she compares the shadows playing upon the landscape to "Moses falling prostrate" before the holiness of God. Instead of the typical biblical pattern as observed by such feminist critics as Alicia Ostriker and J. Cheryl Exum—in which women char-acters are introduced and then buried or forgotten—here Moses, the pri-mary figure of the Exodus story, is literally consigned to the shadows, mentioned once in the poem and then dropped, as the poet turns her focus to Moses' sister Miriam. Moreover, in choosing to allude to the Israelite leader in this way, Bat-Miriam calls to mind those specific bib-lical moments when Moses fell on his face before God: the Korah rebel-lion (Num. 16:4) and the episode where Moses struck the rock instead of talking to it (Num. 20:6). In both instances Moses' authority is severely challenged, even compromised. Her reference to Moses falling on his face clearly reveals Bat-Miriam's hermeneutics of displacement.

In the third and fourth stanzas, she employs the hermeneutics of identification as she reflects upon her adopted name—Bat-Miriam—and imagines herself inhabiting the story of the biblical prophet and poet. She hears Miriam's name rising time and again throughout the generations, "still trembling on the waves of black water." She sees her-self standing by the Nile, like Miriam, her black face (reminiscent both of the appearance of the Shulamite in the Song of Songs and of the phys-ical appearance of the biblical Miriam, as Bat-Miriam must have imag-ined it) "tremulous in the Nile." She then pictures herself dancing and singing along the banks of the Red Sea as Miriam did in Exodus 15, launching "the dance with pipe and joy." Bat-Miriam's use of the phrase *ashlikha et yadi*, evocative of several verses in the biblical book of Exodus—including Pharaoh's decree that all baby boys be *cast* into the Nile (*tashlikhuhu*, Exod. 1:22) and God's commandment to Moses that he cast down his staff (*hashlikheihu artsa*, Exod. 34:3)—indicates a desire to transfer focus and agency from the male leaders to the poet-speaker. Resurrecting her foremother and her "ancient sea song hidden in parchment," these two Miriams dance and sing in response to one another, creating an intergenerational collaboration that fortifies the daughter-poet's claim to a place in Hebrew literary history.

Bat-Miriam's later and more difficult poem "Miriam" amplifies this theme of identification between poetic daughter and foremother:

מרים

עָמְדָה מוּל הַסּוּף וְהַגֹּמֶא
וְנִשְׁמָה כּוֹכָבִים וּמִדְבָּר.
עֵין אַפִּיס עֶגְלָה וְרוֹדֶמֶת
הַצִּיפָה כְּחוֹלָה הַמַּזְהָר

עַל הַחוֹל, עַל אִשְׁתּוֹ הַזּוֹהֶבֶת,
עַל חִיּוּךְ בַּת מְלָכִים הַנִּלְאָט,
עַל שִׂיחַ חַרְטֻמִּים עֲלֵי אֶבֶן
וְזֶמֶר הֵיכָלִים הַמִּצְעָד

מִנֶּגֶד, בְּדֶשֶׁן הַזֵּכֶר,
כִּשְׁפִיפוֹן בְּתַאֲוַת עוֹלָם,
אָמְצָה גֹשֶׁן הַנִּדְרֶכֶת
דְּמִיּוֹן שְׁבָטִים מֵעַמְעָם.

—אִתָּךְ, אִתָּךְ בַּסַּעַר
גּוּפֵךְ מִשְׁתַּרְבֵּב כָּתֹף,
אִתָּךְ בִּמְחוֹלֵךְ מוּל לַהַט
רֵיחַ חוֹלוֹת וְאֵין־סוֹף,

—אֲסַפֵּר מְקֻנְאָה וּמְצֹרַעַת,
אֲסַפֵּר מַלִּינָה עַל עַצְמִי.
הִשְׁבַּעְתִּיךְ בִּנְזִירוּתֵךְ לֹא נִכְנַעַת,
בִּבְדִידוּתֵךְ הַזֹּהוּרָה נָא חֲיִי!

103

עָמְדָה מְהַלַחַשׁ מְנַדְנֶדֶת
כְּמִלְבֵּן פַּעֲמֵי הַגַּל.
גָּחְנָה עַל הַתִּנוֹק כְּנֶדֶר,
כְּצוּ,
כְּפָדוּת,
כְּגוֹרָל.

Miriam

She stood facing the reeds and papyrus
and breathed the stars and desert.
The eye of Apis round and slumbering
flooded its glimmered blue   4

Upon the sand, on its goldening rustle,
upon the smile of a princess hidden,
upon a dialogue of hieroglyphs on stone
and a marched palace song.   8

From afar, in the ashes of memory,
like a horned viper in everlasting desire,
trodden Goshen adopted,
a dim tribal imagination.   12

— With you, with you in the storm
your body protruding like a timbrel,
with you in your dance facing enchantment
smell of sands and infinity,   16

— I shall tell, jealous and leprous,
I shall tell, complaining, of myself.
I adjure you, in your unrelenting seclusion,
in your resplendent isolation, do live!   20

104

She stood rocked by the spell
as by white steps of waves.
She leaned over the baby as a vow,
as command,
as redemption,
as fate.[83] (*Shirim,* pp. 179–80)

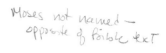

Moses not named —
opposite of possible text

The first in a series of six poetic portraits of biblical figures included in the cycle "Bein hol veshemesh"[84] (Between sand and sun), "Miriam" begins with a picture of the biblical prophet as she stands "facing the reeds and papyrus." This scene remembers Miriam's role in watching over the baby Moses after he is set afloat in a papyrus basket *(teivat gomeh)* hidden by the *suf* (reeds) of the Nile (Exod. 2:3–4). At the same time, Bat-Miriam's reference to *suf* and *gomeh* also sets this story against the background of ancient literary history, alluding to *kriyat Yam Suf* (the parting of the Red Sea), where Moses and Miriam sang their famous songs, as well as to the Egyptian literary tradition of writing on papyrus *(gomeh).* This ancient literary/artistic context is strengthened in line 7, with the reference to a "dialogue of hieroglyphs on stone," a reference to Egyptian pictography.

In this first section of the poem, Bat-Miriam admiringly observes the biblical Miriam as if from afar. In this larger-than-life picture, Miriam emerges as a god-like woman who "breathed the desert and the stars"—evocative, as David Jacobson notes, of God's promise to Abraham that his descendants will be as numerous as the stars in the heavens, as well as of the exodus of the people from Egypt, followed by forty years of wandering in the desert.[85] Miriam's portrait is painted against the background of both Israelite and Egyptian history, as indicated by the description of the eye of Apis, the ancient Egyptian bull god, looking over the scene and flooding its "glimmered blue" upon the various features or inhabitants of the landscape; Miriam assumes a position that incorporates the mythical elements of two important ancient cultures. Bat-Miriam's poem not only combines elements, it displaces them. Ilana Pardes aptly observes in her excellent interpretation of this poem that "While in Exod. 2:4 Miriam's name is not mentioned (she is defined as Moses' sister), here Moses is absent, and Miriam becomes the focus of attention. From mere babysitter she is raised to the status of focalizer, the subject whose perspective the speaker seems to adopt."[86]

At first the speaker maintains a distance from her subject, providing a static overview of the Egyptian cultural, religious, and physical landscape. In the initial three stanzas there are very few verbs; where verbs do appear, they reinforce stasis rather than movement or development. Miriam stands; Apis's slumbering eye floods its glimmered blue, suggesting a sleepy, inert form of background color. The palace song is passively "marched," and downtrodden Goshen, a metonymic reference to the enslaved people of Israel, adopts a dim, ill-defined notion of itself as a reconstituted federation of tribes.[87]

Suddenly, however, in the fourth stanza of the poem, the language becomes increasingly active and intimate. Here it is Miriam rather than Moses who spurs the people on to nationhood. Turning from third-person to second-person voice, Bat-Miriam's speaker announces her spiritual allegiance to the biblical prophet, whose body protrudes "like a timbrel." While the word timbrel recalls the Song of the Sea, the idea of bodily protrusion connotes pregnancy, recalling the rabbinic identification of the Hebrew midwives in Exodus 1 with Miriam and her mother Yokheved[88] and suggesting Miriam's spiritual begetting of her poet-descendant Yokheved Bat-Miriam. Together the mother and daughter enact a fervent dance or a dance of enchantment. Contrary to the biblical account that attributes one line of the song to Miriam and the rest to Moses, here Miriam assumes centrality. The reference in line 16 to the "smell of sands and infinity" recapitulates the earlier reference to stars and desert in line 2, linking Miriam's Song of the Sea with the entire narrative sweep of the Five Books of Moses.

Bat-Miriam then imagines herself participating with Miriam and Aaron in their appeal against Moses' prophetic authority as dramatized in Numbers 12. The Bible judges Miriam harshly for her supposed role as instigator of this insurrection against Moses' authority. Though Aaron, too, was involved in criticizing Moses, only Miriam receives the cruel punishment of leprosy *(tsara'at)* and banishment from the camp for seven days. In Deuteronomy 24:9 and in midrashic tradition—as demonstrated in Genesis Rabbah 45:5—Miriam becomes synonymous with evil speech and the female vice of talkativeness.[89] Even Aaron's plea on Miriam's behalf—"Let her not be as one dead, who emerges from his mother's womb with half his flesh eaten away" (Num. 12:12)—underscores the reversal of her fortune. Miriam, formerly identified with the preservation of the baby Moses, is now compared to a deformed, still-born child.

In contrast to the biblical account, Bat-Miriam celebrates Miriam's revolt. "I shall tell, jealous and leprous," she writes, alluding to Miriam's bid for power and her subsequent leprosy. In contrast to the biblical text that punishes Miriam, Bat-Miriam calls for Miriam to live on and continue in her struggle. *Asaper malinah 'al 'atsmi* (I shall tell, complaining, of myself): this is one of the most puzzling lines in the poem. Who is speaking these lines? What does the speaker mean by declaring her intention to complain about herself? David Jacobson has argued that unlike Miriam in the Bible, the speaker of this poem is directing "her anger not against the masculine authority but against herself. She becomes the object of her own complaint."[90] However, an alternative reading can be advanced based on Bat-Miriam's choice of the word *malinah,* a verb that occurs several times in the book of Numbers following the story of Miriam and Aaron's complaint against Moses and Miriam's subsequent punishment. In Numbers 14, after the return of the twelve spies, we read of the people's complaints against Moses, Aaron, and God, and the verbs used here to connote complaint all come from the same root. In Numbers 14:1, the people complain *(vayilonu 'al)* to Moses and Aaron. Later in the chapter (Numbers 14:26), this verb is repeated three times, as God criticizes the people for their endless complaints *(malinim 'alai).* In this scene of protest, Miriam is conspicuously absent, no longer associated with Moses and Aaron's leadership. In fact, Miriam's name only resurfaces in chapter 20, when the text reports her death and the subsequent lack of water for the Israelites. The biblical text amply records every denunciation of Moses by the people and every denunciation of the people by Moses and God, but no voice is heard to denounce Miriam's banishment from the leadership structure and the text. According to this reading, line 18 of Bat-Miriam's poem constitutes a declaration on the part of the re-embodied Miriam to tell about herself, finish her own story, and complain about the way in which it has been suppressed.

The last stanza returns to third-person voice and to the static opening scene of the poem. Following on the heels of the dramatic resurrection of Miriam in the previous stanza, this choice might seem redundant or anticlimactic. Yet it reinforces the notion of a story told and retold as part of a cycle of commemoration. Here the baby Moses finally appears, albeit unnamed, as if to respond to the unnamed depiction of Miriam

(Moses' sister) in Exodus 2:4. "As a vow, / as a command, / as redemption, / as fate." To what do these four similes, arranged in stepped-form on the page, refer? Are these four words meant to recall the various sets of four that constitute the traditional Passover Seder: the four cups of wine, the four sons in the Haggadah, the four promises of divine redemption? Are they meant to serve as a feminist response to these traditional rituals, offering a way of commemorating female acts of agency and commitment? Tradition remembers Moses as redeemer and lawgiver, but Bat-Miriam's poem reminds us that Miriam committed herself equally to this cause. She played a crucial role in facilitating the redemption of the Israelites and the ultimate delivery of God's commandments on Mount Sinai, and, like Moses, she was chosen or fated for this role. By associating herself with Miriam, Bat-Miriam, re-imagines herself a lead actor in the drama of the Israelite nation-building.[91] According to Ilana Pardes, the arrangement of these last four nouns visually imitates the action of a woman leaning over a baby.[92] By choosing this typographical format, Bat-Miriam also suggests that she as modern poet, and we as modern readers, can lean over the lines of the text and visualize the birth of the People of Israel.[93]

Hannah's Prayer, Hannah's Poetry

Yokheved Bat-Miriam also identified Hannah, mother of the prophet Samuel, as an important literary foremother. The barren wife of Elkanah, she was frequently taunted by her husband's fertile second wife Peninah. At the tabernacle of Shiloh, Hannah prayed for a son silently and innovatively: "only her lips moved but her voice could not be heard" (1 Sam. 1:13). So original was her prayer that Eli, the high priest, was unable to understand this form of spiritual utterance and took her for a drunkard. God granted Hannah's request, and she gave birth to the prophet Samuel. With the institution of rabbinic prayer, now substituting for sacrifice, all of Israel came to emulate her style in the 'amidah, the silent prayer.[94] The text also tells us that Hannah commemorated the occasion of Samuel's birth by composing/singing a song of thanksgiving. Bat-Miriam's poetic invocation of Hannah links her to an empowering—even mainstream—literary history, wherein women create prayers and receive miraculous gifts from God.

In the following poem, Bat-Miriam calls attention to Hannah's role as inventor of Hebrew prayer and precursor to the women writers of the Yiddish *tkhines*. Anticipating the work of feminist historians of religion—such as Chava Weissler—who have turned to the *tkhines* literature for insights into the religious, spiritual, and literary contributions of Jewish women,[95] Bat-Miriam sketches out a female literary/artistic lineage that runs from Hannah to the present day:

מִלְפָנִים, לְפָנִים כֹּה הָיוּ
נָשִׁים כָּמוֹנִי בִּדְמָמָה
תְּחִנּוֹת, לְהָבוֹת חֲבוּיוֹת,
נוֹשְׂאוֹת בְּרוּחַ נִפְעָמָה

הָיוּ—וּבְזַעֲקַת שֶׁבֶר
הִשְׁתַּטְּחוּ עַל קִבְרֵי הָאָבוֹת.
וְנֵרוֹת לְנִשְׁמוֹת הַמֵּתִים
הֶעֱלוּ בְּרֶטֶט לְבָבוֹת.

הָיוּ—לָאֲרוֹנוֹת־קֳדָשִׁים
נָדְבוּ פָּרָכוֹת יְקָרוֹת.
עַל מֶשִׁי וּקְטִיפָה בְּכֶסֶף
נִשְׁזְרוּ גַם תִּקְווֹת נִסְתָּרוֹת.

רַבּוֹת וְשׁוֹנוֹת הַנָּשִׁים
קְשׁוֹת רוּחַ נִכְאָה, שׁוֹמֵמָה.
רַק אַחַת, רַק אַחַת הַיּוֹם לִי
קְרוֹבָה לְנַפְשִׁי הַהוֹמָה: —

חַנָּה שֶׁעָלְתָה לְרֶגֶל
לַמִּשְׁכָּן מִיָּמִים יָמִימָה,
לְפַלֵּל, לְדַבֵּר עַל לִבָּהּ
תְּפִלָּתָהּ בְּלֹא קוֹל וּבְלֹא דִמְעָה.

אַחֶרֶת מִמֶּנָּה אָנֹכִי,
שׁוֹנָה מִנִּיבָהּ גַם נִיבִי
אַךְ כְּמוֹתָהּ כְּמֵהָה בֵּין צְלָלִים
אֶעֱמֹד אֲדַבֵּר עַל לִבִּי - - -

109

Before, in this way, in bygone days,
Women, like me, in silence
would bear supplications *[tkhines]*, hidden flames,
with a throbbibg spirit.   4

They would — and in splintering wails
would prostrate themselves over ancestors' graves.
And raise candles for the souls of the dead
with trembling of hearts.   8

They were — for the holy arks
they would volunteer precious curtains.
On silk and velvet, in silver thread
were interwoven secret hopes.   12

Many and varied were the women
unfortunate, beaten, desolate.
Only one, only one nowadays is
close to my yearning heart: —   16

Hannah who went up for the festival
year after year to the tabernacle,
to pray, to speak her heart,
her prayer without sound and without tear.   20

Different from her am I
and different also is my expression
But like her longing among the shadows
I will stand and speak my heart. (*Merahok,* pp. 123–24)   24

Like Alice Walker, who in her famous essay "In Search of Our Mother's Gardens" unearths in her mother's gardening, quilting, and other domestic arts a formerly unacknowledged African American female artistic tradition,[96] Bat-Miriam endeavors in this poem to uncover the hidden literary and spiritual "flames" of her Jewish female ancestors. The first two stanzas of the poem refer explicitly to the *tkhines* literature as well as to certain related women's rituals. As Chava Weissler explains:

> During the High Holiday season (and also in times of illness and trouble) women went out to the cemetery and measured the cemetery or individual graves with candlewick, all the while reciting *tkhines*. Between Rosh Hashanah and Yom Kippur, and often on the Eve of Yom Kippur, they made the wicks into candles "for the living" and "for the dead," again, reciting *tkhines* as they did so. On Yom Kippur, according to some customs, the candles were burned at home, while, according to others, one or both of them burned in the synagogue. There are hints of this practice in sources going back nearly a thousand years, and it is well attested in literary and ethnographic material over the last three centuries.[97]

Sarah Bas Tovim's famous *Tkhine shloyshe she'orim* (The three gates, eighteenth century) is one of the texts connected with these candle rituals, and so, in referring to these practices, Bat-Miriam pays tribute to a female literary as well as ritual legacy. Bat-Miriam also memorializes other female artistic contributions to Jewish religious life, including the embroidery of curtains used to cover the Holy Ark. Emotional as well as artistic forms of expression intermingle in this poem, suggesting a heritage of unfulfilled or sublimated aspiration. In this context, Bat-Miriam chooses to identify primarily with the biblical Hannah, a spiritual innovator and poet who, in contrast to some of the thwarted women in this tradition, persistently and successfully raised her prayers before God both silently, in her Shiloh visits (1 Sam. 1), and audibly, in her celebratory poem (1 Sam. 2).[98] Even as she praises Hannah's achievement, however, Bat-Miriam asserts her poetic individuality by insisting that she is "different" even from Hannah, that she employs an alternative mode of poetic expression—more secular and less in service of patriarchal tradition.

Notice what Bat-Miriam chooses to mention and what she chooses to omit. In the biblical account, in the midrashic commentaries,[99] and in the *tkhines* literature,[100] Hannah's story is viewed primarily in light of the barrenness motif and the conventional female aspiration for sons. Bat-Miriam's poem completely detaches Hannah's prayers and poems from their procreative context, claiming Hannah first and foremost as an artistic and spiritual precursor. The Bible introduces then drops Hannah from the narrative after mentioning that she sewed Samuel a small coat (1 Sam. 2:19) and then gave birth to three sons and two daughters (1 Sam. 2:29)—all details that confirm her conventional maternal role. But Bat-Miriam memorializes Hannah, specifically for

111

her more iconoclastic contributions, thereby strengthening her own relatively unprecedented move into the realm of Hebrew letters.[101]

Suppressed Voices: Hagar as Poetic Foremother

Latin American feminist biblical critic Elsa Tamez has observed that when speaking about women in the Bible, people tend to focus on such mainstream figures as Deborah, Esther, Sarai and Mary. Seldom do they mention marginal women figures, such as Sarah's maidservant Hagar. According to Tamez, most readers of the Bible have internalized the perception that Hagar is a "negative model."[102] Yet as John Waters has observed, though she is a maidservant, Hagar is no mean figure: "Hagar, as woman, is heir to a promise identical to that of the patriarchs. It is significant that Hagar is the only Old Testament woman who has a recorded theophany and is the recipient of a promise of possession of land and a large number of descendants."[103] Early Hebrew women poets, several of whom wrote poetic revisions of the story of Hagar, anticipate these feminist biblical interpretations, reclaiming Hagar as a bona fide spiritual precursor.

Anda Pinkerfeld-Amir's long poem "Hagar" begins with an indictment of Abraham for his role in Hagar's expulsion. Whereas the biblical text sees Sarai/Sarah as Hagar's chief adversary, Pinkerfeld-Amir emphasizes Abraham's active role in sending Hagar off to an uncertain future. In the epigraph to the poem, she quotes from Genesis 21:14: "Early next morning, Abraham rose . . . and he sent her away. And she wandered about in the wilderness." As in the later episode of the binding of Isaac, Abraham rises early *(vayashkem Avraham baboker),* indicative of an eagerness to do his duty and drive out Hagar and Ishmael as soon as possible. The biblical text specifies that Abraham gave Hagar bread and water and then sent her off to wander in the desert. Pinkerfeld-Amir elaborates extensively on Abraham's cruelty, as intimated in this verse. In the first stanza, Pinkerfeld-Amir targets Abraham by turning the language of barrenness, typically associated with the matriarchs, on this arch patriarch:

וַעֲקָרָה אַבְרָהָם מִלִּבּוֹ,

כַּעֲקָר צֶמַח,

הִשְׁרִישׁ בֵּין חַגְוֵי הַסֶּלַע,

עָמְקוּ מְאֹד שָׁרָשָׁיו.

And Abraham dug her up from his heart
As one digs up a plant
That has taken root between cleft rock,
Sending down very deep roots.[104]

The stanza begins with the word *va'akarah,* a word that recalls the Bible's designation of Sarai as an *'akarah ein la velad* (Gen. 11:30), a barren woman who has no child, hence her need to call upon the services of Hagar. However, the *mapik* in the final *heh* of *va'akarah* indicates that instead of a feminine noun this *'akarah* is a masculine verb with a feminine object: *hu 'akar otah,* he uprooted or deracinated her (Hagar).[105] Hagar's proper name itself does not appear in this first stanza; her grammatical absence mimics her physical uprootedness, which is compared to the digging up of a plant that "has taken root between cleft rock." Pinkerfeld-Amir's reference here to "cleft rock" *(hagvei selah)* alludes to a famous midrash from Genesis Rabbah 45:4: "Why were the matriarchs barren? R. Levi said in R. Shila's name and R. Helbo in R. Johanana's name: Because the Holy One Blessed be He, yearns for their prayers and supplications. Thus it is written, *O my dove, thou art as the clefts of the rock* (Song of Songs 2:14): Why did I make thee barren? In order that, *Let me see thy countenance, let me hear thy voice.*"[106] This section of the midrash answers that God foreordains matriarchal barrenness because he yearns for the prayers of the righteous. The proof text is a verse from Song of Songs that speaks of a lover's desire to gaze upon his beloved's face, to uncover or dig her out from under cleft rock. By imposing barrenness on Abraham rather than Sarah and calling to mind this midrashic meditation on God's role in the matriarchal barrenness narratives, Pinkerfeld-Amir implicates not only Abraham but also God for endorsing Hagar's expulsion.

The God-supported Abraham who emerges from Pinkerfeld-Amir's poem is abusive, even murderous, a man who places his former wife (see Gen. 16:4) and son "in the heart of the desert" to be "lion's prey" *(Gadish,* p. 21) A misused wife who nevertheless persists in loving her husband, this Hagar displays an almost pathological willingness to submit to more abuse, a capacity to love unrequitedly that borders on self-destruction and/or self-sacrifice. This image of Hagar as a love martyr persists in various forms until the very end of the poem. Occasionally, however, self-abnegation yields to anger. At various points in the cycle, Hagar explodes with resentment against Abraham.

The section in which anger and protest are most evident begins with a epigraph taken from a famous *piyyut* by the medieval poet and philosopher, Yehudah Halevi (1075–1141), written as an introductory poem to the *ahavah rabbah* (great love) prayer that precedes the Shema in morning services.[107] Yehudah Halevi's poem culminates with the line "Add to my pain and I'll add to my love, for wondrous is your love to me," and it is this final line that appears in Pinkerfeld-Amir's "Hagar." Both poets express a determination to love in spite of pain and abuse by the beloved. But whereas Halevi addresses his poem to God, Pinkerfeld-Amir dramatizes the story of a woman who allows a man to play the role of God in her life but then has to come to terms with his less-than-godliness. In the following verse, Hagar, in contrast to Abraham, ascends the creative and moral high ground:

2. וְאֵלֶּה שָׂרֵי הָגָר עַד הַיּוֹם הַזֶּה
שָׁם בְּאָהֳלֵךְ מַרְבַדִּים רְבוּדִים,
כַּפּוֹת רַגְלֶיךָ יְלַטֵּפוּ.
כָּל פְּתִיל וְכָל חוּט אֲנִי בָּם שָׁזַרְתִּי,
כָּל צִיץ הֶעֱלָה מִבֹּהוּ הַחוּטִים—
זֶמֶר אֶצְבְּעוֹתַי, לְמַעֲנֶךָ.
כָּל פֶּרַח בָּם קָסְמָה אַהֲבָתִי,
לְעִנֵּג נַפְשֶׁךָ.

וְאֵיךְ לְךָ יֵרְכוּ מַרְבַדִּי,
וְיַרְוּוּ עֵינֶיךָ בְּשֶׁלַל צִבְעֵיהֶם?
אֵיךְ לֹא יִתְלַבּוּ עֲלֵי-פִרְחֵיהֶם
לְלֶהָבָה יוֹקֶדֶת,
תְּלַחֵךְ רַגְלֶיךָ?
אֵיךְ תִּדְרֹךְ שַׁאֲנָן
עַל בִּרְכַּת אֶצְבְּעוֹתַי,
לְךָ שְׁלוּחָה בְּמַרְבַדִּי,
וְשַׁלְוָתְךָ לֹא תִטָּרֵף בְּזַעֲק הֶעָלִים,
בִּבְכוֹתָם חֶרְפָּתִי?

114

2. "And These Are Hagar's Poems to This Very Day"

There in your tent, carpets are spread out,
caressed by the palms of your feet.
Every cord and thread, I wove myself,
every blossom raised from the mass of threads —
my song of fingers for you.
Every flower, made magic by my love
to gladden your soul.

And how can these carpets soften for you,
how can your eyes drink the bounty of their colors?
How is it that the petals don't burst
into blazing flame,
consuming your legs?
How can you walk complacently
on the blessing of my hands,
sent to you in my carpet,
your tranquility unconsumed by the wailing of leaves,
weeping over my disgrace?[108] (*Gadish,* p. 24)

Pinkerfeld-Amir's poetic midrash refuses to see Hagar's role in purely procreative terms. Hagar's labor is also creative and artistic. Unlike the Hagar of the Bible, Pinkerfeld-Amir's Hagar expresses indignation that her handiwork continues to be enjoyed by the patriarch, while she and Ishmael are left to wander the desert in exile. Pinkerfeld-Amir reinvents Hagar not only as an artisan but also as a poet. Notice that her complaint in this section is presented as set of songs or poems that go on to this very day, suggesting a continuous connection between contemporary poets and their biblical predecessors. By lavishing poetic detail on Hagar's psychological state of mind as she progresses through each stage of her exile, she demonstrates a desire to read Hagar's story as a personal rather than a national narrative. By lending a voice to a plea not articulated in the Bible, Pinkerfeld-Amir challenges the ethical assumptions of mainstream biblical interpretation.[109] As Judith Plaskow writes, "Read with new questions and critical freedom, traditional sources can yield 'subversive memories' of past struggles for liberation within and against patriarchy, memories that link contemporary women to a transformative history."[110]

Yocheved Bat-Miriam's "Hagar" similarly uncovers the "subversive memories" of the Hagar story. In contrast to Pinkerfeld-Amir's poem, however, where great emphasis is placed on the idea of Hagar's love for Abraham, Bat-Miriam's "Hagar," part of the same cycle as her "Eve," "Adam," and "Miriam," lays its major stress on Hagar's heroic individualism and visionary qualities. This is indicated by the widespread use of the Hebrew word "to see" throughout the biblical sources on Hagar. Bat-Miriam depicts Hagar's lonely wanderings in the desert after being cast out by Abraham and Sarah[111] as part of a mysterious journey into nothingness, an ecstatic, drunken experience of freedom, solitude, and imagination, where phantom wells murmur and "imaginary treetops . . . rustle":

הגר

אַלְמֻגֶּיהָ תָּלְתָה עַל הַלֵּיל
וַתֵּלֶךְ דַּלָּה וּדְמוּמָה.
יָרֵחַ בְּחוֹמַת הַמַּיִם
צָלַל, הִשְׁתַּקְשֵׁק וְנָע.

לְבַדָּה. רַק הִיא, הַדֶּרֶךְ,
מְנֻשֶּׁבֶת כְּמִלְבֵּן אֱלָהוּת,
כְּכֹתֶבֶת קַעֲקַע מִסְתַּחְרֶרֶת
הִפְלִיגָה מִתִּינוֹק וּבְדִידוּת.

–אֵלֶיךָ לֹא אָשׁוּב, מוֹלֶדֶת,
כַּסְפִּינֶכֶס בְּפֶתַח חַמָּה,
אֶשָּׁאֵר הִנֵּה כָּאן מוּל הֶדֶר
מִדְבָּר, גּוֹרָל וְתַעֲלוּמָה.

בְּדֻוְיָה תְּרַשְׁרֵשׁ הַצַּמֶּרֶת,
בְּאֵר לֹא-קַיֶּמֶת תְּמַלְמֵל.
תִּשְׁכֹּן שַׁלְוָתָם הַמְהֻרְהֶרֶת
בְּמַבָּטִי הַלַּח וּמֻצָּל.

וְעִם זֶה שֶׁנִּשְׁאַר מֵעֵבֶר,
שֶׁחָרַג וְעָבַר אֶת גְּבוּלוֹת
אַהֲבָה יְחִידָה וּמְכֻכֶּבֶת
שְׁתִיקָה, פְּרִידָה וּנְגֹהוֹת –

אַתְּ, אַתִּי מֵאַפְסַיִם,
עִם עַצְמִי בִּשְׁכוֹל וּבְדְרוֹר
אֶכָּנֵף לַאֲחִיזַת עֵינַיִם,
לְדִמְיוֹן מְתַעְתֵּעַ וְשִׁכּוֹר.

נוֹדֵד רְדוּף אִי-מַרְגּוֹעַ,
אָהוּב זָהֲרֵי הַנִּמְנָע –
יְאַמְּצֵנוּ כְּהַגְשָׁמָה וּכְכֹחַ
מַמְלֶכֶת חֲלוֹמוֹ הַנִּשְׁבָּע.
מְתַח-נָא, בְּנִי, אֶת הַשֶּׁלַח.
יַעֲנֶה לַחַץ הַהֵד –
כְּמִקֶּדֶם בִּבְרָכָה מְחֻלְחֶלֶת
וּמַכְתִּיר אֶת שְׁבִילֵי הָאוֹבֵד.

spiny – can be hurtful

She hung her corals on the night
and left, poor and silent.
The moon, in a wall of water,
dived down, clamored and expired.   4

Alone. Only herself, the path,
blown on, as if from the whiteness of God,
like a dizzyingly engraved tattoo,
she sailed from infant and solitude.   8

— I won't come back, my birthplace,
like the Sphinx at the doorway to the sun,
I'll stay here in this splendor of
desert, mystery, and fate.   12

117

Imagined, the tree-tops will rustle,
A well not-there will burble.
Their thoughtful tranquility will dwell
in my moist, shade-giving glance.   16

And with him [as for him] who remained beyond
who drifted and crossed the borders
of a lone love starred with
silence, separation and light —   20

With me, with me, from the far reaches,
with myself in bereavement and freedom
I'll be swept away by delusion,
by drunken chimerical vision.   24

Wandering, chased by restlessness,
in love with the glory of the impossible
he will embrace us as the fulfillment and strength
of the kingdom of his sworn dream.   28

Stretch out the bow, my son.
Let the arrow resound —
as if to welcome tremblingly
and crown my straying path. [112] (*Shirim*, pp. 189–90)   32

The poem begins with a set of water images: Hagar leaves Abraham's household and hangs the corals of her love on the night. The reference to corals conjures up an image of a lush waterscape—as in a coral reef—as well as a life of luxury and jewels, a reference perhaps to the comforts of her former life as wife/concubine of the wealthy Abraham. The moon, symbolic of either a feminine force or some lost sense of inner illumination, dives down into a wall of water, thereby extinguishing itself. The image of a *homat mayim* (a wall of water) plays on the words *hemet mayim*, the skin of water that Abraham gives to Hagar when sending her off to the desert (See Gen. 21:14, 15, 19) and also recalls the miraculous parting of the Red Sea, where the Israelites walked on dry land while the waters of the sea stood up like a wall on either side (see Exod. 14:29). This allusion to the culmination of the Exodus story immediately preceding the Israelites' wandering in the desert points toward Bat-Miriam's desire to read the Hagar story as a narrative of liberation rather than expulsion.[113] Bat-Miriam's description of the moon as diving down and clamoring *(hishtakshek)* resonates further with the text in Gen. 21:19, where God opens Hagar's eyes to a well, from which she refills the waterskin and lets her son drink *(vatashk)*.[114] Like the Israelites walking through the water on dry land, Hagar walks—*vatelekh,* a verb that is repeated three times in Gen. 21 (verses 14, 16, and 19)—through and/or beyond the water-realm, entering a desert wilderness where the movements of her body upon the windswept sands become their own kind of divine writing or spiritual art form; here to discover water means to conjure it up, to subject the environment to her "moist, shady glance" (line 16).

As in "Miriam," Bat-Miriam briefly shifts from third-person to first-person address, and it is here that the hermeneutics of identification with Hagar operate most clearly. Like the exiled Hagar who "crossed the border" from the house of Abraham to the desert, Bat-Miriam has immigrated to this desert land of Israel and committed herself to its mysteries and secrets. And like Hagar in the poem, she has left the comforts of her native land and secure former life to become a poet in the Land of Israel, to wander in the ancient landscape, to experience a life of endless, extravagant vision and drunken imagination. Bat-Miriam's comparison of the Egyptian maidservant Hagar to the Greek/Egyptian "Sphinx at the doorway to the sun" reinforces this image of a desert life of mystery, danger, and majesty. A female monster with the body of a lion and the head of a human with "the habit of asking a riddle and killing anyone who failed to answer it,"[115] the Sphinx is a ferocious and enigmatic figure who uses poetry and imagination as a weapon and a source of protection. In comparing Hagar to the Sphinx, Bat-Miriam endows the biblical handmaid with the mythical power of the word.

In the fifth stanza of the poem, Hagar momentarily glances backward to one who "remained beyond / who drifted and crossed the borders / of a lone love"—presumably to Abraham, who took Hagar in as a second wife, thereby transgressing the borders of monogamy, only to renounce this second love and side exclusively with Sarah. Whereas Anda Pinkerfeld-Amir's Hagar cannot get Abraham out of her head,

Bat-Miriam's Hagar quickly drops the subject of her Abrahamic past, resolving to live independently, to raise her son on her own, to claim his "kingdom of his sworn dream" (line 28). In her moments of loneliness, she will use her visionary powers (evident in the biblical text in the two theophanies experienced by Hagar in Genesis 16 and 21) to conjure up her own form of consolation. Biblical scholar Savina Teubal has written powerfully about the need for Muslim, Christian, and Jewish women to redeem the image of Hagar: "Her courage in the face of adversity, her faith in herself and in her destiny, guided by her own spiritual power must be a revelation for all women. Above all, her close relationship with divinity and her inspiration to forge her own community must not be forgotten."[116] It is precisely these attributes and attainments that are memorialized in Bat-Miriam's poetic portrait. Hardly a passive victim, Bat-Miriam's Hagar emerges as a powerful matriarch, a slave woman set free, a role model, and a visionary.[117]

Multicultural Voices: Leah Goldberg's "Ahavatah shel Teresa de Meun"

In many ways, an analysis of Leah Goldberg's sonnet cycle, "Ahavatah shel Teresa de Meun" (1952), is a fitting culmination to this discussion. It was published later than the others, and it brings together an interest in biblical women along with the broader issue of global women's literary history. Goldberg was a productive, wide-ranging writer whose literary interests encompassed many genres, subjects, and modes. Of all the poets discussed in this chapter, Goldberg was the most erudite and prolific, trained with a Ph.D. in Semitic languages from the University of Bonn (1933), founder and head of the Department of Comparative Literature at Hebrew University, translator of a variety of masterpieces of European literature into Hebrew—including works by Chekhov, Ibsen, Tolstoy, and the sonnets of Petrarch, author of numerous works of criticism, several volumes of poetry, stories, one play, and one novel.[118] A member of the *moderna* movement of Shlonsky and Alterman, Goldberg often resisted the label of "woman writer," so much so that she publicly thanked poet/critic Ya'akov Fichman for granting her the (masculine) designation of *meshorer hadash* in his review of her first book.[119] In general, Goldberg demonstrated less interest in biblical women figures than the other poets discussed in this chapter. In her psychobiography of Goldberg, *El Leah* (Towards Leah, 1995), Amia Lieblikh concludes that she "cannot place Goldberg within the feminist camp"; in general, her poetic themes—small, everyday, personal experiences rather than matters of political or collective concern—cannot be seen as gender specific.[120]

This assertion notwithstanding, there are many moments in Goldberg's corpus where she raises issues of feminist import: the value placed by society on female beauty, mother-daughter relations, and, in the case of her sonnet cycle, "Ahavatah shel Teresa de Meun" (The love of Teresa de Meun), the idea of a female literary tradition. As I consider the place of Goldberg in relation to the other poets discussed in this chapter, a comment made by pioneering feminist critic Ellen Moers about the major women writers of the nineteenth century comes to mind. "Each of these gifted writers had her distinctive style. None imitated the others," Moers writes. "But their sense of encountering in another woman's voice what they believed was the sound of their own is, I think, something special to literary women—perhaps their sense of the surrounding silence, or the deaf ears, with which women spoke before there was such an echo as women's literature."[121]

Of all Goldberg's poems, "Ahavatah shel Teresa de Meun" is the one that concerns itself most with encountering another woman's voice against the surrounding silence of women's literary history. According to the epigraph to the cycle provided by Goldberg, Teresa de Meun, a sixteenth-century French noblewoman, fell in love when she was forty with a young Italian man who tutored her children. She wrote forty-one sonnets attesting her passion, but when the young Italian left her home, de Meun burned the poems and fled to a nunnery. According to the epigraph, "the memory of her poems lived on only as a legend."[122]

In actuality, the legend of Teresa de Meun as presented in the epigraph and the cycle was a product of Goldberg's imagination. In Goldberg's diaries, as transcribed by Amia Lieblikh, Goldberg confesses to inventing Teresa de Meun as a means of giving poetic representation to her own experience of falling in love (at age forty-one) with a younger man, to whom she never expressed her feelings.[123] Though fictitious, the story of Teresa de Meun sheds light on Goldberg's desire to give expression to her unrequited love and to imagine her female poetic precursors. Like Virginia Woolf's Judith Shakespeare, Goldberg's Teresa de Meun attests to a desire to lend a voice to the lost women writers of the past. At the time these sonnets were written and published, Goldberg was also working on a project dealing with the Renaissance Italian poet Petrarch; this resulted in a volume that was published in 1953 and includes a long

121

essay about the poet as well as a collection of her own Hebrew translations of his sonnets. Goldberg's "Ahavatah shel Teresa de Meun" might,
therefore, be seen as a feminist companion to that volume, offering a
glimpse of the unknown contributions women poets might have made
to the European sonnet genre. The sonnets in this cycle also refer to and
reinterpret the stories of biblical women, thereby forging a link with
Hebrew women's literary history.

The first reference to biblical women occurs in the third poem of
the cycle, where de Meun wishes that her fate had been similar to that
of the handmaid, Hagar:

ג.

וְלוּ אוֹתִי גֵרַשְׁתָּ לַמִּדְבָּר
וַתַּפְקִירֵנִי לִבְדִדוּת וָצַעַר,
לְמָוֶת לְרָעָב, לְחַיתוֹ-יַעַר
כְּאַבְרָהָם אֶת שִׁפְחָתוֹ הָגָר,

לוּ, לְעֵינֶיךָ דַּם-לִיבִּי נִגַּר,
לוּ, הִתְעַלַּלְתָּ בִּי כְּבִפְּילֶגֶשׁ,
לֹא כָּךְ הָיָה בִּי מִתְקוֹמֵם הָרֶגֶשׁ,
לֹא כָּךְ הָיָה מְרִיִי–יָבֵשׁ וָמָר.

אֲבָל אֲנִי לְךָ גְּבִירָה רָמָה,
נֶאֱצָלָה וְנַעֲלָה מִגַּעַת,
שֶׁלֹּא תָעֵז לָשֵׂאת לַשָּׁוְא אֶת שְׁמָהּ.

חוֹמָה בְּצוּרָה. הַדֶּרֶךְ חֲסוּמָה.
וּפַחַד הַחֶרְפָּה מֵצֵר כָּל צַעַד
וְאֶגְרוֹפַי מַכִּים עַל הַחוֹמָה.

3.
Oh, if only you had banished me to the desert,
Abandoned me to loneliness and pain,
To death, starvation and wild beasts
As Abraham did to his handmaid Hagar,

122

If only my heart's blood had poured out before you,
If only you had tortured me like a concubine,
Then emotion would not be rising against me this way
Then my defiance would not be like this—dry and bitter.

But to you I am a lofty gentlewoman,
Aristocratic and sublime beyond reach,
One whose name you wouldn't dare pronounce in vain.

Fortified wall. The path is blocked.
And the fear of shame limits every step
And my fists pound against the wall. (*Shirim* 2, p. 158)

In this poem, Goldberg's speaker relocates the handmaid Hagar from her marginal place in biblical history to a central position in the narrative; none of the other biblical matriarchs and patriarchs figure in the cycle, but Hagar's story becomes paramount as an instance of consummate victimization. Hagar's plight is envied here because this allows for pure, unmitigated anger, whereas de Meun's experience of unacknowledged, unrequited love will not permit such emotional release. The poet-speaker craves the power of unbridled rage but remains hemmed in by her social position and unconfessed love. How can she be angry with this young man, who honors her as his superior, who does not shun her as much as he adheres to the rules of his lesser social station?

In addition to the reference to Hagar, poem 3 also alludes explicitly to the biblical Song of Songs, a series of love lyrics in which a young man and woman celebrate and enact a pastoral drama of love. Repeatedly in the song, the brothers of the Shulamite attempt to control or limit her sexual movements. Most famous is the brothers' speech near the conclusion of the song and the sister's bold counter-assertion:

8. We have a little sister,
Whose breasts are not yet formed.
What shall we do for our sister
When she is spoken for?

9. If she be a wall,
We will build upon it a silver battlement;
If she be a door,
We will panel it in cedar.
10. I am a wall,
My breasts are like towers.
So I became in his eyes
As one who finds favor. (Song 8:8–10)

In the biblical poem, the brothers state their intention to guard their sister's innocence and chastity as one who guards an embattled city, setting up architectural fortifications to prevent the penetration of the enemy forces. Rejecting their bid to control her body, the sister asserts that she is no baby—her "breasts are like towers"—and she can fend for herself! At the end of poem 3, Goldberg alludes to this very passage, but instead of celebrating her sexual independence, Teresa de Meun describes herself as a *homah betsurah* (fortified wall) a wall with no outlet, no door.

Much of the tension in this poem cycle derives from the speaker's desire to breach the wall and the social conventions it represents. What happens when one attempts to cross social borders and defy convention? On a literary level, what happens when a female poet such as the fictional de Meun assumes the stance of the male poet of love? The latter theme is especially apparent in poem 5 in the cycle, where, after the manner of classic male masters of the sonnet form, Goldberg's speaker endeavors to express her love in metaphorical form, only to assert the insufficiency of all metaphors. Like Petrarch, who laments that the praises of his beloved Laura exceed his poetic powers,[124] or Shakespeare, who considers comparing his love "to a summer's day" only to conclude that her beauty transcends the meaning of the simile, Goldberg's de Meun likens her love to a "dewy pine" loved only by the hand of the wind and to the "bluish light / trembling delicately in the heart of a flame," but she ultimately concludes that her beloved is "lovely beyond comparison" (*Shirim* 2, p. 160). In adopting this literary convention, wherein the vehicle of poetry is used to consider the limitations of the genre and the deficiencies of metaphor, Goldberg insists on imagining and/or claiming a female literary voice that is capable both of proclaiming love and of meta-poetic reflection.

The next allusion in the cycle to the women of the Bible occurs in poem 6, where de Meun explains that she has not been struck blind by love. She has walked into this emotional experience wide-eyed and naïve, and it is with this same awareness that she greets the prospect of love forever unrequited. In the last stanza of this poem we find the next reference to a biblical woman, when de Meun curses the biblical Eve for her role in creating human knowledge:

הָהּ אִם-כָּל-חַי אַתְּ אֲרוּרָה, חַוָּה,
עֵץ הַחַיִּים נוֹעַד לְאַהֲבָה
וְאַתְּ הִרְעַלְתְּ אוֹתוֹ בִּפְרִי הַדַּעַת?

Ah, Mother of all life, you are cursed, Eve,
The Tree of Life was meant for love
And you poisoned it with the fruit of knowledge? (*Shirim* 2, p. 161)

We thus find ourselves coming full circle to the story of Eve. Goldberg's speaker upholds the notion here of a cursed first woman. Significantly, however, her curse is not related to disobeying God or tempting Adam but to the invention of human knowledge in the realm of love. In eating the fruit of the Tree of Knowledge, Eve brought awareness to love and complicated emotion with intellect. Whereas women are traditionally associated with emotions, in opposition to the male mind, here is Eve, the mother of womankind, who is credited, for better or worse, with the invention of consciousness, subjectivity, and complex feelings.

The final poem of the cycle, poem 12, meant to capture the sense of despair that must have enfolded de Meun's life upon the departure of her beloved, once again returns to the meta-poetic mode. "What is left?" de Meun asks. "Words like ashes / From this fire that has consumed my heart / From my shame, from my poor joy / only letters inscribed in a book" (*Shirim* 2, p. 167). According to Eli Schweid, this moment in the cycle represents a crisis of faith in the value of poetry. "The poetic ideal is presented and held in doubt. Poetry cannot achieve absolute reality. . . . If there is a reality that is whole and concrete, then it is in the domain of faith rather than poetry."[125] But this cycle also functions as part of the project to recuperate a lost female literary voice. Yes, this final poem bewails the deficiencies and limitations of words, yet it does so using carefully crafted, shaped, rhymed words attributed to an imaginary poet from the past. This suggests that beneath the ostensible rejection of poetry is a real belief in the enduring, conjuring power of poetic utterance. In the concluding stanzas of the poem, Goldberg's de Meun compares her love to "corals thrown out to sea," gathered up by fishermen, taken to faraway places, touched by strangers, and played with by time, as if by a child (*Shirim* 2, p. 167). There is a palpable sadness to this image and yet also a great sense of hope: a poetic moment endures; words from an invented past are summoned forth, shaped, and immortalized by a modern Hebrew woman writer gone in search of her lost poetic foremothers.

My Mother, My Land

Female Personifications of the Land of Israel in Hebrew Women's Poetry

Where is she?
Activity/Passivity
Sun/Moon
Culture/Nature
Day/Night

Father/Mother
Head/Heart
Intelligible/Palpable
Logos/Pathos.
Form, convex, step, advance, semen, progress.
Matter, concave, ground — where steps are taken, holding — and
           dumping-ground

<u> Man </u>
Woman
 HÉLÈNE CIXOUS

What can be said about a feminine sexuality "other" than the one
prescribed in, and by phallocratism? How can its language be
recovered, or invented? . . . How can they free themselves from
their expropriation within patriarchal culture? . . . How can they
speak (as) women? By going back through the dominant discourse.
By interrogating men's "mastery." By speaking to women. And
among women.
 LUCE IRIGARAY

Mother, bride, good wife, bad wife, abandoned wife, maiden, daughter.[1]
Since biblical times, male Hebrew prophets have depicted the physical and
spiritual contours of the land and cities of Israel, and, by extension, the
nation itself, by means of female personifications. Common to all these

CHAPTER 3

female personifications, with their heterosexual love plots or their assumptions of female fragility and vulnerability, is their origin in the male imagination. As Tikva Frymer-Kensky explains in her study of biblical transformations of pagan myth, *In the Wake of the Goddesses* (1992), "Zion is a focus of intense passion and longing for the men of Israel. . . . They can express their love directly to this female figure in a way that they cannot have toward the remote, invisible, and masculine God."[2] This masculine tradition of female personifications of Zion and the Land of Israel does not end, of course, with the male biblical prophets; it continues and develops in the gaonic and medieval periods with poets such as Ele'azar Ben Kallir ("Eim habanim"), Yehudah Halevi ("Tsiyyon, halo tishali"), and Shalem Shabazi ("Ahavat Hadassah"). The modern Zionist (male) poets carry on this practice as well, borrowing from tradition or composing their own new female metaphors for the Land of Israel and Jerusalem: a bereaved mother waiting for the return of her sons, a solitary queen,[3] a captive daughter or maiden,[4] or, as in the poetry of Avraham Shlonsky, where the hills and fields of Jezreel are compared to a herd of "young she-camels" clinging to the "breasts" of the Gilboa Mountains, the "milk of rivers flowing over the banks."[5]

I quote Shlonsky here in particular because his poetry about the Land of Israel clearly illustrates the masculine prerogative of this long-standing poetic tradition. Shlonsky's poetic persona, like that of William Wordsworth or Walt Whitman, cavorts about in nature, drawing personal inspiration and spiritual nourishment from the feminized landscape. Female figures are present in this poetry primarily to serve and nurture the male poet's mission and gratify his desires. In the fourth poem of his cycle *'Amal,* for example, a "good mother" figure dresses and adorns her son Abraham in a coat of many colors (reminiscent of the preferential treatment granted to the biblical Joseph), so that he, the son, may embark on his chosen holy work as a "poet-road builder" in Israel.[6] In other similar poems, an open-shirted,[7] hairy-chested[8] male poet is tickled by and nursed from the breast of the land ("behold your milk will flow / and my bones will drink the nectar of Genesis").[9] In these passages, the male poet is the creative center of the universe and all feminine natural forces minister unto him. In other passages, it becomes insufficient for him to draw sustenance and service from the motherland; as a poet, he wants to share, even appropriate, her creative, nourishing powers. Shlonsky's poetic speaker longs to be a partner with her and with female fertility, as in the following excerpts from *Yizra'el* and

128

Adamah (earth or land), where he likens his poetry to breast milk and his poetic creativity to the fertility of land and woman:

> Behold here, my udders have also filled with milk,
> The udders of man *(Adam)*
> And my flesh — a breast flooding all, rising from the land.[10]
> **
> *Adamah!*
> Behold I battled with Elohim
> And was *Adam* (man)
> I — the Flesh
> And you — *Adamah* (earth)
> And who is likened to us, knowers of birth.[11]

The wordplay employed in the *Adamah* excerpt evidently derives from the second account of creation (Gen. 2:7),[12] where God creates Adam from the dust of *adamah*. Shlonsky's speaker consciously alludes to this Creation account because he wishes to displace woman-Eve as primary birth-giver—she is the one "knower of birth" excluded from this poem—and replace her with the male poet-Adam. Despite the seeming honor accorded here to feminine fecundity, the result of Shlonsky's appropriation of female procreativity is that the masculine poet is brought to an even higher level of creative power, while woman-Eve remains below, "fixed in an intermediate position lower on the scale of transcendence" than poet-man.[13] Underlying this analogy between "babies and books," as Susan Stanford Friedman notes in her essay "Creativity and the Childbirth Metaphor," is a simultaneous conflation and separation of procreativity and literary creativity, of reproduction and production.[14] As Friedman explains, at work here is the familiar Western patriarchal dualism (as seen above in the first epigraph to this chapter, taken from Hélène Cixous's "Sorties," *Newly Born Woman*), which typically opposes mind and body, culture and nature, man and woman.[15] In the *Adamah* excerpt, Shlonsky likens man-Adam to the fecund, feminine land only after claiming to have done battle with his peer, the ultimate (masculine) creator, Elohim. The absence of woman-Eve from Shlonsky's list of creative peers rehearses the familiar opposition between the pregnant female body and the pregnant male mind.

How does a woman poet cross over into this kind of tradition? Can "Mother Nature" and "Motherland," cultural tropes that reinforce the conventional association between femininity, nature, and earth, serve as inspiration for women poets? Feminist critics such as Margaret Homans and Annette Kolodny have answered this question in the negative, arguing that the traditions of Mother Nature and Motherland imagery are antithetical to the aspirations of women writers. In her study of nineteenth-century Anglo-American women poets, Homans identifies the Romantic tradition of Mother Nature poetry as a problematic model for women aspiring to be poets, for Mother Nature is "prolific biologically, not linguistically, and she is as destructive as she is creative."[16] Kolodny makes an analogous observation in *The Lay of the Land* and *The Land Before Her,* her twin studies of the land-as-woman symbolization in American literature. According to Kolodny, early colonial (male) writers imagined and established "America's oldest and most cherished fantasy: a daily reality of harmony between man and nature based on an experience of the land as essentially feminine—that is, not simply the land as mother, but the land as woman, the total female principle of gratification—enclosing the individual in an environment of receptivity, repose, and painless and integral satisfaction."[17] Kolodny argues that early American women writers had difficulty participating in this male sexual fantasy of the land-as-woman. Consequently, in their writings about the land, early American women writers were compelled to seek out alternative images, predominantly the more domestic vision of the land as a garden they could nurture and tend.[18]

Based on these usages of the land=woman analogy, one would assume that Hebrew women poets writing about the landscape of Israel would eschew the convention of female personification of the land. Certainly, the masculine nature of this poetic tradition, together with the analogy drawn in Jewish legal texts between the passivity and quiescence of land/earth and the sexual/social passivity of woman, prevents a straightforward acceptance of the metaphor. In B. T. Kidushin, for example, the laws governing the sale of a field are compared to those governing a man's acquisition of a wife.[19] Indeed, the land-as-woman metaphor was so common among the Rabbis that in B. T. Sanhedrin, they conclude that the biblical Esther did not commit an illicit sexual act when she copulated with the Persian King Ahasuerus (even though he was a Gentile and, according to some opinions, she was already married), for she was like *karka 'olam* (natural soil),[20] acted upon, tilled, and sown. Although this statement was pronounced within the specific context of those sins a Jew must be prepared to die for rather than commit in public, the statement *isha karka 'olam hava* ("a woman is merely natural soil") came to have the status of normative truth. Thus, centuries later, in a review of Yokheved Bat-Miriam's first book, *Merahok*, critic Pinhas Lahover was able to argue that women are not usually skilled at abstraction; "nature more than spirit," they typically function as the "*karka 'olam* (natural soil) of everyday life."[21]

Yet one discovers that early Hebrew women poets embraced rather than rejected the masculine habit of feminizing or maternalizing the land. The tradition of personifying the land in feminine terms seems to offer a means for the Zionist woman poet to forge a poetic intimacy and solidarity with her homeland. What happens, then, when these Hebrew women poets take hold of this ancient Jewish literary convention? What does it mean for these women poets to include themselves in a masculine poetic practice that presupposes a male poetic voice addressing a (usually passive) female object of desire or reflection? What does it mean to cross over into an imaginative tradition that depicts (or ventriloquizes through) symbolic feminine figures but offers next to no examples of actual women speakers-poets? How do they clear a space within this tradition for the idea of female creativity, activity, and subjectivity?

To be sure, the three women poets discussed in this chapter—Rachel (Bluwstein), Esther Raab, and Yokheved Bat-Miriam—did not employ in their landscape poetry all the longstanding Zionist metaphors for Erets Yisra'el.[22] They did not typically refer to the land as a young maiden to be betrothed by her new inhabitants. Likewise, they did not portray Zion as "lovely and delicate," or as a helpless mother waiting to be redeemed by her estranged sons, as did the nineteenth-century (male) *Hibat Tsiyyon* poets. In many of the poems analyzed in this chapter, issues of grammatical as well as social gender are placed in high relief. Often a female poetic speaker directly addresses the feminized landscape, and this shift from male to female speaker represents a major departure. The land ceases to be the passive object of a male gaze or a background against which to project a masculine message. Instead, a kind of reciprocal dialogue or relationship opens up between the speaker and the personified land. Roles shift and change, gender and cultural boundaries are challenged, and conventional oppositions are reversed, blurred, or reassessed. As if anticipating the ideas of Luce Irigaray, quoted in the epigraph above, these women poets contest the traditional

131

masculine associations between woman, nature, and land. They do this by "going back though the dominant discourse," uncovering a feminized Land of Israel that is gorgeous and desolate, weak and vigorous, aggressive and nurturing, mercurial and steadfast, palpable and invisible—in short, many different things at once, but "never simply one."[23]

The Poet and the Motherland: Rachel's Poetic "Aftergrowth"

I have chosen to begin my discussion with the poet Rachel Bluwstein because, at first glance, her use of female personifications seems the most straightforward and unoriginal of the three. For decades, readers of Rachel's poetry concentrated almost exclusively on her beauty and her tragic biography and thus read her poetry in overly simplistic terms. An early victim of tuberculosis, Rachel suffered a long lonely infirmity and died at the age of forty-one. This biography of illness and death, loneliness and unrequited love has overshadowed virtually all readings of her poetry. "Her poems are the crystallization of her pure tears shed during lonely days and restless nights," wrote Yosef Seh-Lavan in 1935.[24] "[A] slim shepherdess, blue-eyed, lithe as a gazelle, and lovely as Lake Kinneret," wrote Zalman Shazar, the third president of Israel.[25] Chaste and pure in a white dress; a martyr of fate; a woman robbed of her desire to work the land; who turned to writing "womanly" lyrics that gave controlled and humble expression to her sorrow and disappointment—these are the standard depictions of Rachel and her poetry.

More recently, however, critics have attempted to uncover the more complex features of Rachel's verse—the double meanings and ambivalences that are amply evident in her landscape poetry.[26] Indeed, these poems are never quite as straightforward or simple as they seem. Often Rachel employs female personification not so much to endorse the model in its traditional forms, but to assign new value to feminine qualities typically denigrated in patriarchal culture.

The most common female personification in Rachel's poetry is the Motherland—*immi adamah*. Rachel's conception of the motherland is shaped in large part by the writings of A. D. Gordon, "secular mystic and saint"[27] of the Zionist labor movement. In Gordon's thought, the image of the Motherland assumed a central importance. According to Gordon, there is a "cosmic element in nationality" whereby the natural landscape of the homeland blends with "the spirit of the people inhabiting it."[28] The obligation of the sons and daughters returning from the Diaspora to the Land of Israel is to "form themselves in their Mother's image, the image of *Her* landscape."[29] In her landscape poetry Rachel seizes upon this idea of the metaphorical connection of people and landscape and subtly revises it for her own purposes.

This notion of the children of Israel remaking themselves in the image of their Motherland becomes important in a number of poems, where her speaker's emotions, dispositions, and poetic achievements are likened to the features or products of the landscape. In her poem "Safiah" (Aftergrowth), the title and initial poem of her first published volume,[30] Rachel uses the biblical image of "aftergrowth" as a metaphor for the poetic products of her pen:

סָפִיחַ

הֵן לֹא חָרַשְׁתִּי, גַּם לֹא זָרַעְתִּי,
לֹא הִתְפַּלַּלְתִּי עַל הַמָּטָר.
וּפִתְאֹם, רְאֵה-נָא! שְׂדוֹתַי הִצְמִיחוּ
דָּגָן בְּרוּךְ שֶׁמֶשׁ בִּמְקוֹם דַּרְדַּר,

הַאִם הוּא סְפִיחַ תְּנוּבוֹת מִקֶּדֶם,
חִטֵּי חֶדְוָה הֵם, קְצוּרִים מֵאָז ?
אֲשֶׁר פְּקָדוּנִי בִּימֵי הָעֹנִי,
בָּקְעוּ עָלוּ בִּי בְּאֹרַח רָז.

שַׁגְּשֵׁגְנָה, שְׂגִינָה, שְׂדֵמוֹת הַפֶּלֶא,
שַׁגְּשֵׁגְנָה, שְׂגִינָה, וּגְמֹלְנָה חִישׁ!
אֲנִי זוֹכֶרֶת דִּבְרֵי הַנַּחַם:
תֹּאכְלוּ סָפִיחַ וְאַף סָחִישׁ.

Aftergrowth

Behold I did not plow, I did not even sow,
I did not pray for rain.
And suddenly, look! My fields have grown,
instead of thorns, sun-blessed grain.

Is this the aftergrowth of ancient crops,
wheat of joy, harvested back when?
That visited me in the days of suffering,
burst and secretly rose up in me from then.

Thrive, flourish, fields of wonder,
thrive, flourish, ripen fast.
I remember the consoling verse:
You shall eat aftergrowth and what springs from that. (*Rachel,*
    p. 25)

One way to read this poem is to see it as speaking to the experience of Zionist, agricultural settlement and the miraculous, seemingly sudden regeneration of the land. The opening line of the poem, in which the poet claims *lo harashti, gam lo zarati,* clearly alludes to the chorus of the famous pioneer folk song *Artsa 'alinu* (We've ascended to the Land), which goes *kevar harashnu vegam zaranu / aval 'od lo katsarnu* (We've already ploughed and seeded but haven't yet harvested). In contrast to the pioneer anthem, Rachel's speaker differentiates herself from those working the land, claiming that she hasn't ploughed or sown, suggesting that this poem is using the language of farming to talk about something else, that is, writing poetry. In "Aftergrowth," Rachel does not explicitly link farming and poetry; she also does not explicitly assign a feminine gender to the land. There is, however, a certain stereotypically "feminine" quality to her (poetic) harvest as she describes it, at least in the first stanza. The female poet-speaker claims in this first stanza that she did not intentionally cultivate her poetry or plan for its "growth"; it simply sprang up unpremeditatedly from the landscape of her mind. This image of poetry as "aftergrowth," which sprouts unthinkingly or organically in the mind of the female poet, ostensibly reinforces the association between femininity and procreative rather than creative activity, what feminist critic Mary Ellman refers to as "the most natural and least self-conscious of human experiences."[31]

This image shifts in the second and third stanzas of the poem, where the poetic speaker establishes an additional connection between her poetry and the Bible. In the second stanza, the speaker wonders about the origins of these poetic "grains." Could they be the remnant of some ancient harvest? Is her poetry a carryover from ancient times? Has her reading of the Bible, perhaps, catalyzed this sudden yield of poetry?[32] In this stanza, the poet-speaker still remains a passive entity, "visited" and inspired by the ancient "wheat of joy." By the third stanza, however, the speaker has assumed a markedly active, even prophetic stance. Whereas she initially claimed that her poetry was merely aftergrowth, here she actively commands its growth, referring proudly to her "fields of wonder." The final two lines of the poem, where she invokes the prophecies of Isaiah, support this reading of the poem as moving from a modest, passive, conventionally feminine pose to a more active, prophetic role. Here Rachel quotes from 2 Kings 19:29 (the same line also appears in Isaiah 37:30), where Isaiah assures the people by way of a sign that although they are to be punished, a remnant will survive and regenerate: "And this is the sign for you: This year you eat what grows of itself, and next year, what springs from that; and in the third year, sow and reap and plant vineyards and eat their fruit. And the survivors of the House of Judah that have escaped shall regenerate its stock below and produce boughs above" (2 Kings 19:29–30).[33] It is important to note that Rachel quotes only from the first part of the prophecy—that referring to the aftergrowth (what grows of itself) and that which springs from that—rather than from its entirety. In informing the people that they will eat uncultivated produce, Isaiah acknowledges ongoing hardship, admitting that for two years the people will not be in a position to farm their land; many of them will die at the hands of their enemies, and only the few survivors will eat wild grains. The real consolation comes when this surviving remnant is finally able to sow and reap, to take root, as it were, in the land. Rachel's decision to cull her own prophetic consolation from the "lesser" images of aftergrowth or self-growth suggests both a desire to cross over into the masculine, prophetic tradition and a determination to modify or remake this tradition. As a woman poet without the extensive training in Jewish texts of the likes of a Bialik, Rachel comes to Hebrew poetry as if in the form of an aftergrowth or self-growth; she is an "uncultivated" product of Hebrew literary tradition. In insisting on the importance of "aftergrowth" Rachel's poem elevates the position of women poets such as herself, suggesting that despite (or because of) the disadvantages of their upbringing they have something unique and revolutionary to offer.

In another poem, "Ani me'odi hafakhfekhet" (I am forever fickle-minded, 1927), Rachel's poetic speaker again establishes a link between herself and the habits of nature and (Mother)land:[34]

אֲנִי מְעוֹדִי הַפַּכְפֶּכֶת:
בְּעֶצֶם לִבְלוֹב אֲבִיבָם
רְגָשׁוֹת – כְּעָלִים בְּשַׁלֶּכֶת –
נוֹשְׁרִים, נִשָּׂאִים וְאֵינָם.

רַק בָּךְ לֹא מָעַלְתִּי אַף פַּעַם,
רַק אַתְּ לִי, אִמִּי-אֲדָמָה,
בִּימֵי הָעַצֶּבֶת, הַזַּעַם,
בְּיוֹם בְּשׂוֹרַת-נֶחָמָה.

כְּאָז בַּיַּלְדוּת הַנּוֹהֶרֶת,
רַק לָךְ נֶאֱמָנָה תָּמִיד,
אָבוֹא אֶת לֶחְיִי הַחִוֶּרֶת
אֶל שֹׁזֶף לֶחְיֵךְ לְהַצְמִיד.

I am forever fickle-minded:
in the middle of their blossoming spring
feelings — like leaves in autumn —
fall off, lift away, and are gone.   4

Only you have I never betrayed,
only you are mine, my Motherland,
in times of sorrow, anger,
on the day of consolation.   8

As then, in shining youth,
faithful, only to you, evermore,
I'll come with my pale cheek
to your sunburnt cheek and press close.[35]   12
(*Rachel*, p. 166)

As in the case of "Aftergrowth," this poem seems, at first glance, to support a conventional, masculinist view of women. Rachel's poetic speaker pronounces herself fickle-minded and supports this stereotypical female

image by likening her mood swings to the habits of vegetation. A creature
of nature rather than culture, this speaker seems subject to unpredictable,
hysterical mood swings. Yet a closer reading of the poem suggests this is
no mere natural beast. The female speaker's moods do not mimic the
cycles of the seasons; in her imagination, springtime mixes with autumn;
feelings fall off their "trees" just as they are about to blossom. This is a
speaker who exercises imaginative control over the imagery of nature and
consciously uses the stereotype of female capriciousness as a background
against which to project her enduring allegiance to the Motherland.
Though her unpredictably changeable moods may distance her from people (men?) seeking constancy, they demonstrate her true kinship with the
land. Here we see a relationship between woman and land that is ideological and spiritual rather than biological and material. Of course,
beneath this seemingly optimistic picture of the union of Motherland and
daughter lies the darker, sadder fact of mortality. Despite the speaker's professed dedication to the land, her pledge of allegiance involves a promise
to merge with her Motherland not in life but in death. The image of
Rachel's speaker placing her pallid face against the weathered, "sunburnt
cheek" of the Motherland—a union which can only truly occur when she
is dead and laid to rest—suggests that her efforts to adhere to the habits
of the land while she is still alive have been less than fruitful.

In another poem, "Be'ahad gilgulai" (In a former life, 1929),
Rachel's poetic speaker speculates about past lives and incarnations as if
to explain her present-day personality. Woman as beast, woman as bird,
woman as blade of grass—all these images evoke conventional notions
about the connection between femininity and nature. Again, Rachel
adapts this conventional understanding for her own uses:

בְּאַחַד גִלְגוּלַי

הֶהָיִיתִי חַיָה בֵּין חַיוֹת הַשָׂדֶה
בְּיָמִים רְחוֹקִים, בְּאַחַד גִלְגוּלַי?
וּמֵאָז לִי קִרְבַת הָאָחוֹת לְחַי
וְאֵימַת הָאָדָם הָרוֹדֶה?

אֶפְרַת הַנוֹצָה וַחֲסְרַת הַמָגֵן
גִלְגוּלָה-פִּרְפְּרָה בִּי נִשְׁמַת צִפּוֹר?

מַנְגִּינָה עַגְמוּמִית, אַהֲבַת הַדְּרוֹר -
הֵן מִמֶּנָּה, מִמֶּנָּה שְׁתֵּיהֶן.

וְאוּלַי בַּגִּלְגּוּל הָרָחוֹק-קָדוּם
הָיִיתִי גִבְעַל-עֲשָׂבִים יְרַקְרַק
וְלָכֵן בְּאִמִּי-אֲדָמָה אֶדְבַּק,
וּמְנוּחַי בְּחֵיקָהּ הַשָּׁחוּם.

In a Former Life

Was I once a beast among other beasts of the field
long ago, in a former life?
And from then my sisterly intimacy with the living things
and their fear of tyrant Man?

Grey of feather and defenseless,
does a bird's soul twitch-turn in me?
from her, yes, from her, these both:
my sad song, my love of liberty.

And perhaps in a distant ancient life
I was a greenish blade of grass?
And thus I cling to my Motherland,
and repose in her brown lap. (*Rachel,* p. 196)[36]

Only in the last stanza of the poem does Rachel's speaker mobilize the
metaphor of land-as-woman. Throughout the poem, however, her
metaphors have a feminine trajectory. In the first stanza she wonders
whether in a past life she was a *hayah,* the feminine noun for animal or
beast. Rachel's use of the word *hayah* (animal) is strategic, for it allows
her to exploit the etymological connection between *hayah* and *Havah,*
the biblical Eve, dubbed by Adam in Genesis 3:20 as *eim kol hai,* the
mother of all life. This evocation of Eve fits beautifully into the general
theme of past lives. Imagining herself a *hayah/Havah* in a previous incarnation, the poet speaker identifies herself sororally with the generative
powers of the first woman, Eve, and with femininity in general. Notice

138

that she directly contrasts this generative quality with the destructive agency of *Adam harodeh,* tyrant Adam/man.

The connection established in the second stanza of the poem between the female speaker and the defenseless (feminine noun) *tzippor* (bird) demonstrates a similar combination of the conventional and the iconoclastic. By invoking the image of the (feminine) bird, Rachel joins a longstanding Hebrew literary tradition, dating as far back as the poetry of Yehudah Halevi and finding famous expression in Hayim Nahman Bialik's first poem "El hatsippor" (To the bird), wherein the bird is a symbol of liberty and homecoming. In Bialik's famous poem, the poet-speaker addresses a (female) bird that has returned from her winter migrations in the Holy Land; in contrast to the male poetic speaker, who is stuck in exile in Eastern Europe, the bird is free to fly to *Erets Yisra'el* and partake of its glory. In Rachel's poem, instead of a male poet who offers an imaginative apostrophe to a silent, unanswering female bird, we have a female poet who actively links her sad song *(manginah 'agmumit)* as well as her love of liberty *(ahavat haderor)*—both grammatically feminine nouns—with the habits of the female bird. Poetry and the free spirit are both given a feminine designation here, against the grain of a culture that typically identifies authorship with masculinity and limits the range of female behavior. On the one hand, Rachel's decision to describe this bird as defenseless reinforces a notion of feminine vulnerability and delicateness. On the other, the love of liberty ascribed to the bird implies courage in the face of danger, an idea that modifies the stereotype of the delicate, vulnerable woman.[37]

Rachel completes the metaphorical set in the last stanza, where her speaker imagines a previous life as a blade of grass growing from the lap of the Motherland. Of all the images in this poem, the blade of grass is the most modest and the least animate. Moving from animal to bird to blade of grass, Rachel seemingly conjures up a regressive pattern, one that moves her female speaker down rather than up the evolutionary ladder.

Within the context of the plot of this poem, however—which drives, as in the case of "I am forever fickle-minded," toward the ultimate end of death—this regression makes poignant sense. At the same time, the image of her speaker growing like a blade of grass from the land expresses an intimacy between daughter and Motherland that recalls the writings of A. D. Gordon. "We come to our Homeland," Gordon writes, "in order to be planted in our natural soil from which we have been uprooted, to strike our roots deep into its life-giving substances, and to stretch out our branches in the sustaining and creating air and sunlight of the Homeland."[38] According to Gordon, the need to return to the natural surroundings of the Land of Israel was not only a national but an artistic issue, for outside of nature, one's senses weaken, one's innermost feelings dwindle, the pipelines of creativity are blocked and literary taste is corrupted."[39] In this "Gordonian" sense, the final metaphor of the poem suggests creative regeneration even as it offers intimations of mortality.

Another poem, "Kan 'al penei ha'adamah" (Here upon the land), written the same year as "I am forever fickle-minded," offers an even more *1927* promising and generative vision of the Motherland. In fact, this poem can be read as a poetic manifesto on Motherland-centered Judaism:

כָּאן עַל פְּנֵי הָאֲדָמָה

כָּאן עַל פְּנֵי אֲדָמָה -- לֹא בֶּעָבִים, מֵעָל –
עַל פְּנֵי אֲדָמָה הַקְּרוֹבָה, הָאֵם;
לְהֵעָצֵב בְּעָצְבָּהּ וְלָגִיל בְּגִילָה הַדַּל
הַיּוֹדֵעַ כָּל כָּךְ לְנַחֵם.

לֹא עַרְפִּלֵּי מָחָר – הַיּוֹם הַמּוּמָשׁ בְּיָד,
הַיּוֹם הַמּוּצָק, הַחַם, הָאֵיתָן;
לִרְווֹת אֶת הַיּוֹם הַזֶּה, הַקָּצָר, הָאֶחָד,
עַל פְּנֵי אַדְמָתֵנוּ כָּאן.

בְּטֶרֶם אָתָא הַלֵּיל – בּוֹאוּ, בּוֹאוּ הַכֹּל!
מַאֲמָץ מְאֻחָד, עַקְשָׁנִי וָעֵר
שֶׁל אֶלֶף זְרוֹעוֹת. הַאֻמְנָם יִבָּצֵר לָגֹל
אֶת הָאֶבֶן מִפִּי הַבְּאֵר ?

Here upon the land — not in the clouds on high —
upon this close Motherland
to be sorry with her sorrow and rejoice
in her poor joys that know so well to console.

Not the fogs of tomorrow — today, concrete, in hand,
solid today, warm, firm:

to drink deep of this one short day
here upon our land.

Before evening comes — come one, come all!
A united effort, stubborn and alert
of a thousand arms. Will it be beyond our
reach *[yibatser]* to roll the stone from the well? (*Rachel*, p. 160)[40]

From the beginning of this poem, an opposition is set up between heaven and earth, between the ethereal and the concrete. This opposition coincides with a traditional binary opposition between the qualities of masculinity and femininity. In her book, *Creation and Procreation: Feminist Reflections on the Mythologies of Cosmogony and Parturition,* Marta Weigle calls for scholars and folklorists "to re-value the mundane, *mundus,* this world, as a more feminist complement and counterpart to the usual, largely sexist definitions of *mythos* as numinous, *ganz andere,* other and other-worldly."[41] It is my argument that "Kan 'al penei ha'adamah" uses and adapts biblical materials to make a similar exhortation. This reading of the poem can be supported through an analysis of the various biblical sources interwoven through the poem, beginning with Deuteronomy 30: 11–14, where Moses instructs the people that obedience of God's laws is not in heaven:

> Surely this Instruction which I enjoin upon you this day is not too baffling for you, nor is it beyond reach. It is not in the heavens, that you should say, "Who among us can go up to the heavens and get it for us and impart it to us, that we may observe it?" Neither is it beyond the sea, that you should say, "Who among us can cross to the other side of the sea and get it for us and impart it to us, that we may observe it?" No, the thing is very close to you, in your mouth and in your heart, to observe it.

When Moses says that his instruction is not in the heavens and not beyond the people, he is portraying, through the literary devices of litotes and metaphor, the accessibility of God and the attainability of an obedient religious life. Rachel's poem, in which Moses' words are revised and spoken by a woman, brings the message right down to Mother Earth. Indeed, this poem advocates neither life in the heavens nor in the Torah and the dictates of God the Father but rather "upon this close Motherland."[42] The down-to-earthness spoken of in this poem is not a

141

metaphor for Divine Immanence but down-to-earthness for its own sake, for the here and now, for the firm, warm, accessible, intimate, and nurturing soil of the Land of Israel. Rachel sets up these oppositions, it seems, to add value to the traditionally denigrated, feminine half of the opposition.

This message is reinforced by a micro-allusion to the biblical story of the Tower of Babel in Genesis 11:5–6, an episode that involves an effort on the part of a group of human beings to challenge the separation of heaven and earth: "5) And the Lord came down to look at the city and tower which man had built, 6) and the Lord said, 'If, as one people with one language for all, this is how they have begun to act, then nothing that they may propose to do will be out of their reach *[lo yibatser mehem kol asher yazmu la'asot]*.'" In using the uncommon phrase *lo yibatser*[43] (not out of reach), Rachel evokes the Tower of Babel story and suggests the power inherent in a communal effort here on earth as well as the importance of the here and now, that which is "today, concrete, in hand, / solid today, warm, firm." Rachel strengthens this idea through the image of rolling a stone from a well, an allusion to the biblical account of the first meeting of Jacob and Rachel. In Genesis 29, when Jacob arrives in the vicinity of Haran, he discovers a group of shepherds who are having difficulty rolling a heavy rock from the mouth of a well. Jacob asks them if they are acquainted with his uncle, Laban the son of Nahor; the shepherds answer in the affirmative and point out Laban's daughter, Rachel, who has brought her father's flocks to the well-side. Moved by love at first sight, Jacob lifts the rock from the well and gives water to all of Laban's flock. However, in her glance backward to the Bible, the modern poet Rachel does not re-imagine the advent of a male hero who will accomplish the heroic task of building/irrigating the land all by himself. She does not appeal to the numinous, patriarchal mythos. Instead, Rachel imagines a collaboration, with *elef zro'ot,* "a thousand arms," coming together to accomplish the task.

The Androgynous Vision of Esther Raab

In contrast to Rachel, who uses female personifications of the land and invokes traditional oppositions between masculinity and femininity as a means of valorizing the feminine side, Esther Raab's landscape poetry offers a direct challenge to the oppositions themselves. Like Rachel, Raab is perhaps best known for her poetry about the land. Critic Dov Sadan groups Rachel and Esther Raab together as the two poets who were most "captivated by the magic of Our Land [*artseinu*], whose poetry was ripened by the landscape of our ancient-young homeland."[44] Sadan's metaphorical description of writing ripened by the landscape becomes especially important in the context of a discussion of Raab's landscape poetry because of her singular status as the first native-born Hebrew poet, male or female. Raab stands out over and over again in the critical literature, both early and contemporary, as the first "sabra poet," a designation that again links her with the indigenous fruit and vegetation of the land. Much is made in the literature about Raab—not the least in statements by Esther Raab herself—of her nativeness, her firstness, and the resultant "authenticity" of her landscape depictions.[45] "The Land made me into a poet, her beauty, her immediacy, her wildness," Raab famously said.[46] "I discovered the landscape of *Erets Yisra'el*. I drew it out of my mother's womb, as I emerged into the air of this world. . . . No one else experienced like I did the firstness, the wildness of the Land."[47]

Growing up in the agricultural settlement of Petah Tikvah (often referred to as *eim hamoshavot,* the "mother" of the settlements), where she suffered repeatedly from malaria, Raab experienced firsthand the aggressive quality of her natural surroundings. Significantly, it was the harsh wildness of the landscape that captivated her young imagination, and it was to this harshness that Raab attached her image of the land-as-woman. Raab entitled her first volume of poems *Kimshonim* (Thistles, 1930), a title that attests to her preoccupation with the bristly, sun-parched, and forbidding features of the Israeli landscape. At age nineteen, Raab left Petah Tikvah to join the immigrants of the Second Wave of Zionist immigration in their collective agricultural work at Deganiah, the first kibbutz. Although she did not settle permanently in this Galilee commune, this is where she was exposed to and influenced by the collectivist ideologies of the Second Aliyah—what she termed "my University."[48] Despite her sympathy with the workers' ideology of Berl Katzenelson and A. D. Gordon, Raab sensed a difference between the immigrant perspective and her own. The generation of immigrants in the 20s, Raab observed, fell in love with the land, but they also carried with them memories of a previous homeland. In contrast, she stated, "I am a daughter of my homeland in my every organ. I belong to the land, as a thorn to the field."[49]

If one were to take these statements about Raab's organic, native, vegetal connection to the landscape entirely at face value, it would seem absurd to consider Raab's landscape poetry and her female personifications of the land alongside those of such immigrant poets as Rachel and Yokheved Bat-Miriam. On the basis of the biographical fact of nativeness,[50] critics such as Reuven Shoham, Tzvi Luz, as well as Raab's nephew and biographer Ehud Ben Ezer all argue that Raab's landscape poetry differs utterly from that of her immigrant contemporaries. According to Shoham, "Esther Raab was the first in modern Hebrew literature to look at the land from an entirely different point of view, from inside rather than outside. Her poetry nurses directly, without interruption, from the people and nature of the Israeli landscape; it is neither blocked by memories of the European landscape, nor mediated by biblical sources, and is written in the mother-tongue of Hebrew. And in this sense, Raab opens a new era in modern Hebrew literature."[51] In the same way that Raab herself, in the statements quoted above, genders the land femininely and locates the origins of her poetic vision of the land in her mother's womb, Shoham views both the landscape of *Erets Yisra'el* and Raab's poetic depictions thereof in terms of feminine Motherland imagery. Like a lactating mother, the land and its inhabitants feed Raab's poetic imagination; the language with which she writes issues forth "naturally," even biologically, from these same native, maternal origins. According to Shoham, in the writings of such poets as Rachel and Bat-Miriam, *Erets Yisra'el* is a "stepmotherland" they struggle to adopt as their own. In contrast, Shoham argues, the landscape of Israel in Raab's poetry is never a problem to be overcome; it "exists plain and simple."[52] Ben-Ezer extends the importance of nativeness to Raab's language, contrasting the Hebrew of the immigrant poets with that of Raab, who "burgeoned together with the burgeoning of Hebrew as a live spoken language."[53] Similarly, Luz calls attention to the concreteness of Raab's landscape depictions, the "natural" grounding of Raab's poetic imagery in the "new virgin land."[54]

As Luz's sexualized description of the Land of Israel as a "new virgin land" makes clear, however, poetic language is never really "natural," plain, or simple; it often comes laden with assumptions and associations and should be carefully analyzed as such. Hamutal Tsamir points out that many of Raab's early male readers, particular those of the *moderna* movement in poetry and criticism, accepted these notions of authenticity and biological connection to the Motherland so thoroughly that they completely ignored the sexual/political implications of Raab's use of female personifications of the land.[55] It is indeed naïve to read Raab too much through her nativeness and to take too literally this notion of her poetry sprouting naturally or gestating from the womb of the land, because this leads one to overlook the self-consciousness and feminist implications of Raab's art. Raab's poetry does not just sprout from the land; it is shaped, created, and carefully constructed. The native/immigrant opposition upheld by critics such as Luz and Shoham, and even by Raab herself in some of her interview statements, enforces a stable, transparent notion of identity and place, whereby one's biological and geographical origins ultimately determine the boundaries of the imagination. Yet as I will show here, Raab's landscape poetry consistently questions boundaries and violates conventions—spatial, social, syntactic, and grammatical.

Raab's landscape poetry is admittedly not the product of an immigrant confrontation with the land. Unlike the immigrant poets of her generation, who were strangers, of a sort, in a land they called their own, Raab's childhood experiences growing up in Petah Tikvah enabled her to steep her depictions of *Erets Yisra'el* in indigenous botanical and zoological imagery, in all the flora and fauna of the wild, parched, and thistle-covered landscape of Israel. At the same time, like Rachel and Bat-Miriam, Raab participates crucially in the metaphorical border-crossing into the formerly masculine realm of Hebrew literature. Raab employs various seemingly conventional female personifications of the land in her poetry, but she suggestively mixes feminine and masculine images, thereby reversing or blurring gender boundaries and definitions. In contrast to Shoham, then, who describes the image of the homeland in Raab's poetry as "simply a great vast Mother, in whose bosom it is good to be enfolded and cradled forever,"[56] it is my contention here that Raab's personified landscape is never female or mother, pure and simple. In her many homeland poems, Raab uncovers a kind of *androgynous* beauty and fecundity in the thorns in a way that redefines the femininity of both woman and land, and queries rigid gender categories.

It is important at this point for me to clarify my usage of androgyny,[57] since feminist critics have used the term in very different ways over the course of the twentieth century. "Androgyny," writes Cynthia Secor in the introduction to *The Androgyny Papers* (1974), "is the capacity of a single person of either sex to embody the full range of human character traits, despite cultural attempts to render some exclusively feminine and some exclusively masculine."[58] This union of traits traditionally associated with masculinity and femininity was most famously suggested by Virginia Woolf in her essay *A Room of One's Own,* where she contemplates Coleridge's famous comment that the "great mind is androgynous." Woolf proposes that in speaking of the androgynous mind, Coleridge meant that it "is resonant and porous; that it transmits emotion without impediment; that it is naturally creative, incandescent and undivided."[59] A few pages later, Woolf enlarges on the notion of undividedness by way of a metaphor of heterosexual consummation:

> Some collaboration has to take place in the mind between the woman and the man before the act of creation can be accomplished. Some marriage of opposites has to be consummated. The whole of the mind must lie wide open if we are to get the sense that the writer is communicating his experience with perfect fullness. There must be freedom and there must be peace. Not a wheel must grate, not a light glimmer. The curtains must be close drawn. *The writer, I thought,* once *his* experience is over, must lie back and let *his* mind celebrate its nuptials in darkness. *He* must not look or question what is being done. Rather *he* must pluck the petals from a rose or watch the swans float calmly down the river. And *I saw* again the current which took the boat and the undergraduate and the dead leaves and the taxi took *the man and the woman, I thought,* seeing them come together across the street, and the current swept them away, *I thought,* hearing far off the roar of London's traffic, into that tremendous stream.[60] (emphasis added)

Not all feminist critics have accepted Woolf's notion of the androgynous mind, and the passage quoted here is one that lights their flares. Elaine Showalter, perhaps the most adamant opponent of what she calls Woolf's "flight into androgyny," calls attention to Woolf's choice of a masculine gender for the writer figure in this passage; according to Showalter, at this moment in the text, Woolf transfers her dream of sexual equality to the "mind of the male voyeur"[61] and confirms the idea of masculine sexual/textual dominance. Showalter characterizes Woolf's concept of the androgynous mind as "a utopian projection of the ideal artist" that is "ultimately inhuman" and "represents an escape from the confrontation with femaleness or maleness."[62] Other critics such as Barbara Charlesworth Gelpi take issue with the concept of androgyny because of the tendency in Western culture to privilege the image of the "masculine completed by the feminine" over the converse image of the feminine completed by the masculine, implying that it is "impossible for the female vessel to contain masculine intelligence and spirituality."[63] Still others eschew the notion of androgyny as a fantasy of primordial wholeness, "an image that is rooted in a static image of perfection" and that ultimately privileges a patriarchal unitary subject.[64]

More recently, however, critics such as Toril Moi and Kari Weil have moved to "rescue Woolf" and her concept of androgyny.[65] According to Moi, Woolf's concept of androgyny is not "a flight from fixed gender identities, but a recognition of their falsifying metaphysical nature. Far from fleeing such gender identities because she fears them, Woolf rejects them because she has seen them for what they are. She has understood that the goal of feminist struggle must precisely be to deconstruct the death-dealing binary oppositions of masculinity and femininity."[66] Moi supports this reading by referring to Woolf's recurring playful shifts of subject position throughout *A Room of One's Own*, "leaving the critic no single unified position but a multiplicity of perspectives to grapple with."[67] Note, for example, the recurrent shifts in pronouns which I have highlighted in the passage quoted above from Woolf's essay, as well as the continually moving lens of her writerly gaze: in a few shorts lines Woolf moves from we, to I, to he, and back to I, taking her reader along the "tremendous stream" of her consciousness from the boat, to the dead leaves, the taxi, the man, and the woman. Woolf indeed refers to the writer in this passage as a "he"—perhaps this "he" is the imagined Coleridge of her earlier musings—but before and after doing so, she invokes her own feminine narrative "I," suggesting that this male writer is but a character in her own emergent androgynous fiction. Far from identifying the narrative "I" with the masculine "he," then, these pronoun shifts play with and problematize conventional associations between authorship and masculinity.

Moi's understanding of androgyny as a means of deconstructing and blurring gender differences finds precedent in Carolyn Heilbrun's classic statements on the subject in her pathbreaking 1973 book, *Toward a Recognition of Androgyny.* According to Heilbrun, the "ancient Greek word—from *andro* (male) and *gyn* (female)—defines a condition under which the characteristics of the sexes, and the human impulses expressed by men and women are not rigidly assigned. Androgyny seeks to liberate the individual from the confines of the appropriate."[68] Heilbrun's embrace of androgyny, like Woolf's, is a utopian feminist move that "suggests a reconciliation between the sexes"[69] but not through monolithic unity. On the contrary: Heilbrun emphasizes "the unbounded and hence fundamentally indefinable nature of androgyny."[70]

I have rehearsed this debate on Woolf's androgyny within the context of my discussion of Raab's landscape poetry for two reasons. First,

Woolf and Raab were both important modernist innovators. According to Moi, Woolf's concept of the androgynous mind can be linked stylistically to her modernist practice of writing, with its abrupt shifts in point of view, its ellipses and breaks, its lack of linear order. The same link can be made between what I call Raab's "androgynous vision" and her modernist poetics. As Michael Gluzman notes, as "early as the 1920s Esther Raab was writing poems which seem rather 'strange' in light of the poetry of her mainstream male contemporaries. Raab's early poetry is striking in many ways—her use of free verse, the rejection of the quatrain and regularized rhyme as well as her idiosyncratic syntax and word order."[71]

Second, as in the case of Virginia Woolf, Raab's use of androgyny can be incorporated into a similar feminist critical debate. As Kari Weil explains in her book *Androgyny and the Denial of Difference,* "androgyny has often functioned as a conservative, if not a misogynist, ideal"[72] in Western literature. The same might be said about Raab's androgynous impulses. Like Virginia Woolf, who, in her metaphorical description of literary androgyny as sexual copulation, identifies her writer as "he"—seemingly privileging the masculine side of her literary androgyne over the feminine—Raab frequently seems to valorize the masculine side of the mix. It has become a commonplace among critics of Raab's writing to call attention to her extraordinary identification with her father, Yehudah Raab, one of the founders of Petah Tikvah, a figure whom she raises to a kind of mythic status both in her interview statements and her writing. Repeatedly in her interviews, Raab asserted a stronger identification with her father than her mother[73] and pointed to this masculine/paternal legacy as the source of her poetry. "Poetry is the masculine side within me," Raab famously told the poet Sh. Shifra:

> My foundations are not feminine. I write masculine poems. I have poems of pathos—I'm not speaking here about cheap pathos—and women do not write poems of pathos. Perhaps the element of confusion in my poetry is feminine, but I aspire to be strong. If I were to be born again, I'd want to be born a man. I don't like to be one who concedes. A young man can answer with war. He simply gives a box in the teeth. I want to protect myself. Men allow themselves to do to women what they don't allow themselves to do to men. . . . Women's lives are richer but men's lives are better.[74]

According to this statement, what makes Raab a poet is the greater portion of masculinity she inherited from her father despite her female sex. Throughout these remarks, Raab reinforces misogynist stereotypes, identifying masculinity with strength, valor, and violence, and consigning femininity to the lesser realm of "confusion."

Confusion certainly does not seem to be an enviable feminine trait. Yet in Raab's 1975 essay "Manya Vilbushevitz," a childhood recollection of the visits paid to her house by Manya Shochat, the pioneering founder of the Sejera collective, confusion—gender confusion, to be specific—takes on a crucial strategic function. Here Raab presents a vision of gender differences that ostensibly privileges the masculine over the feminine but in fact gestures toward a celebration of androgyny. In the body of the essay, Raab spells Manya's family name with *bet* rather than a *vav,* punning on the Hebrew word *bilbul* (confusion), thereby intimating an element of bewilderment or blurred boundaries in Manya's gender identification. Raab writes:

> Manya Bilbushevitz used to visit our home. I was a girl of about eight or ten at that time, but I was very impressed by her. She came mainly to visit my father, my mother didn't interest her at all, and she never hid this fact—and my mother felt disgust for her too, she called her: *der hatsi zakhar* (the half-man). . . . Indeed she was masculine. I remember her voice, a kind of low alto, and her dress was masculine, most notably, she always wore a man's hat. Certainly she stood out and was different from all of the soft women. . . . Mom was openly jealous of her, because apparently Dad was attracted to this woman with the masculine personality, and would sit with her for hours in our dim salon—while Mom was doing housework not paying attention to them at all, the two of them immersed in discussion in German, for back then they didn't speak Hebrew yet. . . . When Manya would leave us (I'd get a light pinch on the cheek from her)—silence lingered—and then Mom would say with cleverness and censure: "Nu, what did *der hatsi zakhar* tell you? . . ." One time, I walked into my parents' bedroom and found Mom standing in front of the mirror (the only one in the house), trying on Dad's broad-brimmed hat, turning it in every direction, twisting her face, and looking at herself from various directions—and when she saw me, she burst into laughter and said, "Manya Bilbushevitz!"[75]

Here is a story about what happens when an androgynous woman, one whose identity overtly combines masculine and feminine elements, comes into a conventional domestic setting and provokes play and confusion, as suggested by the punned nickname. On the face of things, this story reinforces stereotypes: Manya is interesting because she is half man or, more accurately, more man than woman. Her manliness makes her

a viable conversation partner for Raab's revered father; her manly interaction with Esther, as represented by the pinch on Esther's face as she
leaves the Raabs' house, designates Esther as a possible future participant
in the masculine conversation. Raab's mother is relegated at first to her
purely feminine domestic place. The story veers in a different direction,
however, when this feminine mother tries on her husband's conventionally masculine hat: the very thing Esther had singled out as the most
salient feature of Manya's manly dress, thereby writing herself unexpectedly into the plot of assumed identities. Whereas the story begins
with the collusion of Manya's father and Esther, it ends with the shared
laughter and play of Esther and her mother, over their own extension of
the gender *bilbul* precipitated by Manya "Bilbushevitz." This piece is
remarkable for the way it plays with and confounds our expectations,
shifting the focus of our identification. At the beginning of the story the
hero appears to be manly Manya, but by the end, Esther's mother, rarely
a character in Raab's poetry or fiction, assumes center stage.

Raab's "Manya Bilbushevitz" is emblematic of a poetics of androgyny that is evident in much of Esther Raab's poetry, especially in her first
and best-known volume *Kimshonim*. It bears repeating that in using the
term androgyny here, I am not referring to women dressing like men or
vice versa but to a literary strategy that involves the mixing of masculine
elements with feminine ones, thereby blurring or confusing rigid gender
designations and oppositions. This understanding of androgyny is predi-
cated on an apprehension of the constructed or performative nature of
gender identity.[76] A similar understanding can be applied to the gendering of landscapes. As feminist geographer Catherine Nash observes, "a
recognition of the constructed nature of identity allows landscape to be
used as a shifting strategic source of identification without implying the
adoption of a masculinist position, or inherent identity, or a restrictive
notion of space."[77] Raab's androgynous gendering of the landscape of *Erets
Yisra'el,* where the land assumes feminine as well as masculine assignations
and is never defined in a truly stable sense, embodies precisely this notion
of constructed rather than essential identity.

One of the most interesting instances of Raab's androgynous gendering of the landscape occurs in her famous poem "La'av" (To the father,
1929), written in honor of the fiftieth anniversary of her father's move to
Petah Tikvah. As in "Manya Bilbushevitz," where the masculinist elements appear at first to undergird rather than break down conventional
gender polarities, Raab's "La'av" provokes a similar initial reading:

לְאָב

במלאת חמשים שנה לעלותו על אדמת פתח תקוה

בְּרוּכוֹת הַיָּדִים

אֲשֶׁר זָרְעוּ

בְּבָקְרֵי-חֹרֶף,

לְאוֹשַׁת זַרְזִירִים עָטִים –

שְׂדֵמוֹת-חֶמְרָה אֲדֻמּוֹת;

אֲשֶׁר הִבְרִיכוּ הַגֶּפֶן בַּעֲנָנָה

וְשָׁתְלוּ אֶקָלִיפְּטִים כְּדִגְלֵי נִיחוֹחַ

עַל מֵי יַרְקוֹן;

אֲשֶׁר רִסְּנוּ הַסּוּס

וְהִצְמִידוּ רוֹבֶה לַלֶּחִי

לְגָרֵשׁ אוֹיֵב מֵעַל סֻכָּה דַלָּה,

סֻכַּת-שָׁלוֹמִים מוֹלֶכֶת

עֲלֵי חוֹלוֹת וְיַמְבּוּט;

וּבְעַיִן יְרֻקָּה עַזָּה

יְפַקַּח עַל הָאֶפְרוֹחִים:

דּוּנְמִים רַכִּים זְרוּעֵי כַּרְשִׁינָה

וּשְׁוָרִים מִסְפָּר רוֹבְצִים בְּמֵי-בִּצָּה...

חוֹרֵשׁ הַתֶּלֶם עַל אַף הַמִּדְבָּר

בּוֹקֵעַ רִאשׁוֹן בְּאַדְמַת-בְּתוּלָה:

בְּרוּכוֹת הַיָּדִים!

To the Father

Fifty years on the soil of Petah Tikvah

Blessed are the hands

that sowed

on winter-mornings,

to the rustle of swooping starlings —

fields of red loam;   5

that caused the vines to bend with fruit

and planted eucalyptus trees like flags of fragrance

along the waters of the river Yarkon;

that bridled the horse

and pressed rifle to cheek   10
to chase off an enemy from a meager hut,
tabernacle-of-peace that reigns
over dune and screw bean;
and a bold green eye
watches over the fledglings: 15
soft dunam seeded with vetch
as a few oxen squat in swamp-water —
plows the furrow despite the desert,
first cleaves virgin soil:
blessed are the hands![78]   20

"To the Father" was a very important poem for Raab. Ehud Ben-Ezer notes that it was published almost ten years after the publication of her first poem, "Ani tahat ha'atad" (I under the thornbush, 1922).[79] Despite this historical fact, Raab insisted to one critic that "To the Father" was her first published poem. As Ben-Ezer notes, Raab's association of this poem with the beginning of her poetic career attests to the depth of her veneration of and identification with her father.[80] Indeed, as Reuven Shoham explains, Yehudah Raab emerges from this poem as a mythical patriarch, "a titanic image, who promises security and success to all who rest in his shade."[81]

Raab's decision to address Yehudah Raab as "the father" rather than more intimately as "my father," detaching him from his specific familial context, supports this reading of "The Father" as mythical farmer-father, one who plants the orchards, tames the horse, shoots the rifle, plants trees as a kind of nationalistic unfurling of "flags of scent," and oversees the household. More than mere flesh and blood, though, the father is seemingly elevated to the position of farmer-God, watching omnisciently, omnipotently, and providently over his soft *dunams* of land as well as his young fledglings. This mythical status is supported by the repeated use of liturgical language in the poem. The adjective *berukhot* (blessed), which begins the first and last lines of the poem, evokes the word *barukh,* the first word of traditional Hebrew blessings. The lines *shatlu ekaliptim kediglei niho'ah al mei Yarkon* (planted eucalyptus trees like flags of fragrance / on the waters of the river Yarkon) brings to mind two similar biblical verses that promise blessings to those who trust in the power of God:

Blessed is the man who trusts in the Lord, and whose trust is the Lord alone. For he shall be like a tree planted by the waters, sending forth its roots by a stream. (Jer. 17:7–8)

Happy is the man who has not followed the counsel of the wicked, or taken the path of sinners. . . . He is like a tree planted beside streams of water, that yields its fruit in season, whose foliage never fades and whatever it produces thrives. (Ps. 1:1, 3)

Read against these biblical verses, the tree-planting carried out by the father in Raab's poem becomes a mythic act signifying security, prosperity, and fertility. Likewise, Raab's depiction of the family hut as a *sukkat shelomim* recalls the depiction of God in the Sabbath Eve liturgy as spreading a Tabernacle of Peace (*pores sukkat shalom*) over the people of Israel and Jerusalem, placing the father in the role of divine protector and provider of physical as well as spiritual shelter.

The second last line of the poem, which refers to the father's role in plowing the first furrow in the "virgin soil," adds a conventional sexual element to this mythic depiction. Here Raab employs a female personification of the land that seems to support a traditional patriarchal concept. In her book *The Green Beast and the New World: Landscape, Gender and American Fiction,* Louise Westling traces the history of land-as-woman images in ancient literature, noting the shifts that take place with the advent of biblical patriarchy. According to Westling,

> the ideology of woman's body as fruitful, spontaneously generating earth gives way in time to a cultural appropriation of the body that responds to and rewrites that primary image. Men claim that they must *plough* the earth, create fields, furrow them, and plant seeds if the earth is to bear fruit. They see female bodies as empty ovens that must be filled with grains and made to concoct offspring. They see the female body as analogous to a writing tablet on which they write; the stylus (plough) carving the lines (furrows) of letters (sown seeds) in the body of the mother.[82]

The image of the furrow ploughed in the virgin soil by the father in Raab's poem ostensibly supports the patriarchal view described by Westling. Yet, as in the analyzed Woolf passage, one cannot ignore the significance of the implied (female) speaker of the poem. What happens when a woman poet writes the story of a man's metaphorical writing upon the body of the feminized land? What happens when she places his narrative of watchfulness and protectiveness under her own watchful poetic eye?

Here, too, as in the case of Woolf's androgyny passage, minute grammatical gender shifts open up possibilities for alternative interpretations. As Chana Kronfeld notes, "Writing as a woman in a language that is her 'father' tongue (and Raab makes that literal point that recurs in her interviews and poems), a language which genders everything, yet treats only the masculine as unmarked, as the norm, compels Raab to thematize, even politicize, the very choice of grammatical gender in her common nouns and adjectives."[83] The poem is addressed to a man and partakes of imagery evocative of the one Father God. Yet it begins with a plural, feminine form of a liturgical adjective (*brukhot,* blessed), modifying a feminine (plural) body part (*yadayim,* hands), thereby creating an androgynous combination of masculine and feminine associations. Raab's choice to use the definite rather than the possessive adjective— blessed are the hands, rather than blessed are *his* hands—becomes significant, for it allows a blurring of grammatical gender boundaries.

Indeed, throughout the poem a grammatical distance is placed between the ostensible subject of the poem—the father—and the actual description. For most of the poem it is not the father who is the subject of the verbs but the (feminine noun) hands or the (grammatically feminine) *sukkah* (hut). In lines 14–15, the father becomes the implied subject of the verb "watches," though he is never introduced explicitly. And even here he oversees through the agency of the (feminine noun) green eye. Notice that the mythic father is presented not as a whole entity but in fragmented body parts. As Hamutal Tsamir aptly notes, "The dismemberment of the father—the classic, national man, the man who loves the mother/bride earth, he who protects and fertilizes—is an additional strategy employed by Raab in order to enter the national masculine conversation, and at the same time to oppose it, challenge it, and to put it simply: to dismember it."[84] What's more, Tsamir suggests, invoking Luce Irigaray, "it is no accident that the father is dismembered specifically into his feminine, paired body parts," transforming an image of the one God into a female "Sex Which Is Not One."[85] The penultimate line of the poem, in which the father cleaves or penetrates the virgin soil, reinforces all the conventional oppositions inherent in the masculine tradition of female personifications of the land. But Raab's decision to begin and end her poem with the line "blessed are the hands" challenges these oppositions, lending a feminine "hand" to the enterprise of poetic depiction.

The poem that opens *Kimshonim,* "'Al ma'arumayikh hogeg yom lavan" (Upon your nakedness white day celebrates), speaks similarly to the need of women writers to recast the masculine tradition of female personifications of the land. As in "L'av," the poem seems, on one level, to reinforce old categories and oppositions. As in the poetry of Abraham Shlonsky, which often imagines the hills and valleys of Jezreel in terms of female body parts, Raab likens the landscape in this poem to a reclining naked woman, passionately aroused and brought to a "continuous and shuddering" climax by the (masculine) noonday sun:

עַל מַעֲרֻמַּיִךְ חוֹגֵג יוֹם לָבָן,
אַתְּ הַדַּלָה וְהָעֲשִׁירָה כֹּה,
נֵד הָרִים קָפָא,
שָׁקוּף כַּחֲזוֹן תַּעְתּוּעִים.
אֶל הָאֹפֶק דָּבֵק.
צָהֳרַיִם, מֶרְחֲבֵי שָׁדוֹתַיִךְ מִשְׁתַּלְהֲבִים
וּלְשַׁדֵּךְ כָּלִיל מִתְלַהְלֵהַּ וְעוֹלֶה
מוּל הַשָּׁמַיִם הַלְּבָנִים,
כְּמָסֵךְ לֹא יִפָּסֵק
נִמְשָׁךְ וְרוֹעֵד.
בְּתוֹךְ הַמִּישׁוֹר
גִּבְעָה, תָּרוֹם כְּשַׁד עָגֹל
וּלְרֹאשָׁהּ קֶבֶר לָבָן חוֹפֵף;
וּבָעֲזוּבַת שָׂדוֹת קְצוּרִים
אָטָד בָּדָד רוֹבֵץ.
וְהָיָה כִּי תִּיעַף הָעַיִן
מִזַּרְמֵי תַּעְתּוּעֵי-אוֹר
וְטָבְלָה בְּיֶרֶק הָאָטָד הַמַּכְחִיל,
כִּבְתוֹךְ בְּרֵכַת מַיִם צוֹנְנִים.
אַתְּ הַדַּלָה כֹּה עַל חֲרִיצֵךְ הַמַּאֲדִּימִים
תּוֹךְ זְהַב הַמֶּרְחַקִים
עִם קַרְקְעֵי נְחָלַיִךְ הַחֲרֵבִים, הַלְּבָנִים –
מַה יָּפִית!

Upon your nakedness a white day celebrates,
so poor and rich you are,
a heap of mountains froze,

155

transparent like a mirage,
cleaving to the horizon.   5
Noon. The expanses of your fields inflame,
your sap going mad and rising
against the white skies,
a never ending curtain
continuous and shuddering.   10
Out there in the plain
a hill rises like a round breast
and at her summit, a white grave covers;
and in the desert of cut fields
a lone thornbush crouches.   15
And as the eye wings
from the streaming illusions of light
it dips into the bluing green of the thornbush,
as if into a pool of cool water.
How poor you are upon your reddening furrows   20
amidst the gold distances
in the soil of your arid white streams —
how lovely you are! (*Kol Hashirim,* pp. 9–10)[86]

According to Reuven Shoham, the female speaker of the poem, as represented by the poetic eye in line 16, reacts ambivalently to the "white day"
and its sexual advances upon the Motherland. Shoham's reading of the
poem is part of a psychobiographical theory about Raab's own ambiguous
sexuality, a subject that Shoham writes about extensively in many places.[87]
Certainly, the image of a white (masculine noun) day celebrating or playing upon the nakedness of the feminized, passively outstretched landscape
suggests a conventional opposition between active male and passive female
sexuality. Yet as Anne Lapidus Lerner suggests, "The land that rises is not
the landscape of male metaphor."[88] As in the case of several of Rachel's
Motherland poems, here both speaker and subject are female, and this
changes everything, allowing for a dialogue between speaker and subject
and for the possibility of switching roles. In her excellent essay on this
poem, Hamutal Tsamir argues that although the land is initially presented

in line 1 as a passive, naked, sexual object, this image changes dramatically in subsequent lines, when the land becomes the subject of a plethora of active verbs—cleaving, inflaming, going mad, rising, continuing, shuddering, and so on. In contrast to the initial opposition, Tsamir points out, there is a gradual blurring of boundaries in the poem between land and sky, between images of frozen mountains and contrasting ones of transparency and hallucination.[89]

This blurring of gender boundaries persists in various ways throughout the poem. Raab's decision to depict the hill as a round breast rising over the plain (line 12) appears to reinforce a masculine habit of maternalizing the landscape. However, an earlier version of the poem, found in the notebooks of *Kimshonim,* points toward a more androgynous vision. In this unpublished version of the poem, the hill ascends from the plain like a *shad 'agulah,* a round (feminine adjective) breast.[90] In reality, the Hebrew word for breast, *shad,* is a masculine noun. In the final, published version of the poem, Raab's initial grammar mistake is corrected and changed to *shad 'agol.* Reading these two versions next to one another, though, one notices this curious fact of Hebrew grammar, which Raab seems to exploit poetically. The body part most closely associated with femininity and maternity, used in this poem to describe a femininely personified hill, ironically turns out to be grammatically masculine, resulting in an unexpected, androgynous combination of masculine and feminine elements. This surprising gender (con)fusion is underscored thematically by the location of a white grave (grammatically masculine), intimating death and desolation, on the summit—the would-be nipple of the breast-hill. In *The Lay of the Land,* Annette Kolodny speculates that American pioneers might have needed to "experience the land as a nurturing, giving maternal breast because of the threatening, alien and potentially emasculating terror of the unknown. . . . In a sense, to make the land woman was already to civilize it a bit, casting the stamp of human relations upon what was otherwise unknown and untamed."[91] Raab does the very opposite in this poem, using the image of the land as maternal breast but deliberately untaming and uncivilizing it, reintroducing into and celebrating the dangerous and threatening aspects of the landscape. While the image of the grave undercuts the typical association of femininity with quiescent and life-giving maternity, the use of the adjective "white" recalls the description of the (male) white day in line 1, further blurring the distinction between land and sky, male and female.

In line 15, Raab further complicates the would-be feminine topography by introducing the phallic *atad* (thornbush) into the landscape. Her description of the thornbush as an *atad badad* (a lone thornbush) is reminiscent of the beginning of the biblical book of Lamentations, where the feminized, destroyed city of Jerusalem sits *badad* (solitary) like a widow. This allusion enhances the androgynous nature of the landscape, linking the phallic thornbush with a well-known biblical instance of female personification.

The biblical association of the *atad* with the parable of Jotham adds another layer of meaning.[92] In Judges 9, Jotham, the one surviving son of Jeruba'al (Gideon), fighting to prevent his murderous brother Abimelekh from being anointed king by the citizens of Shekhem, stands on top of Mount Gerizim and shouts out a parable about a grove of trees seeking to anoint a king. After being rejected by the various fruit-bearing candidates—the olive, the fig, the vine—the trees approach the thornbush and ask him to rule over them: "Then all the trees said to the thornbush, 'You come and reign over us.' And the thornbush said to the trees, 'If you are acting honorably in anointing me king over you, come and take shelter in my shade; but if not may fire issue from the thornbush and consume the cedars of Lebanon!'" (Judg. 9:14–15). Jotham offers this parable to the people of Shekhem as a means of persuading them not to anoint the "thorny" and untrustworthy Abimelekh as king. Unlike the other trees in the parable that are too busy bearing fruit to assume the role of king, the *'atad* lacks all fruit-bearing capacity. It is sterile and dry, good for kindling but little else (hence the reference to a fire issuing from the thornbush). The thornbush does not even provide good shade. Its invitation to the other trees to seek shelter under its shade—like murderous Abimelekh's promises to the people of Shekhem—is, at best, a disingenuous ploy. Raab's decision to move from an exploration of the landscape as breast to the landscape as thornbush turns all this upon its head. Here, the feminized Motherland, which one would more readily associate with the luxurious fruit-bearing trees, is represented by phallic masculinity, danger, violence, even sterility. Raab uses the indigenous plants of Palestine to challenge and complicate traditional associations of land and woman.[93]

This androgynous vision is further amplified in lines 16 through 19. Here the sun-tired eye of the poetic speaker blinks or wings away to take chromatic refuge in the bluing greenery of the thornbush, dipping as if into a (feminine noun) "pool of cool water," a simile which endows the (masculine noun) thornbush—a parched, desert plant, representative of infertility—with thirst-quenching, feminine liquidity. Raab's feminized landscape thus becomes several things at once: masculine and feminine, aggressive and pliant, parched and sumptuously liquid, parched and extravagantly beautiful.

Raab's decision to liken the immersion of the poetic eye in the bluish greenery of the thornbush to a plunge into a pool *(bereikhah)* brings to mind Haim Nahman Bialik's classic nature poem "Habereikhah" (The pool, 1905) and suggests a possible intertextual interpretation of the poem. Raab said in interviews that she had mixed feelings about Bialik's poetry. "Bialik is a giant," she told one interviewer. "'Hamatmid' and 'Habereikhah' are the foundation [of modern Hebrew poetry]. Even so, in my everyday life, in terms of a real human encounter, I felt no real connection."[94] Might Raab's "'Al ma'arumayikh," a poem that celebrates the peculiar landscape of *Erets Yisra'el* and explicitly overturns the tradition of female personifications of the land, be read as Raab's poetic response to Bialik's famous long poem?

"Habereikhah" is organized around a clear opposition between the masculinized and feminized features of the landscape. On the one hand, Bialik introduces the masculinely personified forest, bathed in the grandeur of sunlight or poised heroically during a rainstorm "to face whatever peril is in store."[95] On the other hand, he presents a modest feminized pool, tucked away in the middle of the forest like a "precious royal secret" or like a "hidden princess long ago bewitched," whom the forest guards and protects "until the prince her lover and redeemer / comes in a happy hour, and redeems her."[96] The feminized pool, whose clear waters reflect the surrounding landscape, appears early on in the poem as a metaphor for the reflective, mimetic function of poetry and art. She is a specular entity, however, dependent upon the male reality of the forest for her very essence, a captive woman, waiting to be redeemed or discovered, "dreaming perhaps in secret, who can know? That she is no mere nourisher and image / but the source of his [the forest's] whole being and his growth."[97] Bialik meditates here on the relationship between reality and reflection, suggesting the possibility not that reality creates art but that art creates reality. Throughout, however, the feminine image of the pool evinces a passive character and a dependence upon male poetic agency. Toward the end of the poem, when Bialik's poetic "I" enters into the poem and recalls his artistic awakening in the forest, the metaphor shifts somewhat, with the male poet viewing the feminine pool as a wellspring for his own powers of creative representation or transformation: "Hidden there . . . she seemed to me to be the gazing eye / of the spirit of the forest, deep in thought, / in meditation and in mystery."[98] By describing the pool this way, the male poetic speaker unlocks the secret of the pool; in so doing, he becomes the mythic prince alluded to earlier, the one who finally redeems the princess/pool from her secret captivity.

The thesis of Bialik's poem might pose a problem for a woman poet insofar as it opposes masculine agency and female passivity and figures art or poetry as a feminine pool in which the male imagination enters, plays, and casts its own reflection. It is my contention that Raab's "'Al ma'arumayikh" indicates an awareness of this problem and presents a feminist alternative to Bialik's masculinist artistic vision. As in "Habereikhah," where Bialik introduces the male poetic I/eye as an actor in the poem, the poetic "eye" of Raab's speaker enters into the drama and interacts imaginatively with the landscape. But if Bialik's poem inscribes a conventional opposition between male creativity and female reflexivity, Raab's female poetic "eye" interrupts and challenges this duality. The very presence of a female reflecting eye questions the association of creativity with masculinity. Bialik's poet-speaker actively imagines the passive pool as "the gazing eye of the spirit of the forest." It is he who imaginatively endows the feminine pool with this quality. In contrast, the active, winging, gazing, transformative eye of Raab's female poetic speaker boldly transforms the dry, prickly masculine *atad* into a feminine pool, a metaphorical move that celebrates the indigenous features of the Israeli landscape and makes way for a new androgynous vision.

The image of the *atad* also figures prominently in Raab's first published poem "Ani tahat ha'atad" (I under the thornbush), where the land is represented metonymically by the phallic thornbush. Again, this masculine image takes on androgynous implications in its association with the female speaker of the poem:

אֲנִי תַּחַת הָאָטָד

קַלָּה, זִידוֹנָה,

קוֹצָיו צוֹחֲקֶת

לִקְרָאתֵךְ זָקַפְתִּי;

אוֹר מַכֶּה עַל הַמֶּרְחָב,

כָּל קָפוּל בְּשִׂמְלָתִי

לִי יְלַחֵשׁ:
לִקְרַאת מָוֶת
לְבָנָה וּמְחוֹלֶלֶת
אַתְּ יוֹצֵאָה
אַתָּה מוֹפִיעַ –
וַאֲנִי קַלָּה צוֹהֶלֶת
מְנִיפָה חֶרֶב נוֹצֶצֶת
וּבְעֶצֶם צָהֳרַיִם
בִּשְׂדוֹת לְבָנִים מֵאוֹר
אֶת דִּינֵנוּ גָזַרְתִּי
בְּאַחַת!

I under the thornbush
easy, plotting,
its thorns, laughing,
toward you I raised up;
light strikes the expanse,
every pleat in my dress
whispers to me:
toward death
white and dancing
you go out.
You appear —
and I am lightly exultant
waving a glittering sword
and at high noon
in fields made white by light
I have decreed our fates
as one! (*Kol hashirim*, p. 31)[99]

Raab's use of the preposition *tahat* in the first line of the poem to describe the physical position of the female speaker with respect to the thornbush—a word that can be translated either as "under" (beneath) or as "in place of"—is strategic, suggesting a merging of the female speaker with the phallic feature of the landscape. This image of the woman changing places with or merging with the prickly desert plant is even more apparent in an earlier draft of the poem found in *Mahberot kimshonim*, where lines 3–4 read, *kol kotsav me'al 'ori / likratkha bitshok hakimoti* (all of its/his thorns upon my skin / toward you I raised up.)[100] This portrayal of a woman with thorns sprouting from her skin, thorns she makes erect with the force of her laughter, is enhanced by the title of this earlier version of the poem—"Capricio" [*sic*], which, according to Webster's New Collegiate Dictionary, refers to a lively piece of music in free-form, a "head with hair standing on end," or "a sudden, impulsive, and seemingly unmotivated change of mind."[101] Raab's free verse, experimental poem—which tells of a phallic woman going out in the midday sun to greet her lover, only to deal him a sudden, impulsive deathblow with a sword—speaks to all three meanings. Raab's decision in the final published version of the poem to remove the "Capricio" title, as well as to complicate the syntax and mix verb tenses (I raised up, whispers to me, you go out, I have decreed) suggests a desire to blur boundaries between subject, verb, and object, between past present and future, male and female—in short, a poetics of androgyny. The tortured syntax in lines 3–4 of the final version of the poem (its thorns, laughing, / toward you I raised up), where the female speaker "laughs his thorns," her own emotions materializing or solidifying into thorns, bespeaks a breakdown of regular categories of abstract and concrete, human and plant, masculine and feminine.

The poem also evokes a number of classical stories of female power and warfare. Raab's association of laughter with the solidity and harmfulness of thorns calls to mind the Greek myth of the Medusa, one of the three snake-haired Gorgons who turned to stone all those who looked at them. French feminist critic Catherine Clément's comments on laughter and the Medusa myth resonate remarkably with the subject of this poem: "She laughs, and it's frightening—like Medusa's laugh—petrifying and shattering constraint."[102]

According to poet and critic Shin Shifrah, the plot of a woman who kills her lover at high noon against the backdrop of the Near Eastern desert landscape also brings to mind the stories of the Sumerian goddess Inanna and the death of Dumuzi (Tammuz).[103] In the story "From the Great Above to the Great Below," the goddess Inanna decides to descend into the underworld to attend a funeral. She manages to escape eternal death, but is compelled to offer up someone else in her place. She elects suddenly to sacrifice her husband Dumuzi: "Inanna fastened on Dumuzi the eye of death. / She spoke against him the word of wrath. / She uttered against him the cry of guilt: / *Take him! Take Dumuzi away!*" Shifra's reading of the thorn-woman as Inanna[104] is especially interesting in light of Inanna's role in Sumerian mythology as "the nondomesticated woman," one who straddles social and gender boundaries. According to Tikva Frymer-Kensky, Inanna "is the exception to the rule, the woman who does not behave in societally approved ways, the goddess who models the crossing of gender lines and the danger that this presents."[105] Like the thorn-woman in Raab's poem, Inanna has a role in warfare; her ferocity and love of war are referred to as "manliness."[106] When she marries, Frymer-Kensky explains, she does not assume typical wifely duties.[107] Like Inanna, she "stands at the boundary of differences between man and woman."[108]

Anne Lapidus Lerner astutely identifies a bride motif in the poem, indicated by the repetitions of *likrat* (toward) and *kallah* (with a "kof," meaning easy), a homonym of the word *kallah* (with a "kaf," meaning bride); together the words *likrat kallah* allude to the well-known liturgical hymn for the Sabbath, *lekha dodi likrat kallah* (Go forth my love, to greet the bride).[109] But this thorn-woman, dressed in white, is a bride of a very unconventional sort. Here is a woman warrior who wields a *herev notsetset* (a glittering sword). Once again, as in the case of the *shad 'agol* (the round breast) of "'Al ma'arumayikh," we see Raab's subtle manipulation of grammatical gender to create the effect of poetic androgyny. The word *herev* would appear to be masculine, both in terms of its morphology and its cultural significance. Ironically, it is a feminine noun, taking the feminine adjective *notsetset*. This subtle grammatical point reinforces the androgynous nature of the warrior bride, the female bearer of the sword. Like Inanna, Raab's thorn-woman straddles the boundaries of gender and identity, promising her lover not obedience or conformity but danger, passion, even death.[110]

As in "I under the Thornbush," where the poetic "I" of the poem metonymically merges with the (unexpectedly) phallic features of the landscape, complicating and recasting the convention of female personifications of the land, the poet-speaker of "Tel Aviv" (1928) merges with the landscape, clinging to her hems like a sobbing patch of "parched lovegrass":

תֵּל אָבִיב

אֵיכָה אֵבְךְ וְדִמְעָה אָיִן,
הָלוֹךְ וְטָפוֹף בְּרַגְלֵי מֶרִי
עַל חוֹל אַדְמָתֵךְ – אָתְּ,
לֹא גֹרֶן וְלֹא זַיִת,
עֲרוּגוֹת קְלוֹקְלוֹת,
תִּסְחֲטִי כָּאן,
וְאַבְנֵי־מֶלֶט
עַל חָזֵךְ הָרָזֶה:
עַרְבַּיִךְ עוֹד יְזַלְּפוּ מָה
מֵיץ־כּוֹכָבִיס אוֹ לַחְלוּחִית־יָם;
אֶדְבַּק עִם עֶרֶב אֶל שׁוּלֵי גִּבְעוֹתַיִךְ,
כְּחִלְפָה צְחִיחָה מְיַבֵּבֶת.

Tel Aviv

How [*eikhah*] can I weep when there is no tear
walking and mincing with bitter feet
upon the sands of your land — you.
Neither threshing floor nor olive tree,
meager flower beds
you'll wring out here,
and cement blocks
upon your lean breast.
Your evenings will still leak a little
star-juice or sea-damp;
at evening I'll cling to the hems of your hills
like parched lovegrass sobbing. (*Kol hashirim*, p. 15)[111]

A lament over urbanization, "Tel Aviv" alludes to a host of biblical texts
and thus calls forth many meanings. As Barbara Mann notes, the opening word of the poem, *eikhah*, recalls the beginning of the biblical book
of Lamentations, which mobilizes the metaphor of the city as a profli-
gate, impure woman whose "unfaithfulness" has led to her own ruin
"Jerusalem has sinned therefore she has become loathsome," (*Lam.*

1:8).[112] Similarly, the clause "walking and mincing with bitter feet" alludes to Isaiah 3:16, where the prophet Isaiah castigates the daughters of Zion for their vain habit of walking "with a mincing gait making a tinkling with their feet." Isaiah goes on to imagine, in markedly misogynist terms, the divine debasement of these haughty daughters, who represent, through synecdoche, the people of the Judaean kingdom:

17) My Lord will bare the pates
Of the daughters of Zion.
The Lord will uncover their heads.

18) In that day the Lord will strip off the finery of the anklets, the fillets, and the crescents; 19) of the eardrops, the bracelets, and the veils; 20) the turbans, the armlets, and the sashes; of the talismans and the amulets; 21) the signet rings and the nose rings; 22) of the festive robes, the mantles, and the shawls; the purses, 23) the lace gowns, and the linen vests; and the kerchiefs and the capes. 24)

And then instead of perfume there shall be rot;
And instead of an apron, a rope;
Instead of a diadem of beaten work,
A shorn head;
Instead of a rich robe, a girding of sackcloth;
A burn instead of beauty.
. . .
4: 1) In that day seven women shall take hold of one man, saying
"We will eat our own food,
And wear our own clothes;
Only let us be called by your name —
Take away our disgrace."
2) In that day,
The radiance of the Lord
Will lend beauty and glory. (Isa. 3:17–24, 4:1–2)

Raab's invocation of these sources ostensibly supports traditional misogynist usages of female personification, wherein the city is seen as feminine either in its barrenness, its wantonness, or its menstrual impurity. Raab's speaker, who is ambiguously gendered in the poem, seems to be taking on an identity of lamenter in the masculine mold. The allusion from Isaiah, where female identity and pride are invested primarily in images of fashion and finery, and where the glory of God is revealed through a catalogue of female degradations, offers the strongest evidence for this interpretation.

Yet as Barbara Mann suggests, "Tel Aviv" "both signals a fidelity to the original text and distorts it at every turn."[113] The references to tears in line 1, for example, replays the image of the weeping widow Jerusalem, overflowing with tears, yet lacking a (male) comforter (Lam. 1: 16–17). Raab's speaker announces in line 1, however, that she cannot cry, for she has no tears. While this lack might be owing to the desiccation and dryness of the urban environment, it also suggests the speaker's unwillingness to be incorporated into the masculine tradition of representing the land/city as weeping widow. Line 2 reads as a dangling modifier, such that it is unclear to the reader whether it is the personified city of Tel Aviv or the poet-speaker who is "walking and mincing with bitter feet." The result is a blurred boundary between the speaker and the subject of the poem—another instance of poetic androgyny. According to one possible reading, in absence of (or in opposition to) conventional women's tears, the poet speaker declares her intention to walk on her own "bitter," rebellious, poetic "feet"—the word feet referring to the basic unit of verse or prosody. Later in the poem the speaker will sob, using the word *meyabevet*, which appears only once in the Bible, namely, in the Song of Deborah (Judg. 5), where the mother of Sisera sobs for her lost son. Raab's decision to insert female tears into the poem through an allusion to an exceptional biblical moment of female military heroism and poetic utterance reinforces this reading of the poem as a reinterpretation or reinvention of the Lamentations.

This notion is supported in line 11, where the speaker of the poem announces her intention to cling to the "hems *[shulei]* of your hills," an allusion to Lamentations (1:9), where the "uncleanness" of Zion "clings to her skirts" *(tum'atah beshulehah).* Of course, instead of the male lamenter who gazes upon and mourns over the defiled skirts of the feminine "other," Raab's poem boasts a poet-speaker-lamenter who clings intimately to the skirts of the Motherland, holding out hope for her regeneration.

What is iconoclastic about poems such as "Tel Aviv" is Raab's persistent blending or recasting of traditional masculinist images into new feminist or androgynous forms. Throughout her landscape poems, she celebrates the risk, the danger, the prickly erectness, the violence, the sumptuous femininity of the thistle and thornbush as metonymic representations of the land. "My heart is with your dews, Homeland," she writes in the second poem in *Kimshonim,* "at night upon nettled fields, / and the scent of cypress and moist thistle / I shall spread a hidden wing."[114] In another early poem, "Parats kimosh bahamra" (Thistle burst the red loam), a thistle-bush bursts out of the soil like a swollen maternal breast, spilling white milk over the land.

פָּרַץ קִמּוֹשׁ בַּחַמְרָה
וַיִּשְׁתַּפֵּךְ כְּחָלָב
עַל פְּנֵי אֲדָמָה;
וּבַלֵּילוֹת יְלַקֵּק יָרֵחַ
צַלְּחוֹת חָלָב נָעוֹת
עַל גִּבְעוֹלִים דַּקִּים,
וַעֲנָנִים יִמְשְׁכוּ שֹׁבֶל-לְבָנָם,
יִטְבְּלוּ בְּקֶצֶף קִמּוֹשׁ
פּוֹרֵחַ שׁוֹטֵף,
וּשְׁרַקְרַקִּים יְרֻקִּים בַּהֲמוֹנִים
יְגַרְגְּרוּ וִילַהֲלְהוּ
וִימַלְאוּ כְּרֵסָם
חֲרָקִים רוֹחֲשִׁים
בְּצַלְּחוֹת קִמּוֹשׁ לְבָנוֹת;
סָגְרוּ יַמְבּוּטִים עַל קִמּוֹשׁ
בַּל יְכֻבַּשׁ גַּם הַחוֹל;
רֵיחַ יַמְבּוּט רַךְ, נוֹזֵל
וְרֵיחַ קִמּוֹשׁ חָרִיף מְזֻדְּקָר —
זֶה עַל זֶה בִּדְבֵקוּת מִתְרַפְּקִים
וּמָלְאוּ רַחֲבֵי חַמְרָה
שְׁטוּחָה בְּרַגְבֶיהָ.

A thistle burst the red loam
and overflowed like milk
on the face of the land;
and at night a moon licks   4
saucers of milk moving
on slim stems.
And clouds continue their trail of white
dip in the foam of thistle   8
blooming, teeming,
and green bee-eaters in droves
hoot crazily and gurgle
and fill their bellies   12
with whispering insects
in white saucers of thistle;
Screwbeans closed in upon the thistle
lest the sand too be conquered;   16
the soft fragrance of screwbean spills out
and the sharp fragrance of thistle leaps out —
one upon the other, they cleave and cling
filling the expanses of the loam   20
spread out in its clods. (*Kol hashirim,* p. 18)[115]

Once again in this poem conventional associations, of femininity with pliant passivity and masculinity with aggressive activity, are subverted and blurred. Here the masculine "kimosh" (thistle) takes on a wild, feminine fecundity, spreading out riotously under a moon that licks or suckles from swaying saucers of thistle-milk. As in "Upon your nakedness," the landscape here is charged with erotic energy and activity, the bee-eaters hooting and gargling, the thistle and the screwbean indulging in a kind of sexualized turf war, with the screwbean spilling (as did the thistle earlier in the poem) its fragrance over the land, and the thistle piercing the air with its sharper odors. In this poem the reader is never quite sure whether to assign masculine or feminine attributes to the elements of the landscape. Indeed, everything and everyone in this scene is simultaneously masculine and feminine, moving, jostling, piercing, pouring, feeding, and spreading out over the soil. Once again, verb tenses mix and combine, along with gender assignations, emblematic of a refusal to be confined to the bounds of the "appropriate," an androgynous vision that remains the hallmark of Esther Raab's poetry.

Yokheved Bat-Miriam's *Erets Yisra'el*

Like Esther Raab's, Yokheved Bat-Miriam's poetry challenges the oppositions between femininity and masculinity as expressed in conventional female personifications of the land. But in contrast to Raab's landscape depictions, which are grounded in the concrete—in specific details and names of the flora and fauna of the Land of Israel—Bat-Miriam's poetry hovers in a more mystical, transcendental space. Indeed, of the three poets discussed in this chapter, Bat-Miriam wrote the most numinous and elusive poetry about *Erets Yisra'el*. Through this spiritual, otherworldly image of the feminized land, Bat-Miriam offers her feminist critique and makes her special contribution.

Bat-Miriam's use of female personifications is most evident in her magnificent poem cycle *Erets Yisra'el*. In an admiring essay about Bat-Miriam's poetry, Natan Alterman writes that when one reads certain lines in *Erets Yisra'el*, all other poetic lines about the land are momentarily silenced.[116] Despite this acclaim, the cycle remains relatively underread and underexplicated. In fact, it has become something of a trope in the available critical literature about Bat-Miriam that her poetry has not received the attention it deserves.[117] Various reasons have been adduced for this scarcity of acclaim, but the primary one relates to the highly complex, hermetic quality of her work. Recently, under the influence of feminist theory and gender studies, there has been revived interest in Bat-Miriam's work.[118] Ruth Kartun-Blum's *Bamerhak hane'elam* (1977), the only published book-length monograph on Bat-Miriam's poetry to date, is an invaluable resource on the various themes, symbolism, and technical workings of her poetry, yet it makes no reference to issues of gender and feminist critical practice. Dan Miron's pathbreaking study of the first Hebrew women poets, *Imahot meyasdot, ahayot horgot* (1991), is a treasure trove of literary/historical insights about the development of Bat-Miriam's poetic voice and style in relation to contemporary critical expectations for women's poetry, but as mentioned previously, Miron's essay avoids feminist theory. It is my contention that feminist theory and gender studies offer the strongest argument for the rereading and reengagement of works by poets such as Rachel, Raab, and Bat-Miriam, especially a poem cycle like *Erets Yisra'el,* which represents a conscious, sustained effort on the part of a Hebrew woman poet to take over and recast the Hebrew literary convention of female personifications of the land.

Written toward the middle of Bat-Miriam's career, *Erets Yisra'el* also serves as a thematic and stylistic bridge between her earlier and later work. In the critical literature about Bat-Miriam, much has been made of the difference between her early modernist poetry and her later work. The former was published in Russia when Bat-Miriam was a member of a group of Hebrew writers called the Hebrew Octoberists, who dreamed of creating a revolutionary socialist Hebrew movement in Russia, and the latter was written and published in Palestine, under the influence of the *moderna* movement of Shlonsky and Alterman. Bat-Miriam's early poems—most notably the cycle *Merahok,* published in 1922 in *Hatekufah*—were written in simple, clear language, without meter and rhyme, and they are characterized by themes of overt feminist rebellion.[119] In contrast, her later poetry was written in quatrains with regular rhyme and meter; instead of simple, pared down language and bold assertions, her language is denser and her imagery more complex and elliptical. The differences between her earlier and later poetry are so pronounced that critic Y. Zemorah wrote that he could hardly believe these two bodies of work were written by the same person.[120] According to Ruth Kartun-Blum, the change in Bat-Miriam's poetry after her immigration to Palestine represents a leap forward, particularly in terms of the complexity and originality of the figurative language.[121] For others, such as Dan Miron, Bat-Miriam's later poetry represents a stylistic and thematic retreat, with her subject matter becoming "more confined to the relatively narrow thematic space allotted at that time to women's poetry": passive love, longings, expectations, maternal emotions, and the various folkloric Jewish elements reminiscent of her pious Jewish shtetl upbringing, suitable for a genuine "Bas-Yisroel."[122] Miron calls special attention to Bat-Miriam's own role in creating this pious Jewish persona—critic Dov Sadan dubbed her "the most Jewish of the Hebrew woman poets"[123]—especially her decision not to include in her collected poems, *Shirim* (1963), those early poems that demonstrated an overt erotic interest or a more independent, explicitly feminist voice.[124] According to Miron, Bat-Miriam remade herself and her poetry to conform to a literary ideology that required women's poetry to refrain from being overly rebellious against the norms of female behavior; to express female identity primarily in relation to the male world through images of love, longing, pregnancy, and childbirth; to confine herself to the generic borders of the small lyric; and to employ modernist techniques only in the most conservative sense.[125]

Miron himself acknowledges at the end of *Imahot meyasdot, ahayot horgot* that with *Erets Yisra'el* Bat-Miriam returned, in a sense, to her poetic point of origin, albeit in a different form than the "primitive Expressionism of *Merahok*."[126] *Erets Yisra'el* may be filled with liturgical and biblical references, but this traditional language and imagery takes on a highly innovative, iconoclastic, female-centered form. Insofar as there is an expression here of longing and love for the land, these emotions are dramatized as part of an unusually reciprocal plot in which the female speaker and feminized land pursue each another and unite, break away and chase each other again. And because this plot expresses itself over the course of eleven stylistically challenging lyrics, the poem takes on something of an epic quality.

All this brings to mind similar observations concerning the work of Devorah Baron (1887–1956), the first major woman writer of Hebrew prose fiction, whose fictional oeuvre divides similarly into an earlier, stridently feminist group of stories that Baron repudiated and excluded from her collected works, and a quieter, more restrained, and nostalgic later group of stories that she endorsed and published in various collections.[127] As I shall discuss in chapter 5, many critics have considered Baron's later fiction curiously pious and traditional, static and limited in theme, form, and character development. Only recently have scholars begun to probe Baron's stories for their "modernist techniques and protofeminist content."[128] As in the case of Baron's fiction, the pious content of many of Bat-Miriam's later poems—what Miron describes as a world of "folklore, red kerchiefs, coral beads, dishwashing, laundering linens, and prayers for the well-being of one's sons and daughters"[129]—often conceals other more subversive meanings.

The analogy between Bat-Miriam and Baron is particularly intriguing in light of their remarkably similar biographies. Both writers grew up in Eastern European villages in staunchly religious families and immigrated to Palestine as young adults. Despite their involvement in socialist Zionist activities at a time of prevailing negation of Diaspora life, both remained committed to depicting the landscape, symbolism, religious world, and personalities of the shtetl. Both Baron and Bat-Miriam began their writing careers creating works that included feminist as well as autobiographical themes, only to suppress these early texts from their later

171

collected works. Both demonstrated markedly ascetic life habits: Baron remained a recluse on a very strict and limited diet for some thirty years after her husband's death; Bat-Miriam completely desisted from writing poetry after the death of her son Zuzik in the 1948 war, wearing black and observing various regular fast days to mourn him.[130] In her fiction Baron paid little attention to life in the Land of Israel or other conventional matters of national significance, preferring to concentrate on more marginal "women-centered" forms and themes. In contrast, Bat-Miriam chose to write about her relationship with the land. Still, the picture of the land that emerges in her poetry is almost entirely detached from everyday or national life, rendered instead in strikingly personal, even abstract terms.[131] In short, Bat-Miriam's *Erets Yisra'el*—like a good deal of her later work—demonstrates a willingness to transgress linguistic, thematic, generic, and gender categories; it also exhibits a quality of inventiveness unacknowledged by interpreters of her verse.

Some of this inventiveness can be attributed to the influence of Russian Symbolist poetry, particularly that of Alexander Blok.[132] Russian Symbolist poetry proceeded from the assumptions that "even a passing phenomenon may be understood as a noumenon or as a highly significant symbol," and that "through the mediation and the contemplation of the principle of love"—a concept Blok described as the "Eternal Feminine"—one may "ascend to high heaven from this low world."[133] Throughout Bat-Miriam's poetry—in consonance with the principles outlined by the Russian Symbolists—objects, events, and landscapes are invested with a mysteriously metaphysical feminine quality. Like Blok's "Poems on the Beautiful Lady," Bat-Miriam's *Erets Yisra'el* evokes "an unsubstantial aura, a rarefied atmosphere. The images do not stand in clear and firm outline against the sky, but waver and hover, bodiless and shapeless, in mid-air."[134] *Erets Yisra'el*, in which the land metamorphoses into a female figure who walks, runs, flies, swoops, swoons, tortures and disappoints, nurtures and embraces, also bears the influence of Blok's Mother Russia poetry, where the land is pictured as a spiritual force, "an angel and a demon, a monster of nature and a spirit of the Earth."[135]

This is not to say that Bat-Miriam's poetry merely mimics Russian Symbolist verse. Bat-Miriam not only Hebraizes but also Judaizes Russian Symbolism and its Russian Orthodox religious underpinnings. *Erets Yisra'el*, Bat-Miriam's drama of a female poet's search for the (female) divine presence within the land, is thoroughly Hebrew and biblical, loosely modeled after the biblical Song of Songs and with scattered allusions to the story of Elijah the prophet as well as other biblical narratives. Both the prophetic habit of female personification of the land and the Russian Symbolist cult of the "Eternal Feminine" were fundamentally male-centered poetic practices. In this sense, Bat-Miriam's *Erets Yisra'el*, with its persistent female-centeredness, represents a significant breakthrough.

Some of the themes and poetic figures that figure prominently in *Erets Yisra'el* are already evident in Bat-Miriam's earlier Land of Israel poetry, specifically, "Reihaim shel zahav" (Millstones of gold), which was published as part of her first book of collected poems, *Merahok* (1932).[136] As in *Erets Yisra'el*, the landscape of Israel in "Reihaim shel zahav" is often figured in terms of Jewish textual imagery. In poem 1, for example, a windy Israeli nightscape is compared to a sudden, mystical opening of books of the Talmud, with the movement of winds likened to rabbis engaged in a legal debate (*Merahok*, p. 67). Later in the cycle, the textual metaphors become more explicitly biblical and Near Eastern, as in "Kifsukim hayamim" (Like verses the days), where time and life on the land is depicted through a series of biblical and archaeological similes. Likewise, in poem 9, Bat-Miriam imagines herself part of a group of "desert daughters" who listen to the wonders and miracles of the rocks, thereby bringing to life the marvelous legends of the land, and whose "attentive, vigilant steps" (*Merahok*, pp. 79–80) measure and renew the ancient memories of the nation. It is important to note that the feminine emphasis in these poems, where it appears, remains within the human sphere. While the land is occasionally described in feminine terms, little is made of the female personification. Instead, Bat-Miriam confines herself to imagining the presence of women folk poets who use their poetic and mystical sensibilities to uncover various transcendent features of the landscape. This notion of reflecting on the concrete aspects of the land for the purpose of revealing metaphysical truth assumes a central position in *Erets Yisra'el*. In general, with the notable exception of "Kifsukim hayamim," these ideas play out within a conventional, gender-neutral (even cliché), collective context. For example, in poem 4, the poet speaks for the whole nation, which longs to return to the Jewish homeland: "But one thousand, every thousand [years] are but a day / only yesterday we left our homeland/ yesterday we fell victim upon Her / with the great devotion of a lost soul" (*Merahok*, p. 72).

In the poem "Yerushalayim" (Jerusalem), published in *Musaf davar* in 1936, less than a year before the appearance of the *Erets Yisra'el* cycle,[137] Bat-Miriam's writings about the land and cities of Israel begin to demonstrate the stylistic and thematic features that are so prominent in *Erets Yisra'el*. In contrast to the relatively straightforward and simple language of "Reihaim shel zahav," the language in "Yerushalayim" is denser, more elliptical, and syntactically manipulated. Zion is also clearly feminized, but unlike various biblical feminizations of the land, the city is neither wife nor widow, daughter nor bride, mourner nor mourned. Instead, she is a kind of female wanderer-explorer, whose various movements and ascensions represent the diverse geological and archaeological features of the city. Though cut and inscribed in stone, seemingly static and immovable, the feminized Jerusalem rises, thinks, gropes, and turns; "wrapped" in the sounds of church bells, she "raises a smiling wall, before an ancient remembering tower" (*Shirim*, pp. 175–76). In this poem, all the elements of the city, even those with the greatest ballast and fixity, are depicted as animate and moving. In contrast to "Rehaim shel zahav," where the land remains a largely passive object of reflection, here the city yearns and stands and imagines. With her spaces that "golden and die," she demonstrates an elusive as well as prophetic quality that Bat-Miriam associates with *hazon 'ami*, the biblical/prophetic visions of her people. All these elements reappear in Bat-Miriam's longer work, *Erets Yisra'el*, but in much more amplified and female-centered forms.

On the most basic level, the female-centeredness of *Erets Yisra'el* inheres in the grammar of the poems. Indeed, one of the major problems with translating and writing about *Erets Yisra'el* in English is that one loses the effect of the constant repetition of the second-person feminine pronoun *at*,[138] as well as all the feminine conjugations of the verbs. In some of her other cycles, such as *Midrakhah geshumah* and *Shirei Russyah*, Bat-Miriam's speaker alternates between addressing the object of her love and reflection in masculine and feminine terms. In *Erets Yisra'el*, the entire drama unfolds between the female poet and the feminized land. Like the Bible that endows the personified Zion or Israel with a variety of personae, the feminized land in Bat-Miriam's poem wears many guises, plays many roles, and assumes many forms, both conventional and unconventional.

Female-centeredness may also be identified in the language and style of the poems. Although the influence of (masculine) Symbolist poetry has already been acknowledged, Bat-Miriam's highly elliptical, mystical language, together with the continually shifting and blurring identities of both the land and the female poetic speaker, also seems to

174

anticipate the efforts of French feminist critics such as Hélène Cixous and Luce Irigaray to posit an alternative woman's writing that defies traditional gender binaries and unsettles fixed meanings. In fact, the efforts of French feminist theorists to describe new forms of women's writing and language that partake of and yet deconstruct patriarchal tradition are relevant to the poetic project and poetic style of Bat-Miriam. According to Cixous, writing in her well-known essay "Castration or Decapitation?" what distinguishes a feminine textual body is that it allows "parts, partings, and separations"; it "is always endless, without ending, there's not closure, it doesn't stop, and it is this that very often makes the feminine text difficult to read. . . . A feminine text starts on all sides at once, starts twenty times, thirty times over."[139] Drawing on Lacanian psychoanalysis as well as a female sexual metaphor of the "two lips," Irigaray's theory of feminine behavior and language similarly emphasizes endlessness, changeability, contradiction, even incoherence:

> She [woman] is indefinitely other in herself. This is doubtless why she is said to be whimsical, incomprehensible, agitated, capricious . . . not to mention her language in which "she" sets off in all directions leaving "him" unable to discern the coherence of any meaning. Hers are contradictory words, somewhat mad from the standpoint of reason, inaudible for whoever listens to them with ready-made grids, with a fully elaborated code in hand. For in what she says, too, at least when she dares, woman is constantly touching herself. She steps ever so slightly aside from herself with a murmur, an exclamation, a whisper, a sentence left unfinished. . . . When she returns it is to set off again from elsewhere.[140]

One can quarrel with the essentialist underpinnings of these theories of *écriture feminine;* it is difficult to accept the idea of women's language necessarily and essentially embodying these traits. At the same time, these formulations describe accurately the kinds of feminine identity, movement, and language presented in *Erets Yisra'el.* Echoing—or, more correctly, prefiguring—Cixous's description of the endlessly continuing and recommencing feminine text, Bat-Miriam's poem cycle moves through a series of repeating yet changing, resolved yet endlessly unresolved encounters between the female speaker and the feminine land. In consonance with Irigaray's description of woman and her words in *This Sex Which Is Not One,* the feminized land in *Erets Yisra'el* as well as the language used to describe her is "whimsical, incomprehensible, agitated, capricious," setting off in various directions that defy conventional notions of coherence and meaning. Irigaray's description of woman's "contradictory words, somewhat mad from the standpoint of reason," finds resonance in the plethora of oxymoronic figures and contradictions in terms that occur throughout the cycle. In the second stanza of poem 1, for example, the land is described as possessing a "dropping wing," evident and visible in the "shadows of cities, mountains and desert," and also as a "hidden image" (line 8, *Shirim,* p. 39), "this-but-not-like-this" (line 120, p. 45). In poem 2, the land is self-contradictorily "blazing weary" (line 29, p. 40); it jumps off "helplessly" (line 30, p. 41), and appears "poor" and "illuminated" all at once. One moment the poet speaker is describing the land in terms of its realistic, spare topography: "Mountain, hill, tormented strip of sand / without shade, fountain or tree" (lines 17–18, p. 40). The next moment the terms of reference shift to the lofty and metaphysical—"Deep abysses, visions and glory" (line 33, p. 40)—imagining the land as a reflection of the dreams of an unseen God (p. 40). Throughout the poem, the land both embodies and defies images of femininity that are part of the traditional association between woman and land/earth/city. In poem 2, Bat-Miriam portrays the land in ways that are typical of biblical tradition and modern Hebrew poetry of the Third Aliyah period, calling attention to the harsh sunlight, the "thorn-thistle" (p. 40), the naked landscape, the "mountain, rock, and heaps of desolation" (p. 42).[141] This poor, parched, forsaken land, like the abandoned widow of the Book of Lamentations or the lamenting spirit of Zion in Jeremiah, "beating the breast for sin" (poem 8, line 205, p. 49), and weeps like a small child on the lap of the poetic speaker. This same feminized land, however, also rises above these diminishments, soaring and flying (p. 50) in a kind of flaming, whirling, stormy ecstasy, reminiscent of the bold, rebellious, and ecstatic pronouncements of Bat-Miriam's poetic speaker in her early love cycle *Merahok.*

Flight imagery recurs throughout the poem cycle. "Only your dropping wing leads to / shadows of cities, mountains and desert, / and gathers the ends of my stormy soul / to the arc of your hidden image," writes Bat-Miriam in poem 1 (lines 5–9, p. 39); "Only panting, only breathing and shining / from end to illuminated other / a chariot of fire that swoops and stretches,/ your longing, alighting and excited," she continues in poem 2 (lines 25–28, p. 40).[142] All this brings to mind Cixous's double usage of the French verb *voler,* which means "to fly" as well as *to steal,* in order to describe the ways in which women over the centuries have managed to enter into language and culture despite patriarchal strictures. According to Cixous, women writers have to fly over/steal through generic and gender borders in order to liberate patriarchal language from its disenabling fixities and oppositions and make it their own. "We have all learned flight/theft," Cixous writes, "the art with many techniques, for all the centuries we have only had access to having by stealing/flying; we have lived in a flight/theft, stealing/flying, finding the close, concealed ways-through of desire."[143] In *Erets Yisra'el,* Bat-Miriam's language and feminized land do precisely this: fly and steal in and out of many unexpected or contradictory structures, steal into various (patriarchal) forms of language, and reinvent them for new purposes.

One specific way in which Bat-Miriam flies/steals into patriarchal language is through revisions of masculine God-language and liturgical structures. Throughout the poem, the poetic speaker describes her pursuit of the feminine land as a kind of search for God. "At shokhnah bikhol mekupelet" (You [feminine] dwell in pleated blue), the poem cycle begins, immediately bringing to mind, through the word "shokhnah," the Shekhinah, the traditional (feminine) term for the presence of God. In contrast with traditional Shekhinah imagery, the land is depicted here as an anthropomorphic female deity, stroking and trilling her own, ancient thoughts with a "warm divine hand" (line 3, p. 39). This highly physical and visible representation of the land is not the only version of the female-land-as-God image in the cycle. Repeatedly, almost incantatorily in the poem, the land as the feminine divine is described as simultaneously "revealed and concealed," visible through the features of the landscape but never truly seen or comprehended. Bat-Miriam praises/prays to the feminine land in a modified version of the opening line of the Kaddish, a prayer traditionally recited by mourners, which extols the greatness and splendor of God and his works. The prayer begins with the words *Yitgaddel veyitkaddesh shemei rabbah* (Magnified and sanctified be God's great name). In Bat-Miriam's paean to the feminized Land of Israel, of course, this opening line is reconjugated in the feminine voice—*titgaddel, titkaddash* (line 15, p. 39)—to accommodate the female gender of the land. Bat-Miriam's use of the Kaddish prayer seems at first like a pious Zionist national utterance, but she puts a mysterious and elliptical cast on the traditional prayer that praises God's holy name and calls for widespread recognition of divine majesty and rule. Instead of an image of an "exalted, honored, adored, and lauded" God-king, Bat-Miriam's speaker praises her (feminine) godly land for being infinitely mysterious, incomplete and "unredeemed": *titgaddel, titkaddash lo nig'elet / ta'alumotekh bi la'ad tevuah* (Be

177

magnified, be sanctified, unredeemed, / your mystery forever stamped within me! [lines 15–16, p. 39]).

Also recurrent in the poem are feminizations of the traditional liturgical pronouncements of the oneness of God—*Vehu ehad, ve'ein sheini* (And He is One, and there is none other), as in the well-known liturgical poem "Adon 'olam" (Lord of the world). "In every instance you are one, solitary you," proclaims Bat-Miriam at the beginning of the fourth poem. "There was never anything but you" (line 70, p. 42), "Nothing but you" (line 85, p. 44), she intones, designating the land as the sole object of her devoted worship and pursuit.

As she affirms the all-encompassing, self-contained unity of the land—"From you and back to your streaming self! / Within you and your heralding self!" (poem 5, lines 109–10, pp. 42–43)—Bat-Miriam also allows it an interdenominational, almost polytheistic, multiplicity of form and representation. The land appears as God and as a representation of divine thought (poem 2, line 37, p. 41), as well as a "forging" of "the letters of God's name" (poem 7, line 152, p. 46). Bat-Miriam's feminine land is also seen as encompassing and embodying the wisdom and thought of the "gods of Tyre, Sidon and Canaan," represented in sculpted form with "eyes closed" and "leg and hand lopped off" (poem 8, lines 198–99). These polytheistic archaeological images re-imagine the downtrodden, crippled appearance of the desolate earth as a supernatural entity that transcends the regular, formal order of human life and vision.

One cannot overstress the effect rendered by Bat-Miriam's feminization of these representations and liturgical invocations of the divine in her descriptions of the land. In contrast to Hebrew poetic tradition, where the feminine land is metaphorically imagined as the female consort of the masculine God or of an exiled husband/lover, here the feminized land becomes God herself/selves. If according to patriarchal convention, woman remains fixed in an intermediate position lower on the scale of transcendence than man, Bat-Miriam's *Erets Yisra'el*, where a feminine entity is invested with the features of godliness and metaphysicality, turns all this on its head. At the same time, Bat-Miriam seems unwilling to settle on one particular definition of, or metaphor for, the (female) land. Through the absence of clarifying pronominal antecedents, there is a repeated blurring of the distinction between the female speaker of the poem and the feminized land; often they explicitly switch roles. Once again, this brings to mind the writings of Luce Irigaray. According to Irigaray, women "are engaged in the process of both constructing and deconstructing their identities, their essences, simultaneously."[144] As Diana Fuss explicates Irigaray's argument, "to speak (as) woman is ceaselessly to embrace words and persistently to cast them off. To touch upon but never to solidify, to put into play but never to arrive at a final telos or meaning."[145]

This notion of simultaneously embracing and casting off words and identities, of touching upon but never truly possessing meaning, is dramatized throughout the cycle in the many allusions to the biblical pursuit-evasion plot of Song of Songs. References to the Song of Songs are scattered throughout the poem: Bat-Miriam's cycle begins, as does the biblical Song, with the speaker being led by the wing and drawn into pursuit of her beloved ("Draw me after you, let us run!" [Song of Songs, 1:4]).[146] In poem 3 the poet pursues her beloved land through a metaphorical garden, through the "green efflorescence," climbing and clinging to "the myrrh of your memory" (lines 50, 52, p. 45), a synaesthetic image evocative of the Song (the word "myrrh," which figures throughout the Song, is the marker). Similarly, in poem 6 of the cycle, the land is represented metaphorically as "a gazelle in the shadows of mountains" (line 133), an allusion to any number of gazelle images in the Song of Songs, such as the Shulamite's comparison of her love to a gazelle leaping over the mountains (Song of Songs 2:8–9) or Solomon's comparison of his lover's breasts to "two fawns, twins of gazelle" (Song of Songs 4:5).

The plot of the biblical Song—its sequences of unions and evasions, meetings and misses—is liberally incorporated into Bat-Miriam's poem cycle.[147] Instead of a love story between the male Solomon and the female Shulamite, Bat-Miriam's poem cycle tells the story of a female poet's continual pursuit of a feminine land, and vice versa. If, as Phyllis Trible has suggested, the uniqueness of the Song of Songs inheres in its inclusion of a dominant female voice that opens and closes it[148] and in its representation of mutuality, reciprocity, and harmony in male-female love, Bat-Miriam's poem cycle, which grants this power to two female characters, goes even further. Although the land does not raise her voice and actually speak in the poem as does the poet (and as do the lover-actors in the biblical Song), the land acts, moves, and pursues her poet-beloved. I do not mean to argue that the central plot of *Erets Yisra'el* is necessarily homoerotic: Bat-Miriam's female Land of Israel is not primarily a sexual figure, but it assumes a multiplicity of feminine roles: mother, sister, daughter, and God(dess). Bat-Miriam's cycle does not teem with erotic symbolism and tactile imagery, as does the Song of Songs. But it reads as a powerful female rendition of its themes.

As Ilana Pardes has observed, "Desire reigns in the Song, not fulfillment."[149] Likewise, it is the endurance and recurrence of desire, rather than its consummation, that propels the plot of Bat-Miriam's *Erets Yisra'el*. The poet rises in pursuit of the beloved land, wanders with her "in the radiant blue of paths" (poem 5, line 90, p. 43)[150] or gazes upon the face/surface of the land at "the radiating peaks of Eden-trees" (poem 8, line 211, p. 49), only to retreat and declare that she cannot catch her. She strains to behold and find the land, catches sight of her and offers a description, only to conclude that she cannot be seen at all, or, as in the first poem, that she will only be able to "see" the land when she closes her eyes permanently in death and merges physically with the land, her "dust" covering her "sealed eye" (poem 1, lines 9–11). The land and poet repeatedly unite, only to miss each other again.

This plot of pursuit and evasion operates on both micro- and macroscopic levels in the poem. On a microscopic level, the scenario is dramatized in Bat-Miriam's repeated yoking together of disparate or, more precisely, contradictory, verbs or predicate adjectives. The land is simultaneously "alive" and yet "hidden" (line 83). The poet-speaker says she will "forget" the land, only "to seek" her "in every path" (line 141); she murmurs about the land "what cannot be pronounced" (line 213); pursues the land with "the hope that comes after despair" (line 100); and identifies her "form, like-this-not-like-this" (line 120). The effect of this technique is a continual fortification of descriptive desire and a continual thwarting of its consummation.

On a macroscopic level, the pursuit-evasion theme plays out in the unfolding plot of the cycle. In poem 2, the poet comes close enough to the land to be able to offer a relatively realistic portrait of the Israeli desert landscape, but the land leaps away in mysterious, incomprehensible flight. In turn, in poem 3, the land chases after and pursues the poet, who, lagging and falling in the sand, calls out to her beloved land. The two join together briefly "in the light of the watch, / . . . in confusion and shield" (lines 57–58, p. 42)—an overturning of the plot in the biblical Song, where the meeting of Solomon and the Shulamite is thwarted by the violent intercession of the night watchmen.

Bat-Miriam not only incorporates literal references to the Song, she also adapts the rabbinic allegorical interpretation as a representation of the thwarted, unconsummated relationship between God and Israel and the subsequent exile of the People of Israel. Throughout the cycle, the pursuit-evasion plot of the Song of Songs functions as a narrative representation of Bat-Miriam's complicated relationship with the Land of Israel, her estrangement from and aspired reunion with the land through 'aliyah. In two separate places in the poem cycle, the poet's connection with her adopted homeland of Israel is frustrated by interceding images of her native Russia. In the fourth poem of the cycle, the poet attempts to stave off memories of her beloved former homeland by insisting that "there was never anything but you" (line 70, p. 42). In fact, she attempts to deny completely the allure of the Russian landscape: "the living foreign wing, with longing unquiet," claims the new immigrant Bat-Miriam, "never stroked my nights" (lines 71–72, p. 42). But this attempt at denial cannot dam the rush of memory, and from then on the poet's visions of her past homeland become clearer and more pristine—the white, tempestuous beauty of winter, forests "growing greener and greener" (line 78, p. 43)—all in contradistinction to the parched, desolate appearance of the Israeli landscape, which "crawls" upon its "suffering," as if to be revived by the return of the Jews to her borders.

The "foreign-wing"—literally, the "wing of a foreign land"—reappears again in poem 5, and the immigrant experience, as a narrative of unsuccessful union, is represented in an unsettling, violent manner. Beaten and scorched by the harsh sun of her beloved Israel, the poet closes her eyes and yearns, "with longing great and stirring" (line 103) for the Russia of her dreams. This passage is highly reminiscent of the night scene in Song of Songs 5, where the Shulamite takes off her robe, lies down upon her bed, and gives herself over to her own private dreams, only to be aroused by the knocking of her beloved upon her door. Withdrawn into dreams of Russia, Bat-Miriam's speaker hesitates to answer the call of the Land of Israel. But following the lead of the Shulamite, the poet-speaker awakens and is pulled once again into the pursuit, "as if to return and answer / a sole heart's longing" (lines 106–7).

The Zionist immigrant experience is invoked in very specific terms in poem 9, where the poet gazes upon the scenery, "so simple, so rude and small" (line 220, p. 50), of her beloved new homeland and laments the collective forsaking of the land, which was the Jewish Diaspora. In the first stanza, the poet bewails the abandonment of her beloved land, against the backdrop, in the second stanza, of a Bedouin Arab walking in the desert. The companionship and tribute offered to the land by the Bedouin seem but poor traces of past glories: "only he, who walked and listened / to the secret of a proud-humble camel's sorrow, / binds your sundering glory / in the scattering of his ragged clothes" (lines 226–27, p. 50). The thorn-ridden covering of the land is a further reminder of the dwindled beauty of the land, her "forgotten landscape of palm" (line 228, p. 50). This enumeration of the sufferings and humiliations of the land is another instance of the plot of temporarily frustrated union. These disturbing images, like the beatings of the Shulamite by the night watchmen in Song of Songs 5:7, once again thwart the reunion of the poet and her beloved, divine land. That is, until the poet actively reaffirms her commitment. "Abandoned" is the land, but "never forgotten, / estranged, but within me forever sealed" (lines 232–33, p. 50), she says, recalling the end of Songs of Songs (8:6), where the Shulamite beseeches her beloved to place her "as a seal upon [her] heart, like the seal upon your hand."

Like the Song of Songs, where even this gesture toward consummation does not fully conclude or resolve the plot of pursuit and love—the Song ends not in ultimate union, but with an invitation to enjoy ("Hurry, my beloved, swift as a gazelle or young stag, to the hills of spices"[151])—Bat-Miriam's *Erets Yisra'el* ends unresolved, in mystery, with the intimation of ongoing drama. In poem 11, the Zionist immigration theme recurs one final time, but redemption is still described as a desire "unfulfilled" and unseen. Like the lover running off to the hills of spices, the female land is carried off "unredeemed" in "a chariot of fire amid the mountains of the world" (lines 294–95).

This brings us to the final major set of themes at work in the poem cycle: the motif of prophecy. Throughout the cycle, Bat-Miriam represents the land as a feminine reincarnation of various prophets and leaders—most important, Elijah, the prophet carried off to his death in a chariot of fire, and the figure most commonly associated with the messianic redemption of the children of Israel. The cycle is bracketed at its beginning and its end by references to the story of Elijah. The first reference comes in poem 2, where the land is compared to "a chariot of fire that swoops and stretches" (line 27, p. 40). A more specific allusion to the Elijah narrative occurs in the last stanza of poem 4:

רַק אַתְּ, רַק אַתְּ אֶת הַנּוֹפֶלֶת
בִּקְרִיאָה לְלֹא קוֹל: "אָבִי!" –
עַל שִׁכְמֵךְ מִתְבַּדְּרָה, מִתְעַרְטֶלֶת
אַדַּרְתֵּךְ, שֶׁהִשְׁמִיט הַנָּבִיא!

Only you, only you falling
in a voiceless cry: "My Father!"
On your shoulder, scattered, uncovered
your mantle, cast off by the prophet. (lines 85–88, p. 43)

The specific reference here is to the miraculous death/disappearance of
Elijah as witnessed by his devoted servant Elisha. In Bat-Miriam's revision of this episode, the suffering beaten land is actually re-embodied as
a female version of Elisha, crying, "O Father! Father! Israel's chariots and
horsemen!" (2 Kings 2:12). Elisha's witnessing of Elijah's ascent is both
heartrending and hopeful, for though Elisha has become bereft of his
father-mentor, his ability to see the vision of the chariot of fire is a sign
(prearranged by Elijah) that he has been granted a double portion of
Elijah's prophetic spirit (2 Kings 2:10). As Elijah ascends to the sky, his
mantle, a symbol and instrument of his prophecy and wondrous powers (which functions much like the staff of the great prophet Moses)
drops down to the earth, and Elisha becomes its inheritor—that is,
Elijah's prophetic successor. In Bat-Miriam's poem, the Land of Israel, a
female Elisha, inherits the prophetic mantle and the double portion of
spirit previously accorded to Elijah, the prophetic harbinger of redemption. In other words, the newly regenerating Zionist land has become
the source of wonder and prophetic revelation for the modern children
of Israel, in general, and the female poet, in particular.

In the middle sections of the poem cycle that intervene between
the first "chariot of fire" image and the final one that concludes the cycle,
the female land takes on several other prophetic/messianic guises. In
poem 6, the land prophesies "in the radiant dream" of the "chained messiah" (lines 121–22), namely, the crucified Jesus. In poem 8, the land is
resurrected as a Nazirite pursuing or reinvigorating the previous signs,
wonders, and prophecies of Jesus. In the stanza immediately following
that one, various synecdoches of the land are endowed with
divine/prophetic inspiration:

וּבְרוֹשׁ – קִנְאַת אֵל הַתּוֹבֵעַ,
וּמֵרְחָק – מִמֶּשֶׁה גְּדִי נִמְלָט.
וְאִי שָׁם, בְּדִמְעָתוֹ שֶׁל הוֹשֵׁעַ,
כִּנֶּרֶת – פְּסוּקוֹ שֶׁנִּשְׁמַט.

And cypress — the envy of the demanding God,
And distance — a kid escaped from Moses' flock.
And over there, in the teardrop of Hosea,
Kinneret — his verse that slipped out. (lines 184–87, p. 48)

As in "Kifsukim hayamim," where the features of the landscape are
described in terms of various textual/archaeological similes, here the
indigenous cypress tree is depicted as a sign of the "envy of the demanding God," the jealous protection by the prophets of the supreme oneness of the God. The distances charted by the poet's eye are represented
by the wandering of a goat from the shepherd-prophet Moses' literal as
well as metaphorical flock. Likewise, the waters of the Kinneret, the Sea
of Galilee, are seen as one great embodiment of the tearful, tragic
prophecies of the prophet Hosea.

All these prophetic allusions point to the historical role of the land
as a site of great prophecy and revelation. Toward the end of the poem, the
poetic speaker presents herself as the disciple of the prophetic/poetic land:

שָׁם הָגִיתָ, שָׁם אִמַּצְתָּ לֹא-נִרְגַּעַת,
שָׁם טִפַּחְתָּ, מְיַסְּרָה וּמְקַנְּאָה,
אֶת נַפְשִׁי הַמְזֻנֶּקֶת לֹא-נִכְנַעַת,
אֶת רוּחִי הַגְּדוֹלָה וּכְבֵדָה.

עַד אֶשָּׂא אֶת פָּנַי כְּמֻנְשֶׁבֶת
מֵחֲלַל דִּמְיוֹנְךָ הַנּוֹהֵר,
עַד אֶשָּׂא אֶת פָּנַי כְּמַחְשֶׁבֶת
שֶׁסָּגְרָה חֲלוֹמְךָ הַיּוֹצֵר.

There you spoke, there you adopted unrelenting,
there you nurtured, tormenting and jealous,
my leaping, unsubmissive soul,
my great and heavy spirit.

Until I raised my face as if blown
from the hollow of your streaming imagination,

184

until I raised my face like a thought
sealed within your creating dream. (poem 10, lines 280–87,
  p. 53)

Here, as in the rest of the cycle, the relationship experienced by the
speaker and the land is depicted in strikingly intimate and private terms.
With the exception of the Arab Bedouin who appears in poem 9, the
poem includes no human witnesses to the poet's relationship with the
land and provides little descriptive evidence of Zionist settlement.
Instead, Bat-Miriam offers an account of a personal and reciprocal relationship with the land, setting herself up as a source of prophetic inspiration for her readers. If in poem 9 the land is depicted as a child
weeping on the lap of the poet-speaker, in this poem, the poet-prophet-
land, with her "streaming imagination," becomes mother-mentor to the
poet-speaker, training, nurturing her "leaping, unsubmissive soul" (lines
285 and 282, p. 53).

In contrast to the intimate private descriptions that characterize
the first ten lyrics of the cycle, the final poem evinces a collective,
national tone:

אַרְצִי, אַרְצִי הַמּוּאָרֶת
בַּחֲזוֹן עַמִּי הַנִּדְלָק וְנִשָּׂא
וְזוֹרֶה כְּמִיהַת פְּדוּת לֹא נִפְתֶּרֶת
אֶל עוֹלָם נֶעְלָם וְנִסְעָר.

אִתּוֹ אַתְּ נִשֵּׂאת מְחֻלְחֶלֶת
כִּבְשׁוֹרָה בַּחֲלָלָהּ שֶׁל תֵּבֵל,
אִתּוֹ אַתְּ נִשֵּׂאת לֹא-נִגְאָלֶת,
רֶכֶב אֵשׁ בֵּין הָרְרֵי תֵבֵל.

My land, my land which is illuminated,
in the prophecy of my people afire and exalted
and [which] scatters a desire for redemption unfulfilled
to a turbulent unseen world.

185

With this you are carried suffused,
like tidings in the space of the world,
with this you are carried, unredeemed,
a chariot of fire amid the mountains of the world. (poem 11,
    lines 285–92, p. 53)

Because of the collective tone of this final poem—speaking for "my peo-ple" rather than just for herself—it is often quoted and celebrated in the critical literature as representative of the cycle as a whole. "'A chariot of fire amid the mountains of the world,' is how the Land of Israel rises from this volume," writes poet Natan Alterman, enthusiastically referring to the prophetic reference that closes the poem as typical of Bat-Miriam's poetic portrayal of the land.[152] The collective tone of this poem is enhanced by the traditional association between Elijah the prophet and the ideology of messianic redemption. At the same time, the Elijah references conceal a bold, individual statement wherein Bat-Miriam becomes a successor to Elisha, the prototypical inheritor of prophecy. Like Elisha, who witnesses Elijah's chariot of fire in the Book of Kings, and like the feminized land, which witnesses the same image earlier in the cycle in poem 4, the poet-speaker, as witness to the Chariot(ess) of Fire, inherits the double-portioned poetic/prophetic legacy of the land. But unlike traditional associations between Elijah and messianic redemption, Bat-Miriam's chariot(ess) of fire is carried aloft, unredeemed, representing how endlessly deferred, unfin-ished spiritual quests engender poetry. Bat-Miriam's poet-speaker emerges here in the role of poet-prophet, offering her readers her own, personal form of transcendence.

Barrenness, Babies, and Books

The Barren Woman in Hebrew Women's Writing

> Feminist theorists note that the exclusion of women's writing from
> many of the traditional genres of literature is the result of andro-
> centrically defined criteria of relevance, decorum, and propriety. In
> a male-dominated culture, literary genres, like all cultural produc-
> tions, represent an inescapable male bias. . . . Within a system of
> literary genres that are determined by masculine modes of experi-
> ence, women are obliged to use non-canonical genres.
> DEBORAH L. MADSEN

Consider for a moment the recurrent biblical story of the barren wife. God
creates the world in six days, fashions man and woman in his own image,
commanding them to be fruitful and multiply. The early chapters of
Genesis are filled with "begat" lists of the subsequent fecund generations
of early humankind, litanies of vigorous reproduction, from Adam to
Avram. Suddenly, with the name of Sarai, wife of Avram, the procreative
momentum grinds to a halt. Others may have reproduced effortlessly.
"But Sarai was barren; she had no child" (Gen. 11:30). God repeatedly
promises Avram that his descendants will be numerous, but only when
both he and Sarai are aged, when pregnancy is biologically impossible, is
she finally and miraculously blessed with a pregnancy. The same plot pattern occurs repeatedly in the biblical stories of Rebecca, Rachel, the wife
of Mano'ah (eventual mother of Samson), Hannah, and the Shunamite
woman (2 Kings 4:8–17), where would-be matriarchs are unable to
become pregnant without the agency and intervention of God.[1] As if to
counter all those who might venerate the reproductive powers of woman,
the barrenness stories emphasize the creative primacy of God the Father
who precedes and governs procreation. According to Tikva Frymer-
Kensky, the story of the "once-barren mother repeatedly conveys the message that God—and God alone—can cause conception."[2] "In other

187

words," writes feminist Bible scholar J. Cheryl Exum, the Bible undermines "the chosen mothers' importance by denying the very thing for which they are so highly valued, their reproductive ability."[3]

The previous two chapters considered the ways in which women poets writing in Hebrew stole into the canonical thematic spaces of the Bible and the Land of Israel to offer alternative representations of femininity. In this chapter, we move into the thematic space of the family, examining works of poetry and fiction in terms of the gendered treatment of barrenness and familial (re)generation.

Indeed, Jewish tradition is filled with images of God's generative (masculine) powers projected against an opposing background of a barren femininity. With each repetition of the pattern, the individual accounts of infertility and frustrated maternity join together as part of a larger allegorical narrative about God's role as progenitor of the Jewish national family and redeemer of the exiled People of Israel.

Mary Callaway, author of a critical study of the barrenness motif in biblical and rabbinic literature, detects various allegorical meanings given to the barrenness theme in prophetic and midrashic writings. The first example, Callaway argues, is the story of Hannah (1 Sam. 1–3), which includes a psalm of praise linking the barren woman who eventually gives birth to other instances of God rewarding the righteous and raising up the lowly.[4] According to Callaway, "the use of the barren matriarch as a symbol of the people rather than simply an individual woman, which underlies 1 Samuel 1–3, is developed to its fullest in Second Isaiah."[5] In Isaiah 54, the suffering of the barren woman becomes an explicit metaphor for the exiled People of Israel whom God will ultimately redeem, just as He ultimately gave children to the once barren matriarchs. "Sing, O barren woman, you who did not labor with child," says the prophet, setting the stage for the allegorical understanding of the barrenness theme that figures most prominently in midrashic literature. In *Pesikta de-Rab Kahanah* 20:1, for example, the Rabbis declare that "there were seven barren women: Sarah, Rebecca, Rachel, Leah, Manoah's wife, and Hannah, and Zion." The inclusion of Zion in this list of barren women underscores the view of barrenness as standing for something other than just itself. The choice of the number seven is strategic; there were other barren women in the Bible—Michal the daughter of Saul and the Shunamite woman, for example—but the Rabbis insist upon the number seven because it links these recurrent stories of thwarted (pro)creation with God's creation of the world. There are seven days in the Creation story and there are seven barren women in the history of the nation; Zion's designation as the seventh barren woman places it in the position of the Holy Seventh Day, signifying that the redemption of Zion is the ultimate goal of God's creation of the world.[6]

Consider now S. Y. Agnon's "Aggadat hasofer" (Tale of the scribe, 1919), a story about a pious scribe named Raphael and his barren wife Miriam that draws liberally from various Jewish literary and folk traditions on barrenness. In Genesis Rabbah 45:4, the Rabbis argue that the matriarchs were barren because the Holy One Blessed be He yearns for the prayers of the righteous; Agnon's narrator adduces this same reason as an explanation for Miriam's barrenness.[7] The midrash goes on to suggest, in the name of Rabbi Meir, that one of the benefits of the barrenness of the matriarchs was that their husbands were able to enjoy them sexually for a longer period, "for as soon as a woman becomes pregnant she becomes ugly and repulsive to her husband. Know that for the entire ninety years during which Sarah did not give birth, she was like a bride under the marriage canopy." In "Aggadat hasofer," however, barrenness is neither ordained by God nor instrumental in bringing about increased sexual activity; on the contrary, Miriam is barren for the simple reason that Miriam and Raphael never have sex! Raphael's devotion to his work involves a regime of prayer that "saves him from all lust and desire" (p. 133), impulses that he sublimates into the work of sacred writing.

At the very beginning of the story, we learn that Raphael frequently writes Torah scrolls for men whose wives have died without bearing children. Eventually, Miriam asks Raphael to write such a Torah for them in place of the child they never had, and when she dies an untimely death, Raphael sets out to fulfil her request. For Raphael, writing substitutes, in very real terms, for both sex and birthing, for the bodies of both wife and child. This idea of the Holy Book as surrogate body is made most explicit at the end of the story, when Raphael, after dancing with the Torah scroll he has just completed for himself, sinks down to the floor, his wife's wedding dress "spread out over him and over his scroll" (p. 145).

Remembering that the Hebrew word *sofer* means both scribe and writer, what makes this story so rich is the play of double meaning linking Raphael's erotically charged scribal obsessions with the analogous obsessions of the creative writer. Agnon dedicated this story to his own wife Esther, and what emerges from the narrative is an image of a male scribe-writer whose all-consuming work is enabled and inspired by his all-sacrificing wife. Miriam remains barren so that her husband can sustain and transform sexual desire into text. As Anne Golomb Hoffman observes, throughout most of the story "structures of desire and procreation repeat themselves in the activities of the husband and the wife without coinciding. Miriam's prayers and activities parallel Raphael's devotion to the Torah scroll he is inscribing: she fashions baby clothes as he shapes a text; she prays for fertility, as he sanctifies himself for writing."[8] Miriam's activities are relegated quite literally to a woman's sphere; she engages in all of them behind a partition that separates her husband's work space from her own. Clearly, this story rehearses the familiar dichotomy between the male intellect and the female body, between culture and nature. If Raphael persistently redirects sexual desire toward the production of texts, Miriam clings to her desire for the literal bodies of her husband and the prayed-for child.

There is one moment in the story, however, where this strict separation of male and female spheres is threatened. In general, Raphael and Miriam live a secluded life. Occasionally, however, Raphael receives a visitor, who gives him news of the changing face of modern Jewry: "What should we say and what should we relate, Reb Raphael? If told, it would not be believed. In the house of So-and-So the Scribe, I saw with my own eyes a number of young men sitting day and night writing scrolls, phylacteries and *mezuzot*, thus making factory work of the holy Torah. Not only this, but I have heard that in the house of another even girls sit and write."[9] The ostensible purpose of this passage is to contrast Raphael's rigorous practice of his craft with the permissive practices of other modern scribes. But insofar as "Aggadat hasofer" treats questions of literary creativity, there is more here than initially meets the eye. In referring to the phenomenon of girls who "sit and write" alongside the factory scribes, Agnon seems to be registering a contemporary literary-historical moment, namely, the emergence of Hebrew women's writing. Because they are grouped together with the factory scribes, of course, these women writers are cast in a less than favorable light. Raphael politely praises what he perceives as the "spreading of the Torah"—the rise of modern Hebrew perhaps?—that has necessitated this proliferation of sacred copyists, but given his own strict standards of ritual performance, we know that he is just being kind: these factory scribes are merely scribbling hacks. How much more so for the *sofrot*, the female scribblers, whom Raphael cannot even bring himself to acknowledge in his response! To be sure, female scribes were virtually unheard of in Jewish history, as were Hebrew women writers. Raphael's inability to acknowledge his visitor's report of girls who "sit and write" derives not simply from the unprecedented nature of women's Hebrew writing, but from an explicitly male understanding of the artistic impulse as a form of sublimated male desire inscribed upon a female sexual/textual body.

What happens, then, when women begin to fashion their own Hebrew literary script(s) about the barrenness theme? What happens when they begin to carry on a dialogue not just with sacred Hebrew texts on this theme, but also with such modernist revisions and unsettlings of these texts as S. Y. Agnon's "Aggadat hasofer"?

According to Cordelia Chavez Candelaria, "As politically subordinated subjects, women (and other marginalized political subordinates) must, for survival, know and practice the dominant patriarchal discourse and conventions. But equally manifest is that for survival and maintenance of an unmediated identity of self and class, women and other marginalized groups develop an/other culture and discourse—one not required for the survival of, and therefore largely unavailable to, the empowered members of the dominant class."[10] Following Candelaria's formulation, it is my argument in this chapter that early Hebrew women writers engaged the "dominant patriarchal discourse and conventions" surrounding the barrenness theme, but in doing so demonstrated "an/other culture and discourse." As Deborah L. Madsen writes in the epigraph to this chapter, "Within a system of literary genres that are determined by masculine modes of experience, women are obliged to use non-canonical genres." If the canonical genre used in the treatment of the barrenness theme is that of allegory, early twentieth-century women's representations of barrenness exemplify a non-canonical pattern of literal representation or de-allegorization.[11] To prove this claim, I will examine a numbers of works: Devorah Baron's story "Mishpahah" (Family), which engages the barrenness theme and also resonates distinctly with Agnon's famous tale; a renowned poem by the poet Rachel (Bluwstein) entitled "'Akarah" (Barren woman); a lesser-known poem by Anda Pinkerfeld-Amir, also called "'Akarah"; and finally, "Asonah shel Afyah" (Aphia's plight), a short story by Nehamah Puhachevsky, a farmer, women's rights activist, and Hebrew writer from the First 'Aliyah. All of these texts, as I will demonstrate, shift the narrative focus back to the stories of individual women and thus serve an anti-traditional literalizing function.

Devorah Baron's "Mishpahah"

First published in 1933, "Mishpahah" (Family) is the story of a young orphan woman named Dinah who marries Barukh, the only son of his father Avner Ben Zevil. As indicated by the title, the story concerns the Jewish institution of family, defined here as patriarchal succession, a chain of alternating and repeating male names that link an indivisible collective unit. The concern in this story for continuing the patriarchal family line at all cost is biblical in origin, as indicated by repeated references at the beginning of the story to the early families of Genesis. The members of Barukh's extended family are all noted for being very tall and bulky. A kind of hyper-phallic group, they are known in their community as the "bearded ones" or the "Levites"; both of these are overtly masculine designations, one connoting sagacity and virility, the other religious status and lineage. The phallic physicality of the family is best exemplified by Barukh's father Avner, who was known to carry a walking stick of stout oak that he once used to subdue a band of Gentile hooligans. The notion of masculine learning or wisdom, as suggested in the appellation the "bearded ones" is embodied (albeit ironically) in the person of Avner's cousin Solomon, who, like his royal biblical namesake, had a sage aphorism for every situation.[12]

The masculine virility of this family also manifests itself in a tradition of robust reproduction resulting in incessant generations of Avners, Zevils, Barukhs, and Solomons. That is, until Barukh and Dinah. "Sometimes," the narrator tells us, "it happened that there was no one to continue a family line"—the word choice here for family is *beit-av*, literally meaning house of the father—"as if God had denied them his blessing, and then, it was as if a link has been dislocated and the whole chain was shaken."[13] Naomi Seidman astutely observes that Baron's repeated use of the word *shurah* in this story is deliberate insofar as it also calls to mind a disrupted or disconnected line of text.[14] This idea is made most clear at the end of the story when, after ten years of childless marriage, Barukh is reluctantly persuaded, in accordance with Jewish law,[15] to divorce Dinah and take a new wife. The day arrives, the rabbinical court convenes, a scribe is commissioned to write the bill of divorce. All proceeds toward this sad conclusion until, unexpectedly, a letter falls out of line, causing the bill of divorce to be invalidated. In the wake of this scribal disturbance, Barukh and Dinah are allowed to return to their home still married, and within a year they are miraculously blessed with a son.

If Barukh and Dinah's marriage is threatened by a strict adherence to a text-based legal regime that favors a man's obligation to be fruitful and multiply over his emotional and moral obligation to his wife, it is ultimately saved by a disturbance of this same textual tradition. Fundamentally, Baron's "Mishpahah" is about the idea of breaking or disrupting traditional familial and literary lines for the sake of recasting them in a more compassionate form. As Marc Bernstein notes in relation to another of her stories, Baron "returns the subject to the quotidian and perennial experience of women." As such it represents a kind of women's writing that prizes the individual over the collective, that insists on treating the sufferings of women not only as allegories or national metaphors but also as subjects in their own right.[16]

The de-allegorizing or literalizing function of the story is signaled early on, when we are first introduced to Dinah. A poor teacher's daughter, raised by a stepmother, Dinah is described by the narrator as having the face of an unloved or unpitied child—in Hebrew, *penei tinoket lo-ruhamah.* The use of the words *lo-ruhamah* (a play, perhaps, on the Hebrew word for womb, *rehem*)[17] calls to mind the first chapter of the book of Hosea, where the prophet is commanded to marry a harlot and have children with her. God commands Hosea to call the second child "*Lo-Ruhamah;* for I will no longer accept the House of Israel or pardon them" (Hos. 1:6). Whereas Hosea calls his daughter *Lo-Ruhamah* as a means of allegorically representing the imminent punishment of the people, Baron de-allegorizes and individualizes this designation, making it stand for Dinah herself, for her tribulations alone.

The anti-allegorical stance of the story is especially evident in the way it recapitulates and recasts particular moments from Agnon's "Aggadat hasofer." Critics have already noted the intertextual relationship between Devorah Baron's "Mishpahah" and another classic work of modern Hebrew literature, Y. L. Gordon's feminist poem "Kotso shel yud" (The tip of the yud).[18] Yet to the best of my knowledge, no one has noted the ways in which Baron's barrenness story responds to Agnon's representation of the same theme. In a recent article, Marc Bernstein establishes that Baron and Agnon knew each other well, both professionally and socially,[19] and he offers a persuasive reading of Baron's story "'Agunah'" as a de-allegorizing response to midrashic tradition as well as Agnon's well-known story "'Agunot.'"[20] My reading of "Mishpahah" in relation to "Aggadat Hasofer" extends Bernstein's argument to show how Baron applied this intertextual strategy to other works as well.

Several common details draw together Agnon's "Aggadat hasofer" and Baron's "Mishpahah." Both Dinah and Miriam pine for a child. Married without children, to husbands whose work takes them away for long stretches of time either literally (as in the case of Dinah, whose husband travels to customers) or figuratively (as in the case of Miriam, whose husband's strict work regime leaves her alone on her side of the partition), both women yearn for their past social lives. As is evident from the title of Agnon's story, however, Miriam's concerns are subordinated to Raphael's professional and religious goals. In contrast, Baron's story foregrounds the female protagonist and rejects the notion of a woman being sacrificed for the sake of her husband's aspirations or family obligations.

Sexual awkwardness governs both stories and can in part explain the problem of barrenness that afflicts both families. In "Aggadat hasofer," Miriam and Raphael remain sexually attracted to one another, but a devotion to sacred texts literally prevents sexual consummation, as demonstrated in the following passage:

> When Miriam visits the bathhouse Raphael remains in the House of Study. When she returns home she dresses in fine clothes like a bride on her wedding day, and stands before the mirror. At that moment it seems as if the days of her youth were returning to her. . . . But when she sees reflected in the mirror the east-wall embroidery with its scenes and those two lions with their mouths open, immediately she is startled and shrinks back: "The earth is the Lord's and the fullness thereof."

> And when Raphael returns home after the prayers and sees his wife in her true beauty reflected in the mirror, he is immediately attracted to her. He goes toward her to make some pleasing remark. But when he is near her, His Name, may He be blessed, flashes before him out of the mirror. Immediately he stops and recites devoutly and in holiness: "I have set the Lord always before me," and shuts his eyes before the glory and awe of the Name.[21]

The mirror is a crucial image here. A classic symbol of literary representation, the mirror serves as a medium of reflection as well as deflection, repeatedly redirecting desire away from body and toward text.

Baron's "Mishpahah" includes a strikingly similar two-part depiction of innocence and desire:

> On Friday afternoons she could now wash her hair in private, undisturbed. She would pull the shade over the window, and in the dim half-light, she would let down her copious hair and stand for a while before the mirror, which was also full of shadowy light, like that shimmering light at sunset.

Devorah Baron, courtesy of
Machon Genazim.

Fine steam rose from the basin, and, right there, beside it, on its colored
paper, the "good" soap lay exposed, its embossed surface still showing.

Barukh, peering into her corner, felt something like what he had once experienced when he had walked into the pine forest just as the sun was rising.
He was still young and didn't know how to speak love, but now he truly
understood what that Torah portion of the week meant when it told of Isaac,
who brought Rebecca into the tent of his mother, Sarah, and he loved her
and was comforted after his mother's death.[22]

Here, too, a wife stands before a mirror that reflects her renewed beauty;
a husband catches sight of this wife and experiences awakening passion.
Unlike the Agnon passage, however, where Miriam and Raphael's desires
are both interrupted and absorbed by sacred texts, in Baron's story a textual citation only appears in the paragraph pertaining to Barukh. Dinah
looks in the mirror and experiences uninhibited sensual arousal, as indicated by the images of steam curling up from the washbowl and the
undressed appearance of the "good soap [that] lay exposed, its embossed
surface still showing." Only Barukh's sexual impulses are mediated by the

195

textual tradition. His viewpoint is so inscribed in traditional patterns that he views his wife as surrogate mother as much as lover, like the biblical Isaac, who was comforted over the death of Sarah through his marriage to Rebecca. Implicit here is that while Barukh and Dinah seem to love each other, they may not have figured out exactly how to translate this love into a physical relationship. Of the two, Barukh seems to be the more sexually awkward.[23] This is made explicit later on in the story, when we see Dinah waiting for Barukh to return home for Shabbat, and Barukh is over-awed by Dinah's purity: "When finally his footsteps were heard in the yard on Friday, she burst into the hall and there, between the cellar entrance and the ladder to the attic, she laid her head, her orphaned head, still warm from washing, on his chest, and he, taken aback by the purity that emanated from her, lightly pushed her away and took off his shoes before entering the room."[24] This passage also nods in the direction of Agnon's "Aggadat hasofer." Like Raphael and Miriam in Agnon's tale, Barukh and Dina do not seem to have a sexual relationship. The reference to Dinah's awesome purity calls to mind the obsessive concern for ritual purity that governs the behavior of Raphael and Miriam and keeps them perpetually apart. In Agnon's story, however, the work of the male scribe compensates for this failure to consummate, while Baron's story ultimately seeks compensation or rectification in the disruption of the male script.

Both Agnon and Baron borrow language from biblical and aggadic materials (the latter implied by the title of Agnon's story, "*Aggadat* hasofer"). According to Arnold Band, the seemingly religious language of Agnon's story needs to be read ironically;[25] indeed, Raphael's fanatic devotion to writing is ultimately as narcissistic as it is pious.[26] Agnon's story does not reject allegory, though; it simply replaces one form of allegory with another. Instead of being about God and the people, the allegory in "Aggadat hasofer" is about the modern writer and his obsessive devotion to his art. In contrast, Baron's story rejects allegory altogether, rehearsing biblical and aggadic language for the very purpose of undermining it.

In Agnon's story, Raphael's activities are frequently illustrated and explained by way of a *mashal* (parable); his decision to write a Torah scroll in memory of his wife, for example, is illustrated through the following parable:

A great gardener raised beautiful plants in his garden, and all the officials who were to see the king would first come to his garden and buy beautiful flowers to take with them. Once the gardener's wife was to see the king, and the gardener said: "All others who visit the king take flowers from my garden.

Now that my own wife is to visit the king, it is only proper that I go down to my garden and pick flowers for her."

The comparison is clear. Raphael was a great gardener. He planted beautiful Torah scrolls in the world. And whoever was invited to appear before the King—he took a Torah scroll with him. And now that Miriam's time had come to appear before the King—the Holy One, blessed be He—Raphael immediately went down to his garden—that is, to his pure and holy table—and picked roses—that is, the letters of the Torah scroll which he wrote—and made a beautiful bouquet—that is, the Torah scroll that he had prepared.[27]

The implication of this passage is that if the marriage produced no children and Miriam died childless, all this would be compensated for with a fertile outgrowth of sacred Hebrew texts, themselves a metaphor for Agnon's dedication to production of modernist fiction. Thwarted procreation begets artistic creation.

To be sure, there is a strong element of parody in Raphael's obsessively allegorical depiction of his scribal project, as well as in many other passages in the story that depict Raphael and Miriam's hyper-pious traditional lifestyle. Insofar as "Aggadat hasofer" can be viewed, however, as Agnon's own "aggadah" or "mashal" about the life of the (male) writer and the lengths he will go to sustain his creativity, the story supports the allegorical tradition.

Compare this with the gardening parable offered by Wide Basia in "Mishpahah." In Baron's story, Wide Basia functions as the single greatest promoter of the patriarchy, both on a biological and a literary level; she is noted for having given birth to ten sons and for her allegorical speech patterns, which she inherited from her father, an itinerant preacher or *maggid meisharim*.[28] In the case of the following parable, Basia uses her inherited homiletical manner of speech to induce the family to eject Dinah from their fertile clan: "Once, during the Torah reading, she told the parable of a barren tree in an orchard whose owner decided to chop it down, since it provided him with nothing but a few fallen leaves all year long. She vividly described the way it stood among the fruit trees and how it was chopped down, and as she spoke, she waved her palm so vigorously that Dinah, who was standing nearby, shrank back, as if the hand held a weapon directed at her."[29] Unlike Raphael's consoling *mashal*, Wide Basia's gardening parable has a cruel and murderous aspect. By including this parable, Baron clearly refuses the would-be consolation of allegory, exposing its harsher, dehumanizing aspects.

If Wide Basia exemplifies the tyranny of patriarchal familial and literary tradition—wherein women are compelled to turn against one another in the interest of familial continuity—Dinah stands for an alternate textual as well as social order. When Dinah hears Wide Basia's taunting parable, she quits the women's gallery and resolves from then on to pray alone, like the biblical Hannah. As noted earlier, of all the barren women in the Bible, Hannah was the most independent and innovative, devising her own unique prayer as a means of pleading before God for a child. Unlike Hannah, however, who goes to pray at the tabernacle at Shiloh—a site of priestly and communal worship—Dinah removes herself from the collective, withdrawing into her own home to work out and confront her aspirations.

Both stories have meta-fictional moments, where the narrator comments on the process of writing itself, and it is here that the different approaches to the allegorical treatment of the barrenness theme become most distinct. Toward the end of "Aggadat hasofer," as he grieves over the death of his wife, Raphael suffers an emotional breakdown that impedes his effort to write the Torah scroll in Miriam's memory:

> At times Raphael summoned strength, dipped the pen in ink, and wrote a word, but this did not lead to any more work because his eyes filled with tears. When he sat down to write a single letter in the Torah, immediately his eyes brimmed with tears which rolled down to the parchment.
>
> In vain do builders build palaces
> If a flooding river sweeps away their foundations;
> In vain do people kindle a memorial candle
> If the orphans extinguish it with their tears.
>
> And when he swallowed his tears he said to himself, Now I will work, now I will write, he would reach such a peak of devout ecstasy that his quill spattered droplets of ink, and he was unable to write even a single letter properly.[30]

In this passage, a superabundance of tears invalidates the script. But the outpouring of tears does more than deter Raphael's writing: it also completely interrupts the telling of the story, as the narrator intrudes into the narrative with a meta-fictional poem on the ways in which excessive emotion impedes the creative process. Only when Raphael immerses himself in "icy water on a snowy day" and literally freezes his tears, when he reins in and sublimates emotion, can he proceed with his work and the story can move to its conclusion.

Baron's narrator takes a very different position on tears and their function in the writing process, as evidenced in the following passage, where the narrator interrupts the narrative to reflect on the literary representation and function of sorrow:

> There is a measure of sorrow the poets call a "cask of tears." It is an open vessel that collects the essence of pain, drop by drop, filling as a person's sorrow grows.

> I once thought that it was something like the bucket that stood under the dripping rainspout, but then I was reminded of Dinah, the year of whose divorce had arrived, which was the tenth year after she had first come to live in her husband's house. Hers were actual tears, and they flowed so freely that, as she sat on her doorstep wearing the kerchief that obscured her face, they seemed like rain falling steadily from a cloud. And there was, besides a stormy wind blowing, the kind people don't like, which was another reason they hurried past without slowing down.[31]

Baron's narrator initially supplies a secondary metaphor for the "cask of tears," comparing the cask of tears to a bucket under a rainspout, but then rejects this metaphor, preferring instead to concentrate on Dinah's cask of tears as a subject in and of itself, apart from any broader weather correlatives. The motif of the "cask of tears" appears again during the *get* ceremony, when Barukh's kind-hearted sister Mousha, the person who arranged the marriage between Dinah and Barukh, bursts into sympathetic tears, overflowing the cask. As Baron's narrator observes:

> I have already mentioned the cask of tears, and the way it measures, as it were, a person's portion of suffering. If it overflows and mercy prevails, that is known as divine providence or a miracle, and the custom is to recite a blessing over it, or perhaps record it for posterity in a book. For those adrift at sea it comes in the form of a hand or a board floating on the water; for those trapped in a fire, in the shape of a window, or a break in the wall; here it came in the form of a single letter, which was written improperly and sticking out of its line.[32]

Baron does not actually describe how this scribal mistake came about. Mousha cries and suddenly we learn of the letter gone awry, suggesting something of a causal connection. In both stories, then, tears disrupt the patriarchal writing process, but in Baron's story this engenders a positive outcome, enabling the composition of a more sympathetic script than the traditional Jewish legal one that mandates divorce after ten years of barren marriage.

What, then, about the ending of the story? According to Zilla
Goodman, the "fairy-tale ending" of the story, "which conjures up the
birth of a son to continue the coveted male line that extends from Adam
and Abel and Cain to Avner ben Barukh," represents a perpetuation
rather than a breakdown of the patriarchal order.[33] One way of answer-
ing this objection is to consider the role of the rabbi's daughter-narrator
of the story in relation to her protagonist. Unlike Dinah, whose general ignorance and submissiveness require her, in some sense, to toe the
patriarchal "line," the narrator stands both inside and outside the narrated events. Her role is crucial to any interpretation of the story, for
she is able to take the literary letter into her own hands, bearing witness to Dinah's experiences and authoring her own countertraditional
script. While it is true that this narrator ostensibly offers a fairy-tale
ending, it is also useful to compare this ending to a famous midrash that
conjures up a similarly fantastic conclusion:

> We have learnt elsewhere: If a man has married a wife and lived with her ten
> years and she has not born him a child, he is not at liberty to neglect the duty
> [of begetting children]. R. Idi said: It happened once to a woman in Sidon
> that she lived with her husband for ten years without bearing him a child.
> They came before R. Simeon b. Yohai and requested to be parted from one
> another. He said to them: "On my word, in the same way that you were
> joined together with food and drink, you must separate with food and
> drink." What did they do? They followed his advice, and made themselves a
> holiday and prepared a banquet and drank freely. Feeling in good humor, he
> said to her, "My daughter [my wife], look around and find whatever you
> think is good in this house and take it back with you to your father's house."
> What did she do? After he fell asleep, she signaled to her servants to carry
> him in his bed and bring him to her father's house. At midnight, after the
> effects of the wine had passed, he awakened from his sleep and asked, "Where
> am I?" She replied, "At my father's house." He said, "What am I doing at your
> father's house?" She said, "Didn't you tell me that I could take whatever I
> wanted from the house and bring it to my father's house? There isn't anything
> more precious to me than you." Then they went before R. Simeon b. Yohai
> and he stood and prayed for them and they were "visited" [she became preg-
> nant]. What does this teach us? That in the same way that God makes bar-
> ren women fertile so the righteous can make barren women fertile. See, it is
> a *kal vahomer.* If a human being says to another flesh and blood being, there
> is nothing more precious to me than you, and they are remembered, how
> much more so in the case of the people of Israel who are waiting for salva-
> tion from God, and every day they declare that there is nothing more pre-
> cious to them than God, that they too will be remembered.[34]

Both Baron's story and this midrash feature a divorce that never comes to be and a miraculous birth of children to a once-barren couple. Note, however, the allegorical thrust of the midrash; the entire narrative drives toward the ending, where a comparison is made between the pregnancy of the barren woman from Sidon and the hoped-for redemption of the nation of Israel. Baron's story makes no such analogy; on the contrary, the story stresses the importance of the individual in the face of collective institutions such as nation and family. According to Judith Baskin, the lesson of this midrash is that "barrenness is never more than a presumption, nor should one despair of the efficacy of prayer."[35] Baron's story certainly teaches the former point, but it remains silent on the latter. R. Shimon is the obvious hero of the midrash, insofar as he prepares the ground for the wife to make her poignant expression of love and then intercedes on the couple's behalf with his efficacious prayer. The rabbi in "Mishpahah," however, saves the couple not by praying but by invalidating or negating a Jewish legal text. The midrash refers to the eventual pregnancy of the woman from Sidon in the traditional language of divine remembrance or visitation, just as in Genesis 21, where God "remembers" or "visits" (pakad et) Sarah with pregnancy. Baron avoids the language of divine intervention, refusing to re-inscribe the story in biblical patterns.

Even so, Goodman makes a strong case, one that is not easy to dispel. If Baron really wanted to disrupt the patriarchal script, why not give Dinah a daughter[36] instead of the son required by the phallic family? It is a curious fact, actually, that for all their countertraditional elements, almost all the female-authored texts on the barrenness theme from this period rehearse the traditional theme of the barren mother yearning for a son even as they repudiate its allegorical, national aspects.

Rachel Bluwstein's "'Akarah"

Rachel's famous poem "'Akarah" (Barren woman, 1928) is a case in point:

עֲ קָ רָ ה

בֵּן לוּ הָיָה לִי ! יֶלֶד קָטָן,

שְׁחֹר תַּלְתַּלִּים וְנָבוֹן.

לֶאֱחֹז בְּיָדוֹ וְלִפְסֹעַ לְאַט

201

בִּשְׁבִילֵי הַגָּן.
יֶלֶד.
קָטָן.

אוּרִי אֶקְרָא לוֹ, אוּרִי שֶׁלִּי!
רַךְ וְצָלוּל הוּא הַשֵּׁם הַקָּצָר.
רְסִיס נְהָרָה.
לְיַלְדִּי הַשְּׁחַרְחָר
— "! אוּרִי"
אֶקְרָא!

עוֹד אֶתְמַרְמֵר כְּרָחֵל הָאֵם.
עוֹד אֶתְפַּלֵּל כְּחַנָּה בְּשִׁילֹה.
עוֹד אֲחַכֶּה
לוֹ.

Barren Woman

If only I had a son! A little boy,
black-curled and clever.
Just to hold his hand and stroll slowly
Through park lanes.
A boy.
Small.

Uri, I'd call him. My Uri!
Soft and clear is this short name.
A bit of light. My dark-haired boy,
"Uri!"
I'd call!

Still, I'll be embittered like Rachel.
Still I'll pray like Hannah in Shiloh.
Still I'll await
Him. (*Rachel,* p. 189)

Note the way in which each stanza moves from longer to shorter lines, creating a persistent emphasis on smallness both in form and content. This is a tiny poem, with short words, speaking of a small child, a bit of light. Is Rachel's use of smallness here part of a poetics of duplicity, masking large ambition with a veneer of self-diminution? Can this stress on the diminutive also be understood as an effort to reduce the barrenness theme to smaller, more personal proportions? It is important to note that while Rachel's speaker casts herself in the mold of the biblical Rachel and Hannah, she does not imagine calling her child Joseph or Samuel. Though the name Uri appears in the Bible (the biblical artist Betsalel is identified as the son of Uri[37]), the name Uri nods in the direction of the Russian name Yuri, reflecting Rachel's own bilingual and bicultural ties. "Uri" also can also be seen as alluding to the Hebrew word *uri* (with an ayin rather than an aleph) meaning "wake-up," as in Isaiah 52:1, where the prophet urges a feminized Zion to "wake-up, wake-up, and dress in splendor," emblematic of a general strategy of female personification that also includes the representation of Zion as a barren woman (Isa. 54:1). But unlike Isaiah, Rachel dramatizes a personal rather than a national quest, an idea implicit in the possessive personal form of the name "Uri," meaning "*my* light." The notion of personal rather than national yearnings is underlined in the last two lines of the poem ('*od ahakeh / lo,* Still I'll await / Him), which allude to the liturgical statement of belief in the coming of the messiah—*ahakeh lo bekhol yom sheyavo* (I'll wait for him whenever he comes). But instead of a statement of national religious belief in the eventual coming of the messiah, Rachel's clipped usage of liturgy depicts the individual yearnings of a woman for a son.

While it might be argued that the biblical/liturgical references in this poem indeed situate the speaker's yearning for a child within the national context, the emphasis on smallness and the repetition of possessive adjectives and pronouns strengthen the personal over the national reading. Note as well that Rachel (Bluwstein) selects very deliberately from the biblical barrenness stories. While Hannah is invoked for her iconoclastic prayer, the matriarch Rachel is recalled primarily for her bitterness, seen primarily in her speech to Jacob in Genesis 30:1, "Give me sons or else I'll die." According to Robert Alter, "It is a general principle of biblical narrative that a character's first recorded speech has particular defining force as characterization. Surprisingly, although Rachel has been part of the story for more than a decade of narrated time, this is the first piece of dialogue assigned to her. It is a sudden revelation of her simmering frustration and impulsivity: in fact, she speaks with impetuousness reminiscent of her brother-in-law Esau who announced to Jacob that he was on the point of death if Jacob did not immediately give him what he wanted."[38] In choosing to memorialize the biblical matriarch's deferred emergence into speech, the poet Rachel also registers the idea of women's belated entry into Hebrew literary history. More than that, in valorizing rather than repudiating Rachel's bitternessness and impetuousity—indicative of Esau-like personality traits not generally applauded by the rabbinic commentaries—Rachel betrays a desire to tell a barrenness story but, as Emily Dickinson famously wrote, to "tell it slant."[39]

These countertraditional elements notwithstanding, Rachel's "'Akarah," like the various biblical barrenness stories, is all about waiting for a son. The Bible fails to give us a single extended account of the birth of a daughter (let alone, a story of unsolved fertility), and in this regard Devorah Baron and Rachel follow in the footsteps of the biblical tradition.[40]

Anda Pinkerfeld-Amir's "'Akarah"

Though published around the same time as Rachel's "'Akarah," Anda Pinkerfeld-Amir's similarly titled poem(1928) has been all but forgotten, completely eclipsed in the minds of the Hebrew reading public by Rachel's oft-sung poem. In her review of *Yamim dovevim* (Whispering days), Bluwstein herself ignores Pinkerfeld-Amir's "'Akarah,"[41] preferring instead to quote from a poem that appears later in the collection, in which a woman praises God for giving her a son.[42] In general, Pinkerfeld-Amir was recognized by Israeli readers more as a children's writer than as a poet.[43] When critically discussed, her poetry was praised largely for what was perceived as its conventionally feminine aspects. To take one example, critic Bentsion Benshalom observes in a review esssay that Pinkerfeld-Amir's "heart, the heart of a woman, is filled with softness and sympathy. So meager is life, so pitiable are people. She as a woman, wants to comfort, to calm, to straighten that which God has made crooked."[44] Throughout his essay, Benshalom insists on the womanliness of Pinkerfeld-Amir's verse and even attempts to adduce proof for this poetic womanliness from the poem "'Akarah."[45] Despite Benshalom's attempts, "'Akarah" and the following three, untitled but thematically related poems in the volume, hardly demonstrates a conventional feminine desire to comfort, calm, or straighten the crooked. These are poems in which a woman cries out against God, refusing all traditional forms of comfort. Written in simple language but concealing hidden complexity, Pinkerfeld-Amir's poems employ biblical and liturgical allusion to argue strenuously against the image of the barren woman being miraculously and blessed with a son by a magnanimous (masculine) and all-powerful deity:

עֲ קָ רָ ה

עֲקָרָה בִּרְכַּי חִבַּקְתִּי,
נִדְנַדְתִּין הֵנֶּה – הֵנָּה,
נוּם-נוּמֵינָה – שַׁרְתִּי לָמוֹ.

בָּכוּ בִרְכַּי כָּאֶפְרוֹחִים,
לְאֵם נַפְשָׁם יִשָּׂאוּ –
– וְאָנֹכִי עֲקָרָה –
שָׁדַי לֹא יִתְבָּרְכוּ.

*

לֹא שָׁקְטָה נַפְשִׁי בְּשִׁקְטֵי-הַלַּיְל,
בְּקִסְמֵי-יָרֵחַ וְכֹכָבִים,
לֹא תְשֻׁלֶּה בְּבִרְכַּת-אִמָּהוּת.

הוֹמִיּוֹת, הוֹמִיּוֹת תְּהוֹמוֹת,
אֵמֶת סֵבֶל-עוֹלָם צוֹעֶקֶת.

אֵיכָה אֶשְׁלָו?

*

מָרוּ הַדְּמָעוֹת, לֹא נָאוּ כַּנָּהָר מִגְּדוֹתַי-עֵינַיִם,
מַר כְּאֵב-לֹא-הֻגַּד מְנַצֵּחַ עַד נֶצַח.
וִיחִי עוֹד אִלֵּם מֵעֵבֶר לַחַיִּים
תַּחַת תַּכְרִיכִים בְּחָזֶה חָרֵב.

*

אָסוֹן, אָסוֹן
צִלְצֵל בָּעוֹלָם פַּעֲמוֹן,
צָרַח.
בָּכָה גֶּבֶר קְשֵׁה-הָעֹרֶף, שָׁאָג.
הָאֵל שֶׁבַּשָּׁמַיִם הִסְתִּיר פָּנָיו.

וּלְאַל-הָאָסוֹן אֵין פָּנִים.
מֵאָה יָדַיִם-חוֹנְקוֹת לוֹ.
עַל בּוּלֵי-רַגְלָיו יִשְׁרֹץ, יִגְלֹשׁ,
וְיִצְרַח בָּעוֹלָם.

Barren Woman

Barren, I embraced my knees,
swayed them to and fro,
hush, hushabye — I sang to them.

My knees wept like chicks,
their souls were borne away for a mother —
— and myself, I am a barren woman—
my breasts have not been blessed.

*

My soul was not stilled in the night-stillness
by moon-magic and stars,
it will not be misled by motherhood-blessing.

Roaring, roaring depths,
She screams the truth of everlasting pain.
How ever can I be tranquil?

*

The tears were bitter, but did not rise like a river from eye-banks,
bitter untold-pain from eternity to eternity.

206

And it lived on speechless beyond life
under shrouds in a dried-up chest.

*

Disaster, disaster
Rang out in the world like a bell,
Shrieked.
A stiff-necked man wept, howled.
God in Heaven concealed His face.

And the disaster-god has no face.
Rather a hundred strangling arms.
On his lump of legs he creeps and slides,
and shrieks throughout the world.[46]

In "'Akarah" and the ensuing poems, Pinkerfeld-Amir invokes the biblical
representation of infertility as a way of exposing its silences and omissions.
If biblical barrenness typically ends happily with a divinely ordained pregnancy, Pinkerfeld-Amir's poem addresses the more somber question of
how one copes with infertility that is never remedied, what she refers to in
the third poem as *mar ke'ev lo-hugad* (bitter untold pain). In the first poem,
the repeated use of the word *birkai* (my knees) calls to mind the biblical
language of procreation and barrenness: the idea of a baby being born on
a father or mother's (or grandfather's) "knees" (see Gen. 50:23) or of a
handmaid bearing a child "on the knees" of a barren matriarch, as in
Rachel's suggestion to Jacob that he take her handmaid Bilhah, "that she
may bear on my knees" (see Gen. 30:3). In Pinkerfeld-Amir's poem, of
course, there is neither handmaid nor divine intervention. Instead, the
infertile woman withdraws into her ceaseless pain, desperately embracing
her knees and rocking them wishfully like a baby.

Note that the word *birkai* also plays on the idea of devotion to God
(getting down on one's knees)[47] as well as on the Hebrew word for blessing *(berakhah)*, as seen in the last line of the first poem, where the speaker
laments that her breasts *(shadai)* haven't been blessed. Pinkerfeld-Amir's
use of the word *shadai* enacts yet another wordplay, calling to mind the
divine appellation *El Shaddai,* which appears several times in the book of
Genesis in the context of fertility blessings[48] (see Gen. 48:3 and 49:25).

The unblessed breasts of the speaker thus also emphasize the conspicuous absence of a God who blesses the breasts and wombs of the people.

In the second poem, the female speaker refuses to be consoled by "moon-magic and stars," referring to God's promise to Abraham that his offspring will be as countless as the stars in the night sky (Gen. 15:5). An even more intertextual allusion to biblical (in)fertility occurs in this same poem (line 3), where the speaker insists that her soul will not be deceived *(lo tishleh)* by the blessing of motherhood; this recalls the Shunamite woman's complaint to Elisha, who intervened before God on her behalf so that she could have a son. In the wake of that same son's death, the Shunamite woman confronts Elisha with the fact that she did not asked him to intercede on her behalf before God for a child; she specifically asked him not to mislead or deceive *(lo tashleh oti)* her with vain promises of motherhood (2 Kings 4:28). In contrast to the biblical account, where the prophet resurrects the once-barren Shunamite woman's child, the speaker in Pinkerfeld-Amir's poem refuses the very idea of a pregnancy ordained by God.

Indeed, in these poems Pinkerfeld-Amir relentlessly repudiates all biblical fertility promises. This utter rejection of the biblical God is most explicit in the last quoted poem. Here, after the manner of the biblical book of Lamentations, which begins with a female speaker and shifts to a male speaker (*Ani hagever, ra'ah 'oni beshevet 'evrato* [I am the man who has known affliction under the rod of His wrath], Lam. 3:1), Pinkerfeld-Amir introduces a "stiff-necked" male sufferer who cries out to God. But in contrast to the male speaker in Lamentations who is eventually consoled, the face of the would-be benign God is concealed from the sufferer, and no consolation can be found. Instead of an all-god, all-powerful *El Shaddai* or *El Adon* (masterful God), the God who emerges in this poem is an *El ason*, a "disaster god," who creeps around the world, shrieking and wreaking havoc upon the undeserving.

Nehamah Puhachevsky's "Asonah shel Afyah"

Nehamah Puhachevsky's "Asonah shel Afyah" (Aphia's plight, 1925[49]) similarly refuses the consolation of the biblical barrenness plot. Puhachevsky was the author of two collections of stories, *BiY'hudah hahadashah* (In the New Judah, 1911) and *Bakefar uba'avodah* (In the village and at work, 1930), which offer depictions of "a broad spectrum of women (farmers, workers, domestic helpers, kibbutz members)," but it is her first collection, which pays particular attention to the lives of Jewish Yemenite women in Palestine. Half of the stories in this 1911 collection depict the Yemenite community, including a story titled "Aharei simhah" (After happiness), a story about a barren woman named Adyah, whose husband, Salim, takes a second wife. Puhachevsky's later story, "Asonah shel Afyah," extends and enlarges upon the issues introduced in "Aharei simhah." According to Puhachevsky's granddaughter Ruth Arbel, both stories were based on a real-life incident involving a Yemenite woman named Adyah who lived in Puhachevsky's basement in Rishon Le Tsiyyon.[50] Adyah was barren for many years, but she finally became pregnant and had a protracted and dangerous labor. Fortunately, Nehamah Puhachevsky sought medical help for Adyah, and in the end the baby (a son) was born healthy.

In adapting this story for fiction, Puhachevsky chose to end it tragically, in conformity with the bleak endings of most of her stories.[51] In the 1925 story, the name Adyah becomes Afyah. She is the young wife of Moussa, a manual laborer and also something of a *talmid hakham,* who likes to quote from scripture and rabbinic literature. Despite his blatant misogyny, Afyah respects and admires her husband for his scholarship as well as his hard-working habits. In contrast, Moussa evinces little respect for his child-bride, openly reveling in the fact that he was able to "buy" her so cheaply. He encourages her to remain illiterate, spouting various misogynist catchphrases from rabbinic literature to support his beliefs about the need to refrain from teaching women how to read. Afyah is naïvely willing to put up with this bluster, but when words turn to blows and Moussa beats her brutally for failing to return some escaped chickens to their coop, Afyah flees their house and goes to stay with her relatives in the city. Initially, Moussa goes off looking for her armed with a revolver, indicative of his explosive demeanor. He eventually calms down and resolves to appease her with gifts. He is shocked to discover that she will not be easily mollified.

Part of what this story investigates is the transformation that overtakes a woman as a result of crossing geographical and social borders. While Moussa remains tied to the old-world customs of Yemen even after immigrating to Palestine—both in terms of his religious observances and his attitudes about women and marriage—Afyah is progressively influenced by the ways of her Ashkenazic neighbors. Even after Moussa convinces her to come home, Afyah insists on staying in the city for at least one more month so that she can bathe in the sea; she has heard from the Ashkenazic women that the waters are known

Nehamah Puhachevsky, courtesy of
Machon Genazim.

to "build up barren women" and is convinced that these women understand the mysteries of birth (p. 93). When Afyah finally does become
pregnant, she prays for a daughter rather than a son. She vows that
when her daughter grows up she will not be sold away in marriage but
will be allowed to choose her own husband, according to the practice
of the Ashkenazim (p. 96).

To be sure, there is something disquieting about Puhachevsky's
decision to designate the Ashkenazic Jews as the source of enlightenment
for Afyah, as if the Jews of Eastern Europe did not have their own forms
of backwardness and misogyny. That said, Puhachevsky also criticizes
the tendency of the Eastern European community in Palestine to look
down on their Yemenite neighbors and regard them as social inferiors.
Ultimately, "Asonah shel Afyah" is a story about a character doubly
marginalized, as Yemenite and as woman, and her abortive efforts, both
literally and figuratively, to improve her lot.

Nehamah Pukhachvsky, courtesy of
Machon Genazim.

Indeed, Afyah's situation continues to deteriorate. Throughout her
pregnancy she is afflicted with nightmares in which harm befalls either
her or the baby. As the months go by, she becomes more and more convinced that her husband is going to take a second wife in her stead,
according to Yemenite polygamous custom. When she finally goes into
labor, complications arise, but since it is the Sabbath, Moussa is unwilling to seek medical assistance, citing a verse from the prayer for the ill
that is recited in synagogues as part of the Sabbath liturgy: *Shabbat hi
meliz'ok, vrefu'ah krovah lavo* (Today is the Sabbath. There is no need for
alarm, deliverance [healing] will come soon).[52] In the context of the
liturgy, this verse means that even though on the Sabbath we are forbidden from crying out, we make an exception and ask God to bring a
speedy recovery to the sick people in our midst. Moussa clearly distorts
the meaning of this verse, marshalling it as an argument against calling
for medical help on the Sabbath, despite the obviously life-threatening
circumstances. Instead of calling for a doctor, Moussa loosely quotes
from a Talmudic passage from B. T. Ta'anit 2a, "Three keys are in His

211

hands [that were never handed over to an emissary]: for rain, for resurrecting the dead, and for bringing forth life" (p. 97). This text displaces woman from her central birth-giving role, transfering all the power and agency to God.

However, Afyah refuses to give in to Moussa's reading of the text and of the act of parturition. Against his will, she calls for her previous (Ashkenazi) mistress, who brings a midwife and a doctor; with this medical assistance, Afyah's life is saved, though her baby boy is born dead. Moussa blames Afyah and her violation of the Sabbath for the death of the child, and he prepares to take a second wife. Afyah's worst fears materialize.

Throughout history, Jewish communities have evolved various superstitions and folk customs concerning barrenness and birth.[53] Puhachevsky links Afyah to this superstitious tradition, yet at the same time she invests Afyah's fears with a measure of truth. In contrast, Moussa's uncompromisingly strict interpretation of and adherence to the law is exposed as a complete fraud. Moussa's community criticizes him harshly for intending to take a second wife, but, as is his habit, he offers a scriptural retort: "Man's steps are decided by the Lord; what does a man know about his own way?" (Prov. 20:24). Through this scriptural citation, he attempts to claim divine authority for his selfish behavior, an indication of the ways in which sacred texts can be manipulated for less than holy purposes.

The ending of "Asonah shel Afyah" exposes in stark terms the need for a new way of reading scripture and provides an alternative, female-centered portrayal of such experiences as barrenness, childbirth, and marriage. The next two chapters extend this idea, investigating prose and poetry by women that challenge the boundaries of Jewish women's lives and envision alternative forms of community.

"In What World?"

Transgressed Boundaries and Female Community in Early Hebrew Women's Fiction

> As a recurrent literary image, a community of women is a rebuke to the conventional ideal of a solitary woman living for and through men, attaining citizenship in the community of adulthood through masculine approval alone. The communities of women which have haunted our literary imagination from the beginning are emblems of female self-sufficiency which create their own corporate reality.
>
> NINA AUERBACH

In her now classic study of British women novelists, Elaine Showalter makes a plea for the study of neglected women novelists. "Criticism of women novelists," Showalter argues,

> while focusing on these happy few [Jane Austen, the Brontës, George Eliot, and Virginia Woolf] has ignored those who are not "great," and left them out of anthologies, histories, textbooks, and theories. Having lost sight of the minor novelists, who were the links in the chain that bound one generation to the next, we have not had a clear understanding of the continuities of women's writing, nor any reliable information about the relationships between the writers' lives and the changes in the legal, economic, and social status of women.[1]

This chapter, which includes a discussion of two so-called "minor" writers (Sarah Feige Meinkin Foner and Hava Shapiro) alongside a more canonical one (Devorah Baron), follows Showalter's lead and brings to feminist Hebrew literary studies the same conviction about the importance of "the minor" in constructing a literary history to the study of Hebrew women writers. Here our exploration moves from issues of literary convention to images of space and place, focusing on the ways early women writers of modern Hebrew prose documented the idea of women's crossing into new geographical, intellectual, and social spaces. On the most basic level, this chapter investigates what Showalter refers to as the relationship between "writers' lives and the changes in the legal, economic, and social status of women."

"Wasn't Rachel a Shepherdess?": Sarah Feige Meinkin Foner's Transgressive Passages

In 1919, Sarah Feige Meinkin Foner, the first modern Hebrew woman novelist, published an article, entitled "From My Childhood Memories," about how she came to learn Hebrew.[2] According to this account, Foner's father and mother were both literate in Hebrew sources. Her father, a former student of the Volozhin Yeshiva,[3] "studied Talmud day and night," while her mother spent every Saturday studying the *parashah* of the week with the commentaries of Rashi and Ibn Ezra.

Despite her mother's facility with the Hebrew language, young Sarah turned to her father, not her mother, to teach her Hebrew, a decision explained, at least in part, by a story she tells about visiting the house of a Jewish servant named Miriam. One day, Sarah's mother tells her to go to Miriam's house and ask Miriam to come as soon as possible to help prepare a special meal. If she finds Miriam in the middle of saying prayers, she should wait until she has finished before disturbing her with this request. When Sarah arrives at Miriam's house, she indeed finds her engrossed in prayer, and as she waits for Miriam to finish, she hears her recite a Yiddish prayer taught to young children: "May blessings and success fall on my little head, *Amen selah.*"[4] Five-and-a-half-year-old Sarah immediately deduces that there was something wrong with Miriam's liturgical education: "When she was a little girl, her mother taught her to recite 'May blessings and success fall on my little head,' and she still repeats these words today without any understanding. A prayer like that is a *tefilat shav* [an invalid or vain prayer] and I don't want to be like her. When I get home I will ask my father to teach me to read from the *siddur* so I will know how to pray properly."[5] In this vignette, Foner clearly designates Hebrew as the literate father-language of prayer and legal scholarship over Yiddish, the mother-tongue of housework and ignorance. When her father returns home from the *beit midrash* (study house), she runs outside to greet him, takes his "*tallis* and *tefillin*"[6] from him—representative of a desire not only to learn the language but to take possession of the various *mitsvot* (commandmants) associated with this language—and insists he buy her an *aleph-bet* so she can begin learning to read Hebrew. Throughout the story, an opposition is enacted between home, the province of mothers and their daughters, and the *beit midrash*, the province of fathers and their sons. Sarah's father teaches her Hebrew during the narrow band of time when he returns home from the *beit midrash* to eat breakfast or lunch. Hers is a home-bound form of learning, set against a feminine domestic background.

But Sarah refuses to accept these spatial and temporal limitations. After her first lesson, her father exhorts her to "go and play," promising to teach her more when he returns again. Instead of going to play, Sarah sits on the porch—a liminal zone between the domestic space of the home and the outside world—and reviews her *aleph-bet* until she knows it by heart and can read a short prayer on her own. When her father returns, he discovers "this wonder"[7] and shares the news of Sarah's accomplishment with her uncle, who announces that it's a shame she is a girl, for "if she were a boy, she would have been a *gaon* [great sage] in Israel."[8] This misogynist pronouncement, a sort commonly documented in stories by Jewish women of this period,[9] represents an effort to reassert gender difference within the context of Jewish learning, the very distinction the story aims to undercut and blur. "And a girl can't become a *gaon?*" young Sarah asks naïvely.[10] Sarah's father and uncle laugh at her response, but in the end she triumphs. Her father delivers her from her life of home-schooling to the *heder,* where she is allowed to study alongside the boys, many much older than she: "Every half year, I passed from grade to grade, until I acquired a knowledge of Tanakh and Talmud, and when I left there I began to read every Hebrew book that came to my hands. When I was twenty-five years old, I wrote a Hebrew story, the first of my published books, *Love of the Righteous.*" Foner's decision to close this reminiscence with the title of her first novel indicates a desire to impress upon her reader the "righteousness" of her pursuit as well as to publicize her work. The story suggests that learning a language commonly associated with boys and men enables a young girl to inhabit new religious, intellectual, and literary spaces and that this is a fundamentally good thing, past practice notwithstanding.

It is worth noting that of all Foner's written works, "From My Childhood Memories" is the only one that offers such a sanguine view of the "transgressive passage." Both her novel *Ahavat yesharim* and her novella *Beged bogdim* offer groundbreaking images of "new Hebrew women" who attempt to break down gender boundaries and challenge the

הַיְלָדִים יָצְאוּ מֵחֲדַר הָאַלְמָנָה
וְכַעֲבוֹר רְגָעִים אֲחָדִים בָּא אָבִי שְׁמוּאֵל
וּבְיָדוֹ אֶת הַחוֹלָה, וְעַמָּנוּאֵל הֵבִיא
אֶת סַמֵּי הָרְפוּאָה.

כַּעֲבוֹר יָמִים אֲחָדִים יָרְדָה שָׂרָה
מִמִּטָתָהּ וְשָׁבָה לְאֵיתָנָהּ[2]. כְּמִקֶּדֶם
הָיְתָה עוֹמֶדֶת לִפְנֵי הַתַּלְמִיד תּוֹרָה
וּמוֹכֶרֶת פֵּרוֹת, כְּעָכִים, מַמְתַּקִים
וְשׁוֹקוֹלָד. וּבְכָל פַּעַם אֲשֶׁר רָאֲתָה
אֶת שְׁמוּאֵל, יִצְחָק וְעַמָּנוּאֵל עוֹלִים
עַל מַדְרֵגוֹת בֵּית הַסֵּפֶר הִבִּיטָה אֲלֵיהֶם
בְּאַהֲבָה רַבָּה.

— רַחֲמָנִים הֵם, בְּנֵי רַחֲמָנִים!—
אָמְרָה שָׂרָה בְּלִבָּהּ.

_____

מִזְכְּרוֹנוֹת יְמֵי נְעוּרִי

מֵאֵת

שָׂרָה פֵיינֶה פוֹנֶר.

בְּרֵאשִׁית מַמְלֶכֶת אֲלֶכְּסַנְדֶּר הַשֵּׁנִי
בְּרוּסְיָה, בִּשְׁנַת ה' תרט"ז, נוֹלַדְתִּי בָּעִיר זַגֶר.
אָבִי הָיָה מְלָמֵד בְּתוֹרָה וּבְחָכְמָה וְהָגָה יוֹם
וָלַיְלָה בְּתַלְמוּד, וְאִמִּי יָדְעָה גַם הִיא הֵיא עִבְרִית,
וּבְכָל יוֹם שַׁבָּת אַחַר הַצָּהֳרַיִם לָמְדָה אֶת

פָּרָשַׁת הַשָּׁבוּעַ עִם פֵּירוּשֵׁי רַשִׁ"י וְאִבְּן עֶזְרָא.
וְאַתֶּם הֲלֹא יְדַעְתֶּם, קוֹרְאַי הַצְּעִירִים,
כִּי לִפְנֵי שָׁנִים הָיוּ הַהוֹרִים מְלַמְּדִים אֶת
בְּנֵיהֶם תּוֹרָה וְתַלְמוּד, אַךְ לֹא אֶת בְּנוֹתֵיהֶם.

שרה פיינה פונר היא אשה כבת ששים
וחמש, מלמדת בתורה ובתלמוד ובספרות
העברית. היא מדברת עברית יפה וכתבה
ספרים עברים אחדים.
היא גרה בהרלם אשר בניורק ומקדישה
את כל ימיה ללמוד הספרות העברית,
העתיקה והחדשה. בשעות הפנויות היא
מקבצת תרומות מאת מכיריה, ואת הכסף
הזה היא נותנת לבתי הספר העברים,
למען תהי להם האפשרות ללמד לבני
עניים חנם אין כסף.

אֶת הַבַּת לִמְּדוּ רַק לִקְרֹא בְּסֵפֶר הַתְּפִלּוֹת
וְלִכְתּוֹב מִכְתָּב בִּיהוּדִית. הַנְּעָרוֹת הָיוּ טְרוּדוֹת
כָּל הַיָּמִים בַּעֲבוֹדוֹת הַבַּיִת, וְהַהוֹרִים חָשְׁבוּ
לְמוֹתָר לְלַמֵּד אֶת בְּנוֹתֵיהֶם תּוֹרָה.

examined [1] ; to her strength [2].

accepted separation of feminine and masculine spheres. In both these works, the obstacles and disappointments faced by the female protagonists point strongly to the societal limits placed on female social mobility.

In *Ahavat yesharim* (Love of the righteous, 1881), boundary transgression is presented first and foremost through the speech and action of the heroine, Finalia. In the opening chapter of the novel, we find Finalia, having stayed out late to counsel a tormented friend, walking unaccompanied in the streets of Milan on a dark, starless night. Her willingness to walk alone with only the hood of her coat to protect her exposes her to unmistakable danger; like Little Red Riding Hood, she is ready prey for stalking male predators. In contrast to Little Red Riding Hood, however, Finalia refuses to succumb naïvely to the lure of the [male] wolf. "In the dark, we cannot discern between wolves and men," she says to her pursuer Victor, "because sometimes we meet a wolf in the guise of a man, and therefore we must be cautious."[11] Victor attempts to woo her with flattery, telling her the stars have refused to come out this evening because of fear that her glowing beauty would dim their light. Finalia rejects his flattery outright, showing a frank unwillingness to be vulnerable and quiescent and using the occasion to display the full extent of her learning and wit. She discourses ably on the nature of dreams and their interpretation, quotes freely from a variety of biblical sources, and offers the following scientific description of the heavenly bodies as a means of keeping herself resolutely off the romantic pedestal:

> "Behold this is known to all," said the maiden, "that the majority of the heavenly bodies are dark. They only receive their light from the sun and without her they wouldn't illuminate anything. And what have they to do with me or I with them? Can I fire the heavens, am I not of the earth? Can we lower the planets to the earth and distance them from the sun? Would not both they and I then be dark? And if they sought later to fly upwards, then in the end they would fall back because others would have taken their places. Therefore, leave them in the sky to receive light from the sun and illuminate each other and not come to me, because I am on the earth, from which I was taken and to which I shall return."[12]

Finalia's remarks here are impressive for both their resolution and their cheek; she will not be taken in by hackneyed metaphors that compare her to the stars and raise her to the heavens. She insists on speaking her mind and being taken for what she is—an educated human being. Victor eventually proves himself to Finalia as a worthy suitor, and before long the two (somewhat implausibly) pledge their eternal love.

Throughout the novel, Finalia and Victor are forced to contend with men who have malicious designs against them or their families. In the meeting scene described above, Finalia's intelligence, eloquence, and strength of character offer a redemptive model of the enlightened Jewish woman. At the end of the day, these attributes fail to ensure Finalia's safe passage from one social space to another. Repeatedly, we are introduced to predatory men—a Galician Hassid, a Polish nobleman, an Italian-Jewish district officer—who, half-crazed by Finalia's beauty, conspire to seize her for themselves. Even Victor, her devoted lover, shows a disturbing jealous streak. Despite Finalia's independent spirit and willingness to violate convention, she is immobilized by the masculine forces arrayed against her, a fact tragically illustrated when she is kidnapped by a suitor and carried off to his home in Galicia.

A similar pattern can be detected in Foner's historical novella *Beged bogdim* (The treachery of traitors or The cloak of traitors, 1891). *Beged bogdim* is loosely based on Josephus's account in *The Antiquities of the Jews* (Book 13, Chapter 7:4) of the murder of Simon, the king and high priest of Judah, by his son-in-law Ptolemy. Josephus reports that Ptolemy also killed his wife and put his two sons in chains. Foner's novella, as she explains in her "Word to the Reader," is a kind of "midrash" on Josephus, in that it attempts to explain what motivated Ptolemy to commit such a heinous crime. To this end, Foner creates the character of Helena, princess of Egypt, a woman of uncommon beauty and intelligence, who convinces the Hellenist Ptolemy to kill the Judaean king (his father-in-law) in exchange for her hand in marriage. Helena is credited in the novella with using her beauty and wisdom to accomplish what her male compatriots were unable to achieve with their swords. "You fled before the Jews, fleeing the sword and the slaying," she says. "I, a young maiden who has never held a sword and scorned a javelin, who has worn neither armor nor helmet, I myself will deliver you all the champions and great men of Jerusalem, even the King of Judah."[13] In calling this foreign princess Helena, Foner is clearly alluding to the Homeric Helen of Troy, the face that launched a thousand ships and was allegedly responsible for the epic war between the Greeks and the Trojans. At the same time, Foner is also punning on the term "Hellenist." Foner's Ptolemy is a Hellenist in both senses of the term. He loves Greek culture and he lusts after a foreign princess named Helena, who, in her alliance with the Greeks, ultimately betrays him.

In opposition to the ruthless Helena, Foner offers a positive example of enlightened womanhood in the person of Judith, daughter of a wealthy farmer from Modi'in named Aviezer, a staunch supporter of the Hasmonean dynasty. Judith, whose name evokes both the militant heroism of the biblical Judith in subduing the Assyrian Holophernes and the idea of Jewishness, is beautiful, intelligent, and good. Like Helena, Judith dares to tread on the territory of men but for solely constructive purposes.

Every year, on the anniversary of the death of Mattathias, Judith's father Aviezer invites the king and his retinue to his estate for refreshment after their visit to their ancestral grave site. On one such anniversary, Judith returns home late, thereby missing all the fanfare of the king's visit. She explains to her mother that she had wanted to come home early enough to help serve the guests but could not abandon the sheep left in her care. Judith's mother assures her that her help was not needed, but she expresses alarm over the thought of her daughter tending sheep: "But what's this my ears hear that you were watching the flocks? Have your parents made you a shepherd? Won't your father be wroth with you if he hears about this, because your parents didn't bring you up to watch the sheep" (*Beged bogdim,* pp. 10–11; *A Woman's Voice,* p. 115). Judith's mother's remarks derive from her sense of upper-class feminine propriety and social aspiration. Because Judith involved herself in the seemingly masculine, lower-class work of watching sheep, she missed the visit of the king and the other dignitaries, thereby losing an opportunity to advance herself in aristocratic society. Judith explains to her mother that she watched the sheep because all the regular shepherds were either sick or absent; she had no choice but to lend a hand. During the course of the day, she nursed and substituted for an ailing shepherd. "I regret very much that I am so late," Judith tells her mother, "but I am comforted by the fact that I saved a man from harm, and who wouldn't have done as I? Besides I do not understand, is it shameful, my dear mother, to herd sheep? Wasn't Rachel the Matriarch a shepherdess? (*Beged bogdim,* p. 11).[14]

Judith's ostensibly respectful questions conceal a frank rejection of aristocratic values and norms of female social location and/or occupation. Judith's mother insists there is no shame in being a shepherd, but if the daughters of Jerusalem knew that she herded sheep they would despise her for it, thereby lessening her prospects. Judith refuses to tailor her behavior to the urban aristocratic specifications of the daughters of Jerusalem. Instead, she opts for the agrarian model of the biblical Rachel who works with sheep in the open air (and in so doing meets her lover Jacob).

Indeed, a few pages later, Judith's Jacob appears on the scene, in the person of Johanan, the son of Simon the king/high priest. Judith and her brother Judah converse with the prince and inquire after the welfare of his sister, whom Johanan describes as wretched, having been married off, for political reasons, to the wicked Ptolemy. Judith answers with a learned play-on-words based on a biblical verse, provoking her brother to say "If only my sister had been a man . . . by now without doubt she would be learned and wise and a wonder in Israel." Johanan replies that if she were born a man, "she wouldn't be able to make happy the man that she chooses" (*Beged bogdim*, p. 14; *A Woman's Voice*, p. 119). Johanan's comment, intended as a compliment to Judith, contains a darker aspect. As in the case of the learned and accomplished Finalia in *Ahavat yesharim*, who is viewed by the men of the novel as little more than a feminine love object to be pursued, trapped, and guarded, Judith's reason for living, as stated even by the worthy Johanan, is to make a man happy. None of the men of the novella consider Judith's need to set her own agenda and parameters.

Judith eventually marries Johanan, and after Ptolemy murders Simon, she becomes queen, thereby achieving a position comparable to Helena's. The Sukkot festival arrives, lifting the spirits of King Johanan (renamed Hyrcanus after his heroic ascent to the throne) and his subjects after these tragic events. Judith stands alone, however in her ongoing despondency:

> But one person who should have been happier this festival than all the rest of Israel was sad-spirited. She was Judith, the daughter of Aviezer, the wife of Hyrcanus the king and high priest. When tidings came from Jerusalem that Ptolemy had slain Simon the High Priest, her father Aviezer couldn't bear this great pain. He sobbed bitterly over the loss and became bedridden, and after a couple of weeks, he died. . . . And Judith, despite all the honors she received now, took no comfort and was depressed and mourning for her father, because he would never see with his own eyes all the honor that the Lord had granted to his beloved daughter. (*Beged bogdim*, p. 33; *A Woman's Voice*, p. 139)

Judith's sorrow derives chiefly from the loss of her beloved father, but there is something else at work here. The narrator has just finished describing the gruesome murder of Simon, and then of his wife and daughter. The Hasmoneans have been thrown into a state of war, and, impossible as it seems, the people of Israel have put aside their sorrow to celebrate the holiday of Sukkot. Foner quotes the relevant passage from Josephus that sums up this moment: "And these were the events that made the festival happy and joyful for the Jews, and *they forgot the evil that had occurred to them*" (*Beged bogdim*, p. 33; *A Woman's Voice*, p. 139; emphasis added). All but Judith. A woman of action and high principle, Judith finds herself unsuited for the social life at court. Married now to a king and living in aristocratic Jerusalem, this ingenuous daughter of the countryside discovers she has crossed into a social and/or moral realm that she does not know how to inhabit.

In the fiction of Sarah Feige Meinkin Foner, enlightenment offers women a modicum of social mobility but no real power to determine the ultimate direction of their lives. Women in her fiction achieve intellectual or romantic success and cross into new spaces, but in doing so they become aliens in worlds not their own. Even while advocating female enlightenment, Foner's depictions of women manifest a palpable sense of disappointment with its social consequences.

Hava Shapiro's Clipped Wings

Hava Shapiro's short fiction demonstrates a similar desire to expand women's boundaries, both socially and intellectually, as well as a frank recognition of the many obstacles in the paths.[15] In an important essay entitled "Demut ha'isha besifruteinu" (The image of woman in our literature), one of the first examples of "images of women" criticism in Hebrew literary studies, Shapiro points out the various deficiencies and strengths in the ways that modern Hebrew (male) writers have depicted women in their fiction, looking forward to the entry of women into the Hebrew literary arena: "I believe in the talents and the spirit of our nation's writers—what has not yet been accomplished in this generation will be accomplished in the next generation—until a generation of female Hebrew writers rises up and begins to compete with their male counterparts in this task of filling in that which is lacking in our literature—the image of the New Hebrew [Jewish] Woman."[16] Shapiro's own 1909 collection of sketches, *Kovets tsiyyurim* (A collection of sketches), is filled with compelling portrayals of new Hebrew women, written in a concise and subtle style that represents a major step forward for Hebrew women's prose writing. As in the case of Foner's fiction, Shapiro's collection of sketches is filled with portraits of unconventional girls and women who stake a claim to their own spiritual or intellectual territory but who find themselves even more isolated and despondent as a result.

Kovets tsiyyurim includes a number of allegorical sketches that figure women in the stereotypically feminine guise of birds and flowers. The use of allegory allows the author to demonstrate in clear terms the ways in which women have been held captive by culturally constructed images of femininity masked as "nature." In one sketch, entitled "Ketsutsat kenafayim" (Clipped wings), a *deror*—the Hebrew word for sparrow as well as freedom—attempts to actualize her potential as suggested by her name by ascending ever higher in flight, searching unceasingly for "the course of her happiness, the goal of her longings and aspirations."[17] Only once does she stray from her course, to rest on the branch of a tree. This break, however, is enough to put an end to her quest: mischievous boys capture her, clip one of her wings, and place her in a cage so that she can sing for their pleasure. Again, as in Foner's fiction, we see a critique of a masculine culture that preys upon accomplished and talented females, that views them solely as tools for masculine desire and amusement. Alienated from the sources of her creativity, the *deror* languishes in the cage, and the dissatisfied boys are on the verge of abandoning her when she sees some other birds through the window and lets out a sorrowful song. Ironically, this (literary) expression of discontent thrills the boys, who resolve to keep her so that she will sing some more. On another occasion, the sparrow sees a bird outside on a branch, but within seconds she hears a loud noise and the bird falls dead to the ground, evidence, the cynical boys tell her, of the dangers of the outside world—dangers they themselves help perpetuate as a means of solidifying their control over the so-called "weaker sex." At the end of the sketch, the door to the sparrow's cage accidentally opens, enabling the bird to escape. The sparrow slips out the window and attempts to ascend in flight, only to remember that her wing has been clipped. At best, this is an allegory of domestication, at worst, of prostitution. A feminine free spirit is captured in matrimony or in the sex trade; her natural inclination is to express herself in song, a common metaphor for literary production, and in flight, an image of mobility and personal advancement. But when finally given the option to do so, she finds that the experience of emotional/sexual incarceration has stripped her of the equipment—physical, emotional, intellectual, or financial—to actualize her innate potential.

In another, non-allegorical sketch entitled "Haholemet" (The dreamer), the *deror*'s longings to ascend, fly, and sing are rendered in human form, offering the first female-authored Hebrew "portrait of the artist as a young woman":

> Already as a young girl, she demonstrated an inclination toward fantasy. She'd sit in a corner, apart from the games of the other children her own age, and any effort they made to entice her to join their play was futile. In time, they distanced themselves from her, calling her melancholic. But when she'd agree to their request to tell them stories, all would come forward and surround her.
>
> There was a wonderful quality to her stories. She told of things obscure, incredible events, all in vivid color, with such strong enthusiasm that her listeners were unwittingly drawn into the storyteller's fantasy. Suddenly it was as if they themselves saw, with their very own eyes, the magnificent pictures she described.
>
> As she grew older, not only did she tell stories; she also defended her dream: One law and equal rights for both sexes in society. She rebelled against every limitation and every law that lessened the value of the "weaker sex." . . . She dreamed and preached, that a time would come when there were no laws to keep "the weaker sex" consigned to a lower level, to a narrow, limited circle. When there were no obstacles or limitations on their rights, allowing them finally to reach the highest levels in society and humankind. (pp. 40–41)

What is so significant about this passage is that it suggests a direct link between female literary creativity and the feminist transformation of society. Because the "dreamer" has the ability to transport herself fantastically to another sphere and imagine incredible scenarios that transcend the quotidian, she is also able to envision the advent of equal rights and opportunities for women. In situating the feminist aspirations of this young storyteller within the realm of dreams and the fantastic, Shapiro hints already that these views are not easily sustained in the "real" world. In time, the dreamer marries and experiences a complete ideological turnaround. Now, instead of composing stories and preaching equal rights for women, she focuses all her energy on her "God-given" maternal role, becoming the exemplary "anti-feminist woman," to borrow Adrienne Rich's well-known term.[18] Naomi Caruso reads "The Dreamer" as an endorsement of the traditional feminine pursuit of marriage and children,[19] but this seems to overlook the elements of protest and disappointment so evident in the story. Rather than advocating marriage and motherhood, this tale offers a realistic depiction of what can happen to a woman who dares to take an unconventional route. Eventually, social pressures bear down so hard that she must cross over to the other side, ideologically speaking. As a young girl, the dreamer's unique qualities set her inexorably apart from other children; in her current, antifeminist incarnation, she can rely on the comforts of the mainstream, but only at the expense of her solidarity with other women. Previously she had joined with other young women in a quest to transform the world, but now she preaches that "only those who are unfulfilled as women can be given over to the ideas and aspirations that I once promoted. . . . We have special rights and privileges of our own that we must not betray" (*Kovets tsiyyurim*, pp. 41–42). Her conversion to patriarchal norms is so complete currently that her greatest dream is to supplement her family of three daughters with a son: "None of her dreams were as sought after, expected and hoped for as this one" (*Kovets tsiyyurim*, p. 43). Whereas she once imagined the impossible, her dreams now follow a prescribed patriarchal script, in which personal aspiration is completely subsumed by one's maternal role.

In another sketch, "Betulah zekeinah" (The old maid), we meet another female figure who experiences a crucial conversion. The protagonist here is an unmarried woman—independent, with a career—who feels bitter and alienated from the adult world at large. Childhood friends call her "Old Maid," a badge of shame and a torment, especially given her loneliness and her desire for children. Something happens in the end to change everything:

> The landlady was stunned. . . . She told all her neighbors that a change had come over the "Old Maid." . . . She no longer despises the young women *[tsi'irot]*. . . . Her voice calls out with joy. . . . She stands tall. . . . The assistant *['ozer]* from her office comes to see her every now and again. . . . She asks the young mother surprising questions. . . . Strange words come out of her mouth. . . . She repeats that she no longer pays attention to what people say. . . . The "Old Maid" looks to the future, prepares for "the event" of her life. (Kovetz tsiyyurim, p. 26)

According to Carole Balin, this ending indicates that the protagonist finally makes peace with her circumstances, thereby providing a model of a successful border-crossing into a life "free of societal expectations."[20] An equally plausible reading is that the turnaround isn't a sign of inner peace but of the protagonist's newfound love interest with the (male) assistant in her office. According to this reading, at the end of the sketch,

Hava Shapiro, courtesy of the
Montreal Jewish Public Library.

the former "Old Maid" is readying herself for the possibility of love, marriage, and/or motherhood. Whether the protagonist will manage to carry over her professional achievement and independence to her new married life is a question left unanswered.

In terms of the feminist struggle to cross over or steal into new linguistic and ritual spaces, the most significant sketch in the collection is the closing piece, "Kiddush levanah" (Sanctification of the moon), a story told from the perspective of a young girl who protests her exclusion from the monthly ritual of sanctifying the moon. The female narrator was accustomed to joining her brothers in all the ritual activities of the Jewish calendar. Suddenly—owing perhaps to her growth into puberty and the advent of her menses—she finds herself cast out from the sacred inner circle, unable to participate in a ceremony that is likened in the Talmud to "greeting the face of the Shekhinah" (B. T. Sanhedrin 42a).

There is an implicit irony in the narrator's exclusion from the moon sanctification ceremony, given the traditional biological and mythological connection between women and the lunar cycle. The notion of excluding women from the practice of sanctifying the moon might have originated in a Talmudic discussion about the *kiddush levanah* liturgy, where R. Aha quotes in the name of R. Ashi that it is the custom of those in the West to say a short blessing, *Barukh mehadesh hodashim* (Blessed is He who renews the months). This short blessing is rejected as a "woman's blessing" in favor of a much longer one.[21] It is important to note that while a definite bias against women and their Hebrew linguistic capacities is evident from this passage, the Talmud does not forbid women from participating in the moon ritual.

Indeed, in Shapiro's story, the exclusion of women seems grounded more in superstition than in law. Not only is the narrator forbidden from joining in the blessings, her brothers tell her that if she even looks at those praying she will suffer excruciating, God-given torments. Eventually, the narrator decides she can no longer tolerate exclusion. A religious outlaw, she steals into the forbidden space of masculine prayer: "I stole outside *[hitganavti]* and purposely stood in front of those sanctifying the moon to listened to the sound of their melodies. . . . And my brothers terrified me, saying that surely some disaster would befall me. . . . At the beginning, I paid no attention to what they were saying, but within a few days, I became frightened of the sound of every 'driven leaf'" (*Kovets tsiyyurim*, p. 62). As the days pass, her dread increases. Lying in bed one night, she suddenly hears footsteps approaching the closed door of her bedroom and is terrorized by the thought that someone has come to punish her. In the end, the footsteps turn out to belong to the Gentile gatekeeper who had been instructed, during the cloudy month of Heshvan, to announce to all the men in the household when the moon was out so that the sanctification could begin. He mistakenly knocks on the door of the girls' room instead of the boys.'

The conclusion of this sketch is not entirely clear. Does the gatekeeper recognize his mistake and retreat from the girls' room (thereby debunking misogynist superstition) or does something dark and sinister actually take place? Is the purpose of the ending to suggest that the masculine "gatekeepers" of secular Gentile culture are more receptive than their Jewish counterparts to women who cross the gender divide? Is Shapiro intimating that Gentile culture is "knocking on the doors" of young Jewish feminists, luring them away from the strictures of Jewish tradition?

A later essay by Shapiro, called "Yemei Hanukah" (Chanukah days, 1924), can serve as a postscript to the ending of "Kiddush Levanah." Here Shapiro looks back nostalgically at her childhood experiences of

Chanukah as representative of a traditional lifestyle she left behind so long ago. Some fifteen years after the publication of *Kovets tsiyyurim,* she now yearns for the religious days of her youth, the very times that are represented as so oppressive to young women in "Kiddush Levanah"! "Ah! Where are you, where are those days of faith, happiness, and joy!"[22] Lamenting that in her current surroundings "there is no place where people still light Chanukah candles," Shapiro shines a critical "light" on her own quest for education and emancipation.

What is so intriguing about this essay is the way in which Shapiro juxtaposes these insights against her memories of her educated mother reading Hebrew books. In contrast to Foner, who traces her Hebrew education back to her father, Shapiro, who dedicated her *Kovets tsiyyurim* to her mother, singles her out as her intellectual model:

> And here is my beloved mother. She was like a stranger in this environment. Book learned she was, finding her solace and calm in the reading of Hebrew literature and journalism, which were completely unacceptable *[pesulim]* in the eyes of her entire family. There was a tacit agreement *[berit]* between us children and her that we not disturb her as she read, and because of this she always did our bidding. On Sabbath evenings, by the great chandelier that hung in the middle of the dining room and next to the many burning Sabbath candles that were on the table, she sat before a book, with her right hand affixed to it, as if afraid that someone would take it away from her, her left hand on her chin and her cheek, completely absorbed in her reading and in her world,—and we, in our corner, silent and tranquil, looking jealously from afar at the tiny letters that our mother held mastery over almost like the men. On Chanukah evenings, though, even she became involved, as if stripping off her seriousness, and giving herself over to the frivolity *[kalut da'at]* of the commandment *[mitzvah].*[23]

The plethora of light-related imagery in this paragraph highlights the importance of the sketch as a reflection on the consequences of enlightenment. A woman who sits intellectually apart from the rest of her Hassidic family under the glow of the chandelier and the slowly extinguishing Sabbath candles, Shapiro's mother exudes the alternative light of Hebrew literature and reading. The tacit agreement or *berit*—a word evocative of biblical notions of the covenantal relationship between God and Israel—that binds Mrs. Shapiro with her children points to a new "covenantal" commitment of Jewish youth to the dictates of the Hebrew *Haskalah.* For this serious Hebrew woman reader, involvement in traditional Jewish ritual such as the lighting of Chanukah candles is frivolous, a kind of *kalut da'at* or intellectual light-headedness that ironically overturns the rabbinic assertion of light-headedness of women (*nashim da'atan kalot 'aleihen*) in B. T. Kiddushin 80b.

But if Shapiro's mother represents the potential high seriousness and sacred mission of women's learning and Haskalah over and against the "frivolity" of old-world legalism and ritual, Shapiro's essay suggests that much has been lost in this brave new intellectual world and little gained. Closing her essay with an impressionistic depiction of her student days, Shapiro displaces the "frivolity" of the commandments onto cosmopolitan university life, casting a disturbingly critical eye on the whole enterprise of (female) intellectual development: "And here, another environment. Figures, shadows and impressions rising from the confusions of memory. Male and female students gathering in a tavern. A large brightly lit auditorium. Lectures and speeches and brave efforts to kindle the heart; to diffuse the desolation and arouse the sleeping spark. Delighting, dancing, singing and humming, trying to amuse themselves. . . . Yet the joy is not true joy." Alas, here are the youth who have been lured away from Jewish practice by the intellectual promise of secular, Gentile culture (as intimated by the ending of "Kiddush levanah"), depicted as having dissipated their lives in meaningless, dizzy talk and merriment.

Exile and Community in the Fiction of Devorah Baron

Up to this point I have been analyzing two Diaspora-based writers who portrayed the female attempt to transgress social and ritual borders, documenting their various successes and disappointments. In moving the discussion to Devorah Baron (1887–1956), I turn to a writer whose career was played out both in the Diaspora and in the Land of Israel, thereby encompassing the additional elements of Zionist border-crossing or aliyah. One of the primary focuses of previous critics of Baron's fiction is her ostensible failure to engage the central issues of the early Zionist experience. According to critics such as Eli Schweid, Hillel Barzel, and Dan Miron, Baron portrayed neither the young intellectual Jew's alienation from tradition and community, the social upheavals in Eastern Europe caused by mass migrations of Jews to Palestine and America, nor the reality of the new life in *Erets Yisra'el*. Despite the fact that Baron experienced these disruptions and dislocations herself, moving from the role of rabbi's daughter to that of writer and teacher, from shtetl to city, from Eastern Europe to Palestine, her fiction largely bypasses these experiences. In contrast to the fiction of S. Y. Agnon, for example, which portrays life in Palestine as well as Poland, and which depicts modernity from the point of view of tradition and tradition from the point of view of modernity, Baron's fiction is perennially and statically rooted—as if outside time—in a mythical version of the shtetl, ensconced within its sacred texts and genealogies.[24]

By treating Devorah Baron in relation to the theme of transgressed boundaries, my goal is to challenge prior assessments of her work. In doing so, I join a growing group of critics and scholars who have begun to reread her fiction from the perspective of modernism, postmodernism, feminism, and gender studies: beginning with Baron's pioneering biographer, Nurit Govrin, and more recently, and most notably, Naomi Seidman, whose *A Marriage Made in Heaven: The Sexual Politics of Hebrew and Yiddish* (1997) includes a masterful discussion of Baron's Hebrew and Yiddish fiction through the metaphor of the women's section of the synagogue;[25] and Amia Lieblikh, whose *Rikmot* (Embroideries, 1991), a postmodern psychological "biography" of Baron written as a series of fictional encounters between Baron and Lieblikh, has been published in English translation also by Seidman.[26] There is no question that Baron's fiction, which often thematically bypasses the new homeland of Palestine in favor of the Lithuanian shtetl and which seemingly seeks out scriptural continuities between the old world and the new, differs from her contemporaries. But this does not mean, as Schweid has argued, that "Baron is completely unaware of the problematic that agitates the writers of her generation."[27] As Seidman aptly observes, "For a literary audience accustomed to and eager to recognize the collective apostasy narrative in a literary text, Baron's work might well have seemed timid, outdated, and populated with the ignorant small-town folk the new generation of Hebrew writers longed to leave behind. Baron's work, though, is neither conservative nor nostalgic."[28] On the contrary, it is written in a style that mixes midrashic homily with modernist invention, and conventional folktale structures with elements of social realism, often revealing in subtle yet powerful ways the gaps and disjunctions between tradition and modernity. Even as they portray and memorialize the traditional Jewish world, Baron's stories clearly respond to the problematic of early twentieth-century Jewish women's experience, providing significant insights into the phenomena of change, separation, alienation, and border-crossing from a woman's point of view.

To be sure, in comparison with the work of the early Hebrew women poets, who embraced the Land of Israel and the experience of immigration as primary sources of female literary and creative inspiration, Baron's fiction, which often leaves its protagonists in the Diaspora, represents a very different kind of writing. While the poetry of Rachel (Bluwstein), Esther Raab, and Leah Goldberg celebrates the new motherland of Israel and grieves over its poverty and its parched, unfamiliar landscape, Baron's fiction (when it touches upon these topics) typically depicts Zionist immigration either as a male phenomenon from which women are excluded or as a thoroughly futile exercise.[29] Baron's fictions of female "non-immigration," as I call them, often employ and overturn fairy-tale motifs, thereby demystifying all happily-ever-after notions of upward and lateral mobility, and frequently portray women whose lives remain woefully circumscribed by the conditions of domestic servitude and exile.[30] In one story after another, the reader encounters women who are anchored to the threshold, in limbo between outside and inside, the old world and the new, widowhood and marriage, *galut* and the Land of Israel.

This is not to say that Baron was the only Hebrew writer who depicted exile or denied the utopian promise of immigration. In his novel *Shekhol vekishalon* (Breakdown and bereavement) as well as in many of his other stories and essays, Y. H. Brenner repeatedly portrays life in Palestine as if nothing significant had changed from life in the Pale: "The same ghetto with all its attributes!" writes Brenner in "Mikan umikan."[31] In his novel *Temol shilshom* (Only yesterday), S. Y. Agnon offers a similarly pessimistic picture of the Zionist immigrant experience, portraying an immigrant protagonist (Yitshak Kummer) who achieves none of his Zionist goals of working the land but who instead retreats into the shtetl-like environment of the old *Yishuv* in Jerusalem and meets an absurd death as a result of a dog bite.

What differentiates Baron's writing from these male writers is her persistent focus on female non-immigration and her preference of exile rather than homecoming as the site of her woman-centered fiction. To adapt Sandra Gilbert and Susan Gubar's observations about nineteenth-century Anglo-American women writers, Baron both participated in and "swerved away" from the central sequences of Hebrew male literary history, "enacting a uniquely female process of revision and redefinition that necessarily caused her to seem 'odd'"[32] but that also offered great benefit. Like Mary Carmichael, Virginia Woolf's persona in *A Room of One's Own*, who, when denied entrance into the Oxbridge library, contemplates "how unpleasant it is to be locked out" but "how it is worse perhaps to be locked in,"[33] Baron seems to have been aware of the aesthetic benefits of remaining outside the mainstream. As Nurit Govrin suggests,

> The choice to remain within the realm of the Lithuanian *shtetl,* and to barely touch upon the Israeli reality was a means of placing a barrier between herself and the prevailing trends of fiction in Israel, especially after World War I. Thus, she emphasized her special position, and declared her own private fictional territory. . . . This was a bold step, a kind of individualistic declaration of independence . . . in this generation, the Zionist politics and education of which preached a complete rejection of the Diaspora.[34]

By resisting the dominant trends of Hebrew fiction of her day, Baron effectively resisted assimilation into the mainstream of male Hebrew letters. Instead she carved out her own distinct literary space. Paradoxically, it was from this self-created outside vantage point that Baron depicted and protested (especially in her earlier stories) the marginal, outsider status of Jewish women, offering important countertraditional versions and explanations of their lives.

Baron's fictional corpus comprises two parts: a collection of forty-three collected stories, which she endorsed and published in various book collections—most important, a 1951 collection entitled *Parshiyyot;* and a roughly equal number of published but uncollected stories that she selected out of her canon and which were unavailable to the general reading public until Nurit Govrin published a full collection in 1988.[35] As Baron's daughter Tzipporah Aharonovitz relates in her introduction to *Agav orha* (Incidentally),[36] Baron repudiated all her early stories, dubbing them *smartutim* (rags) and scorning all commentators who mentioned them in their critical essays.[37] Ironically, in one of these early texts, a story called "Genizah" (Burial, 1908),[38] Baron employs this same word, *smartut,* to refer to those "women's texts" that are unjustly cast aside by masculine tradition as ragged, unholy remnants. In this story, a young rabbi's daughter (often seen as a depiction of Baron herself) fights for her right to store her mother's old torn *tkhines* book—a volume that her rabbi-father regards as a worthless *smartut*—among the *shemos* (names), those sacred Hebrew texts mentioning the name of God, which, when tattered or worn, must be buried in the communal *genizah,* a synagogue or community storeroom.[39]

Critics have attempted to account in various ways for Baron's decision in the second half of her career to repudiate her earlier "women's texts," to marginalize those very works that protest female marginality and exclusion from mainstream male experience. According to Nurit Govrin, many of the early stories are aesthetically inferior to her later, more polished works; others divulge too much personal, autobiographical information, deal too explicitly with erotic themes, or protest too stridently against the oppression of women in shtetl society in comparison with her later, more subtle treatments of the subject.[40] According to Lily Rattok, Baron's decision to disavow her earlier, more overtly feminist work represents a problematic "acceptance of a patriarchal script."[41] In contrast, Naomi Seidman discusses the importance of cloth remnants and castoffs for female crafts and considers the possibility that Baron's decision to call her earliest stories "rags" is "more evidence of self-irony" than "self-denigration." Seidman's analysis of Baron's thematic reworking of these earlier fictional *smartutim* in her later work points to a kind of "feminine ingenuity in creating art from the discarded and outworn."[42] A related possibility, I believe, is that by distancing herself from those earlier texts that loudly protest the exclusion of women from mainstream male experience, Baron allowed herself in her later work to transform marginality from a vice into a virtue. In many of the earlier stories, including the ones examined in this chapter, Baron's female protagonists protest but also conspire in their own detested marginality, fostering a dependence on male agency and authority, yet her later protagonists begin to find solace in the notion of a separate female community of experience. By rereading her later work in light of the earlier stories, we begin to appreciate the ways in which these stories creatively reinterpret—rather than repudiate—her former attempts to protest fiction and women-centered "marginal" prose. A re-examination of these stories in terms of issues of space and place, center and margin, location and dislocation provides a graphic picture of which cultural and social borders Baron's fiction attempts to transgress or reinforce.

One early story by Baron that addresses the subject of female location and dislocation is "Tiyyul 'ivri" (Hebrew outing), published in 1904, when Baron was seventeen years old and teaching, writing, and participating in Zionist organizations in Kovno. Nurit Govrin has described "Hebrew Outing" as "an exemplary Zionist story" that depicts Baron's involvement with the women Hebrew-speakers association.[43] But if this is a Zionist story, it is notable not for nationalist enthusiasm and hope but for its expression of unfulfilled promise, estrangement, and despair. Written as a lament over the recent death of Theodor Herzl some two months before, the story tells of the young female narrator's experience on a boat and hiking trip with a group of other Hebrew-speaking women on an excruciatingly hot and sunny day. The entire story is characterized by a mood of disquietude and discomfort. The narrator reluctantly accepts an invitation to join this field trip. During the boat ride, she becomes noticeably homesick for her hometown and rather bored by the Hebrew conversations of her peers. Upon disembarking from the boat, the young women in the group hurry to escape the sun by climbing up a mountain *(har)* where they relax in the shade *(tsel)*—two Hebrew words that when combined spell the name of the Zionist hero "Herzl." For a brief moment, the protective *har-tsel* (shady mountain), symbolic of Herzl's ideology of nationalist Zionist regeneration, together with the Hebrew conversations of her female peers, fills the narrator with a fleeting sense of promise and faith, an enthusiastic yearning for "a beautiful land, a wonderful land, a land of milk and honey beyond the mountain" (*Parshiyyot mukdamot,* p. 368). This Zionist epiphany is enlarged through a reference to a midrash the narrator hears from the mouth of an old religious man sitting next to her (or imagines herself hearing in a nostalgic backward glance to her hometown). In this midrash on Song of Songs 4:8, taken from Exodus Rabbah 23, a mountain called Amana—which can be variably pronounced as *emunah,* the Hebrew word for "faith"—is identified as the geographical dividing line between Israel and the countries that border it. In adducing this midrashic reference, Baron's narrator seems to equate Herzl, as represented by *Har-tsel,* the shady mountain, with the very concept of faith. Baron's introduction of this fleeting expression of Zionist faith through the figure of a traditional Jew (ironically?), juxtaposing Herzlian Zionism with traditional Jewish theology and text, indicates the multiple gaps of faith and conflicting viewpoints experienced by this female narrator as she scales the Zionist heights of the mountain. Indeed, the narrator's moment of Zionist elation soon dissipates. The boat whistle blows, and the young women are called away for the return ride, during which they pass by a farming village where women farmers are harvesting wheat and singing a Russian folk song about the motherland. In a moment of nationalist yearning, the narrator attempts to translate their song into Hebrew but cannot; she is alone and bereft of her "mother" (land). The essential loneliness of the narrator of this story despite the company of her Hebrew-speaking female peers, her evanescent sense of contentment and sisterhood experienced only during a moment of identification with a deceased male Zionist leader, and the ever present hot sun beating down on her head all suggest futility and exile, rather than belief in Jewish (female) border-crossing or homecoming.

In "Tiyyul 'ivri," a community of women presents no remedy for the narrator's feelings of estrangement from her environment, while her association of visions of the motherland with the male Herzl/*har-tsel* hints at her identification with the agency of a male leader or representative. In another early story, entitled "Fedka" (1909),[44] Baron develops this idea of female exile and dependence on masculine agency in her depiction of the lives of shtetl women left behind in the old world while their men emigrate to distant lands. Almost all the Jewish townsmen have abandoned their female loved ones and sailed away, creating a community of *'agunot* (living widows), who are suspended somewhere between marriage and widowhood, between the past and an uncertain vision of the future. The sense of suspended and undirected time in this story is reinforced by the narrative technique of habitual exposition. Time passes and yet recurs in this portrayal of the everyday lives of the Jewish townswomen. Day after day the women greet and project all their repressed desires on Fedka, the Gentile postman who brings them letters from their husbands.

Virtually the only adult male in the town, Fedka becomes a surrogate husband/lover for the Jewish women. He is portrayed as a creature of immense masculinity and allure, narcissistically thriving on the attentions of the abandoned females. His towering height is described in language reminiscent of descriptions of the biblical Saul[45]—"from his shoulders and upward he was taller than any of the group around him" (*Parshiyyot mukdamot*, p. 444); a subtle irony is embedded in this allusion, for Fedka is considered tall only in relation to the community of women that surrounds him. Baron lavishes descriptive attention on the details of Fedka's would-be imposing physical appearance and sexual presence—a trumped-up fantasy of Gentile male sexuality. His attractive postal uniform with its shiny buttons and stripes, an almost parodic version of a heroic soldier's uniform; his dark complexion; his black curly hair, which bounces as he walks, "striking against his forehead, all at once scratching-tickling, scraping-caressing" (*Parshiyyot mukdamot*, p. 444): all these details heighten the sexual tension and energy inherent in Fedka's relations with the Jews.

Throughout the story Fedka's movements and actions remain highly tactile and sensuous. As he delivers the letters to the women, he lingers and teases like a lover, fingering, folding, and crushing the letters sitting in his satchel. The Jewish women willingly embrace this fantasy of the Gentile male, participating in a love-plot that mixes audacious female sexuality with conventional notions of female weakness and passivity. As Fedka approaches the Jewish neighborhood, he finds the women in their flimsy house clothes, situated by various doorways, corridors, and balconies—architectural openings that suggest female erotic receptivity. They rush out blushingly to greet him, and he, in turn, penetrates into the physical center of his admiring "flock."

Fedka repeatedly engages in acts of penetration or unlocking on behalf of the women, and the women respond with all the features of erotic excitement. He pulls out a letter from his pack and calls out the name of its recipient: "the woman stretches out all her ten fingers toward the letter, her blood pulsing through her veins" (*Parshiyyot mukdamot*, p. 444). Fedka opens the letter for her, and his slow, lingering movements highlight the meaning of this act as a form of seduction or disrobing of the private matters of this woman's personal life. Often as he passes out the letters, a flushed and panting woman will come forward, asking him to help her pull the cork out of a bottle, another erotically charged act, symbolizing the masculine opening up or unlocking of a sealed, private space.

The women praise Fedka's strength in terms ironically reminiscent of Jewish liturgy. *Habriyyot mekalsot;* (The creatures praise); *Yedei gever, yedei gever!* (The hands of a man, the hands of a man! *Parshiyyot mukdamot*, p. 445). The women chant their praises using language both sexual, in its emphasis upon hands and masculine virility, and liturgical, in its allusion to traditional praises of the strength of God. Together, the postman and the women act out a fantasy in which the super-virile Fedka becomes pseudo-Jewish lord of every household. He playfully recites the Hebrew blessing over the bread; likewise, the women imagine him reciting the kiddush, emphasizing their willing dependence on male religious as well as sexual power. When fires break out in the town, and the frantic Jewish women curse their luck and throw up their hands in despair, it is Fedka who comes to their rescue. "How will I ever pay you back for all your kindness, Fedka? Perhaps on your wedding day" (literally, "on the day of your canopy," p. 446), suggests one woman, intimating a reciprocation through female sexual favors, perhaps even marriage. The implausibility of this arrangement of reciprocity is immediately suggested through the use of the term *hupah* to connote the wedding ceremony. Of course, all these women have already entered into the

235

Jewish *hupah* of marriage. Fedka provides his own refutation to this idea, in an outwardly playful, but inwardly serious, way: "But how would I ever get married when I am cared for by tens of women?" (p. 446). In reality, Fedka is (and like the stereotypical playboy, wants to be) everyone's, and at the same time, no one's, lover. He is a completely unattainable object, and in their devotion to him, the women's static, liminal position is reinforced. The story begins with a description of Fedka rising with the sun and facing the east, symbolic of Jewish prayer (facing east) and redemption, yet it ends at night, with the ominous ringing of church bells, and with a description of Fedka's usual angry reaction to the visit/return of an immigrant Jewish husband. Baron thus depicts a recurrent, futile scheme of approach and retreat, of quasi-erotic union between Fedka and the women, and then a break in their relations.

Curiously, Baron's own experience of immigrating to Palestine in 1910 did not drastically alter her approach to the subject of the female "non-immigrant" experience. In such stories as "Be'eizeh 'olam?" (In what world?) and "Ke'aleh nidaf" (As a driven leaf), both of which were published in Palestine rather than Eastern Europe, Baron's female heroines imagine alternative realms but remain largely dependent upon Fedka-like male figures to bring messages or take them back across the border. Both these stories employ and revise folktale motifs as a means of questioning utopian fairy-tale notions of immigration and social mobility. Like a "Sleeping Beauty" who never wakes up, the heroines of these stories assume a tragically liminal status, belonging neither to the old world nor to the new.

"Be'eizeh 'olam?" (1910), the first story Baron published after immigrating to Palestine, echoes the concern shown in "Tiyyul 'Ivri" for women left in exile when the men in their lives immigrate to better places. As the title itself suggests, the story deals with the predicament of a young woman who is caught between two worlds: Russia and Palestine, reality and fantasy. The protagonist of the story is a young girl named Rachel, whose *teacher* father has died and whose mother has been forced to take on a demeaning job as a live-in domestic servant for a wealthy Jewish family. An imaginative and intellectually ambitious young woman, Rachel constantly dreams of a better life. She fantasizes about leaving her hometown to study in the city in the *gymnasium*. She pictures the sudden acquisition of great wealth or intellectual attainment that would allow her and her ailing mother some social mobility. Finally, she imagines being whisked away to Palestine by a Zionist "Prince Charming" named David.

The story is told in first-person, present-tense time by Rachel, and it closely follows Rachel's thoughts as they shift back and forth between reality and fantasy. An avid reader of the Bible as well as of secular folklore, Rachel fashions her dream-visions out of a mix of biblical stories and fairy-tales. Her Zionist friend David spurs her on to these imaginings, urging her to see her life within the biblical/legendary context of Jewish redemption and Zionist return. He shows her pictures of the grave of her namesake, the matriarch Rachel, who was buried on the road to Efrat—a reference to unfulfilled desire and mortality that serves as a subtle omen that all will not go well with this budding relationship. David shares with her his own plans to immigrate to Palestine, showing her pictures of his Zionist female cousin riding bareback in Petah Tikvah. Rachel ignores this hint that he may have another romantic interest and fantasizes about his taking her with him. Like Fedka, who revels in the devotions of the Jewish townswomen, David encourages these imaginings by telling Rachel a Rapunzel-like Jewish fairy-tale of love that transcends class boundaries, a story of redemption and immigration:

> Once upon a time there was a prince, who fell in love with the daughter of his wet nurse and arranged to meet with her every day. When his father, the king, discovered this, he decreed that his son be removed from the palace, and as for the wet nurse and her daughter, he shut them up in a tall, dark tower. What did the prince do? He secluded himself in his house of worship, cried, and prayed for three days and three nights. He prayed for God to perform a miracle on his behalf—that wings should sprout from his back. On the third day, his wish was granted. Two wide wings, white like snow, suddenly grew out of his back. That very same night the prince rose up to the sky and flew between heaven and earth toward the tall tower, where he tapped against the window.
>
> "Who are you?"
>
> "My child, my child, how your face glows!"
>
> "My light comes from the splendor of your face, my Lord Prince."
>
> "My child, my child. With what have you been busying yourself all this time?"
>
> "Hair after hair I have pulled from my head. One by one I have intertwined them to make a case for your prayer shawl, my Lord Prince."
>
> "And what else have you done, my beautiful bride?"
>
> "Thin threads I have spun. Day and night I have woven them, to make us a blue *[tekhelet]* marriage canopy, my Lord, my Prince."
>
> Immediately the prince embraced his beloved, and spread his white wings, flapping them once, twice—and lo and behold, they ascended between heaven and earth, flying and floating in the sky like the angels, until they reached a large solitary island, a huge garden in the middle of the ocean. (*Parshiyyot mukdamot*, pp. 530–31)

Baron's insertion of this fairy-tale plot into a story otherwise characterized by realistic stream-of-consciousness narrative creates a stark contrast, emphasizing the gap between Rachel's romantic hopes and her real prospects. If the Jewish townswomen in "Fedka" endeavor vainly to escape the boredom and uncertainty of their lives through a form of fantastic eroticism that can never truly be consummated, Rachel similarly attempts to escape poverty and stasis through the medium of fairy-tale romance, literal and literary.

By interpreting David's story as an allegory of his love for her and a Zionist pledge to bring her and her mother to the Land of Israel, Rachel glosses over a whole series of disturbing class and gender elements in this tale, beginning with the prince's choice to address his beloved as "my child," suggesting an ongoing disparity in their status. This imbalance in the relations between the prince and the girl is compounded by her willingness to subject herself to self-sacrifice—pulling the hairs out of her head—to create a piece of female handiwork to encase his prayer shawl, a ritual object traditionally used only by men, the Jewish ritual elite. As in the Rapunzel story, the young girl puts her body, specifically her hair, in the service of a man. Unlike in the fairy tale, however, in which Rapunzel grows her hair and, as Bruno Bettelheim explains, finds "the means of escaping her predicament in her own body," indicating that one's body can provide a sense of security,"[46] the young girl in David's story violates the integrity of her body, tearing out her hair in a manner evocative more of mourning rituals (as we will see later in this chapter) than strategies of escape. The prince's godlike ability to transcend the norms of nature, to grow wings and miraculously breach the tower of her solitude, suggests the extent to which he remains the source of spiritual and physical power in the tale. Moreover, his decision to transplant his beloved and her mother from one site of female solitude (the tower) to another (a solitary island) signals that she has not been liberated; instead, proprietary rights have shifted from one male sovereign (the king) to another (the prince). Nevertheless, Rachel allows herself to merge imaginatively with the protagonist of the fairy tale. The borderline between fantasy and reality blurs completely when Rachel, like the masochistic young maiden in the legend, embroiders a beautiful case for David's prayer shawl as a pledge of her love. David finally immigrates to Palestine to join his uncle (and presumably to marry his uncle's daughter) in Petah Tikvah.

The tragic ending of her story, a harsh revision of David's fairy tale of princely redemption, finds Rachel, orphaned now of both her father and mother, living and working secluded (as if in a tall dark tower, like Rapunzel) with David's widowed mother, who has also been left behind. Instead of crafting a *tallit* bag or marriage canopy, as in the fairy tale— a lofty, religiously inspired form of work—their job involves cutting pieces of paper and rolling them into cigarettes for a local factory, occasionally rereading an old letter from David to break the monotony. Each time she rereads the letter, Rachel conjures up impossible images of herself picking oranges in a Jaffa orchard, and of David—a modern incarnation of the biblical shepherd-king—standing at the top of a hill next to the ruins of an ancient fortress, shepherding his large flock, and she momentarily loses her sense of reality. "My God, my God, what world am I in?" Rachel asks. "And in what world will I be?" The ending of this narrative, which gives the story its title, is both clumsy and hyperdramatic, yet it encapsulates Rachel's predicament: caught between imagination and grim reality. Unlike David, who manages to actualize his dream of immigrating to Palestine, Rachel is stuck in the old world, living her dreams vicariously.

"Be'eizeh 'olam?" was originally published as a children's story in *Moledet: Yarhon livnei hane'urim.* It was roundly criticized by contemporary critics for its Diasporic emphasis, as well as for its failure to provide "a lively and refreshing" depiction of the new generation and new life in the Land of Israel.[47] These negative responses to Baron's story clearly reflect her marginal position, not only as a woman writer of Hebrew prose but as a writer unwilling to subscribe to the orthodoxies of the Zionist literary world of which she was an active member—as literary editor of the Labor Zionist *Hapoel Hatza'ir,* and later as the wife of activist/editor Yosef Aharonovitz.

Baron's later story, "Ke'aleh nidaf" (1948), goes even further in its rejection of Zionist literary orthodoxy by transplanting the exilic angst of earlier stories such as "Tiyyul 'ivri," and "Be'eizeh 'olam?" to the Land of Israel itself. The story's title, derived from a verse in Job 13:24–25, in which the unfairly stricken Job queries God about the justice of his pursuit of a man already defeated as "a driven leaf," intimates a plot of innocent suffering and uprootedness. A quieter and more restrained but no less tragic tale of failed immigration, "Ke'aleh nidaf" tells the story of a young female immigrant to Palestine named Mirl, who, like Rachel in "Be'eizeh 'olam?" comes to stake her life's hopes on the attentions and redemptions of a man. Mirl has immigrated to Palestine very reluctantly, at the behest of her mother, who, seeing the young people stream out of their town, became worried about her daughter's *takhlis* (literally, her "end" or "goal," and figuratively, her marriage prospects). After hearing a fairy-tale story about the cobbler's daughter Hava-Rachel, who immigrated to Palestine and married a wealthy landowner, Mirl's mother encourages her daughter to sacrifice the security of home for the sake of her marriage prospects. Little good results from the move, however: the daughter meets her "end" indeed, but not in the way her concerned mother had hoped.

As in the shtetl, here, too, Mirl works as a domestic servant, in a house furnished and decorated in a manner reminiscent of the house where she lived and worked before immigrating to Palestine. The similarity of the furnishings heightens the sense of futility surrounding Mirl's immigration, intensifying her feelings of loneliness and nostalgia. Fortunately, she makes friends with an aging cook who lives across the street, a woman of similar class, who remains nameless throughout the story, addressed and mentioned only as "the cook," or "the helper"— symbolic of her own nameless status in her community. Mirl pours out her heart to the cook, sharing her sense of alienation from everything she ever knew or cared about; this is epitomized by the experience of her voyage, during which she sat alone on the ship, feeling a Job-like disconnection from her former life, "forever detached, like a torn thread, or . . . like a leaf that has fallen from a tree."[48] Mirl's sense of alienation as a result of her Zionist immigration recalls the feelings of estrangement experienced by the narrator of "Tiyyul 'Ivri," but stands in stark contrast to the Zionist and romantic longings of Rachel in "Be'eizeh 'olam?" What emerges from a joint reading of these stories is a sense of deep ambivalence about the issue. On the one hand, Diaspora life is associated with class discrimination, purposeless, and rootlessness; on the other hand, life in the Land of Israel seems to offer no real alternative to this condition. The cook consoles Mirl by telling her if she has "ascended" (immigrated) to the Land of Israel, so can her mother "ascend," compelling Mirl to direct all her energies toward achieving the goal of bringing her mother to Palestine: a counterpoint to her mother's goal of Mirl's finding the perfect husband in Israel.

Indeed, Mirl keeps her new goal uppermost in her mind until the spring—the traditional season of romantic desire—when Borik, the youngest son of her mistress, comes to visit his mother, and Mirl gradually falls prey to marriage fantasies of her own. Borik's arrival underscores her position as an outsider in the household, a lowly servant, yet Mirl is inspired by this reunion of mother and child. She also is moved by the romantic interest shown her by Borik. Like David, Rachel's would-be redeemer in "B'eizeh 'olam?" Borik fills Mirl with hopes for better things. Mirl is particularly affected by Borik's reaction to a cut she gets while cleaning out a drawer. Here a wound, which would otherwise be considered a minor mishap, becomes fraught with meaning: "Once, when she was straightening out his drawer in the washroom, she cut herself on his razor, and he came to dress the wound. It was amusing to see his alarm when a drop of blood spurted out, as though she had never cut herself before in her mistress' house with the choppers and knives, every one of which was as sharp as the razor" (*Parshiyyot,* p. 551). Mirl is amused both by Borik's upper-class ignorance of the realities of domestic service and his extravagant concern. Still, this incident has a dark, foreboding aspect. Reminiscent of folktale pricking scenes (i.e., the beginning of the story of Snow White, where the queen pricks herself with a needle in the course of sewing, subsequently gives birth to Snow White, and dies in childbirth), this account of penetration and bloodletting becomes a two-edged metaphor, signifying both sexual initiation/awakening and death. In the same way that bleeding leads to light-headedness and disorientation, Mirl's cut and Borik's subsequent attentions throw her off her balance and direction. Throughout the story, she is reminded of this initial pricking incident, and each time she becomes dizzy and unsteady, "the visions of the world darken[ing] and blur[ring] before her" (*Parshiyyot,* p. 558). Mirl's disorientation before Borik—her social superior—reminds her of the feeling she experienced back in Russia when she crossed the wobbly bridge over the river from her town toward the countess' estate—symbolic of her desire for class mobility as well as for sensual gratification. Like the countess' garden, filled with delicate flowers, fragrances, and lush greenery, Borik's attentions hold forth a promise—albeit illusory—of beauty and luxury.

As the story progresses, Borik continues to pursue Mirl, despite this class barrier—despite the fact that a match has already been arranged for him with the daughter of a wealthy orchard owner. Thus he is identified with reckless, fiery, animal passion, an image reinforced by the burning cigarette that hangs constantly from his mouth. When a friend from Mirl's native town brings his brother to meet her and Borik sees the two of them chatting on the street outside the house, "his eyes, beneath his angry brow, ignite like the cigarette in his mouth," and he stares at Mirl as "a wolf would a lamb" (*Parhiyyot,* p. 553). In interpreting the story of Little Red Riding Hood (another folktale about sexual initiation, as signaled by the blood-red color of the girl's cap), Rudolf Meyer decodes the wolf as a symbol of "the attractions of the sense-world"; Little Red Riding Hood herself represents the "young soul-power" who goes to visit the grandmother, symbolic of the "primal ancestor," but "can no longer find the primal wisdom when she reaches down into her own depths: the wolf has seized the formative forces within her."[49] In venturing out of her mother's house into the home of the old widow in Palestine, Mirl becomes a kind of Little Red Riding Hood, but without the protective agency of the kind woodsman. So long as she maintains her goal of bringing her mother to Israel, she is safe; as soon as she allows the lure of sensual/sexual passion as represented by Borik to replace this goal, she is consumed.

During the Passover celebrations, Borik continues to flirt with Mirl, showing her his picture albums by candlelight, leaning over and "breathing warmly on her bare neck" (*Parshiyyot*, p. 556). A few days later, however, Mirl learns of his engagement to the orchard owner's daughter. (Here, the orange grove, part of Rachel's Zionist fantasy in "Be'eizeh 'olam?" becomes the site of thwarted desire.) Mirl's friend the cook is not home to console her, and thus she is left utterly alone to face her disappointment. Recapitulating the initial pricking incident one last time, Mirl takes up one of Borik's razors and digs into her old scar, extending it until it becomes a fatal wound: "From among the linens that her mother gave her for that day 'when her luck would shine,' she took out a towel and wrapped her arm, went out and sat down on the bench outside, where, as during her sad lonely moments on the ship, there was nothing but stars and evening silence; as in that time, she felt as though she was floating lightly in endless space, alone and forever detached, as a leaf fallen from a tree" (*Parshiyyot*, p. 558).

Mirl's immigrant experience is thus framed, at its beginning and its tragic end, by her sense of herself as floating endlessly and inescapably toward oblivion. She does not come in or "ascend" (*la'a lot* in Zionist Hebrew parlance). For Mirl, the act of border-crossing thus becomes the ultimate exercise in futility, symbolized by her use of the linens designated for her *takhlis* as a bandage to stave off her inevitable death. As a "driven leaf," she has been severed forever from her roots, tossed about, and battered, but unlike the biblical Job, who used the same metaphor to plead his case before God, Mirl never hears God's voice in the whirlwind. She has come to the Jewish homeland, but contrary to the Zionist dream, she has no hope of being replanted and revivified in this new soil.[50]

As my readings of "Be'eizeh 'olam?" and "Ke'aleh nidaf" suggest, Baron's interest in the idea of failed immigration continues in her later fiction, despite her decision to immigrate to Palestine and her commitment to Zionist ideals. Almost all Baron's later fiction is set in the Jewish exile of the shtetl rather than in Palestine, and these stories all deal just as persistently with the exilic or liminal condition of women. Even the novella *Le'eit 'atah* (For now), part of which is set in the Palestinian *Yishuv*, is more about exile than homecoming; ninety percent of the work deals with the Turkish expulsion of Jewish settlers to Egypt during World War I. Likewise, "A Day in the Life of Rami," a story about a child who wanders off from home and gets lost in the Tel Aviv streets, focuses primarily on homelessness and empty, childless homes.

A number of significant changes or revisions do appear in Baron's later, more canonical stories. On a stylistic level, the overt tone of protest disappears and is replaced by a subtler, more restrained, and, in some cases, more optimistic treatment. In terms of plot and thematic development, Baron's later female protagonists often demonstrate greater personal agency, if not complete control, over their fates, and they are frequently rewarded for their trials. In such stories as "Mishpahah" (Family)—discussed in the previous chapter—"Derekh kotsim" (The thorny path), and the novella *Le'eit 'atah*, the hardships or failures suffered by women are compensated through the successes of their (most often, male) children.[51] In other stories, the margins of female exclusion are broadened to encompass alternate social roles, realms of beauty and promise, and the consoling company of female community. Like Baron's idiosyncratic, non-mainstream subject matter—and like her eccentric thirty-three years of seclusion in a Tel Aviv apartment with Israeli society growing and building up all around her—the fictional women of Baron's later stories remain in the margins, mustering their efforts and achieving their consolations within a private outsider world of women.

In two such stories, "Masa" (Journey, 1951) and "Ketanot" (Little things, 1933), Baron's dire depictions of female abandonment begin to offer some form of consolation. Both these stories are presented as a female narrator's recollections of her summertime visits to her aunt's house in the nearby town of Khmilovka, a narrative structure that points toward the redemptive possibilities both of female story-telling and female community. The niece-narrator is an adventurous young girl. Her aunt is the daughter of a miller, whose youth was abruptly cut short when she was married off to the weak and sickly rabbi of Khmilovka.[52]

243

An unhappy martyr of a system of prearranged marriages (in "Ketanot" Baron compares her to the biblical female martyr, Jephthah's daughter),[53] she now lives a lonely life with her sickly scholar-husband, yearning, like Emma Bovary, for a better, more beautiful life.[54]

Reminiscent of the allegorical treatment of Zionist yearning and journeying in "Tiyyul 'Ivri," "Masa" is an allegory of failed border-crossing or aliyah. The narrator tells us that every summer she and her aunt would take walks down in the valley by the Usha River. Together they would look longingly (like Mirl in "Ke'aleh nidaf") at the countess' estate across the river, a "green mountain" that the young girl compares to the Garden of Eden. The aunt's longings begin to enter into and cleave to the heart of the young niece-narrator. When she returns to her aunt's house in the early spring and once again walks along the river, she notices a great spread of ice floes, arranged in rows like the scales of a fish, flowing together southward, as if toward some sort of goal that seems to beckon her: "When I glanced across to the 'green mountain,' and I saw that the gate at the entrance of the estate was open, and none of the guards was standing by, I mounted *['aliti]* one of the pieces of ice that seemed solid to me, and floated along with the others, a clod of earth among other clods, conjoined with them in my similar aspiration toward a goal" (*Parshiyyot,* p. 201). One obvious interpretation of this story concerns the notion of class mobility: the disappearance of the guards at the gate suggests a temporary weakening of class barriers, which the narrator hopes to transgress.

A close reading of the language that Baron employs here to describe the young narrator's "journey" points to another possible rendering of this story as an allegory of Zionist aspiration. While the Land of Israel and the Zionist project are never directly mentioned in the story, Baron's prose ripples with Zionist undercurrents. Her description of the ice floes migrating southward as if toward some *matarah,* some great collective purpose; her depiction of herself as "ascending" *('aliti)* onto the ice floes, as one who ascends to the Land of Israel, and conjoining with a larger collective purpose; her comparison of herself to a clod of earth among other clods, which suggests a melding of purpose with that of the earth or "Land"—these elements suggest that this short piece is about the disappointments of Zionist immigration and the impossibility of reaching the great goals trumpeted by the collective movement.

For although the ice floes seem directed toward some ultimate, certain destination, they do not allow the young narrator to achieve her own purpose. The stability of her ice floes proves illusory, and the aspiring narrator never achieves her goal of crossing the river to the open gates of the countess' estate. Instead, she falls into the river divide, only to be fished out by farmers from a nearby village, and forced to run a gauntlet of disapproving family members and derisive children. "Only my aunt looked out at me with a sense of shared understanding," the narrator recalls:

> For she, with her inner wisdom, understood—and later I came to understand this as well—that this, in essence, was a very daring act on my part, an effort to cross over from a troubled world to one that was better. Granted, the "sailboat" that I chose for my journey was strange. And yet people, in their eternal aspirations for what is good, often choose varying modes of transportation. Departing for that desired place, one will sit on a handkerchief spread out over the waters; another will take off in a chariot of fire; and even Jacob, on that wondrous night in Bethel, we know not the nature of his ladder, and yet it was the means he used to reach the very presence of God. (*Parshiyyot,* p. 201)

In this passage, a simple act of childhood mischief or transgression is raised to a mythical level, with the young narrator being compared at once to a hero riding a magic handkerchief, to Elijah in his chariot of fire—an image associated with messianic redemption—and to Jacob ascending a ladder to the heavens. These analogies augment the transgressiveness of the "journey," in that they juxtapose female domestic and personal striving with traditional male narratives of ascent and transcendence. The role of the rabbi's wife as friend and mentor to the narrator suggests shared female striving and commiseration. Although the young narrator fails to achieve her stated goal and is derided by the mainstream community, she receives solace from her aunt, who understands the importance and significance of her quest.

As in "Masa," the focus in the longer story "Ketanot" is on the power of female community as an antidote to the predicament of spiritual exile. The title of the story, which can be alternately translated as "Small [feminine] things" or "Small [feminine] ones," ironically points out the negative evaluation assigned by the mainstream community both to women and to matters of feminine concern. In comparison to the word *masa,* which conjures up various (masculine) heroic notions of journeying and exploring, this story announces from the outset its concern with marginal matters. Insofar as "small things" are valorized and writ large in the story, the negative mainstream evaluation of things marginal and feminine is challenged and subverted.

The narrator of "Ketanot" is the niece of a *rebbetzin* (rabbi's wife), who is presumably the focus of the story. Yet the tale begins digressively with several "small" incidental portraits: the *rebbetzin's* father, whose greatest affections are given to his cows (in marked contrast to his moderate interest in his granddaughters); and the *rebbetzin's* mother-in-law, a harsh, male-identified, lineage-conscious woman who accepts her bumpkin daughter-in-law into the family only grudgingly. These character sketches seem to displace the rabbi's wife from her central position in the story; in actuality, they help emphasize her extreme loneliness in light of her mismatched marriage and the fact that she has disappointed everyone by repeatedly giving birth to daughters and no sons. Baron amplifies this one "small" story of female alienation by adducing a similar but more extreme one. Next door to the rabbi and his wife live the cobbler and his wife, Elka-Sarah, who has continued to give birth only to daughters and thus is regularly beaten by her husband. In describing Elka-Sarah's fate, the niece-narrator quotes Isaiah 54:6: "For the Lord has called thee a woman forsaken and grieved in spirit."[55] Significantly, in this story the narrator does not include the consoling second half of the verse: "But as a wife of youth, can she be cast off? For a small moment, I have forsaken you but with great mercies will I gather you." For Elka-Sarah, there are no verses of consolation. Every year she gives birth to yet another daughter, and each time her husband beats her mercilessly and then drags her to the rabbi's house (the narrator's uncle) demanding a *get*, a bill of divorce. Every year the rabbi offers various reasons why the cobbler and his wife should remain united in marriage. Despite the rabbi's efforts to bring peace to the household, no reconciliation ever occurs between Elka-Sarah and her husband. The narrator's association of her aunt with Elka-Sarah and of Elka-Sarah with images of Jewish exile is enlarged by the coincidental fact that Elka-Sarah gives birth to her daughters every summer during the three weeks of Jewish mourning for the destruction of the Temple in Jerusalem. Her biological cycle thus mimics, even supersedes, the Jewish national experience of exile. If in masculine tradition marginal female figures—the widow, abandoned wife, and barren woman—are used as metaphors for the suffering People of Israel, in this story the sufferings of Israel become a metaphor for the persecution of an unwanted daughter or wife.

As if to compensate for this condition of female marginalization, Elka-Sarah and the narrator's aunt discover sympathy, kinship, and "small things" of wonder and beauty within the private society of other women. Literally as well as figuratively, it is in the women's gallery of the synagogue that Elka-Sarah is able to reveal her beaten arms to her friend the rabbi's wife, confess her misery, and seek female sympathy. Similarly, it is in the company of other women that the rabbi's wife is able to nourish and keep alive her aspirations for beauty and fulfillment. During a visit to the narrator's home in Zhizhikovka, the rabbi's wife sees, in her city-born sister-in-law's dowry chest, a pair of embroidered house slippers, a symbol for this beauty-starved *rebbetzin* not only of dazzling beauty but also of distant places, freedom, and homecoming. The narrator comments: "By dint of their imagination—a gift, that like the sunlight, is vouchsafed not only the fortunate—those stricken by fate may compensate for what life has denied them. Thus, the prisoner may see himself walking about free of his chains, and the exile may again cherish his native soil. . . . Never having seen anything of the wide world, she imagined that its mystery and magic lay in those wondrous slippers, which she had seen with her own eyes and fondled with her own fingers" (*Parshiyyot*, p. 42).[56] Like the narrator's misunderstood journey across the river in "Masa," these "trifling" slippers feed this woman's hungry imagination. Likewise, her friendship with Elka-Sarah's eldest daughter, Hannah-Gittel[57]—a young woman who has been sent away to the city to work as a domestic servant for a wealthy Jewish city family—soothes her lonely soul. On the eve of Shabbat Nahamu (the Sabbath after the fast day of Tish'a Be'av, which is named *Nahamu*, "Be comforted," after the traditional *Haftarah* chanted on that Sabbath, taken from the consolation prophecy in Isaiah), Hannah-Gittel returns home for a short visit to comfort and aid her mother, who has given birth to yet another baby girl. At night the *rebbetzin* sneaks out of the house to join Hannah-Gittel in conversation. "Was this a sin," she asks herself, betraying an awareness of the transgressive power of female friendship, "to take a stroll in the fresh evening breeze with a neighbor's daughter?" (*Parshiyyot*, pp. 46–47; *The Thorny Path*, p. 54). Together, these two young women sit for hours, as Hannah-Gittel tells of the wonders and splendors of the big city. For the *rebbetzin,* these hours with Hannah-Gittel on Shabbat Nahamu, like her image of the slippers, provide a welcome respite from her monotonous life—in Nina Auerbach's terms, "an imaginative rebuke to the conventional ideal of a solitary woman living for and through men, attaining citizenship in the community of adulthood through masculine approval alone."[58]

Throughout "Ketanot," the personal experiences of women follow or supersede various observances of the Jewish calendar. In the same way that Elka-Sarah's tribulations coincide with the commemorations of Jewish sufferings, and the consoling conversations between Hannah-Gittel and the *rebbetzin* coincide with Shabbat Nahamu, the *rebbetzin* is unexpectedly summoned to appear in the district court, during the traditional period of divine judgment, the Ten Days of Repentance before Yom Kippur. As in other instances where the significance of a day shifts from national/metaphorical concerns to the literal sufferings of individual women, the transcendent notion of prayer and divine judgment is displaced by the experience of an individual woman testifying on behalf of another woman in an actual court of law. When the *rebbetzin* arrives at the district courthouse, she is shocked to discover that her friend Hannah-Gittel has been accused of committing a robbery in the home of her employers on the same Shabbat Nahamu when they spent the night in each other's company. The *rebbetzin's* friendship with Hannah-Gittel, which had previously lifted her out of her dolorous life, now compels her literally to cross from the shtetl into the big city, into a realm of female advocacy and personal discovery. The *rebbetzin* testifies on Hannah-Gittel's behalf, and the girl is exonerated. Emerging with Hannah-Gittel from the solemnity of the courtroom, the *rebbetzin* finds herself in the heart of the city, amid the tall, red-roofed buildings, the bustling streets, and the lamp-lit roadways. There, in a street-side shop window, she discovers a pair of lovely embroidered slippers, precisely like those she saw at the home of her sister-in-law. Among the jumble of dusty objects in the window (symbolic, perhaps, of the *rebbetzin's* own dull, dreary life), "the slippers shone out like a rainbow through a cloud, and for a long time she stood gazing at them, an expression of pious awe in her face, as indeed one gazes at the rainbow before saying the prescribed benediction" (*Parshiyyot*, p. 54; *The Thorny Path*, p. 65).

The trauma of Hannah-Gittel's arrest gives way to a great fulfillment, likened no less to a rainbow, the covenantal sign sent by God to Noah after the Flood. The *rebbetzin* buys the slippers and returns home. This is how the story ends: not with a permanent solution to the plight of the abused wives nor with a flourish of prophecy, but with a small, thisworldly consolation, shared among women. In "Ketanot" women find pleasure and consolation in the marginal world of female experience.

Throughout her career, Baron remained obsessed with representing the marginal status of women in Jewish culture. In her earlier stories she fought with her pen to write women into the "malestream." In her later writing she abjured protest and opted for strategic retreat, writing powerfully subversive fiction from within the small places and partitioned spaces, the conversations and commiserations of Jewish women's experience.

The Rabbi's Daughter
in and out of the Kitchen

Feminist Literary Negotiations

> Spaces can be real and imagined. Spaces can tell stories and unfold
> histories. Spaces can be interrupted, appropriated, and trans-
> formed through artistic and literary practice.
>
> BELL HOOKS

Do women write differently than men? Asked this question in a rare
interview published in the 1950s, Hebrew prose writer Devorah Baron
gave the following answer: "No. I didn't see a difference between the
writing of men and women. But women might be more capable, perhaps, of describing the life of a woman from the inside, while male writers see women only from the outside. Yes, the woman writer is better at
recognizing certain aspects of a woman's life—*all that is connected to the
kitchen, to foodstuffs, the nursery, and so on*"[1] (emphasis added). The
kitchen? The nursery? By invoking these stereotypically feminine
"inside" spaces, what did Baron mean to say about the potential distinctiveness of women's writing? Was she being ironic or flip, offering a
parodically simplistic answer to what she considered a simplistic question? Or was she honestly delineating the spaces in which so many
women's lives, and so many women's stories, have unfolded? Was she situating her own writing within this domestic realm?

One way to unravel the meaning of Baron's statement is to consider the symbolic importance of the kitchen as a marginal space that
can serve, as bell hooks has described, not just as a site of repression but
a place of resistance, a location of "radical openness" and possibility.[2] To
be sure, the primary responsibilities traditionally assigned to women—
preparing food, keeping the house, feeding and raising children—have
seriously limited their opportunities to do creative work. Yet as anthropologist Carole M. Counihan has noted, "The predominant role of

women in feeding is a cultural universal, a major component of female identity, and an important source of female connections to and influence over others. Although there are other components of female identity and other sources of their authority, the power of women has often derived from the power of food."[3] In this sense, Baron's observation about the ability of a woman writer to depict "all that is connected to the kitchen, foodstuffs, the nursery" might be interpreted as an acknowledgment that these traditional areas of female agency, authority, and power are potent sources of literary inspiration.

This chapter will interrogate the idea of kitchen-based literature through an analysis of works by three Hebrew women writers across three generations. Rachel Morpurgo's "Anaseh akh hapa'am" (Once again I'll try, 1866) represents the earliest treatment of this topic. Devorah Baron's "Mah shehayah" (What once was, 1939), a novella about the kitchen-based friendship of a young rabbi's daughter and a female baker named Mina, represents the next variation on the theme. Finally, I shall examine the poem, "Hedra shel ima hu'ar" (My mother's room is lit, 1967) by the poet Zelda (Schneerson Mishkovsky, 1914–1984), a figure whose life straddled the traditional and the avantgarde and whose literary work bridged the older and newer generations of Hebrew women's poetry. All these works feature a female protagonist or speaker who hails from a rabbinic or scholarly family and moves in and out of the kitchen in particularly symbolic and suggestive ways.[4]

Throughout Jewish history, the Rabbi's daughter has occupied a gender "borderland." Latin American feminist critic Gloria Anzaldúa explains the notion of the "borderland" in these terms: "Borders are set up to define the places that are safe and unsafe, to distinguish us from them. A border is a dividing line, a narrow strip along a steep edge. A borderland is a vague undetermined place created by the emotional residue of an unnatural boundary. It is in a constant state of transition. The prohibited and forbidden are its inhabitants . . . those who cross over, pass over, or go through the confines of the normal."[5]

As a borderland figure, the Rabbi's daughter enjoyed a privileged exposure to the world of Jewish scholarship and ritual leadership, presenting an alternative to the traditional binary divisions of Jewish gender roles. Situated at the center of Jewish learning and communal responsibility, she often passed over "the confines of the normal," gaining access to a depth of religious education and involvement usually denied women in traditional Jewish circles. In many instances the

Rabbi's daughter was a happy exception to the rule of female religious illiteracy and Hebrew literary silence. Indeed, of the few women who attempted to write in Hebrew, from the post-biblical era until the nineteenth century, virtually all were rabbis' daughters and/or rabbis' wives.[6] Still, as a daughter rather than a son, the Rabbi's daughter remained confined in certain crucial ways to the "women's gallery" or "kitchen-spaces" of Jewish scholarly and literary activity. On some occasions she might successfully cross into the male scholarly realm, but at other times this opening might be blocked off. Hers was a mixed identity and a scholarly potential that, if actualized, had problematic, even transgressive implications.

Emblematic of this representation of the Rabbi's daughter as a transgressive borderland figure, to be revered as well as feared, is the legend about Beruriah (second century), the famously learned daughter of Rabbi Haninah ben Terdiyion and the wife of Rabbi Meir.[7] In the B. T. Avodah Zarah 18b, we read that Rabbi Meir, husband of Beruriah, fled to Babylonia. Two explanations are offered for Rabbi Meir's flight, each of which carries interesting gender and sexual implications. The first explanation concerns the efforts of Rabbi Meir to rescue Beruriah's sister from a whorehouse, where she was incarcerated by the Romans as a punishment for her father's persistent public teaching of the Torah. This introduces a notion of sexual vulnerability in the public role of the Rabbi's daughter and her need for male protection and heroic intercession. The second reason adduced for Rabbi Meir's flight concerns the "story of Beruriah," which is left unelaborated by the redactors of the Talmud. We learn the details of this story only from exegetical marginalia, specifically in the commentary of Rashi. According to Rashi, "on one occasion, Beruriah scoffed at the sages who claimed that 'women are light-headed.'[8] In response Rabbi Meir swore that in the end, Beruriah would agree that they were right. Rabbi Meir then went and ordered one of his pupils to seduce her. For many days the student entreated her, until she finally relented. When she realized what she had done, she hanged herself. Rabbi Meir then fled to Babylonia."[9]

"What is there to say" about this story, laments Israeli novelist Ruth Almog, "but that Beruriah dared trespass onto men's territory—that of wisdom, that of spiritual intellectual activity—and was punished by her very own husband, the father or her children."[10] I chose to quote Almog here specifically because of the way she configures Beruriah's story in terms of images of space and place: the notion of female intellectualism as an encroachment on masculine space. The appearance of this episode within the context of a story of a great sage's flight from the land of Israel to Babylonia underscores the spatial or geographically symbolic elements of the story. Implied (disturbingly) in this tale is the idea that a blurring of boundaries between men and women's spaces leads to a further blurring of sexual/moral boundaries and, inexorably, to tragic exile from the Land of Israel.

A modern version of the Beruriah story, set in the context of nineteenth-century Eastern Europe, can be discerned in a story by Hebrew writer Jacob Steinberg (1884–1947), entitled "Bat haRav" (The rabbi's daughter).[11] Sarah, the rabbi's daughter in the story, is a reader of Russian novels, and thus she has rendered herself unfit for a match with a pious scholar. Eventually she is betrothed to a tobacco shop owner, an ignorant brute of a man who seduces her before their wedding and impregnates her. When the rabbi's daughter discovers she is pregnant, she initially contemplates having an abortion, but when her fiancé fails to show up to accompany her to the procedure, she jumps off the roof of her parents' house and kills herself.[12]

In this story the Rabbi's daughter is no scholar. On the contrary, she is depicted as a feminine stereotype, more emotional than intellectual, and given to neurotic outbursts and chronic toothaches, all due to her seeming inability to secure the right husband. She is, however, a reader of secular books, at a time when, as Iris Parush has shown, Jewish women gained access to secular culture that was often off-limits to men. According to Parush, "the underestimation of women's talents which led to permissiveness on the part of traditional society regarding the provision of secular education for women also led to a lack of concern about what they read. Whereas a man who wished to read a work of fiction had to do so in secrecy and, if caught, was suspected of rank heresy, literate women were permitted to read virtually anything they wished."[13] If Torah learning has a transgressive power, Steinberg's story extends this power to women's reading of secular texts. As a result of her reading, Sarah has moved beyond the pale of daughterly piety. Reading has inflamed her passions, as evidenced by numerous images throughout the story of heat and fire: the recurring depiction of Sarah and her fiancé Berl sitting by a stoked oven, the repeated references to cups of hot drink; and, of course, Berl's work as owner of a tobacco shop. Ultimately, Sarah's inflamed passions lead to her moral downfall, indicating again the dangers that beset women in the intellectual or literary borderland.

What happens, however, when women begin to author their own portraits of learned and literary women? What happens when the modern daughters of rabbinic or scholarly *(Maskilic)* families begin to sketch their own destiny and describe their own pursuit of enlightenment?

Pots, Pans, and Poetry: Rachel Morpurgo's "Anaseh akh hapa'am"

We return to the poetry of Rachel Morpurgo, who struggled her entire life to live up to her literary aspirations and at the same time adhere to a traditional Jewish lifestyle.[14] In a late poem, "Anaseh akh hapa'am" (1866), Morpurgo dramatizes in stark terms the ongoing conflict between her traditionally feminine role in the home and her spiritual/ literary goals, postulating a solution only in her ultimate release from physical existence:

אנסה אך הפעם

אֲנַסֶּה אַךְ הַפַּעַם
אִם אוּכַל לָשִׁיר,
מֵאֵצֶל הַסִּיר
רָחַקְתִּי מֵרֹב זָעַם:

מָאַסְתִּי הוֹן וָהֶבֶל
וְלָצֵאת מִסֵּבֶל
יְכוֹנוּ רַגְלָי
צוּרִי יִגְמֹל עָלָי

בְּרְכוֹתָיו יְרְעֲפוּן
אֶל טוּב הַצָּפוּן
אֲקַוֶּה אֶל הַחֶבֶל

הִנֵּה יוֹצֵר הָרִים
מַתִּיר אֲסוּרִים
יַתִּיר לִי מִכָּל־חֶבֶל.

וּבְיוֹם מִיתָתִי,   הוּא יוֹם שִׂמְחָתִי

בִּמְקוֹם קִינָה   גִּילָה רִנָּה

וּתְמוּר שַׂקִּים   לְבְשׁוּ נָאִים

גַּם אֵל מָחוֹל   מָחוֹל אֱמְחוֹל

כִּי גֵרוּשִׁי   הֵם נִשּׂוּאָי

Once again
  I'll try to **sing**
  I've left the **pot**
  Behind in anger.

I despise wealth and **vanity**
  And long to escape
  My suffering.
  God shall reward me.

His blessings will drizzle down
  Toward the hidden good
  I await my lot to come.

The creator of mountains
  And freer of slaves
  Will loosen all my **bonds.**

And the day of my **death**   will be the day of my **mirth**
In place of a dirge   joy and song
And instead of sackcloth   finest dress
Even in renunciation   I shall surely dance[15]
For my divorce   is my marriage.[16]
[emphasis added]

The poem begins with the speaker's departure from the kitchen in an effort, once again, to compose poetry. The typographical arrangement of the poem, wherein the second, third, and fourth line of the first four

256

stanzas are set apart from or farther ahead than the first, underlines this idea of spatial dislocation, of attempting to move from one sphere to another. The movement in the third and fourth stanzas from a quatrain form to a three-line form, as well as the breaking up of the lines in the final stanza into shorter, choppier units, creates a rhythmic sense of quickening, a sense of flight or escape.

This conflict at the heart of the poem can be identified in the rhyme of *sir* (pot) and *lashir* (to sing or compose poetry), two words that sound alike, but which Morpurgo experiences as antithetical entities.[17] In choosing to represent the kitchen through a metonymic reference to the *sir,* Morpurgo calls to mind a host of negative biblical associations. In Exodus 16:3, the People of Israel rue the day they left Egypt, saying, "If only we had died by the hand of the Lord in the land of Egypt, where we sat by the *fleshpots,* where we ate our fill of bread! For you have brought us out into this wilderness to starve this whole congregation to death." In this verse, the *sir habasar* is associated with crass, slavish materialism, a willingness to forego spiritual freedom so long as one's basic physical urges are readily satisfied. Elsewhere the image of the *sir* is associated with the threat of exile (as in Jeremiah 1:13, where the prophet sees an image of a "steaming pot, tipped away from the north," signifying the menace of military attack by a northern enemy kingdom) and with the evils of moral corruption (as in Ezekiel 24:6, where the prophet depicts a bloody city and a filthy pot).

In stanza two, the speaker announces she is tired not only of pots and pans but of all vain material pursuits. She rejects both the feminine domestic role and a feminine identity grounded in materialism and the body. Longing for release from this earthly bondage, she yearns for death, which she envisions as a kind of divine reward—a liturgical dance of sorts, as indicated by the punned usage in the poem's second last line of the word *mahol,* which means both "dance" and "forgiveness" or "renunciation." As Yaffa Berlovitz explains: "Morpurgo translates death not only as a liberation from compulsions and obligations, but also as liberation from her life as a woman (with all of its attendant degradations). . . . Her longing for death becomes a longing not just for freedom but also for poetry, insofar as she describes death as a completely optimistic celebratory situation."[18]

Indeed, one possible way to interpret the speaker's move away from the "*sir*" (pot) toward *shir* (song) is as a fast or hunger strike, using the medium of food (or the renunciation thereof) to rail against as well as transcend her societally imposed limitations. According to Caroline Walker Bynum, writing in her book *Holy Feast and Holy Fast: The Religious Significance of Food to Medieval Women,* "to prepare food is to control food. Moreover, food is not merely *a* resource that women control; it is *the* resource that women control—both for themselves and for others. In the long course of Western history, economic resources were controlled by husbands, fathers, uncles or brothers. Yet human beings can renounce, or deny themselves, only that which they control."[19] Women's traditional control of food preparation, then, can be a vital source of power and self-expression. Bynum notes that "for the ancient Hebrews, food abstention was an expression of grief and repentance, a plea for deliverance from some test or chastisement, a sign of confidence in God's mercy, and intercession and preparation for meeting God."[20] All these ideas can be inferred from Morpurgo's poem. In temporarily renouncing food and food preparation, she finds a way to express grief over her lost creative opportunities, make a plea for deliverance from torment, proclaim her confidence in God's mercy and goodness, and ready herself for meeting God in the afterlife. This last event is celebrated in the jubilant final stanza, a kind celebratory poem-within-the-poem. It is formally set off from the rest of the poem typographically as well as metrically. Thematically, it represents the climactic moment of *nisu'im* (marriage or elevation), when the poet departs from her mundane existence and is lifted aloft to heaven. According to this reading, Morpurgo's poem reinforces the traditional opposition between masculinity and femininity. The poet-speaker's desire to escape bodily materiality into disembodied spirituality amounts to a preference for the traditionally masculine mode over the feminine.

I'd like to propose an alternative based on another set of intertextual references from chapter 7 in the biblical Book of Ecclesiastes. Consider the following excerpted verses:

ד) לֵב חֲכָמִים בְּבֵית אֵבֶל וְלֵב כְּסִילִים בְּבֵית שִׂמְחָה:

ה) טוֹב לִשְׁמֹעַ גַּעֲרַת חָכָם מֵאִישׁ שֹׁמֵעַ שִׁיר כְּסִילִים:

ו) כִּי כְקוֹל הַסִּירִים תַּחַת הַסִּיר כֵּן שְׂחֹק הַכְּסִיל וְגַם-זֶה הָבֶל:

[...]

כה) סַבּוֹתִי אֲנִי וְלִבִּי לָדַעַת וְלָתוּר וּבַקֵּשׁ חָכְמָה וְחֶשְׁבּוֹן וְלָדַעַת רֶשַׁע כֶּסֶל וְהַסִּכְלוּת הוֹלֵלוֹת:

כו) וּמוֹצֵא אֲנִי מַר מִמָּוֶת אֶת הָאִשָּׁה אֲשֶׁר הִיא מְצוֹדִים וַחֲרָמִים לִבָּה

אֲסוּרִים יָדֶיהָ טוֹב לִפְנֵי הָאֱלֹהִים יִמָּלֵט מִמֶּנָּה וְחוֹטֵא יִלָּכֶד בָּהּ: כח) אֲשֶׁר עוֹד-בִּקְשָׁה נַפְשִׁי וְלֹא מָצָאתִי אָדָם אֶחָד מֵאֶלֶף מָצָאתִי וְאִשָּׁה בְכָל-אֵלֶּה לֹא מָצָאתִי:

4. Wise men are drawn to the house of mourning, and fools to the house of mirth.

5. It is better to hear the wise man's rebuke, than to listen to the *song [poem]* of fools.

6. For the levity of the fool is like the crackling of nettles under *a pot* and that too is *vanity;* for cheating may rob the wise man of reason and destroy the prudence of the cautious. . . .

25. I put my mind to studying, exploring, and seeking wisdom and the reason of things, and to studying wickedness, stupidity, madness and folly.

26. Now I find woman more bitter than death; she is all traps, her hands are *fetters* and her heart is snares. He who is pleasing to God escapes her, and who is displeasing is caught by her fire. . . .

28. As for what I sought further but did not find, I found only one human being in a thousand, and the one I found among so many was never a woman. [emphasis added][21]

The need to reckon with Kohelet 7 as a traditional source that demeans and limits women is underscored by the willingness of modern Jewish *maskilim* to embrace the misogyny of the text, despite their otherwise enlightened dispositions. As Shmuel Feiner notes in an important article about Haskalah attitudes toward modern women, Moses Mendelsohn, in his commentary on Kohelet, explicitly endorses the derogatory pronouncements of Kohelet 7, drawing a direct connection between the observations about foolishness and false virtue that appear at the beginning of the chapter and verse 26, which pronounces woman "more bitter than death."[22]

It is my contention that "Anaseh akh hapa'am" can be read as a retort to the "wisdom" of Kohelet as well as its latter-day enlightened interpreters. As indicated by the italicized words, Morpurgo's poem incorporates a number of elements from Ecclesiastes 7: the emphasis on death, the twin references to *sir* and *shir* (pot and poetry); the complaint against vanity; and the use of the word *asirim* (fetters or bonds). Of course, the poem recapitulates Ecclesiastes with several major differences.

The speaker Kohelet claims that it is better to hear the rebuke of the wise than the song *[shir]* of fools; by describing womankind later in the chapter as a force that fetters and snares the good man, he essentially binds women to the realm of foolishness and categorically excludes the possibility of female moral or religious seriousness. In contrast, Morpurgo daringly sets out to write a highly serious poem grounded in her experiences as a woman, in which she imagines God untying her spiritual bonds and releasing her into the realm of liturgical poetry. By declaring her intention to offer a song or poem despite Kohelet's association in this chapter of *shir* with *sir,* that is, foolishness, Morpurgo self-consciously adopts an alternative feminine mode and provides her own wise woman's rebuke to the misogynist rant of the biblical "wise" man. Her angry move away from the *sir*/pot can thus be construed as a rejection not of femininity but of Kohelet's definition thereof. According to this reading, if Ecclesiastes 7 establishes a strict dichotomy between man, wisdom, and the solemnity of death, on the one hand, and woman, levity, and the foolishness of song or poetry, on the other, Morpurgo subverts and breaks down this division, making a song out of death, mixing levity with gravity, and invading the solemn male disembodied death space of Kohelet 7 with her unfettered femininely foolish song.

Baking Memories: Baron's "Mah shehayah"

This alternate reading notwithstanding, it is clear that Morpurgo identifies a location of "radical openness" and possibility outside rather than inside the kitchen. In contrast, Devorah Baron's novella "Mah shehayah" (What once was, 1939) tells a story of interpersonal growth, resistance, and creativity that takes place in the kitchen, within the company of other women.[23]

The plot of this novella contradicts certain facts of Baron's childhood and early adulthood, which typically found her among boys and men. The daughter of the rabbi of the town of Uzda in Lithuania, she received an education in Jewish sources, albeit within a framework that placed her, both literally and figuratively, in the women's gallery. While her father gave lessons to the boys in the synagogue, young Devorah sat behind a partition in the women's section, following along with the lessons, occasionally calling across the partition for an explanation of a difficult passage.[24] Her presence in the study house indicated her privileged status; her spatial location behind the partition, however, was a constant reminder of the traditional limitations on her movement. She published her first Hebrew stories at the astonishingly young age of fifteen. Around the same time she left home to study, first in Minsk, then in Kovno and Mariampol, undertaking a lifestyle atypical for a rabbi's daughter of her day. She settled in Palestine when she was only twenty-four years old and became literary editor of *Hapo'el hatsa'ir,* a weekly newspaper edited by her husband Yosef Aharonovitz. In Zionist literary circles she was often a lone woman in an overwhelmingly male group. But as Naomi Seidman has aptly observed, "Baron alternated between transgressing the borders and gendered (and generic) spaces assigned to women and retreating . . . to the generic and stylistic 'women's section.'"[25] "Mah shehayah," a story of self-development and transformation that occurs specifically within the conventionally female domain of the kitchen, records one occasion of strategic retreat.

The protagonist of the story is an awkward, illiterate young baker named Mina, whom the narrator befriends and teaches to read, thereby helping her discover inner reserves of strength and self-respect. Mina, in turn, tells kitchen-spun stories of her life to the narrator, unknowingly supplying lessons about what constitutes a good storyteller. The kitchen might be an improbable birthplace for literary art, but from the very first paragraph of the novella, Baron's narrator drops aphorisms asserting that beauty often comes from the most unlikely places. Her best friend Mina, she tells us, "was hardly what one might call a pretty girl; but, we all know the saying that it is in the earthenware jar that the best wine is preserved, and have we not seen the living word of God inscribed in a simple scroll?"[26] This sentence is a crucial one, in that it links food/wine preparation with the art of (sacred) writing.

Throughout "Mah shehayah" women's personal stories are shared against the background of kitchen work. Images of food, drink, and the preparation of meals are yoked with meta-fictional musing. Mina offers a vivid description of her family's former mansion in the city while she "pounds the cinnamon with a mortar" (*Parshiyyot,* pp. 128–29; *The Thorny Path,* p. 81). She tells the sad story about how her family came to be reduced in their financial circumstances while she is "getting the cake-tins ready so as to save time for the next morning" (*Parshiyyot,* p. 129; *The Thorny Path,* p. 81). The harrowing story of how she came to have such unconventionally short hair (the result of a painful altercation with her cruel mother), comes out "[o]ne day, as [they] were sitting together in the kitchen" (*Parshiyyot,* p. 132, *The Thorny Path,* p. 85). The vivid, realistic, albeit unembellished detail of all these stories impresses the narrator in her role as writer-in-training, although it takes her several years to crystallize these lessons into a poetics. "It was much later," she reflects, "that I realized that the good narrator does not labor his subject and encumber it with explanations, which only obscure it" (*Parshiyyot*, p. 128; *The Thorny Path*, p. 80).

Indeed, through the story of the narrator's relationship with Mina, Baron identifies the kitchen as a vital origin of culture. Anthropologist Claude Lévi-Strauss famously argued that "the conversion of the raw into the cooked represents a conversion process from nature to culture."[27] Building on the ideas of Lévi-Strauss, Renée Hirschon, in her research about houses and home life in urban Greece, contends that "it is woman, who in dealing with the raw 'natural' substances of the 'outside' world, acts as the agent in the cultural process and by extension, the man is designated to 'nature' through his activities outside the home."[28] These ideas are directly represented in Baron's novella: Mina's role as an agent of culture, according to Hirschon's formulation, is symbolized through her eventual marriage to Avraham Itzi Hacohen, a miller from Libidov. Whereas Avraham Itzi's work situates him within the realm of the raw—he produces flour—Mina's work situates her within the realm of the cooked. It is her job to take her husband's raw products and transform them into cakes and pastry "fit to be served up at religious feasts and to have benedictions pronounced over them" (*Parshiyyot*, p. 127; *The Thorny Path*, p. 79). Baron's novella also suggests that the culture-forming function of the kitchen can serve as a metaphor and/or as an inspiration for women's writing and reading. It is from the illiterate Mina that the narrator begins to understand the principles of fiction writing. And it is from the rabbi's daughter-narrator that Mina finally learns how to read.

Significantly, Baron's novel also acknowledges the need for women to move beyond the kitchen in order to abet their development. The progress of Mina's reading lessons eventually necessitates a deliberate spatial relocation: "As we couldn't find a quiet place for ourselves in the house, we moved to the upper vestibule of the synagogue, and there, in the dim half-light, the wonders of Creation were gradually unfolded to her: there was light at God's command, and the heavens were created out of the formlessness and the void, and day followed day, and man came to live on the earth, he and, with him, all that complexity of actions and struggles that makes up human life" (*Parshiyyot*, p. 134; *The Thorny Path*, p. 89).

Mina's movement beyond the kitchen for these Bible lessons enables her to contemplate the origins of creativity, as represented by the biblical account of divine creation. Note, however, that Baron situates this occasion of female development not in a masculine space but in a kind of communal borderland, the upper vestibule of the synagogue, presumably leading to the women's gallery. Here, in this liminal space, the narrator imparts to Mina the biblical lessons that her rabbi-father gave to her, opening Mina's mind to the wonders of knowledge and the complexities of human interaction.

In time, the narrator, like Baron herself, also relocates, leaving her hometown to pursue higher studies and eventually settling in Palestine. Before departing, she and Mina look back on their shared experiences:

> We recalled our first talks, our strolls together through the fields, how I had first taught her the letters of the alphabet, which she had then described as being "like rows of dishes set out along cupboard shelves," and from which she had drawn so much spiritual comfort. In the days preceding my departure we would share our reminiscences as she busied herself in a corner of the kitchen, or stood over her washing-tub, and we promised to make a point of letting one another know how we fared. (*Parshiyyot*, p. 178; *The Thorny Path*, p. 150)

In this scene of reminiscences, the centrality of the kitchen as a site of female work, friendship, and shared intellectual development is repeatedly confirmed. She recalls her first lessons on the alphabet through the kitchen-based image of "rows of dishes set out along cupboard shelves." They share their memories as Mina washes clothes or works in another corner of the kitchen. Baron makes it clear that Mina's familial and domestic obligations limit her mobility; she cannot leave home and study in the city like her beloved friend, for she has responsibilities to others. Yet Baron's depiction of Mina's life and work is a tribute to the ways in which shtetl women cared for their families—in good times and bad. As time goes by, the narrator loses touch with Mina, but one day Mina's son Ephraim, named after Mina's younger brother who died in childhood, comes to visit her in *Erets Yisra'el,* linking her new world with the old and offering an image of familial continuity despite the disruptions and dislocations of early twentieth-century Jewish history. In telling the stories of Mina and her family, the narrator offers her own version of continuity, showing how the raw materials of her hometown kitchen, its fragrances, textures, and tastes, can be preserved and cooked into great fiction.

Perhaps the greatest irony about this fictional tribute to the old world kitchen is that Baron wrote it during that long period of her life (from approximately 1922 to her death in 1956) when she lived in self-imposed isolation (with her only daughter), adhering to a strict diet that amounted to self-starvation. Scholars continue to puzzle over the riddle of Baron's life.[29] Psychobiographer Amia Lieblikh writes that for Baron, "fiction was a kind of 'monastic creed,' an end to justify all means."[30] Critic Lily Rattok similarly asserts that "Baron apparently imprisoned herself in her own house in order to achieve spiritual freedom at the expense of freedom of movement and worldly pleasure. This strange way of life was the only way she had to free herself from the accepted role of a woman in a patriarchal culture."[31] All this recalls our discussion of Morpurgo's poem, where the poet-speaker renounces the kitchen and/or food and announces a desire to retreat entirely from the material world, to embrace spirituality, poetry, and death.

Clearly, Morpurgo and Baron both recognized the conflict between pots and poetics, between a desire to pursue a life of letters and the pressures to conform to a predetermined gender role. Baron's "Mah shehayah" offers a more positive portrayal of the feminine space of the kitchen. Read with a knowledge of her life story, the novella also paints a picture of a writer who successfully cooked her experiences into fiction—but literally starved herself in the process. According to anthropologist Carole Counihan, "giving food connects women to close relatives through an extremely intense emotional channel; women become identified with the food they offer."[32] In Baron's case, this idea found poignant expression in her fiction, but not in her life.

Zelda's "Hedra shel immi hu'ar"

Finally we come to "Hedrah shel immi hu'ar" (My mother's room is lit), by Zelda (Schneerson Mishkovsky), a descendent of rabbis and a prolific contemporary poet.[33] Zelda was born in Russia to a prominent rabbinic family, relatives of Rav Menachem Mendel Schneerson of Lubavitch. In 1925 the family, persecuted by Communist authorities, settled in Jerusalem, where Zelda became a teacher and painter.[34] Though a chronological contemporary of earlier writers such as Leah Goldberg, Zelda emerged as a poet much later than Goldberg. While she began writing poems in the 1940s, her first collection of poems (*Penai,* Leisure) did not appear until 1967, when she was fifty-three.

Surprisingly, despite her age and religious orientation, Zelda was embraced by younger avant-garde poets such as Meir Wieseltier and Yona Wallach.[35]

Zelda was a unique personality in Israeli letters, one whose work straddled the older and newer generations of Hebrew poetry and appealed to secular and religious readers alike. In contrast to the majority of women writers examined in this study, who grew up in traditional households but abandoned religious practice, Zelda remained staunchly observant her entire life, seeing no inherent conflict between a life of tradition and a life of poetry, between a Jewish woman's conventional role and her intellectual aspirations. "What difference does it make?" she asked: "A poet and a religious woman? There is no contradiction in this. Sure, it provokes public curiosity. I know that. It makes for 'entertainment.' But I don't think that when a woman covers her hair this affects her ability or inability to write poetry."[36] Her early poem "Hedra shel immi hu'ar," published in her first collection of poems, makes a similar assertion:

חדרה של אמי הואר

הַסִּיד הַחִוֵּר מָזַג בְּסִיד הַלֵּחַ
וֶרֶד דַּק שֶׁבְּדַק,
זִיו שֶׁל נִצַּת הַתַּפּוּחַ, חִיּוּךְ שֶׁל עוֹלָל.
אֶשְׁכְּלוֹת כֶּסֶף שָׁם וְכִתְרֵי פְּלִיֵּי חֲקוּקִים
בְּפָמוֹטוֹת הַיְרֻשָּׁה, מְנַצְנְצִים עַל גַּבֵּי הַשִּׂידָה,
נִשְׁקָפִים בִּרְאִי עָגֹל,
(פִּרְדְּסֵי אַהֲבָה מָדוֹר לְדוֹר וְעַטְרוֹת הַיִּחוּס וְהַדְּמָעוֹת).
וְעַל הַשֻּׁלְחָן – בְּמַעֲשִׂיּוֹת חֲסִידִים, בְּסִפּוּרֵי הַזָּהָב
(שֶׁהָרַב זֵוֶין לִקֵּט, אָסַף),
מֵעֲלֵעַל אַט-אַט רוּחַ הָרִים
וּמְעַרְבֵּב נוֹפֵי שֶׁלֶּג בְּנוֹף שָׁרָב.
אִמִּי מִתְפַּלֶּלֶת – עַל רֹאשָׁהּ מִשְׁבְּצוֹת מֶשִׁי.

הַחֶדֶר הַגָּדוֹל, הַפְּנִימִי, אָפֵל
כִּמְעָרַת רַבִּי שִׁמְעוֹן בַּר יוֹחַאי,
בּוֹ שְׁתִיקָה שֶׁל יָם –
שַׁבָּת בּוֹ, מֵעֵין הָעוֹלָם הַבָּא.

265

בְּכָל הַדִּירָה דְּמָמָה.
בַּעֲלִי הָלַךְ לַמִּשְׂרָד. אִמִּי בְּהֵיכַל תְּפִלּוֹתֶיהָ.
אֲנִי בַּמִּטְבָּח.
וּבַפַּח עוֹלֶה עַל גְּדוֹתָיו גַּרְנִיּוֹם כְּעֵין הַדָּם.
בְּחָצֵר הַמְרֻצֶּפֶת לְיַד הַצְּמָחִים
פּוֹסַעַת חָתוּל כְּבַעֲלַת-אֶחֱזָה מִן הַדּוֹר הַיָּשָׁן.
אַט-אַט
נִפְתַּחַת הַדֶּלֶת
לְחָלָב , לְלֶחֶם, לְנֵרוֹת,
לְמֵסִים, לָאִגֶּרֶת.
יוֹם שִׁשִּׁי הוּא יוֹמָהּ שֶׁל עַיִן צוֹחֶקֶת קְרוּעָה בַּפּוּךְ,
וְיוֹמוֹ שֶׁל הַפֶּה הֶעָצוּב.
יוֹס שִׁשִּׁי הוּא יוֹמָם שֶׁל הָעֲנִיִּים.
כָּךְ עוֹבְרִים הַיָּמִים,
כָּךְ שָׁנִים עוֹבְרוֹת.
דַּק שֶׁל זִיו יְכַסֶּה יִסּוּרִים, אָזְלַת יָד,
מְשׁוּגוֹת.
כָּךְ עוֹבְרִים הַיָּמִים וְהַחַיִּים הַהוֹמִים
שׁוֹפְעִים תְּשׁוּקוֹת, נִצָּנִים, תִּינוֹקוֹת, יַמִּים וִיעָרוֹת,
אוֹזְלִים בַּלָּאט מֵאֵיבָרַי, נִגָּרִים כַּדָּם.
כְּשֶׁאָמוּת –
יִפְרֹם אֱלֹהִים רִקְמָתִי
חוּט-חוּט,
וְהַיָּמָּה יַשְׁלִיךְ צִבְעֵי
אֶל מַחְסָנָיו שֶׁבַּתְּהוֹם.
וְאוּלַי יַהַפְכֶם לְפֶרַח וְאוּלַי יַהַפְכֶם לְפַרְפַּר
כֵּהֶה-לֵילִי-רַךְ, כֵּהֶה-לֵילִי-חַי.

My Mother's Room Is Lit

The pale plasterer mixed into the damp plaster
the slightest tint of rose,
radiance of apple blossom, smile of infant.

266

Silver clusters there and crowns of copper carved
in the heirloom candlesticks, sparkling on the chest-of-drawers, 5
are reflected in a round mirror,
(groves of love passed down from generation to generation and
    the crowns of lineage and tears).
And on the table — in Hasidic stories, in the golden tales
(that Rav Zevin collected, compiled),
a mountain wind slowly turns pages   10
and mixes landscapes of snow with landscape of *hamsin.*
My mother prays — on her head checkers of silk.

The inner great room is as dark
as the cave of Rabbi Shimon bar Yohai.
In it, the silence of the sea —   15
within, Sabbath, a hint of the world to come.
Stillness fills the flat.
My husband has gone to the office. My mother is in the
    sanctuary of her prayers.
I am in the kitchen.
And on the plate a geranium overflows like a fountain blood. 20
In the paved courtyard next to the plants
a cat paces, like a noblewoman from an older generation.
Little by little,
the door is opened
to milk, to bread, to candles,   25
to taxes, to a letter.
Friday is the day of a laughing eye painted with mascara,
and the day of the sad mouth.
Friday is the day of the poor.
So pass the days,   30
so the years pass.
A thin veneer of radiance covers over torments, helplessness,
missteps.
So pass the days and the tumultuous life

abounding in longings, buds, babies, seas and forests,   35
flowing out quietly from my limbs, pouring out like blood.
When I die —
God will unravel the tissue of my being
thread by thread,
and hurl my colors seaward   40
into His storerooms in the abyss.
And perhaps He'll turn them into a flower and perhaps He'll
    turn them into a
butterfly
Dark-nightly-soft, dark-nightly-live.[37]

Like Morpurgo's "Anaseh akh hapa'am" and Baron's "Mah shehayah," Zelda's poem engages issues of feminine versus masculine space, of religious and intellectual legacy, and the idea of death as a form of spiritual or creative release. The poem begins in the speaker's mother's room, which has been painted or plastered. Inside, her pious mother, her head covered in silk, is engrossed in prayer. Her room is literally being lit or lightened by paint; it is also being metaphorically illuminated by the poet's eye that lovingly captures all the details of space and mood. The complicated syntax of the first stanza, which includes images of reflection as well as illumination, suggests the poet's meta-poetic awareness of the complex nature of literary representation.

The two references in the poem to literary rabbis—Rav Zevin (1890–1978, author, among other works, of *Sippurei hassidim*) and Rabbi Shimon bar Yohai (second-century Talmudic and mystical sage, author of the *Zohar*)—situate this poem within a masculine Hassidic/mystical literary tradition. At the same time, the centrality of the praying mother in the poem, reminiscent of the holy grandmothers in Esther Raab's "Savtot kedoshot biY'rushalayim"[38] indicates the poet's desire to fashion a literary/religious lineage that combines both masculine and feminine aspects. Notice that the speaker places herself in the kitchen (line 19), in contrast to the husband in his office and the mother who dwells in the spiritual realm of her prayers. How does this domestic geography affect or shape her vision?

The words *ani bamitbah* occur roughly halfway through the poem, in a sense representing a turning point in its development. Until this

Zelda, courtesy of Machon
Genazim.

point, the poem has concerned itself largely with external physical
description: the color of the paint, the silence of the flat, the engraved
heirloom candlesticks, the mother's checkered silk kerchief, the snowy
landscape of Russia, where the poet's family and Rabbi Zevin (a
Jerusalem rabbi-scholar of Russian origin) originated (see line 11) mixing, as it were, with the parched dry heat and landscape of Israel. After
line 19, when the poet-speaker describes her location, the poem moves
inward, focusing more on her idiosyncratic or metaphysical view of life.

As in Baron's "Mah shehayah," in which the sights, smells, and
conversations of the kitchen give rise to fiction, the speaker's location in
the kitchen paradoxically affords a poetic perspective, mixing the mundane with the otherworldly. A geranium plant becomes animated and
overflows like blood, an image that combines the force of life with death
and depletion; an alley cat paces outside like a noblewoman, indicating
the extent to which animal nature lords over the human realm. This
kitchen is the site of routine, commonplace activity, where people pour
milk, open letters, prepare tax forms. Yet from this domestic, seemingly
mundane location, the poet meditates on the meaning of life and the
inevitability of death.

Beginning with line 27, the poet shifts her focus from space to time. "Friday is the day of a laughing eye painted with mascara, / and the day of the sad mouth. / Friday is the day of the poor." In these three lines, the sixth day of the Jewish week is variably associated with laughter, sorrow, and the charity-seeking poor, a mixed bag of associations and emotions representing the ever-shifting importance and meaning of time.

As the poem progresses, the poet's focus widens to encompass considerations of an entire lifetime, with diverse emotions and achievements. Earlier in the poem, in line 20, Zelda uses the image of blood to depict a red, efflorescent geranium. In lines 33 through 35 the blood image expands to encompass various physical and metaphysical pieces of one's life—"longings, buds, babies, seas and forests"—all envisaged in terms of blood flowing out of and collecting in the veins. Through this image, the physical stuff of blood becomes metaphysical, and the metaphysical is reincorporated as part of the natural cycle of life.

As in the concluding section of Morpurgo's "Anaseh akh hapa'am," the conclusion of "Hedra shel immi hu'ar" celebrates death. In her effort to picture her own death, the poet imagines God unraveling her *rikmah*, the tissue or embroidery of her being, an image evocative of feminine handicrafts and the complex design that is human biology. Zelda imagines God hurling the colors of her embroidered life back into the abyss, an image of reverse-creation, evocative of Genesis 1:2, and then recycling them into a new living (art) form.

What is remarkable about this poem, especially in comparison to Morpurgo's poem and Baron's story, is the sense of continuity of space and time. Morpurgo's poem sets up a clear opposition between the limited opportunities for female spiritual and intellectual development in this world and the unbounded life of the spirit that awaits us in the next. Baron finds a way to rehabilitate the domestic realm as a source of literary inspiration, but she implies that the stuff of the kitchen cannot become literature unless one leaves the kitchen for other spaces. In contrast, Zelda's speaker paints a broad poetic canvas from the vantage point of her kitchen. She expresses no need to escape physically from the confines of her traditional existence in order to live a life replete with poetry and spirituality. The poem moves seamlessly from the Hassidic stories of Rav Zevin to milk, bread, candles, and letters in the kitchen, to yearnings, children, torments, to the kabbalistic idea of *gilgul neshamot* (reincarnation of souls). The spiritual, the domestic, and the poetic meld freely here, with no contradiction or tension. The conclusion of the poem, in which the poet-speaker imagines her reincarnation, expresses a belief in the afterlife not as a form of refuge from the limitations of this one but as a natural extension of the many creative transformations enacted in life, especially by the artist. If the poem initially presents a gendered geography of space—with the husband out in the world of work and the women at home, involved in traditionally feminine acts of private prayer and food preparation, it concludes with a female-generated larger-than-life perspective that explodes (or unravels) all notions of fixed space and place. This latter-day Rabbi's daughter travels as far as possible from the kitchen, yet she never leaves it.

AFTERWORD

In his recent verse novel, *Oto hayam* (The same sea), the narrator, a prize-winning writer who lives in Arad and has written such novels as *To Know a Woman*—in other words, a postmodern stand-in for Amos Oz himself—recalls his school days and the advice of a woman teacher who later became a well-known poet:

> Fifty-years have passed:
> in Jerusalem, on Zechariah Street, in a two-room flat, a private
> school belonging to Mrs. Yonina. My teacher was Mrs. Zelda,
>   Zelda
> who some years later wrote the poems in *The Spectacular*
>   *Difference* and
> *The Invisible Carmel.* Once, on a winter day, she chose to say
> to me softly: If you stop talking sometimes
> maybe things will sometimes be able to talk to you. Years later
> I found it promised in one of her poems that *trees and stones*
> *Will respond Amen.* A spectacular difference she promised,
> Between stones and trees, to anyone who is prepared to listen.[1]

The narrator's-Oz's invocation of Zelda comes as he reflects on the writing process, and it constitutes an important moment in Israeli literary history. In her 1994 afterword to *Hakol ha'aher,* Lily Rattok discerns a gender dichotomy in Israeli letters, arguing that while Israeli women write "to express themselves," male writers such as Amos Oz aspired to serve as "tribal witch doctors," writing to heal the collective ills of Israeli society.[2] Yet here is that same "witch doctor" male writer, composing a highly personal, lyrical, almost "womanly" novel in which he repeatedly invokes the influence, counsel, and inspiration of a female predecessor poet!

Long ago, in the early days of Hebrew women's writing, when one or two or, at best, a handful of women wrote alongside scores of male poets and prose writers, women writers were not typically consulted as arbiters of literary truth or sources of inspiration for male prose writers or poets. Aware of the novelty and extraordinariness of their status, early Hebrew women writers and poets often turned to one another for inspiration,[3] reviewing each other's work and dedicating poems to one another. Rachel reviewed Anda Pinkerfeld-Amir's first book of poetry[4] *(Yamim dovevim);* Elisheva Bihovsky reviewed Pinkerfeld-Amir's 1936 volume *Gitit;*[5] and Leah Goldberg reviewed Devorah Baron's collected stories *Parshiyyot.*[6] Anda Pinkerfeld-Amir and Rachel Bluwstein both dedicated lyrics to Yocheved Bat-Miriam.[7] Bat-Miriam composed a heartrending elegy to Rachel in the wake of her death from tuberculosis[8] as did Pinkerfeld-Amir and several other contemporary women poets.[9] Esther Raab wrote a poem "To Leah Goldberg,"[10] as did Dahlia Ravikovitch, a poet of the Statehood generation.[11]

To be sure, much has changed since those early days. Whereas Israeli literature (like Israeli politics) was once dominated by secular Ashkenazi male writers, a new pluralism characterizes the Hebrew literary scene, encompassing Sepharadic, Arab, and ultra-Orthodox writers, with women represented in all three categories. The rise of feminist studies in the Israeli academy, the creation of writing workshops at various Israeli universities, and the influence of postmodern experimentation have affected and changed the way Israeli writers write and the way Israeli readers read.[12]

Since the 1980s the Hebrew literary scene has witnessed an explosion of poetry and prose by women, prompting one critic to consider whether Hebrew literature has undergone a "feminization."[13] Reflecting on the rise of women poets in the eighties, critic Ariel Hirschfeld concludes, "There are no longer one or two women poets alongside an entire generation of male poets and writers, but an abundance."[14] Hirschfeld goes on to enumerate a long list of women poets, among them Leah Ayalon, Maya Bejerano, Hedva Harcavi, Galit Hazan-Rokem, Amira Hess, Agi Mishol, and Hamutal Bar-Yosef.[15] Most striking is the ever-increasing list of women novelists. In addition to older, more seasoned writers such as Amalia Kahana-Carmon, Shulamit Hareven, Ruth Almog, Yehudit Hendel, and Shulamit Lapid, the Hebrew literary scene has seen the rise of numerous important and influential young writers, among them Orly Castel-Bloom, Yehudit Katzir, Savyon Liebrecht, Ronit Matalon, Dorit Rabinyan, and Tsruya

Shalev. Predictably, this boom in Israeli women's writing has given rise to something of a backlash, with one threatened male critic devoting an entire book to the cause of discrediting the influential feminist literary essays of Amalia Kahana-Carmon[16] and downgrading the achievements of contemporary Israeli women writers.[17]

To be sure, some of the trends, themes, and patterns noted in this book are present in contemporary Israeli women's writing. Not unsurprisingly, women poets and prose writers in Israel remain interested in recasting the images of women as seen in biblical and rabbinic sources,[18] and they continue to be inspired and fascinated by the work of their literary predecessors and sisters.[19] By dramatizing the inequities that beset women in their communities, contemporary writers hailing from the Orthodox sector of Israeli society (Yehudit Rotem, Yokheved Brandeis, Mira Magen) are carrying on a practice initiated by earlier poets and prose writers. Yet as Yael Feldman has noted, Israeli women novelists evince skepticism as to "their heroines' ability to live up to the work and love ideal of classical feminism,"[20] a notion that finds ample precedent in the works of Foner, Shapiro, and Baron.

That said, Hebrew women's writing has changed dramatically. In 2000, at the opening ceremony of *Shavua hasefer ha'Ivri* (Hebrew Book Week), novelist Yehudit Katzir declared, "The former droplets of women's writing have now become a mighty river with many streams, facets and voices."[21] In writing *And Rachel Stole the Idols,* I have attempted to gather and preserve several, if not all, the droplets. Mapping the uncharted literary streams and tributaries of this writing and assessing them in terms of their relationship to Jewish feminism and Jewish literature both in Israel and in the Diaspora will be the work of literary historians for many years to come.

APPENDIX

Erets Yisra'el
Yokheved Bat-Miriam

The Hebrew text of the poem cycle can be found in Yokheved Bat-Miriam, *Shirim* (Tel Aviv: Sifriyat Po'alim, 1972), pp. 39–53. I am very grateful to Professors Robert Alter and William Cutter for their helpful comments on this translation. Unfortunately, I was not able to reproduce Bat-Miriam's ABAB rhyme scheme.

1

You [feminine] dwell in pleated blue   1
and hum like the slumbering violin.
A warm divine hand embellishes
your swooning ancient thoughts.

Only your dropping wing leads to   5
shadows of cities, mountains, and desert,
and gathers the ends of my stormy soul
to the arc of your hidden image.

I shall not catch you, revealed-concealed one,
I shall not plumb the full extent of your thoughts,   10
your dust will touch my sealed eye,
like an explanation for me understood.

And distant, unclaiming, unbeckoned
I shall stand like the frozen question.
Be magnified, be sanctified, unredeemed,   15
your mystery forever stamped within me!

277

2
Mountain, hill, tormented strip of sand
without shade, fountain or tree.
The image of a slowly-moving camel hovers
in the soft naked landscape, golden and white.   20

Like this, you are lifted and pursuing,
where to, where to ascend?
Your yearnings melted-fainting
in droplets of brilliance and light.

Only panting, only breathing and shining,   25
from one end to the illuminated other
a chariot of fire that swoops and stretches
your longing, alighting and excited.

In your flight, blazing weary
you jump off helplessly somewhere within   30
to be forgotten among the thorn-thistle, dying
of fainting thirst and leading astray . . .

Deep abysses, visions and glory
One-unseen dreams you up.
You are the vision of after-image returning   35
to be reflected in otherworldliness of blue.

Embodied in you is the thought of the Creator-God,
His footsteps within you, tremble and pulse.
You are my land, the poor and illuminated
upon the thresholds of hidden worlds . . .   40

3
And from there you turn and chase
after me to ask, to see.

Here I am, failing and lagging.
in the dust paths and sands.

Where are you, I shall not see you, concealed one,   45
only the blue scarf of your nights
makes your breath blow in a muttered voice
upon the road and lane.

After you, from *hamsin* lapped in flame
and scent of your green efflorescence —   50
I shall climb loving and clinging to
the myrrh of your memory, hidden and distant.

Between mountains, on some uncovering peak
cool, abounding with light,
with a bluing monument crown   55
I shall find you, for me you stayed behind and waited.

And with you in the light of the watch,
with you in confusion and shield,
I shall remain devoted and at rest
with you in your radiant light.   60

Up beyond the standing whispering corn
in perfect green modesty —
your simple image, concealed,
will clarify, revealing and stirring.

      4
In every instance you are one, solitary you,   65
mountain, rock, and heaps of desolation,
and the opening simplicity of huts
in submissive devotion, concealed.

Like this to see you and know:
there was never anything but you;   70
the living foreign wing, with longing unquiet,
never stroked my nights;

A confused white wandering
never led to the raging tempest
where springtimes stepped, in the awakening rustle,   75
like storks in the meadow,

where forests stood as if on the borders
of the well growing green and greener,
as if hiding at the edge of the sky
the drawn out rustling of the earth.   80

Nothing but you, who bends over
your reflected suffering to revive
your image, alive and hidden
in fleeting slivers of light.

Only you, only you falling   85
in a voiceless cry: "My father!"
On your shoulder, scattered, uncovered
your mantle, cast off by the prophet!

5
With you to wander and stride,
in the radiant blue of paths.   90
To sink and step in the sands
Still stretched out like living creatures;

to stick close to a smiling fence,
that lifts its face in innocent

faith against fear zigzagging   95
nights that kneel upon the deep.

With you in a slender-peaked inscription,
in joy flourishing and hidden,
to draw green and streaming
the hope that comes after despair.   100

And blighted from your suffering, as if distanced,
my eyes suddenly close,
with longing great and stirring
for the foreign wing flapping in my dream: —

Trickling forth, faint and pulling,   105
as if to return and answer
a sole heart's longing, that goes
calling from shore to shore.

From you and back to your streaming self!
Within you and your heralding self!   110
With you, devoted and silent,
I'll be merged with your guarded anticipation — —

    6
Twilight, whispers and laments
and prayer as if frozen in the mouth.
And facing the gravestones   115
a candle stretches, leads astray.

And you cover yourself disappear,
like distant glows in the river.
Flaring up somewhere and fading
your form, like this-not-like-this.   120

Prophesying in the radiant dream,
that was dreamed by your chained messiah,
you spread out my yearnings in your flight
that stretches from border to border.

And rising wrapped in longing   125
and devouring my eyes like smoke,
tottering old and longed-for
as if spun into chariots of cloud.

Further, still further bending over,
and from what is destined to be —   130
bearing his radiated thought,
to dress the footsteps of your path.

You are a gazelle in the shadows of mountains!
You are a branch in a landscape bestarred!
In the skies of luminous other-world space —   135
a full moon silvery and dreaming!

Embracing like a dream and then closing,
like a vision of bereaving redemption,
you realize yourself and withdraw
the revelation of your marvelous mystery.   140

I shall forget you—to seek you in every path!
I shall forsake you—to find you for myself forever!
And to redeem with never-ending longing
the hidden reaches of your majesty.

Drawn, abounding, bluing,   145
sparkling amid tear and thought,
drawn, abounding as hope —
O, please, let me live and die with you!

7

But lofty, you rise as if fleeing
from me, from yourself and from shade,   150
stretched out in the naked landscape space
forging the letters of God's name.

Your horizons are deliberately confounded
yearning vainly to rise,   155
rising, in a longing that seeds
your breath in the radiance of roads — —

And I, I am the wearied
in the dimming sorrow of generations — —
What to remember, I do not know,   160
deceived by the convulsion of visions.

Perplexity, prophecy, and fear
and disappointed glory, impoverished.
With you, like you, only emanating
the hope of my despair, unredeemed,   165

and binding to your height of your steps
echo-steps, tidings and redemption,
the light of end-of-days—in your distances,
that prophesy with sign and destiny —

Circuit within closed circuit,   170
circle spinning within circle,
with you, attached to you,
my longing goes round like a lark —

And summoning in echo, without direction.   175
And summoning in bereavement and awe,
gather me, enclose me in the glory
of your naked, poor wing — —

8

Another mountain, desolations of sand and path,   180
as a Nazirite that breathes following
a thought that slid down from Nazareth
to be embodied in signs and wonders.

And cypress—the envy of the demanding God
and distance—a kid escaped from Moses' flock.   185
And over there, in the teardrop of Hosea
Kinneret—his verse that was left out.

Great light, expectation and hope,
drawn to the edges of revelation,
in you walk and guide unredeemed   190
tidings without meaning, without deliverance.

And with the splendor of your bluing nights,
like an echo, torn off
from shading dreamlands somewhere,
and upon a feast unseen and alluring,   195

a smile quivers, unsubmissive,
with the concealed wisdom and unending thought
of the gods of Tyre, Sidon and Canaan,
eyes closed, leg and hand lopped off;

Spinning and weaving the expression   200
of your invisible and blinding brilliance,
of the rays of your despairing reproof
and the suffering of my atoning sin —

and like this, abounding and sacred,
prostrate and beating the breast for sin,   205
you murmur to my heart and are whispered,
like a threshold of separation stretched out endlessly.

Glimmering, like a path upon the water,
like autumn leaves shedding from somewhere,
you are a path to what is hidden from the eye   210
that floods and draws forth in effulgence.

Upon your surface, slipping-marked out
amid shadeless shadow and line
the radiating peaks of Eden-trees
like reddish golden fruit.   215

Murmuring what cannot be pronounced,
Calling out for what is nameless.
To you, cleaving, like imagination facing
my yearning final and silent . . .

    9
So simple, so rude and small   220
unto weeping for your pains, and to weep,
I remember and yet fail to recall
how I abandoned you to desolation and sand.

And only he, who walked and listened
to the secret of a proud-humble camel's sorrow,   225
binds your sundering glory in
the scattering of his ragged clothes.

And only thorns, and the forgotten landscape of palm
your thoughts continuing to think,
and you, rising as if lit   230
and sobbing in hallucinatory visions.

Abandoned, but never forgotten,
estranged, but within me forever sealed, —
the eye of God, blue and open,
Gazing before my own wide-open eye — —   235

To your soaring, rising wing
to cover your footprints unseen,
in devotion, in brilliant submission
I shall be embraced in hope and tears.

Until I find you, and you are weeping and radiant   240
within my bosom, weaned in light,
the simple, rude and small
unto weeping for your pains, and to weep — —

10
A wind [blows] the entire length of the journey,
as if fleeing from herself, detached,   245
a wind familiar and other
spreading forth your distant image.

Caught amid the branches of palm,
some yesterdays winging aloft
carry your stirring desires   250
in dusty, listened-to flight,

and an inflamed *hamsin* whirling
from a dance between desert and snake,
a deranged and mocking grin
blows fiercely, desolate and stormy.   255

And wandering, weary and stammering,
in the footsteps of foreign nations,
who sought to cloak their barren ruin
in your embodied mystery.

You shall enwrap yourself amid shrub and wind,   260
amid the tribes and sands of the desert,
there sliding down is your risen sun
precious as an ostrich feather.

Slumbering, silent and drawing out
your guttered firebrands,   265
weary, weathered and walking
Amid your plague-struck wild-grass desolation . . .

Engraved as a tatoo in copper,
sealed as an amulet upon the heart,
a living, faint rustle   270
murmurs from dream to dream.

From dream to dream adjoining
like a rainbow upon water and shade,
you are a tassel of corn, swaying in the wind!
A greenish lightning bolt in the night!   275

Abounding, distant, ungrasped,
disappearing from border to border
smiling to me ancient and despairing
from distances of place and time.

There you spoke, there you adopted unrelenting,   280
there you nurtured, tormenting and jealous,
my leaping, unsubmissive soul,
my great and heavy spirit.

Until I raised my face as if blown
from the hollow of your streaming imagination   285
until I raised my face like a thought
sealed by your creating dream.

11
My land, my land which is illuminated
by the prophecy of my people afire and exalted

and [which] scatters a desire for redemption unfulfilled   290
to a turbulent unseen world.

With it you are carried suffused
like tidings in the space of the world,
with it you are carried, unredeemed
a chariot of fire amid the mountains of the world.   295

NOTES

INTRODUCTION

1. Allegra Goodman, "The Story of Rachel," *Genesis: As It Is Written: Contemporary Writers on Our First Stories* (San Francisco: HarperSanFrancisco, 1996), p. 173.

2. In *Narrative Art in Genesis* (Amsterdam: Van Gorcum, 1975), J. P. Fokkelman observes the repetition of the verb to steal and suggests that "Rachel is a true Jacoba, related by nature to Jacob" (p. 163). In contrast, Esther Fuchs focuses on the differences between these two acts of theft, Rachel's being literal and Jacob's figurative. According to Fuchs, while the narrator justifies Jacob's act of deception, Rachel's theft of her father's *teraphim* appears arbitrary and unjustified, placing Rachel's "already weak moral stature in an even more negative light." See Esther Fuchs, "'For I Have the Way of Women': Deception, Gender, and Ideology in Biblical Narrative," *Semeia* 42 (Atlanta: Scholars Press, 1988), pp. 68–83.

3. See, for example, *Bereishit Rabbah* 74:32, *Aggadat Bereishit* 52:1, and *Pirkei de Rebbi Eliezer* 35. In a number of midrashim Rachel is adduced as a negative archetype of female thievery and therefore deserving of this death sentence. See, for example, *Bereishit Rabbah* 18:2, 45:5, and 80. Note that in *Bereishit Rabbah* 80, Rachel is designated specifically as a *memashmeshanit* (handler), a word related to the verb *vayemashesh*, which is assigned in this chapter not to Rachel but to Laban as he gropes around in the tent looking for the *teraphim*. In using this word, the midrashic author intimates a behavioral similarity between Laban and Rachel—in other words, like father, like daughter. In terms of contemporary Orthodox readings of Rachel, Adin Steinsaltz views Rachel's sins and character flaws as emblematic of those of the (feminized) People of Israel. According to Steinsaltz, "Rachel is 'daughter of Jerusalem . . . daughter of Zion' (Lamentations 2:13), not only because she was the young love, the 'partner' of the Lord (the accepted image throughout the Bible), but because she was also the wayward and capricious woman." Here again, Rachel has been the archetype of the people of Israel for most of its history, during the period of the Kingdom of Judah and Israel and at various times later. See Adin Steinsaltz, *Biblical Images: Men and Women of the Book* (New York: Basic Books, 1984), p. 52.

4. One of the most famous and strident articulations of this taboo can be found in Nahmanides' interpretation of Genesis 31:35. Nahmanides explains that Rachel does not rise before her father because "in ancient days menstruants kept themselves very isolated. They were described as *niddot* (the banned ones) because they neither approached nor spoke with people. For the ancients in their wisdom knew that their breath is harmful, their gaze is injurious and makes a bad impression, as the philosophers have explained" (Moses ben Nahman [Nahmanides], *Commentary on the Torah,* trans. Charles Chavel [New York: Shilo, 1974], 2:177). For an analysis of this commentary as

well as Nahmanides' other writings on the "polluting function of the menstrual flow," see Sharon Faye Koren, "The Woman from Whom God Wanders": The Menstruant in Medieval Jewish Mysticism (Ph.D. diss., Yale University, 1999).

5. See, for example, Rashi, Genesis 31:19, "*Vatignov Rachel et haterafim.*"

6. See Moshe Greenberg's reading in "Another Look at Rachel's Theft of the Teraphim," *Journal of Biblical Literature* 81:3 (September 1962): 239–48.

7. See, for example, Rashbam, Genesis 31:19, "*Vatignov Rachel et haterafim.*"

8. See E. A. Speiser, *Genesis: The Anchor Bible* (Garden City, N.Y.: Doubleday, 1964), p. 250. See also Ilana Pardes, *Countertraditions in the Bible: A Feminist Approach* (Cambridge: Harvard University Press, 1992), p. 70; and J. Cheryl Exum, *Fragmented Women: Feminist Subversions of Biblical Narratives* (Valley Forge, Pa.: Trinity Press International, 1993), pp. 128–29.

9. Mieke Bal, "Tricky Thematics," *Semeia* 42 (Atlanta: Scholars Press, 1988), p. 152.

10. Along these lines, Bruce Vawter rejects the hypothesis that Rachel stole the *teraphim* as a way of transferring authority over the clan from Laban to Jacob on the grounds that "Jacob seems to be totally unaware of what is going on. . . . He is not only ignorant of Rachel's action, he thinks the idea that anyone should have done such a thing preposterous and ludicrous." Moreover, he notes that "in Nuzi law the household gods descend and have their efficacy after the testator's death, not while he is yet alive." See Bruce Vawter, *On Genesis: A New Reading* (New York: Doubleday, 1977), pp. 338–40.

11. J. E. Lapsley, "The Voice of Rachel: Resistance and Polyphony in Genesis 31.14–35," *Genesis: A Feminist Companion to the Bible,* 2d series, ed. Athalya Brenner (Sheffield: Sheffield Academic Press, 1998), p. 238.

12. Ibid., p. 242.

13. Alicia Suskin Ostriker, *Stealing the Language: The Emergence of Women's Poetry in America* (Boston: Beacon Press, 1986), pp. 210–11.

14. Benjamin Harshav, *Language in Time of Revolution* (Berkeley: University of California Press, 1993), p. 81.

15. According to Shaul Stampfer, in Eastern Europe "frameworks existed in which girls could, and did study, but there was no standard pattern for women's education as there was for boys." In some cases, Stampfer notes, special *hederim* operated for girls. In general, however, girls studied for fewer years and their education was practical rather than Torah study for its own sake. See Shaul Stampfer, "Gender Differentiation and Education of the Jewish Woman in Nineteenth-Century Eastern Europe," in *From Shtetl to Socialism: Studies from Polin* (London: Littman Library of Jewish Civilization, 1993), pp. 187–211.

16. See the discussion of Shapiro's biography in Carole Balin's *To Reveal Our Hearts: Jewish Women Writers in Tsarist Russia* (New York: Hebrew Union College Press, 2000), pp. 51–83.

17. Nurit Govrin, "Nefesh miRishon LeTsiyyon homiyah," *Devash misela* (Tel Aviv: Misrad Habitahon, 1989), p. 119.

18. Ruth Kartun-Blum, "Immi Yokheved Bat-Miriam," *Yediot ahronot* (19.1.90): 22.

19. Yael Feldman briefly compares the common experiences/lifestyles of Virginia Woolf and Hebrew prose writer Devorah Baron in her book *No Room of Their Own:*

Gender and Nation in Israeli Women's Fiction (New York: Columbia University Press, 1999), p. 26 and p. 246, note 21. Otherwise, her study focuses on the influence of Woolf on contemporary Israeli women writers rather than the earlier figures studied here.

20. Virginia Woolf, *A Room of One's Own* (New York: Harcourt Brace Jovanovich, 1929), p. 43.

21. Sandra M. Gilbert and Susan Gubar, *The Madwoman in the Attic: The Woman Writer and the Nineteenth-Century Literary Imagination* (New Haven: Yale University Press, 1979), p. 49.

22. Ibid., p. 72.

23. For a sampling of the various theoretical approaches that arose at this time, see, for example, Diana Fuss, *Essentially Speaking: Feminism, Nature and Difference* (New York: Routledge, 1989); Donna Haraway, "A Cyborg Manifesto: Science, Technology, and Socialist Feminism in the Late Twentieth Century," in *Simians, Cyborgs and Women: The Reinvention of Nature* (New York: Routledge, 1991, pp. 149–81; *Feminism/Postmodernism,* edited and with an introduction by Linda J. Nicholson (New York: Routledge, 1990); and Ann Brooks, *Postfeminisms: Feminism, Cultural Theory and Cultural Forms* (London; Routledge, 1997).

24. See Elaine Showalter, "Feminist Criticism in the Wilderness," in *The New Feminist Criticism: Essays on Women, Literature, Theory,* ed. Elaine Showalter (New York; Pantheon, 1985), p. 248.

25. Judith Butler, *Gender Trouble: Feminism and the Subversion of Identity* (New York: Routledge, 1997), p. 1.

26. Linda Alcoff, "Cultural Feminism versus Poststructuralism: The Identity Crisis in Feminist Theory," *Signs* 13:3 (1988): 407.

27. For a review of these two books, see Naomi Sokoloff, "Feminist Criticism and Hebrew Literature," *Prooftexts* 8 (1988): 143–56. For a general overview of the development of feminist scholarship in Hebrew literature, see also Naomi Sokoloff, "Modern Hebrew Literature: The Impact of Feminist Research," in *Feminist Perspectives on Jewish Studies,* ed. Lynn Davidman and Shelley Tenenbaum (New Haven: Yale University Press, 1994), pp. 224–43.

28. Yaffa Berlovitz, *Sifrut nashim benot ha'aliyah harishonah* (Tel Aviv: Tarmil, 1984); Nurit Govrin, *Hamahatsit harishonah: Devorah Baron, hayeha veyitsiratah* (Jerusalem: Mossad Bialik, 1988); and Nurit Govrin, *Devash misela: mehkarim besifrut Erets Yisra'el* (Tel Aviv: Misrad Habitahon, 1989), pp. 45–52, 114–71, and 354–92.

29. Dan Miron, *Imahot meyasdot, ahayot horgot* (Tel Aviv: Hakibbutz Hameuchad, 1991), p. 46.

30. Ibid., pp. 153–77.

31. See, for example, Ziva Shamir, "Ahot rehokah: Miri Dor—hameshoreret hamodernistit harishonah," *Sadan* 2 (1996): 247–50. Shamir rejects Miron's argument that there were no women poets until the 1920s because they could not meet the literary expectations of Bialikite poetics. She argues that the dearth of Hebrew women poets during Bialik's generation was because the women of that generation learned Yiddish and Russian, not Hebrew. For an objection to his reading of the politics of literary reception as it pertained to Esther Raab, see Tzvi Luz, *Shirat Esther Raab* (Tel Aviv: Hakibbutz Hameuchad, 1997), pp. 11–12; and Ehud Ben Ezer, *Yamim shel la'anah udevash: sippur hayeha shel hameshoreret Esther Raab* (Tel Aviv: 'Am 'Oved, 1998), pp. 419–21.

32. See, for example, Michael Gluzman, "The Exclusion of Women From Hebrew Literary History," *Prooftexts* 11:3 (1991): 259–78; see also his recent book, *The Politics of Canonicity: Lines of Resistance in Modernist Hebrew Poetry* (Stanford: Stanford University Press, 2003), pp. 100–140; Tova Cohen, "Betokh hatarbut umihutsah lah: al nikhus sefat ha'av kederekh le'itsuv intellectuali shel ha'ani hanashi," *Sadan* 2 (1996): 69–110.

33. For a critique of Miron's "distaste for and suspicion of contemporary feminist research," see Naomi Seidman, "Gender Criticism and Hebrew-Yiddish Literature: A Report from the Field," *Prooftexts* 14 (1994): 305.

34. Miron, *Imahot*, pp. 86–87.

35. Ibid., p. 56.

36. See *Gender and Text in Modern Hebrew and Yiddish Literature*, ed. Naomi B. Sokoloff, Anne Lapidus Lerner, and Anita Norich (New York: Jewish Theological Seminary of America, 1992). This volume also includes an annotated bibliography of feminist writing on Hebrew literature. For a more recent overview of various developments in this field, see Sokoloff, "Modern Hebrew Literature," pp. 224–43.

37. Chana Kronfeld, *On the Margins of Modernism: Decentering Literary Dynamics* (Berkeley: University of California Press, 1996); Gluzman, "Exclusion of Women."

38. Feldman, *No Room of Their Own*, p. x.

39. See *The Defiant Muse: Hebrew Feminist Poems from Antiquity to the Present*, ed. Shirley Kaufman, Galit Hasan-Rokem, and Tamar S. Hess (New York: Feminist Press, 1999); and *Dreaming the Actual: Contemporary Fiction and Poetry by Israeli Women Writers*, edited with an introduction by Miriyam Glazer (Albany: State University of New York Press, 2000). See also Glazer's earlier anthology of Israeli women's poetry, *Burning Air and a Clear Mind* (Athens: Ohio University Press, 1981).

40. A considerably abridged version of this book was issued in English translation under the title *Ribcage: Israeli Women's Fiction (A Hadassah Anthology)*, ed. Carol Diament and Lily Rattok (Hadassah: Women's Zionist Organization of America, 1994).

41. See Lily Rattok, "Deyokan ha'isha kemeshoreret Yisra'elit," *Moznayim* (May 1988): 56–62; Lily Rattok, "Hahipus ahar ha'em hashirit," *Shedemot* 110 (1989):129–31.

42. Lily Rattok, afterword to *Hakol ha'aher: sipporet nashim 'Ivrit* (Tel Aviv: Hakibbutz Hameuchad, 1994), p. 264; translation taken from Rattok's introduction to *Ribcage*, p. xvii.

43. Rattok, "Deyokan ha'isha kemeshoreret Yisra'elit," p. 59.

44. Translated from Cohen, "Betokh hatarbut umihutsah lah," p. 73.

45. Rattok, *Hakol ha'aher*, p. 264.

46. Sidra DeKoven Ezrahi, *Booking Passage: Exile and Homecoming in the Modern Jewish Imagination* (Berkeley: University of California Press, 2000), p. 15. I am grateful to Laura Levitt for calling my attention to this reference to Rachel and the *teraphim*.

47. As a result of the thematic organization, and the concentration on the idea of stealing the language of the father, I was not able to include readings of all the women writers who wrote Hebrew poetry and prose from 1850–1950. Most conspicuously absent is a discussion of the poetry of Elisheva, whose work does not explicitly engage biblical/rabbinic tradition or demonstrate conspicuously Jewish content. For an

extended discussion of the poetry of Elisheva, see Miron, *Imahot,* pp. 25–31. Lily Rattok includes Elisheva's short story "Ha'emet" in *Hakol ha'aher,* pp. 227–35; see also Rattok's afterword in this volume, pp. 267–68. See also Yaffa Berlovitz's new anthology, *She'ani addman ve'adam* (Hakibbutz Hameuchad, 2003), which includes many other Hebrew women prose writers, including several not covered in this book.

CHAPTER 1

1. Ostriker, *Stealing the Language,* p. 15.

2. S. D. Goitein, "Women as Creators of Biblical Genres," *Prooftexts* 8:1 (1988): 1–33 (trans. Michael Carasik from *Iyyunim ba Mikra: behinato hasifrutit vehahevratit* [Tel Aviv: Yahneh, 1957]). Also published in *Nashim baTanakh,* ed. Y. Zemorah (Israel: Mahberot Lesifrut, 1964), pp. 519–51.

3. Ibid., p. 4. For an in-depth analysis of the question of female authorship in the Bible and the gendering of texts, see Athalya Brenner and Fokkelien Van Dijk-Hemmes, *On Gendering Texts: Male and Female Voices in the Hebrew Bible* (Leiden: E. J. Brill, 1993).

4. For an overview of feminist approaches to Biblical scholarship, see Tikva Frymer-Kensky, "The Bible and Women's Studies," in *Feminist Perspectives on Jewish Studies,* ed. Davidman and Tenenbaum, pp. 16–39; Bible and Culture Collective, "Feminist and Womanist Criticism," in *The Postmodern Bible* (New Haven: Yale University Press, 1995), pp. 225–71. See also Adele Reinhartz's review of the series *A Feminist Companion to the Hebrew Bible,* ed. Athalya Brenner (Sheffield: Sheffield Academic Press, 1993–2001) in *Prooftexts* (Special Issue: Reading through the Lens of Gender) 20:1–2 (2000): 43–60.

5. Goitein, "Women as Creators," p. 26.

6. In a recent article, Tova Cohen also attributes the absence of women from "canonical Hebrew literature" to a Jewish doctrine of female modesty—based on the verse, "The King's daughter is all glorious *within,*" Psalms 45:14—that limited the activity of women to the private sphere. Cohen notes that there were parallel attitudes in the broader European "patriarchal" culture, but the Jewish version was more extreme in form. See Tova Cohen, "Min hatehum haperati el hatehum hatsibburi: kitvei maskilot 'Ivriyot bame'ah ha-19," in *MiVilna li Y'rushalayim: mehkarim betoldoteihem uvetarbutam shel Yehudei Mizrah Eiropah, mugashim leProfessor Shmuel Verses* (Jerusalem: Magnes Press, 2002), p. 237.

7. According to Boyarin, the Palestinian Talmud offers a different interpretation of the concept of merit, suggesting that for Ben Azzai, the merit in question is actually that of Torah study. In contrast, in the Babylonian Talmud this interpretation is completely suppressed. See Daniel Boyarin, *Carnal Israel: Reading Sex in Talmudic Culture* (Berkeley: University of California Press, 1993), pp. 169–80.

8. Ibid., pp. 169–70. For a compilation of Hebrew sources on women and Torah study see Getzel Ellinson, *Ha'isha vehamitsvot* (Jerusalem: Alpha Press, 1974), pp. 143–65; and Rachel Biale, *Women and Jewish Law: The Essential Texts, Their History, and Their Relevance for Today* (New York: Schocken Books, 1984), pp. 29–41. For sources supportive of women's involvement in Torah story see Susan Handelman, "Women and the Study of Torah in the Thought of the Lubavitcher Rebbe," in *Jewish Legal Writings by Women,* ed. Michah D. Halpern and Chana Safrai (New York: Lambda, 1998), pp. 143–78.

9. See Maimonides, *Mishneh Torah*, Hilkhot Talmud Torah 1:13.

10. See Rabbi Moses Isserles' notes on the *Shulhan Arukh*, Yoreh Deah 246:4.

11. Beruriah, the wife of Rabbi Meir and the daughter of the martyr Rabbi Haninah ben Teradiyon, was purported to have "studied three hundred laws from three hundred teachers in one day" (B. T. Pesahim 62b). In B. T. Berakhot 10a, she offers a better midrashic interpretation on a verse from Psalms than her illustrious husband. Similarly, in *Tosefta Kelim* Bava Kama 4:17, a question arises as to when one can go about purifying an oven that was plastered in purity but later became impure; the answer provided by Beruriah is accepted over that of her brother. Beruriah's incisiveness is also memorialized in a passage from B. T. Eruvin 53b: Rabbi Yossi the Galileean, approaches Beruriah on the road and asks the seemingly benign question, "By what path can one go to Lod?" "Stupid Galileean," Beruriah answers trenchantly. "Don't you know that the sages admonished that a man should not speak too much to a woman? You should have asked 'How to Lod?'" What is so remarkable about this passage is its duplicity, simultaneously upholding and subverting rabbinic attitudes toward the idea of men conversing with women. Here Beruriah is seen as hoisting a rabbi by his own petard! For sources on Imma shalom, see B. T. Shabbat 116a, Eruvin 63a, Nedarim 20a, Bava Metzia 59b, and J. T. Shvi'it 6:36c. See also Sondra Henry and Emily Taitz, *Written out of History: Our Jewish Foremothers* (New York: Biblio Press, 1988) pp. 48–53. This book has recently been updated and published as *The JPS Guide to Jewish Women*, Emily Taitz, Sondra Henry, and Cheryl Tallan, eds. (Philadelphia: Jewish Publication Society, 2003). For references to Yalta, see B. T. Berakhot 51b, Beitsah 25b, Gittin 77b, Hulin 109b, Niddah 20b.

12. Judith Baskin, "Jewish Women in the Middle Ages," in *Jewish Women in Historical Perspective*, 2d ed. (Detroit: Wayne State University Press, 1998), pp. 116–17.

13. See Henry and Taitz, *Written out of History*, pp. 175–83.

14. According to Avraham M. Habermann, "only a handful of Hebrew women poets are known to us from the Middle Ages, most of what we know of them comes by way of legend, and we do not know whether there is a kernel of truth to these legends." See Avraham M. Habermann, *Mipri ha'et veha'et* (Jerusalem: Reuven Mass, 1981), p. 93. According to one of these legends, the daughter of Rabbi Yehudah Halevi (eleventh to twelfth centuries) was a Hebrew poet.

15. See James Mansfield Nichols, "Qasmuna the Poetess: Who Was She?" *American Oriental Society* 103 (1983): 423–24.

16. See Pellegrino Ascarelli, *Debora Ascarelli Poetessa* (Rome: 1925). See also Cecil Roth, *The Jews in the Renaissance* (Philadelphia: Jewish Publication Society, 1959), p. 57, quoted in Howard Adelman, "Italian Jewish Women," in *Jewish Women in Historical Perspective*, p. 154.

17. For information about Sarah Copia Sullam, see Adelman, "Italian Jewish Women," p. 154; Israel Zinberg, "Writings in Yiddish by Women," in *A History of Jewish Literature*, vol. 7, trans. Bernard Martin (New York: Ktav, 1975). For her polemical letters see Franz Kobler, ed., *Letters of the Jews through the Ages*, vol. 2 (New York: East and West Library, 1952), 436–48. Also see *Four Hundred Years of Jewish Women's Spirituality*, ed. Ellen Umansky and Diane Ashton (Boston: Beacon Press, 1992), pp. 45–47.

18. Deborah Hertz, "Emancipation through Intermarriage?: Wealthy Jewish Salon Women in Old Berlin," in *Jewish Women in Historical Perspective*, pp. 193–207.

19. Shmuel Niger, "Yiddish and the Female Reader," translated and abridged by Sheva Zucker, in *Women of the Word: Jewish Women and Jewish Writing*, ed. Judith R. Baskin (Detroit: Wayne State University Press, 1994), p. 75.

20. Ibid., p. 72.

21. Ibid., p. 75.

22. Naomi Seidman, *A Marriage Made in Heaven: The Sexual Politics of Hebrew and Yiddish* (Berkeley: University of California Press, 1997), p. 9.

23. Quoted in Henry and Taitz, *Written out of History*, p. 94. For a reprint of the original Yiddish text of *Menekes Rivkah*—which until recently was almost entirely lost, save for one copy in the library of the Jewish Theological Seminary of America—see *Ateret Rivkah: Arba'ah sifrei tekhinot nashim im targum lelashon hakodesh*, ed. Meir Wunder (Jerusalem: Hamakhon Lehantsahat Yehudei Galitsiyah, 1991); this edition also includes an essay by Khone Shmeruk, "Hasoferet haYehudit harishonah bePolin—Rivka bas Meir Tiktiner vehiburehah," pp. 148–57.

24. Quoted from Shmeruk's transcription as printed in *'Ateret Rivkah*, p. 150. My translation.

25. See, for example, the rhymed preface to Nahmanides' commentary on the Torah.

26. In "Hasoferet haYehudit harishonah bePolin" Shmeruk observes that from "the rhymed Hebrew preface one can deduce that she knew Hebrew well," but he makes no further comment on this preface as a piece of Hebrew poetry. See *'Ateret Rivkah*, p. 151.

27. For Tiktiner's "A simchas toyre lied" as well as poems by Royzl Fishls (sixteenth century), Toybe Pan (seventeenth century), and Hannah Katz (seventeenth and eighteenth centuries) see Ezra Korman, *Yiddishe dikhterins: antologye* (Chicago: Verlag L. M. Stein, 1928), pp. 5–38. Meir Wunder also includes a copy of "A simhes toyre lied" in *'Ateret Rivkah*, pp. 155–58.

28. See *The Memoirs of Glückel of Hameln*, trans. Marvin Lowenthal (New York: Schocken Books, 1977).

29. See Natalie Zemon Davis, *Women on the Margins: Three Sixteenth-Century Lives* (Cambridge: Harvard University Press, 1995), p. 60.

30. Chava Weissler, *Voices of the Matriarchs: Listening to the Prayers of Early Modern Jewish Women* (Boston: Beacon Press, 1998), p. 7.

31. Ibid., p. 7.

32. For a translated excerpt, see ibid., pp. 177–78.

33. According to Weissler, a certain measure of uncertainty surrounds the historicity of this author. Ibid., p. 94.

34. Weissler notes incidentally that Leah Horowitz was a poor Hebrew stylist. Ibid., p. 110.

35. Ibid., p. 107.

36. Ibid.

37. *The Defiant Muse* includes a very useful historical overview. This greatly influenced the shape of my own historical discussion, for it introduced me to some writers of whom I was not yet aware, such as Merecina of Gerona, Freyha bat Yosef, and Asenath Barzani. See the discussion below.

38. For the Hebrew original of this poem as well as an English translation, see *Defiant Muse*, pp. 62–63.

39. Ezra Fleischer, "'Al Dunash ben Labrat ve'ishto uvno," in *Mehkerei Yerushalayim besifrut 'Ivrit*, ed. Dan Pagis (Jerusalem: Magnes Press, 1984), p. 199. My translation.

40. See Avraham M. Habermann, *Studies in Sacred and Secular Poetry of the Middle Ages* (Jerusalem: Reuven Mass, 1972), pp. 265–67. For the Hebrew original as well as a translation of the poem, see *Defiant Muse*, pp. 64–65. Also see the introduction to the volume, p. 6.

41. From Jacob Mann, *Texts and Studies in Jewish History and Literature*, vol. 1 (Cincinnati: Hebrew Union College Press, 1931), p. 483.

42. Yona Sabar, *The Folk Literature of Kurdistani Jews: An Anthology* (New Haven: Yale University Press, 1982), p. 123.

43. Again, for the Hebrew original as well as an English translation by Peter Cole of Asenath's poem, see *Defiant Muse*, pp. 66–69, as well as the introduction to the volume, pp. 7–8.

44. For more on Freyha see Yosef Chetrit, "Freyha bat Yosef: meshoreret 'Ivriah beMorocco beme'ah ha-18" in *Pe'amim* 4 (1980): 84–93; Yosef Chetrit, "Freyha bat Rabbi Avraham," *Pe'amim* 55 (1995): 124–30. For the text of two poems by Freyha and English translations thereof, see *Defiant Muse*, pp. 74–75, as well as the introduction to the anthology, pp. 8–9.

45. Kaufman, Hassan-Rokem, and Hess, introduction to *Defiant Muse*, p. 9.

46. According to Yitzchak Haim Castiglioni, who wrote a short account of Rachel Morpurgo's life as an introduction to his edited collection of her poems *'Ugav Rachel*—first published in Cracow in 1890 and reprinted in Tel Aviv in 1943—her education was primarily in the Jewish Holy Books. "Until age 12 she studied the Pentateuch. . . . At age fourteen she began learning the Babylonian Talmud with the great rabbi, Ben-Nadiv from Mantua" (Tel Aviv: Hapo'el hatsa'ir, 1943), pp. vii–viii. For an English paraphrase of Castiglioni's short biography, see Nina Davis Salaman, *Rachel Morpurgo and Contemporary Hebrew Poets in Italy* (London: George Allen and Unwin, 1924). Salaman also provides English translations of three of Morpurgo's poems. For more recent biographical articles on Morpurgo, see Howard Adelman, "Women's Voices in Italian Jewish Literature," in *Women of the Word*, pp. 62–65; Yael Levine Katz, "Rachel Morpurgo," *Judaism* 49:1 (winter 2000): 13–29.

47. Morpurgo published a poetic exchange with her cousin S. D. Luzzatto on the subject of her refusal to marry anyone else but Jacob Morpurgo, the man she loved. See *'Ugav Rachel*, pp. 66–67.

48. Vittorio (Yitshak Haim) Castiglioni, introduction to *'Ugav Rachel*, p. vii–xii.

49. For an excellent analysis of the poems written by male *maskilim* in "praise" of Morpurgo's poetry see Yaffa Berlovitz, "Rachel Morpurgo: hateshukah el hamavet, hateshukah el hashir," *Sadan* 2 (1996): 11–40, particularly pp. 11–21.

50. "Ve'eileh divrei Rachel" published in *Kokhavei Yitshak* 11 (1847): 3–4. Reprinted in *'Ugav Rachel*, p. 45. My translation. For another translation, see *Defiant Muse*, pp. 78–79. In order to reproduce the rhyme scheme, I have taken some liberties with the literal meaning of a few of the words. All future citations from *'Ugav Rachel* will be noted by page number within the body of the text.

51. See Tova Cohen, "Betokh hatarbut umihutsah lah: 'al nikhus sefat ha'av kederekh le'itsuv intellectuali shel ha'ani hanashi," *Sadan* 2 (1996): 69–110. The poem by

Ibn Gabirol that is alluded to in Morpurgo's sonnet is titled "Shelishit shokedet meshaleshet tsevahah"; here a femininely personified "Kenesset Yisra'el" is waiting and calling for divine redemption, which itself alludes to Jeremiah 48:11

52. Here I am incorporating comments made by Cohen in a letter to me, dated February 2003.

53. *The Talmud of the Land of Israel: A Preliminary Translation and Explanation* (Volume 2, Yebamot), trans. Jacob Neusner (Chicago: University of Chicago Press, 1987), pp. 390–91.

54. Berlovitz, "Rachel Morpurgo," p. 33.

55. See B. T. Kiddushin 80b.

56. For more on this, see Berlovitz, "Rachel Morpurgo," pp. 17–19.

57. For the Talmudic source for this misogynist dictum (there is no wisdom to women except the spindle), see B. T. Yoma 66b.

58. See Zemorah's preface to the 1943 edition of *'Ugav Rachel,* p. v.

59. Ibid., p. 5.

60. Dan Miron, *Imahot meyasdot ahayot horgot* (Tel Aviv: Hakibbutz Hameuchad, 1991), pp. 11–12.

61. Michael Gluzman, "The Exclusion of Women from Hebrew Literary History," *Prooftexts* 11 (1991): 259–78.

62. Iris Parush, "Women Readers in Jewish Society of Nineteenth-Century Eastern Europe," *Prooftexts* 14 (1994): 17. For an extensive treatment of the "woman question" in Haskalah writing, see Shmuel Feiner, "Ha'ishah haYehudiyah hamodernit: mikreh-mivhan beyahasei haHaskalah vehaModernah," in *Eros erusin ve'issurim,* ed. Y. Bartal and Y. Gafni (Jerusalem: Mercaz Zalman Shazar Letoldot Yisrael, 1998), pp. 253–303, esp. pp. 268–81. Feiner's article originally appeared in *Zion* 58 (1993): 453–99.

63. See the *Letters of Y. L. Gordon,* vol. 2 (Warsaw: Shuldberg Brothers, 1894), pp. 157–58. For a fascinating article on the Hebrew letter-writing by *maskilot* that examines an array of Hebrew letters written by women to friends, family members, male *maskilim,* and *Haskalah* journals, see Cohen, "Min hatehum haperati," pp. 235–58.

64. Ibid., pp. 330–40.

65. Gordon's "The Tip of the Yod" was first published in *Hashahar* 7 (1875). For more on the poem, see Michael Stanislawski, *For Whom Do I Toil* (New York: Oxford University Press, 1988), pp. 125–28. For a discussion of feminism and Hebrew literature of the Haskalah, see Ben Ami Feingold, "Feminism and Hebrew Nineteenth Century Fiction," *Jewish Social Studies* 49:3–4 (1957): 235–50.

66. Balin, *To Reveal Our Hearts,* p. 17. Again, for more on this issue, see Feiner, "Ha'ishah haYehudiyah hamodernit," pp. 253–303. Also see Tova Cohen's analysis of this issue in "Min hatehum haperati," pp. 235–58.

67. Balin, *To Reveal Our Hearts,* pp. 48–49.

68. Sarah Feige Meinkin Foner, *Ahavat yesharim o hamishpahot hamurdafot* (Vilna: Katsnelenbogen, 1881). Foner's great-grandson Morris Rosenthal has translated most of her writing. See *A Woman's Voice: Sarah Foner, Hebrew Author of the Haskalah,* trans. Morris Rosenthal (Wilbraham, Mass.: Daily International, 2001).

69. The fantastic plot elements in *Ahavat yesharim* and its polemical aspects (targeting the Galician Hassidic movement with its adoration of the *tsaddik* as well as the

Jesuit community) are all in keeping with the narrative trends in Haskalah novels. For more on this see David Patterson, *The Hebrew Novel in Czarist Russia: A Portrait of Jewish Life in the Nineteenth Century* (Lanham, Md.: Rowan and Littlefield, 1999).

70. See David Frischmann, review of *Ahavat Yesharim o hamishpahot hamurdafot,* in *Haboker or,* ed. Avraham Ber Ha-Cohen Gottlober (May–June 1881): 387–91. For an English translation of this review, see the web translation by Morris Rosenthal at www.fonerbooks.com.

71. Translation adapted from Rosenthal's translation as cited in note 69.

72. Patterson, *Hebrew Novel in Czarist Russia,* p. 234.

73. See Rosenthal's translation in *A Woman's Voice,* pp. 83–104 and on Rosenthal's Web site at www.fonerbooks.com/index.htm.

74. Sarah Feige Meinkin Foner, *Begged bogdim* (Warsaw: Druk Von A. Ginz, 1891). See Rosenthal's translation, "The Treachery of Traitors" in *A Woman's Voice,* pp. 105–42.

75. Sarah Feige Meinkin Foner, *Mizikhronot yeme yalduti: o, mar'eh ha'ir Dvinsk* (Warsaw: Hatsefirah, 1903). See Rosenthal's translation in *A Woman's Voice,* pp. 1–72.

76. Information gleaned from personal conversations with Morris Rosenthal.

77. See Y. S. Weiss, "Hahozeret biteshuvah," in *Tiltulei Gever* (Tel Aviv: 1948), pp. 46–48.

78. See Foner, *Mizikhronot yeme yalduti,* chapter 10. One can look as far back as *Beged bogdim,* her novella about the evils of Hellenism, which can be read as a veiled polemic against the assimilationist excesses of her own, enlightened generation.

79. For more information on Foner see Haim Leib Fuchs, *Lodish shel ma'alah* (Tel Aviv: Y. L. Perets Verlag, 1972), pp. 258–59; Yankev Glattshteyn, "Studentisher sleng in medinas yisroel," *Yiddisher Kempfer* (Friday, January 15, 1965), p. 11; Getzel Kressel, *Leksikon hasifrut ha'Ivrit badorot ha'ahronim* (Merhaviah: Sifriyat Po'alim, 1965–1967), p. 586; Joseph Jacobs, *The Jewish Encyclopedia* (New York: Funk and Wagnalls, 1906), p. 148 (in the entry for the city Lodz); Alter Esselin, *Leksikon fun der nayer Yiddisher literatur* (New York: Congress for Jewish Culture, 1968), p. 306. For a rather favorable overview of Foner's work, see E. Ben-Ezra, "Sofret 'Ivriot BeAmerikah," *Hado'ar* (Twenty-Fifth Anniversary Edition, 4 Sivan 5707/ 23 May 1947): 847–48. See also Patterson, *The Hebrew Novel in Czarist Russia,* and *A Phoenix in Fetters: Studies in Nineteenth- and Early Twentieth-Century Hebrew Fiction* (Totowa, N.J.: Rowan and Littlefield, 1988).

80. Hava Shapiro (Eim Kol Hai), *Kovets tsiyyurim* (Warsaw: Y. Edelstein, 1909), p. 4.

81. For a later essay on the subject of the image of women in Hebrew literature see Dr. Hava Shapiro, "The Female Image in Our Literature," *Hatekufah* 26–27 (1930): 617–33. In this article Shapiro argues that in contrast to other world literatures, Hebrew literature has conspicuously lacked real female characters.

82. For sources on Hava Shapiro, see Naomi Caruso, "Chava Shapiro: A Woman Before Her Time," M.A. thesis, McGill University, 1991. Also see Balin's chapter on Hava Shapiro in *To Reveal Our Hearts,* pp. 51–83. Relatively little was written about Shapiro during her time. An exception to this is an article by Yosef Klausner, "'Al 'bat hayehidah'," *Hado'ar* (23 Kislev 5699), p. 107, but even this was written well after the publication of *Kovets tsiyyurim.*

83. See, for example, "Ketsutsat kenafayim," *Kovets tsiyyurim,* pp. 14–16.

84. Balin, *To Reveal Our Hearts,* p. 69.

85. From Shapiro's diary, 1927. Quoted in ibid., p. 78.

86. Y. Klausner, "'Al 'bat hayehidah,'" *Hado'ar,* p. 107.

87. Caruso, "Chava Shapiro," p. 178.

88. For a collection of women's writings from the First Aliyah, see *Sippurei nashim benot ha'aliyah harishonah,* edited and with an afterword by Yaffa Berlovitz (Israel: Sifriyat Tarmil, 1984). See also Yaffa Berlovitz, "Ha'isha besifrut nashim shel ha'aliyah harishonah," *Katedrah* 54 (December 1989): 107–24.

89. This is the Hebrew pen name for Elizabetha Zirkova, a Russian poet who took an interest from her youth in matters Jewish, began writing poems in Hebrew after her marriage to the Zionist Shimon Bihovsky, and subsequently settled in Tel Aviv in the second half of the 1920s.

90. For an excellent discussion of Miri Dor, see Ziva Shamir, "Ahot rehokah: Miri Dor, hameshoreret hamodernistit harishonah," *Sadan* 2 (1996): 241–63.

91. Along with another woman poet, M. Bat-Hamah (née Malka Schechtman, 1898–1979), Yokheved Bat-Miriam participated in a Communist Hebrew literary movement known as the Hebrew Octoberists. As part of this movement both Bat-Miriam and Bat-Hama contributed to an anthology of Hebrew poems and essays titled *Bereishit* and published in Russia in 1926. For more on this movement, see Yehoshua Gilboa, *Octobera'im 'Ivrim: toldoteha shel ashlayah* (Tel Aviv: Tel Aviv University Press, 1974).

92. Berlovitz, *Sippurei nashim,* p. 187.

93. Deborah Bernstein, *The Struggle for Equality: Urban Women Workers in Pre-state Israeli Society* (New York: Praeger, 1987), p. 1.

94. See Hemdah Ben-Yehudah, *Ben-Yehudah: hayav umif'alav* (Ben-Yehuda: His life and works) (Jerusalem: Ben-Yehudah Hotsa'ah La'or, 1940), p. 118.

95. Taken from Nurit Govrin's essay on Hemdah Ben-Yehudah in Nurit Govrin, *Devash misela,* p. 47. Translation mine.

96. For an interesting treatment of the sexual politics surrounding Ben-Yehudah's promotion of Hebrew, see Seidman, *A Marriage Made in Heaven,* pp. 102–14. For more on Hemdah Ben-Yehudah, see Yoffa Berlovitz, "Literature by Women of the First Aliyah: The Aspiration for Women's Renaissance in Eretz Israel," in *Pioneers and Homemakers,* ed. Deborah S. Bernstein (Albany: State University of New York Press, 1992), pp. 49–74.

97. For a discussion of Bat-Miriam's use of images of space, distance and color, see Ruth Kartun-Blum, *Bamerhak hane'elam: 'Iyyunim beshirat Yokheved Bat-Miriam* (Tel Aviv: Massada, 1977).

98. Yokheved Bat-Miriam, *Merahok* (Tel Aviv: Hakibbutz Hameuchad, 1985), pp. 5–6. Translation mine. All further citations from *Merahok* will be noted by page number within the body of the text.

99. Kartun-Blum, *Bamerhak hane'elam,* p. 76.

100. Ibid., p. 74.

101. See "Tsafririm," in Chaim Nachman Bialik, *Selected Poems* (Bilingual Edition), trans. Ruth Nevo (Jerusalem: Dvir and the Jerusalem Post, 1981), pp. 10–13.

102. See Marjorie Slome, *Dreams in the Bible,* Rabbinic Thesis, HUC-JIR, 1987, pp. 22–23.

103. David Jacobson, "Religious Experience in the Early Poetry of Yokheved Bat-Miriam," *Hebrew Annual Review* 5 (1981): 53.
104. Ibid., p. 54.

CHAPTER 2

1. Robert Alter, "The Double Canonicity of the Hebrew Bible," in *Insider/Outsider: American Jews and Multiculturalism,* ed. David Biale, Michael Galchinsky, and Susannah Heschel (Berkeley: University of California Press, 1998), p. 143.
2. Ibid., pp. 132–33.
3. Ibid., p. 144.
4. Ibid., p. 137.
5. See Eli Schweid, "Shirat yahid bema'agal rabim: hatanakh beshirat Rachel," in *Rachel veshiratah,* ed. Shimon Kushnir and Mordekhai Snir (Tel Aviv: Davar, 1971), p. 212.
6. Ibid., p. 213.
7. Ibid., p. 212.
8. Lori Lefkowitz, "Eavesdropping on Angels and Laughing at God: Theorizing a Subversive Matriarchy," in *Gender and Judaism: The Transformation of Tradition,* ed. T. M. Rudavsky (New York: New York University Press, 1995), p. 160.
9. For a discussion of the concepts of poetic power or "gevurah" in mainstream male Hebrew poetry, see Lily Rattok, "Deyokan ha'isha kemeshoreret Yisra'elit," *Moznayim* (May 1988): 56–58.
10. Alter, "Double Canonicity," p. 136.
11. Shulamit Kalugai, *Nashim: shirim* (Tel Aviv: Yavneh, 1941), pp. 7–8. All further citations from *Nashim* will be noted by page number in the body of the text.
12. Gilbert and Gubar, *The Madwoman in the Attic,* p. 49.
13. Elisabeth Schüssler Fiorenza, *Sharing Her Word* (Boston: Beacon Press, 1995), p. 76.
14. In her analysis of British and American women's poetry about the Bible, Alicia Suskin Ostriker argues that "biblical revisionism takes three sometimes overlapping forms: a hermeneutics of suspicion, a hermeneutics of desire, and a hermeneutics of indeterminacy." See (*Feminist Revision and the Bible* (Cambridge, Mass.: Blackwell, 1993), p. 57. Ostriker's terminology and analysis are very useful and, indeed, applicable to Hebrew women's poetry. I have elected, however, to use my own terms, in an effort to delineate some of the distinctive aspects of Hebrew women's poetry in comparison with women's poetry in other languages.
15. Some poems written by women in this period seem to uphold rather than subvert "patriarchal" ideology. For example, if, as feminist biblical critic Cheryl Exum asserts, "the phallocentric message of the story of Jephthah's daughter is . . . submit to patriarchal authority" (Cheryl Exum, *Fragmented Women* [Valley Forge, Pa.: Trinity Press International, 1993], p. 34), Anda Pinkerfeld-Amir's "Bat-Yiftah" upholds this patriarchal message. See "Bat-Yiftah" in *Gittit* (Tel Aviv: Davar, 1937), pp. 25–28. The same might be said about the first version of Pinkerfeld-Amir's "Avishag," a poem about female renunciation, where Avishag learns to accept her lamentable lot as consort to the

aging King David. See "Avishag," in *Yuval: Shirim* (Tel Aviv: Davar, 1932), pp. 86–92. The later version of this poem, however, revises this message; see Anda Pinkerfeld-Amir, *Gadish: Shirim* (Tel Aviv: Dvir, 1949), pp. 69–74. This version includes a dramatic middle section called "Kinnor David" (David's harp), in which Avishag demonstrates a heroic, spiritual, and creative disposition that contrasts with her otherwise submissive, self-effacing behavior. For a discussion of this poem see Yitshak Akavyahu,"Avishag haShunamit," in *Lifnim meshurat hashir* (Tel Aviv: Akad, 1975). Reprinted in *Anda: kovets ma'amarim, reshimot, vedivrei sifrut aherim im nisphah bibliographi 'al Anda 'Amir-Pinkerfeld*, ed. Zahavah Beilin (Tel Aviv: Akad, 1977), pp. 119–30.

16. Miriam Peskowitz, "Engendering Jewish Religious History," in *Judaism since Gender*, ed. Miriam Peskowitz and Laura Levitt (New York: Routledge, 1997), p. 29.

17. See, for example, Anda Pinkerfeld, "Yuval," in *Yuval*, where the poetic speaker expresses a strong sense of identification with Yuval, the biblical figure described in Genesis 4:21 as the first musician. See also Rachel, "Eliyahu," "Yonatan," "Minneged," and "Tanakhi patuah beSefer IYYon," all of which express identification with male figures. See *Rachel: Shirim, mikhtavim, reshimot, korot hayehah*, ed. Uri Millstein (Tel Aviv: Zemorah Bitan, 1985), pp. 179, 190, 215, 238; Yokheved Bat-Miriam, "Sha'ul," "Adam," and "Avraham," in *Shirim* (Tel Aviv: Sifriyat Po'alim, 1972), pp. 181–82, 183–84, 187–88; and Leah Goldberg, "Kismei yare'ah," in *Shirim*, vol. 1 (Tel Aviv: Sifriyat Po'alim, 1986), p. 169; "Kuttonet passim" and "Ahavat Shimshon" in *Shirim*, vol. 2 (Tel Aviv: Sifriyat Po'alim, 1971), pp. 148, 169.

18. See the various poems included in *Nashim baTanakh*, ed. Y. Zemorah; for example, Saul Tchernihowsky, "Parashat Dinah," and B. Mordekhai, "Sarah," pp. 271–73 and p. 428, respectively.

19. Y. Karni, *Shirim*, vol. 3, ed. Dan Miron (Jerusalem: Mossad Bialik, 1992), pp. 76–77.

20. Y. Fichman, *Kitvei Ya'akov Fichman* (Tel Aviv: Dvir, 1959), p. 37.

21. Fichman's attribution of divine wisdom to Adam (to the exclusion of Eve) echoes Don Isaac Abravanel's interpretation of Genesis 1:27. According to Abravanel, the verse "And God created man in His image, in the image of God He created him; male and female he created them" suggests that only man was created in God's [intellectual, spiritual] image, while woman was created for procreative purposes, as indicated by the verse that follows (Gen. 1:28), which includes the blessing to "be fruitful and multiply." See *Abravanel al haTorah* on Genesis 1, p. 69.

22. In the closing passage of *A Room of One's Own*, Virginia Woolf exhorts her readers "to look past Milton's Bogey." Sandra Gilbert and Susan Gubar have explained this phrase as a reference to Milton's misogyny (representative of the patriarchal tradition of biblical interpretation), as expressed in his rendering of the story of Adam and Eve in *Paradise Lost*. See "Milton's Bogey: Patriarchal Poetry and Women Readers," in *Madwoman in the Attic*. Also see the introductory chapter to Margaret Homans, *Women Writers and Poetic Identity* (Princeton: Princeton University Press, 1980). For feminist discussions of the biblical account itself, see Phyllis Trible, *God and the Rhetoric of Sexuality* (Philadelphia: Fortress Press, 1978), pp. 72–143; Carol Meyers, *Discovering Eve: Ancient Israelite Women in Context* (New York: Oxford University Press, 1988); Mieke Bal, *Lethal Love: Feminist Literary Readings of Biblical Love Stories* (Bloomington: Indiana University Press, 1987); Pardes, *Countertraditions in the Bible*; and Adrien Janis

Bledstein, "Are Women Cursed in Genesis 3.16?," in *A Feminist Companion to Genesis*. For a comprehensive discussion of Eve and her various representations in the Hebraic literary tradition, see Nechama Aschekenasy, *Eve's Journey* (Philadelphia: University of Pennsylvania Press, 1986).

23. Elizabeth Cady Stanton, *The Woman's Bible* (New York: European Publishing, 1898), p. 7

24. See, for example, the selections on Adam and Eve in *Modern Poems on the Bible: An Anthology*, ed. David Curzon (Philadelphia: Jewish Publication Society, 1994), especially Susan Donnelly, "Eve Names the Animals," pp. 62–63, and Stevie Smith, "How Cruel Is the Story of Eve," pp. 77–78. Also see Alicia Suskin Ostriker's discussion of poems by Christina Rossetti, Maurya Simon, Linda Pastan, Stevie Smith, Kathleen Norris, and Ursula LeGuin in *Feminist Revision and the Bible*, pp. 69–71 and 80–83.

25. The Hebrew original of this poem, "Havah," can be found in Anda Pinkerfeld-Amir, *Gadish: shirim*, pp. 9–11. It was first published in Anda Pinkerfeld, *Me'olam: demuyot mikedem* (Tel Aviv: Adi, 1942), pp. 13–17. In writing this translation I consulted Sue Ann Wasserman's translation in *Four Hundred Years of Jewish Women's Spirituality*, p. 168. For an extended reading of this poem, see Chaya Cohen, *Anda Pinkerfeld-Amir: Monographyal*, Doctoral dissertation, Bar-Ilan University, 1999, pp. 194–200.

26. See line 65, "through it I shall be redeemed."

27. Yokheved Bat-Miriam, *Merahok*, p. 61. All translations from *Merahok* are mine unless otherwise indicated. Future citations will be indicated by page number within the body of the text.

28. Originally published as "Bein hol vashemesh," *Mahberot lesifrut* 1:1 (Shevat 1940): 21–24. Reprinted as part of an expanded poem cycle under the same title in Yokheved Bat-Miriam, *Shirim*, pp. 183–86. Translation mine. All further citations from *Shirim* will be indicated by page number within the body of the text.

29. David Jacobson, *Modern Midrash: The Retelling of Traditional Jewish Narratives by Twentieth-Century Hebrew Writers* (Albany: State University of New York Press, 1987), p. 126.

30. See Sue Ann Wasserman's translation of "Havah" in her 1987 Hebrew Union College rabbinical thesis, "Women's Voices: The Present through the Past," p. 12.

31. See Kalugai, *Nashim*, pp. 17–20.

32. This reading of the story is similar to a midrash from Genesis Rabbah 20:8 that attempts to explain the use of the word "voice" in the verse "And to Adam He said, 'Because you listened to the voice of your wife and ate of the tree'" (Gen. 3:17). The rabbis suggest that Eve used her voice to cry and scream to Adam, thus persuading him to eat with her.

33. For other poems alluding to the Eve story by twentieth-century Hebrew women poets, see Esther Raab, "Shirat isha," "Al gehonkha tizhol," and "Benot Havah" in *Kol hashirim*, ed. Ehud Ben Ezer (Tel Aviv: Zemorah Bitan, 1988), pp. 194, 247, and 384, respectively; Ella Amitan, "Meshirei Havah," *Pirhei neshiyah: shirim* (Tel Aviv: Aleph, 1963), pp. 22–24. See also *Bat kol: 'olamah shel meshoreret*, ed. Gila Uriel and Edna Mittwoch-Meller (Tel Aviv: Yaron Golan, 1995), pp. 17–19.

34. For more on this tradition see Daniel Boyarin, *Carnal Israel*, pp. 94–96.

35. See, for example, Elyakum Zunser, "Shivat Tsiyyon," and Yitshak Leib Barukh (Borkhovitz), "Evel Tsiyyon," in *Hashirah ha'ivrit bitekufat hibat Tsiyyon*, ed. Ruth Kartun-Blum (Jerusalem: Mossad Bialik, 1969), pp. 162–64 and 203–4 respec-

tively. Anthropologist Susan Starr Sered has written about the development of what she calls "the Cultic Rachel" during the nineteenth century. See Susan Starr Sered, "A Tale of Three Rachels, or, The Cultural *Her*story of a Symbol," *Nashim: A Journal of Jewish Women's Studies and Gender Issues* 1 (winter 1998): 5–41.

36. Morpugo, *'Ugav Rachel,* p. 28.

37. See "Shir tehillah" in *'Ugav Rachel,* pp. 29–30.

38. I'd like to thank Carole Balin for sharing this insight with me.

39. See also my discussion of "Ad lo zakanti" in the Introduction. The word/name Rachel also figures in two later poems by Morpurgo, but in a very different context. Whereas here Rachel is remembered for her voice and sympathetic tears, in these later poems Morpurgo marshals the literal meaning of the Hebrew word "*Rachel*" (ewe) as a figure of female poetic muteness, as in Isaiah 53:7, where the prophet describes a man who is submissive and mute, "like a ewe that is dumb before those who shear her." See *'Ugav Rachel,* pp. 45, 49.

40. For another translation, see Peter Cole's translation in *Defiant Muse,* p. 79.

41. For another reading of this poem see Yoffa Berlovitz, "Rachel Morpurgo: hateshukah el hamavet, hateshukah el hashir," *Sadan* 2 (1996): 28.

42. For the complete text of Ibn Gabirol's poem see *Shirei hahol shel Shelomo Ibn Gabirol,* ed. Haim Brody and Haim Schirmann (Jerusalem: Schocken, 1975), pp. 30–32. In searching out this allusion to Ibn Gabirol, I am indebted to Tova Cohen, who demonstrates in her brilliant analysis of another poem "Ve'eleh divrei Rachel," that Morpurgo includes linguistic elements from a *piyyut* by Ibn Gabirol called "Shelishit shokedet." Cohen notes that Morpurgo's cousin, Shemuel David Luzzatto (SHaDaL) was a collector of medieval *piyyutim* and that Morpurgo had access to this liturgical material through his collection. See Tova Cohen, "Betokh hatarbut umihutsah lah: 'al nikhus safat ha'av kederekh le'itsuv intelltuali shel ha'ani hanashi," *Sadan* 2 (1996): 69–110. It is difficult to establish with certainty that Morpurgo had similar access to such lesser known *shirei hol* (secular poetry) as "Afales ma'agali." According to H. Schirmann, S. D. Luzzatto published several editions of Ibn Gabirol's secular poetry; see H. Schirmann, *Toledot hashirah ha'Ivrit biSepharad haMuslamit* (Jerusalem: Magnes Press, 1996), p. 258. And while Brody and Schirmann seem to take the text of "Afales ma'gali" from manuscript sources discovered after Luzzatto's time, the possibility remains that Luzzatto and Morpurgo both knew of this poem from another source.

43. See "Eliyahu," in *Rachel: shirim, mikhtavim, reshimot, korot hayehah,* ed. Uri Millstein (Tel Aviv: Zemorah Bitan, 1985), p. 179. All quotations from Rachel will be noted by page number within the body of the text by the title *Rachel.*

44. See "Iyyov," in *Rachel,* p. 238

45. Schweid, "Shirat yahid bema'agal rabim," p. 213.

46. For a male-authored poem that reads the story of Rachel in terms of a shift from shepherdess to wife, see Mordekhai Goldberg, "Rachel" in *Nashim baTanakh,* p. 406.

47. See, for example, Rachel's famous plea in Genesis 30:1 to Jacob for sons, "Give me sons or else I will die," as well as various competitive naming speeches of Leah and Rachel in the ensuing verses.

48. I'd like to thank Aaron Panken for pointing out the interpretive possibilities in the words "*darki*" and "*shemurim.*"

49. *Rachel,* p. 140.

50. See *Petikhta d'Eikha Rabbah* 25 (Vilna edition).

51. For more on the biblical story of Rachel as a narrative of thwarted desire, see Pardes, "Rachel's Dream: The Female Subplot," in *Countertraditions in the Bible*, and Adin Steinsaltz, "Rachel," in *Biblical Images* (New York: Basic Books, 1984).

52. The biblical matriarch figures once again in a later poem titled "'Akarah" (Barren woman). I will discuss this poem in chapter 4, which focuses on the barren woman motif in Hebrew women's writing.

53. Leah Goldberg, "Ya'akov veRachel," *Shirim,* vol. 1, ed. Tuvya Ruebner (Israel: Sifriyat Po'alim), pp. 163–64.

54. For a discussion of café life in the poetic circle of Alterman, Shlonsky, and Goldberg, see Amia Lieblikh, *El Leah* (Tel Aviv: Hakibbutz Hameuchad, 1995), pp. 97–98. Lieblikh cites Menahem Dorman's biography of Alterman, *Pirkei Biographyah* (Tel Aviv: Hakibbutz Hameuchad, 1986), pp. 114, 117, 118.

55. Here, instead of the JPS translation, which translates "'*einayim rakkot*" as "weak eyes," I quote from Robert Alter's translation of Genesis (New York: W. W. Norton, 1996), p. 153.

56. Woolf, *A Room of One's Own*, pp. 48–51.

57. Biblical scholars have done a good deal of work in the past years trying to reconstruct images of biblical women singers, musicians, and poets. See, for example, S. D. Goitein, "Nashim keyotsrot sugei sifrut bamikra," in *Nashim baTanakh*, pp. 519–51; and S. D. Goitein, "Women as Creators of Biblical Genres," *Prooftexts* 8 (1988):1–33.

58. '*Ugav Rachel,* p. 45. Special thanks to Peter Cole for his help with this translation.

59. I'd like to thank Yael Levine Katz for pointing me in the direction of this source.

60. See, for example, Jerusalem Talmud Pe'ah 2:17:1, Megilah 4:74:4; *Shemot Rabbah* 10; *Vayikra Rabbah* 22; and *Kohelet Rabbah* 1.

61. See, for example, *Shut Rivash* 341 (beginning with the words "od lanizkar") and *Shut Yabia Omer* 2, Even Ha-ezer 7.

62. *Keter,* the highest *sefirah,* shares the same root as *koteret. Tif'eret,* another one of the *sefirot,* refers to a mixing of color and form into a creation of great beauty. It also is associated with mercy and compassion, and thus is a fitting appellation for a figure like the biblical Deborah, who was a poet as well as a great judge.

63. In using the relatively uncommon word "*tahalah*" (error or folly), Morpurgo seems to allude to Eliphaz's speech in Job 4:18, where he explains that God charges even the angels with folly; how can human beings expect to emerge unscathed? This reference to Job seems to insert an element of unfair punishment or precariousness into the poem.

64. In using this expression "Rachel ne'elamah," Morpurgo might also have been alluding to a poem by Solomon Ibn Gabirol called "Yotser leshabbat hamishit ahar pesah," in which a femininely personified *Kenesset Yisra'el* (together with the poetic speaker, the *meshorer*) begs God for salvation. In the sixth stanza of this poem, the *Kenesset Yisrael* speaker announces that she is sick with hopelessness and has become dumb like a sheep [ewe]—"*ne'elamti kerachel.*" See *Selected Poems of Solomon Ibn Gabirol* (Philadelphia: Jewish Publication Society, 1952), p. 26.

65. Esther Raab, *Gan sheharav,* ed. Ehud Ben Ezer (Israel: Sifriyat Tarmil, 1983), p. 104.

66. Esther Raab, *Kol hashirim,* p. 14. Hereafter all citations from Esther Raab will be indicated by page number within the body of the text.

67. Anne Lapidus Lerner, "The Naked Land: Nature in the Poetry of Esther Raab," in *Women of the Word,* p. 252.

68. Raab had a number of relatives who lived in the *Yishuv hayashan,* the old settlement in Jerusalem; her father moved from Jerusalem to become one of the founders of the agricultural settlement of Petah Tikvah.

69. See, for example, "Etsel Savtah" (At grandmother's house), where Raab recalls these healing visits to Jerusalem, including words and details that recapitulate the motifs of this poem. In particular, Raab's description of the grandmother includes agricultural images that suggest a melding rather than an opposition between pious Jerusalem and pioneering Petah Tikvah: "She is straight-backed, thin and erect, her face like a field furrowed with wrinkles, velvet wrinkles that I sometimes pass a finger over, and above are two blue eyes like two chicory plants suddenly sprouting in a plowed field. Her head is wrapped in a starched English lace kerchief. Everything about her rustles with starch and cleanliness. Freshness, and the fragrance of apples rises from her. Only on Friday does this scent mix somewhat with the naphthalene that clings to Sabbath clothes" (Raab, *Gan sheharav,* p. 57).

70. Lily Rattok, "Kemo mayim hotsevet: He'arot al me'afyenei hakol nashi bashirah ha'Ivrit," *Sadan* 2 (1996): 194.

71. For two more female-authored poems that comment on the story of Deborah (and Yael), see Anda Pinkerfeld-Amir, "Ya'el," in *Gadish va'omer* (Tel Aviv: Dvir, 1960), pp. 49–56. See also Elah Amitan,"Tsavah" in *Lakh ulekha: shirim* (Tel Aviv: Masada, 1949), p. 5.

72. See *Rachel veshiratah,* p. 91. Reprinted in Dan Miron, *Imahot meyasdot, ahayot horgot* (Tel Aviv: Hakibbutz Hameuchad, 1991), pp. 144–45.

73. Ziva Shamir disputes this reading of Bialik's eulogy, arguing that Bialik spoke out of a compassionate regard for Rachel's achievements, in no way seeking to belittle or disparage her poetry. See Shamir, "Ahot rekokah: Miri Dor—hameshoeret hamodernistit harishonah," *Sadan* 2 (1996): 252–54.

74. Miron, *Imahot,* p. 147.

75. Taken from an interview with Mariassa Bat-Miriam Katzenelson conducted by Ruth Kartun-Blum, titled, "Immi Yokheved Bat-Miriam," *Yedio't ahronot,* January 1, 1990. Reprinted in *Sadan* 2 (1996): 153–63. According to Ilana Pardes, Yokheved Zhelezniak decided to take the name Bat-Miriam because her biological mother's name was Miriam. In this sense, her name change represents a critique of the "patrilinear naming system," as well as of a culture in which "literary tradition, like names, is passed down from father to son." See Ilana Pardes, "The Poetic Strength of a Matronym" in *Gender and Text in Modern Hebrew and Yiddish Literature,* pp. 41–42.

76. See, for example, Ostriker, *Feminist Revision and the Bible,* pp. 43–44.

77. Ibid., p. 49. J. Cheryl Exum similarly observes that "the matriarchs step forward in the service of the androcentric agenda, and once they have served their purposes they disappear until such time, if any, they might again prove useful." See J. Cheryl Exum, "The (M)other's Place," in *Fragmented Women,* p. 97.

78. Alice Bach, "With a Song in Her Heart: Listening to Scholars Listen to Miriam," *Women in the Hebrew Bible,* ed. Alice Bach (New York: Routledge, 1998), p. 419. See also Phyllis Trible, "Bringing Miriam Out of the Shadows"; J. Gerald Janzen,

"Song of Moses, Song of Miriam: Who Is Seconding Whom?"; "Some Recent Views on the Presentation of the Song of Miriam"; and "Miriam the Musician"; these essays are all included in *A Feminist Companion to Exodus and Deuteronomy,* ed. Athalya Brenner (Sheffield: Sheffield Academic Press, 1994), pp. 175–230.

79. The scroll text at issue here is a biblical reworking, numbered 4Q365. For more on this, see George Brooke, "Power to the Powerless: A Long Lost Song of Miriam," in *Biblical Archaeology Review* 20:3 (1994): 62–65. Brooke also refers to Philo's description in *On the Contemplative Life* of the practices of an Egyptian Jewish group (the Theraputae), that references Miriam and the Song of the Sea. According to Philo, the Theraputae celebrated a "holy all-night festival," in which separate male and female choruses were assembled to sing hymns to God. Later in the evening the two choruses were mixed into one, "in imitation of what happened long ago beside the Red Sea" (Brooke, "Power to the Powerless," p. 65).

80. Yokheved Bat-Miriam first published "Kifsukim hayamim mizmorim nignazu" in *Musaf davar* 4:28, 26 Adar I, 5689 (8 March 1929), the same year she immigrated to Palestine. For a complete bibliography of Yokheved Bat-Miriam's publications in Hebrew periodicals, see Ruth Kartun-Blum, *Bemerhak hane'elam: 'iyyunim beshirat Yokheved Bat-Miriam* (Tel Aviv: Masada, 1977), pp. 165–75.

81. I had considerable difficulty translating the words *"sha'avah vakir."* The word *kir* typically means wall, but the bringing together of wax and wall in this line seems confusing. My colleague Joel Hoffman suggested that the word *kir* here might mean "wax" not wall. According to Hoffman, in Greek *kiros* means wax, and this word seems to have made its way into Rabbinic Hebrew/Aramaic as *kira* or *kir.* There is also a Russian word *syrguc,* which apparently means sealing wax. These may be connected, says Hoffman, which might explain how Bat-Miriam knew this rare word. The problem with translating *sha'avah vakir* into English is that if both words mean wax, English does not have two separate words to connote the same thing.

82. This translation has been developed from a partial translation of the poem by Ilana Pardes in her chapter, "The Poetic Strength of a Matronym," in *Gender and Text,* p. 41; it is reprinted with the permission of the translator and the Jewish Theological Seminary Press.

83. This translation is a slightly revised version of Pardes's translation in "Poetic Strength of a Matronym," pp. 45–46. Used with the permission of the translator and the Jewish Theological Seminary Press.

84. For a discussion of two other poems in this cycle, "Adam" and "Eve," see chapter 2 in this volume.

85. Jacobson, *Modern Midrash,* p. 116.

86. Pardes, "Poetic Strength of a Matronym," p. 46.

87. For a scholarly treatment of ancient Egypt as a culture of stasis, see E. A Speiser, "The Biblical Idea of History in Its Common near Eastern Setting," in *The Jewish Expression,* ed. Judah Goldin (New Haven: Yale University Press, 1976), pp. 1–17.

88. For a comprehensive discussion of the rabbinic portrayal of Miriam, see Devora Steinmetz, "A Portrait of Miriam in Rabbinic Midrash," *Prooftexts* 1:8 (1988): 35–65.

89. See Deuteronomy 24:9, where the people are reminded to remember what God did to Miriam after they left Egypt. Classical exegetes have typically viewed this as an admonition against sins of *lashon harah,* evil speech or gossip.

90. Jacobson, *Modern Midrash,* p. 118.

91. According to Lily Rattok, "the infant that Miriam leans over can be seen not just as Moses but as the Nation of Israel that is born with the Exodus from Egypt." See Lily Rattok, "Hahipus aharei ha'em hashirit," *Shedemot* 110 (August 1989): 132. For more on birth imagery and its relevance to the Exodus story, see Ilana Pardes, *The Biography of Ancient Israel* (Berkeley: University of California Press, 2000), pp. 16–39.

92. Pardes, "Poetic Strength of a Matronym," p. 55.

93: For another reading of this poem, see Haim Snir, "Ahavat Miriam," *Dimui* 5–6 (winter 5753/1993): 106–10.

94. Both Rachel Adler and Leila Leah Bronner have called attention to the irony that the rabbis credit a woman with the invention of the silent "'amidah" prayer, yet women are neither granted a substantive role in the communal worship nor counted as part of the prayer quorum. See Leila Leah Bronner, *From Eve to Esther: Rabbinic Reconstructions of Biblical Women* (Westminster; John Knox Press, 1994), p. 104; and Rachel Adler, *Engendering Judaism: Toward an Inclusive Theology and Ethics* (Philadelphia: Jewish Publication Society, 1998), p. 65.

95. See Chava Weissler, *Voices of the Matriarchs.*

96. See Alice Walker, "In Search of Our Mother's Gardens," in *In Search of Our Mother's Gardens* (New York: Harcourt Brace, 1983), pp. 231–43.

97. Weissler, *Voices of the Matriarchs,* p. 133.

98. Ruth Kartun-Blum argues that Bat-Miriam's admiration for Hannah derives from an aesthetic/spiritual ideology that prizes silence, abstinence, and *nezirut* (asceticism). Kartun-Blum bases this argument on an examination of the themes of silence and *nezirut* in Bat-Miriam's early poem cycle *Merahok.* See Ruth Kartun-Blum, *Bamerhak hane'elam,* pp. 85–86. In contrast to this position, I would argue that the emphasis in this poem is on speaking one's heart rather than upholding a form of abstinent silence. For another reading of these themes, see David Jacobson, "Religious Experience in the Early Poetry of Yokheved Bat-Miriam," *Hebrew Annual Review* 5 (1981): 57, note 10.

99. See, for example, B. T. Berakhot 31b, *Aggadat Bereishit* 43:3 and 53:3, and *Pesikta deRav Kahana* 20:1.

100. See *Out of the Depths I Call to You: A Book of Prayers for the Married Jewish Woman,* ed. and trans. Nina Beth Cardin (Northvale, N.J.: Jason Aronson, 1995), pp. 21–23. According to Chava Weissler, Hannah is frequently associated in the *tkhines* literature with the women's commandments of separating the hallah, ritual immersion in the *mikvah,* and lighting Sabbath candles. See Weissler, *Voices of the Matriarchs,* pp. 29 and 71.

101. The poet Rachel also alludes to the story of Hannah in her well-known poem "'Akarah" (Barren women), in *Rachel,* p. 189. See my discussion of this poem in chapter 4.

102. Quoted from Kwok Pui-Lan, "Racism and Ethnocentrism in Feminist Biblical Interpretation," in *Searching the Scriptures: A Feminist Introduction,* vol. 1, ed. Elisabeth Schüssler-Fiorenza (New York: Crossroad, 1993), p. 105.

103. John Waters, "Who Was Hagar?" in *Stony the Road We Trod: African American Biblical Interpretation* (Minneapolis: Augsburg Fortress, 1991), p. 198.

104. Pinkerfeld-Amir, *Gadish: shirim,* p. 20. My translation. All future citations will be indicated by page number within the body of the text.

105. I would like to thank my student Rachel Goldenberg for bringing this point to my attention.

106. *The Midrash Rabbah,* vol. I, trans. H. Freedman and Maurice Simon (London: Soncino Press, 1977), pp. 381–82.

107. See Yehudah Halevi, "Yitav be'einekha," in *ShaDal megiish mishirei RiHal,* ed. Joseph Hauben (Tel Aviv: Yaron Golan, 1996), p. 164.

108. My translation. For the Hebrew text, see *Gadish: shirim,* pp. 20–35.

109. For a contemporary Hebrew poem about Hagar that has much in common with Pinkerfeld-Amir's long poem see Zerubavela, "Shevuat Hagar bamidbar," in *Kor'ot miBereishit: nashim Yisra'eliyot kotvot al neshot Sefer Bereishit,* ed. Ruti Ravitzky (Tel Aviv: Yedi'ot ahronot, 1999), pp. 153–55.

110. Judith Plaskow, *Standing Again at Sinai: Judaism from a Feminist Perspective* (New York: Harper and Row, 1990), p. 15. For an excellent article that investigates the subversive quality of Anda Pinkerfeld Amir's reworkings of the stories of marginal biblical women, see Yohai Oppenheimer, "Nashiut ule'umiut: shirat Anda Pinkerfeld-Amir bishenot ha'arba'im vehahamishim," *Mikan* (2001):142–64. In this article, Oppenheimer detects in many of Pinkerfeld-Amir poems on marginal biblical women (Lot's wife, Yael, and Delilah) a note of protest against the national/religious values of the Bible. Oppenheimer contrasts this with Pinkerfeld-Amir's later poetry, published in the 1940s and 50s, which conforms to hegemonic national values.

111. Hagar wanders in the desert twice in Genesis. The first instance occurs in Genesis 15, when Sarai gives her Egyptian maidservant to Abram (before he is renamed) and Hagar bears him a son. Jealous of Hagar's child, Sarai begins to mistreat Hagar, and Hagar flees to the wilderness, where an angel finds her by a spring and urges her to return to her mistress. The second occasion occurs in Genesis 21:9–21, when the renamed Sarah tells Abraham to banish Hagar and her child from their household and Abraham does her bidding. Hagar wanders in the wilderness of Beersheba and is once again visited and saved by an angel of God.

112. This translation is mine, although in revising it I have consulted with Zvi Jagendorf's translation in *Defiant Muse,* p. 109.

113. My thanks again to Rachel Goldenberg for identifying this allusion in a presentation given for my seminar on the Bible and Modern Hebrew Women Writers at Hebrew Union College-Jewish Institute of Religion, New York, fall 2002. For an excellent discussion of the linguistic and thematic connections between the Hagar narratives and the Exodus story, see Phyllis Trible, "Hagar: The Desolation of Rejection," in *Texts of Terror* (Philadelphia: Fortress Press, 1984), pp. 9–35.

114. Thanks to my students Jeff Saxe and Michael Friedman, respectively, for identifying the "hemet mayim" and "vatashk" references.

115. *Webster's New Collegiate Dictionary,* ed. Henry Bosley Woolf (Springfield, Mass.: G. & C. Merriam, 1979), p. 1111.

116. Savina J. Teubal, *Ancient Sisterhood: The Lost Tradition of Hagar and Sarah* (Athens: Swallow Press/Ohio University Press, 1990), p. 200.

117. In the same cycle, "Bein hol veshemesh" (Between sand and sun), Bat-Miriam also includes a poem titled "Avraham," which looks at the story from Avraham's perspective and explicitly addresses Hagar. See *Shirim,* pp. 187–88. See also Ahuvah Bat-

Hannah (pseudonym of Ahuvah Rudnik, author of three books of Hebrew poetry since 1959), "Hagar," in *Nashim baTanakh,* p. 305.

118. For a chronology and selected bibliography of the works of Leah Goldberg, see *Leah Goldberg: mivhar ma'amarim al yetsiratah,* ed. A. B. Yafeh (Tel Aviv: 'Am 'Oved, 1980), pp. 239–46.

119. Quoted in Hayah Shaham, "Meshoreret bekahal meshorerim: 'al hitkablut shiratan shel Leah Goldberg veDalia Ravikovitch 'al yedei bikkoret zemanan," *Sadan* 2 (1997): 204.

120. Amia Lieblikh, *El Leah,* p. 246.

121. Ellen Moers, *Literary Women: The Great Writers* (New York: Oxford University Press, 1977), p. 66.

122. Leah Goldberg, "Ahavatah shel Teresa de Meun," *Shirim,* vol. 2, p. 156. All future citations from this cycle will be indicated by page number within the body of the text.

123. Lieblikh, *El Leah,* p. 210.

124. See Petrarch, Sonnet XVIII, "To Laura in Life," in *The Sonnets, Triumphs and Other Poems* (London: Henry G. Bohn, 1859), p. 16.

125. Eli Schweid, "El hashir—umimenu vehal'ah: Ahavatah shel Teresa de Meun me'et Leah Goldberg," in *Leah Goldberg: mivhar ma'amarim 'al yetsiratah,* p. 118.

CHAPTER 3

1. List taken from Tikva Frymer-Kensky, *In the Wake of the Goddesses: Women, Culture, and the Transformation of Pagan Myth* (New York: Free Press, 1992), p. 168.

2. Ibid., p. 178.

3. See Yehuda Leib Levin, "Meshir tsiyyon" (From the song of Zion), and Elyakum Zunser, "Shivat tsiyon" (The return to Zion) in *Hashirah ha'ivrit bitekufat hibat tsiyyon,* pp. 112, 162.

4. See Avraham Ber Gotlober, "Nes Tsiyyonah," in ibid., p. 42.

5. Avraham Shlonsky, "Yizra'el," in *Shirim,* vol. 2, p. 37.

6. See Shlonsky, "'Amal", in *Shirim,* vol. 2, p. 15.

7. Shlonsky, *Shirim,* vol. 2, p. 41.

8. Ibid.,p. 46.

9. Ibid., p. 27

10. Ibid., p. 37.

11. Ibid., pp. 29–30.

12. This account is generally thought by feminist critics to be the more antifeminist version, for here Adam is created first from the earth; Eve, formed from Adam's rib, is the secondary creature. For differing views see Phyllis Trible, *God and the Rhetoric of Sexuality,* pp. 72–105, and Mieke Bal, *Lethal Love,* pp. 104–30.

13. Sherry Ortner, "Is Female to Male as Nature Is to Culture?" in *Woman Culture and Society,* ed. Michelle Zimbalist Rosaldo and Louise Lamphere (Stanford: Stanford University Press, 1974), p. 75.

14. Susan Stanford Friedman, "Creativity and the Childbirth Metaphor," in *Speaking of Gender,* ed. Elaine Showalter (New York: Routledge, 1989), p. 75.

15. Ibid.

16. Margaret Homans, *Women Writers and Poetic Identity,* p. 13.

17. Annette Kolodny, *The Lay of the Land: Metaphor as Experience and History in American Life and Letters* (Chapel Hill: University of North Carolina Press, 1975), p. 4.

18. As Kolodny writes, "Neither paradisal nor gendered, the vocabulary of the garden and gardener evaded the disappointments inherent in the male fantasies." See Annette Kolodny, *The Land Before Her: Fantasy and Experience on the American Frontier* (Chapel Hill: University of North Carolina Press, 1984), p. 7.

19. B. T. Kiddushin, chap. 1.

20. B. T. Sanhedrin, ed. I. Epstein (London: Soncino Press, 1969), p. 74:b.

21. See P. Lahover, "Shirei Bat-Miriam," *Moznayim* 4, 18:13 (13 Tishrei 5692 / September 1932): p. 10.

22. For another Land of Israel poem that employs female personification, which is not discussed in this chapter, see Andda Pinkerfeld, "Yuval," in *Yuval: shirim,* pp. 7–12.

23. See Luce Irigaray, *This Sex Which Is Not One,* trans. Catherine Porter (Ithaca: Cornell University Press, 1985), pp. 30–31.

24. Yosef Seh-Lavan, "'Otsvah shel Rachel," *Bama'alah* (April 29, 1935).

25. Zalman Shazar, "Her Undimmed Light," in *Morning Stars,* trans. Shulamith Nardi from the Hebrew original (titled *Kokhvei boker* [Tel Aviv: 'Am 'Oved, 1950]) (Philadelphia: Jewish Publication Society, 1967), p. 215.

26. See for example, Michael Gluzman, *The Politics of Canonicity,* pp. 100–140.

27. Arthur Hertzberg, "Aharon David Gordon," in *The Zionist Idea,* ed. Arthur Hertzberg, ed. (New York: Atheneum, 1984), p. 369.

28. A. D. Gordon, "'Avodateinu me'atah," in *Kitvei A. D. Gordon,* vol. 2 (Tel Aviv: Hapo'el Hatsa'ir, 1925), p. 43. Translated as "Our Tasks Ahead," in *The Zionist Idea,* p. 379.

29. Einat Ramon, "The Zionist Myth of the Mother: The Land of Israel in the Thought of A. D. Gordon." Paper delivered at the Association of Jewish Studies Annual Conference, Boston, MA, December 14, 1993, p. 5.

30. Rachel, *Safiah: shirim* (Tel Aviv: Davar, 1927), p. 3.

31. Mary Ellmann, *Thinking about Women* (London: Virago, 1979), p. 61.

32. For a discussion of the importance of the Bible in Rachel's poetry see Eli Schweid, "Shirat yahid bama'agal harabim," in *Rachel veshiratah,* pp. 208–19; see also Havivah Yannai, "Minhat hashir: 'al zikkot lamikra bisheloshah shirim shel Rachel," *Be'eri* 1 (1988): 91–99; and Yair Mazor, "Hoi Kinneret sheli, kama kehulah ume-tuhkemet," *Hado'ar* 73:16 (1994): 18–22.

33. This translation is adapted from *The Prophets* (Philadelphia: Jewish Publication Society, 1978).

34. The poem "Temurah," also written in 1927, amplifies this notion of spiritually merging with the Motherland in death. Here Rachel foresees the decomposition of her lifeless, illness-ravaged body, its melding into fertile soil, and the eventual sprouting of grass from her eyes. See *Rachel: shirim, mikhtavim, reshimot, korot hayehah,* p. 163. Also see "Im tsav hagoral," the poem in which Rachel asks that she if can no longer work the land near the Kinneret, that she at least be permitted to be buried in "her cemetery." Here it is the Sea of Galilee that is femininely personified (*Rachel,* p. 178).

35. My translation. For another translation see Ruth Finer Mintz's translation in

Modern Hebrew Poetry: A Bilingual Anthology (Berkeley: University of California Press, 1966), p. 112.

36. My translation. For another translation that remains faithful to the rhyme pattern of the original Hebrew, see *Flowers of Perhaps: Selected Poems of Ra'hel*, trans. Robert Friend (London: Menard Press, 1995), p. 40.

37. The mixed meanings that attach to the symbol of the (female) bird are similarly evident in a poem by Rachel's contemporary, Esther Raab, titled "Portret shel ishah" (Portrait of a woman). See Esther Raab, *Kol hashirim*, ed. Ehud Ben Ezer (Tel Aviv: Zemorah Bitan, 1988), p. 85. For a translation, see *Poems: Esther Raab*, trans. Harold Schimmel (Tel Aviv: Institute for the Translation of Hebrew Literature, 1996), p. 53. In this poem, Raab identifies among the first principles of wisdom the need of a woman to heed her man, "as a bird heeds its flight." On the face of things, this poem supports a very traditional view of a woman's role in a relationship. On the other hand, as Lily Rattok has observed, birds do not submit easily to limitations; the liberating image of a bird flying is antithetical to the very idea of obedience or subservience. See Lily Rattok, "Portret shel isha—shiratah shel Esther Raab im hofa'at *Kol hashirim*," *Itton 77* 12 (1988): 18.

38. Gordon, "'Avodateinu me'atah," p. 51 ("Our Tasks Ahead," p. 381).

39. A. D. Gordon, *Ha'adam vahateva* (Tel Aviv: Hapo'el Hataza'ir, 1951), p. 41–47.

40. My translation. For another translation see Mintz's translation in *Modern Hebrew Poetry*, pp. 112–13.

41. Marta Weigle, *Creation and Procreation: Feminist Reflections on the Mythologies of Cosmogony and Parturition* (Philadelphia: University of Philadelphia Press, 1989), p. xi.

42. The message of this poem is once again reminiscent of the teachings of A. D. Gordon. In Gordon's writings, the land assumes a historically primary position, before the teachings of Moses, for it was "in this Land . . . and in the image of her landscape that monotheism emerged. Hence it was [the Motherland] who gave humanity the highest idea of all, the idea of the unity of God and all creation." Einat Ramon, "Zionist Myth of the Mother," p. 9. See, for example, A. D. Gordon's "Ha'adam vehateva," in *Kitvei A. D. Gordon*, vol. 3, p. 131, where Gordon speaks about monotheism being the "son of the desert."

43. The word *yibatser* occurs only twice in the Hebrew Bible. The first is in the story of the Tower of Babel, as cited above. The second is in the Book of Job (42:2) where Job answers God and says, "*yadati ki kol tuchal, lo yibatser mimkha mezimah*" (I know that You can do everything / That nothing You propose is impossible for you.) In contrast to the Job reference, however, Rachel's poem emphasizes not the power of God but the power of human beings.

44. Dov Sadan, *Orhot ushevilim* (Tel Aviv: 'Am 'Oved, 1977), p. 44.

45. See, for example, Ehud Ben Ezer, "Leilot levanim bePetah Tikvah," *Ha'arets* (November 9, 1984); Reuven Shoham, "Bein 'olam hapardesim lenerot shel shabbat venaftalin," *Shedemot* 58 (1976): 20–26. For an excellent and thorough analysis of the use of these concepts of truth, authenticity, firstness, naturalness, and nativeness in the critical literature about Raab, especially that which was published in the 1960s after the publication of *Shirei Esther Raab* (1963), see Hamutal Tsamir, "Ahavat moledet vesiah hirshim: shir ehad shel Esther Raab vehitkabluto hagavrit," *Te'oriah uvikkoret* 7 (1995):

125–45. According to Tsamir, the Israeli-born *moderna* generation of critics and poets who read Raab's poetry, rediscovered, praised and emphasized these qualities in Raab's poetry as part of their own effort to promote a new, nativist, modernist poetics.

46. Naomi Gottkind, "Esther Raab, hatsabbarit hameshoreret," *Hatsofeh*, May 22, 1969, p. 5.

47. Moshe Dor, "Ani giliti et hanof ha'Erets Yisra'eli," *Ma'ariv*, October 3, 1971, p. 14.

48. Quoted in Ehud Ben Ezer, *Yamim shel la'anah udevash*, p. 182.

49. Quoted in Reuven Shoham, "Esther Raab veshiratah," in *Esther Raab: yalkut shirim* (Tel Aviv: Yahdav, 1982), p. 15. My translation.

50. Reuven Shoham argues in *Kol udeyokan: tahanot behitpathut deyokan hadover bashirah ha'ivrit hahadashah* (Haifa: Haifa University Press, 1988), p. 114, that "anyone who knew Esther knows the extent to which it is impossible to separate her poetry from her person." His reading of Raab stems from this experiential conviction that the best way to understand Raab's poetry is to have known her. My reading here tends to complicate this assertion of a direct correlation between biography and poetic creation.

51. Reuven Shoham, "Bat ha'arets," *Shedemot* 56 (1975): 89.

52. Ibid., p. 90.

53. Ben Ezer, *Yamim shel la'anah udevash*, p. 420.

54. Tzvi Luz, *Shirat Esther Raab: monografyah* (Tel Aviv: Hakibbutz Hameuchad, 1997), p. 15.

55. Tsamir, "Ahavat moledet vesiah hirshim," p. 130.

56. Shoham, *Kol udeyokan*, p. 118.

57. Yael Feldman argues in *No Room of Their Own* that the "invention of Israeli androgyny coincided, interestingly enough, with the controversies that erupted within Western (mostly Anglo-American) feminism over Woolf's legacy" (p. 91). In her book Feldman devotes two chapters to Woolf's concept of androgyny and the way it was received by such writers as Shulamith Hareven, Netivah Ben-Yehudah, and Ruth Almog. My own discussion of androgyny also touches on Woolf's concept, but it shows how the idea of androgyny plays out in the work of a much earlier Israeli poet, who may or may not have been exposed to the writings of the great British modernist and feminist.

58. Cynthia Secor, "The Androgyny Papers," in *The Androgyny Papers*, ed. Cynthia Secor, *Women's Studies* 2 (1974): 139.

59. Woolf, *A Room of One's Own*, p. 102.

60. Ibid., p. 108.

61. Elaine Showalter, *A Literature of Their Own: British Women Novelists from Brontë to Lessing* (Princeton: Princeton University Press, 1977), p. 288.

62. Ibid., p. 289.

63. Barbara Charlesworth Gelpi, "The Politics of Androgyny," in *Androgyny Papers*, pp. 151–52.

64. Cynthia Secor, "Androgyny: An Early Appraisal," in *Androgyny Papers*, p. 164.

65. Weil's chapter, "Androgyny, Feminism and the Critical Difference" in her book *Androgyny and the Denial of Difference* (Charlottesville: University Press of Virginia, 1992), pp. 145–69, provides an excellent critical overview of the feminist debate about androgyny, and I found it invaluable for this chapter. Weil's special contribution to this debate includes a reading of Woolf's novel *Orlando,* which Woolf was writing at the same time as

A Room of One's Own. Weil contends that in contrast to the essay, where Woolf seems to present a notion of androgyny as a "fusion of male and female resulting in an ideal of wholeness and unity," *Orlando* uses gender indeterminacy to question "the patriarchal construction of woman as different from man" as well as "the androgynous ideals of psychological equilibrium and aesthetic harmony" (Weil, p. 156).

66. Toril Moi, *Sexual/Textual Politics: Feminist Literary Theory* (London: Routledge, 1985), p. 13.

67. Ibid., p. 2.

68. Carolyn Heilbrun, *Toward a Recognition of Androgyny* (New York: W. W. Norton, 1993), p. x.

69. Ibid.

70. Ibid., p. 14.

71. Michael Gluzman, "The Exclusion of Women from Hebrew Literary History," *Prooftexts* 11:3 (1991): 271. Reprinted in *The Politics of Canonicity,* p. 125.

72. Weil, *Androgyny and the Denial of Difference,* p. 2.

73. From Rut Bondi, "Shevil hayahid shel Esther Raab," *Davar shavu'a,* 21.4.67. Quoted in Shoham, *Kol udeyokan,* p. 115.

74. Sh. Shifra, "Re'ayon im Esther Raab: ka'asher ani meriha ahava ani rotsa shoshanim," *Masa* (June 1, 1973): 1, 7.

75. Esther Raab, "Manya Vilbushevitz," in *Kol haprosah,* ed. Ehud Ben Ezer (Tel Aviv: April 1994), pp. 73–74. My translation.

76. See, for example, Butler, *Gender Trouble.*

77. Catherine Nash, "Remapping the Body/Land: New Cartographies of Identity, Gender, and Landscape in Ireland," in *Writing Women and Space: Colonial and Postcolonial Geographies,* ed. Allison Blunt and Gillian Rose (New York: Guilford Press, 1994), p. 238.

78. Esther Raab, *Kol hashirim,* p. 17. All future citations from Raab's collected poems will be noted by page number within the body of the text. "La'av" is translated by Harold Schimmel, © Translation Institute, and appeared in *Thistles: Selected Poems of Esther Raab* (Jerusalem: Ibis Editions, 2003), pp. 46–47.

79. Originally published in *Hedim* 2 (1922): 41.

80. Ehud Ben Ezer, *Yamim shel la'anah udevash,* p. 264.

81. Shoham, *Kol udeyokan,* pp. 115–16.

82. Louise Westling, *The Green Beast and the New World: Landscape, Gender and American Fiction* (Athens: University of Georgia Press, 1996), p. 27.

83. Chana Kronfeld, *On the Margins of Modernism,* p. 71.

84. Tsamir, "Ahavat moledet vesiah hirshim," p. 142.

85. Ibid.

86. This is my translation, but I consulted Harold Schimmel's translation in *Thistles: Selected Poems of Esther Raab,* pp. 39–40, and Anne Lapidus Lerner's translation in "The Naked Land: Nature in the Poetry of Esther Raab," in *Women of the Word,* pp. 248–49.

87. See, for example, Shoham, *Kol udeyokan,* pp. 121–22.

88. Lerner, "Naked Land," p. 249.

89. Tsamir, "Ahavat moledet vesiah hirshim," p. 136.

90. *Mahberot kimshonim,* ed. Ehud Ben Ezer (Tel Aviv: June 1999), p. 53.

91. Kolodny, *Lay of the Land,* p. 9.

92. For more on the significance of the parable of Jotham in Raab's poetry see Dan Miron, *Imahot meyasdot, ahayot horgot,* p. 21; also Lerner, "Naked Land," p. 247.

93. For an excellent discussion of Raab's poetic treatment of the Israeli landscape, including her incorporation of botanical knowledge, see Barbara Mann, "Framing the Native: Esther Raab's Visual Poetics," *Israel Studies* 4:1 (1999): 234–57.

94. "Esther Raab, Ne'urei hashirah be'erets lo zeru'ah: re'ayon shene'erakh b-9.5.1971 'im hameshoreret Esther Raab," *Hadarim* 1 (spring 1981): 104.

95. Chaim N. Bialik, *Selected Poems,* trans. Ruth Nevo (Dvir/Jerusalem Post, 1981), p. 124.

96. Ibid., p. 122.

97. Ibid., p. 120.

98. Ibid., p. 132.

99. For other translations, see Schimmel, *Thistles,* p. 56; Lerner, "Naked Land," p. 246; and Kronfeld, *On the Margins of Modernism,* p. 77.

100. *Mahberot kimshonim,* p. 5

101. *Webster's New Collegiate Dictionary,* p. 163.

102. Hélène Cixous and Catherine Clément, *The Newly Born Woman,* trans. Betsy Wing (Minneapolis: University of Minnesota Press, 1986), p. 32.

103. Diana Wolkstein and Samuel Noah Kramer, *Inanna, Queen of Heaven and Earth: Her Stories and Hymns from Sumer* (New York: Harper and Row, 1983), p. 71.

104. Shin Shifrah, "Hakayits hu peragim ahronim: mikra beshirei Esther Raab, hamesh shanim lemotah," *Itton 77* (September–October 1986): 80–81.

105. Frymer-Kensky, *In the Wake of the Goddesses,* p. 25.

106. Ibid., p. 30.

107. Ibid., p. 26.

108. Ibid., p. 29.

109. Anne Lapidus Lerner, "Nature in the Poetry of Esther Raab," p. 247.

110. For a poem on a related theme see "Lo ah ve'esh kirayim," in *Kol hashirim,* p. 30. Also see Kronfeld, *On the Margins of Modernism,* pp. 72–74.

111. Again, this translation is mine, although I have consulted other translations. See Barbara Mann's translation in "Framing the Narrative: Esther Raab's Visual Poetics," *Israel Studies* 4:1 (1999), p. 243.

112. Mann, "Framing the Narrative," p. 243.

113. Ibid.

114. Raab, *Kol hashirim,* p. 11.

115. For other translations, see Schimmel, *Thistles,* p. 48 and Mann, "Framing the Narrative," pp. 247–48.

116. Natan Alterman, "Kamah devarim besha'ah gedolah leshirateinu," in *Bema'agal: Ma'amarim vereshimot* (Tel Aviv: Hakibbutz Hameuchad, 1971), p. 84.

117. Ruth Kartun-Blum, *Bamerhak hane'elam,* p. 7. See also Dan Miron, "Kanfot ha'arets: He'arot leshirat Y. Bat-Miriam," *Gazit* 16 (1958–1959): 7–8.

118. See, for example, Ruth Kartun-Blum, "Immi Yokheved Bat-Miriam," *Yediot ahronot,* January 19, 1990, pp. 22, 23, 27; also Ilana Pardes, "Yokheved Bat-Miriam: The Poetic Strength of a Matronym," in *Gender and Text in Modern Hebrew and Yiddish Literature,* pp. 39–63.

119. Ibid., p. 220.
120. Quoted in Kartun-Blum, *Bemerhak hane'elam,* p. 23.
121. Ibid., p. 49.
122. Miron, *Imahot,* p. 221.
123. Dov Sadan, "Ge'ulat kissufim" in *Orhot ushevilim,* p. 44.
124. Miron, *Imahot,* p. 166.
125. Ibid., pp. 161–72.
126. Ibid., p. 176
127. Baron's early works were made available to the wider reading public only after her death, through the publication of Nurit Govrin's *Parshiyyot mukdamot,* a biographical account of Baron's early life and career, that includes a collection of her previously uncollected early works, edited by Avner Holtzman (Jerusalem: Mossad Bialik 1988). For an account of Bat-Miriam's determination not to include anything from *Merahok* in her collected works (*Shirim,* 1963), see Dan Miron, "Hitvad'ut limeshoreret," *Mahberot lesifrut, lehevrah, ulevikkoret* 2 (February 1980): 7–12.
128. Naomi Seidman, *A Marriage Made in Heaven,* p. 72. See also Wendy Zierler, "In What World?: Devorah Baron's Fiction of Exile," *Prooftexts* 19 (1999):127–50.
129. Miron, *Imahot,* p. 106.
130. For details, see Kartun-Blum, "Immi Yokheved Bat-Miriam," p. 22.
131. Reuven Shoham argues that the abstract quality of Bat-Miriam's landscape descriptions in *Erets Yisra'el* is typical of the landscape poetry written by the immigrant Hebrew poets of her generation. According to Shoham, immigrant poets such as Bat-Miriam, Y. Karni, and A. Shlonsky longed to embrace their new homeland in all its aspects, but they suffered from a sense of estrangement and yearning for the Russian landscape of their youth. This prevented them, Shoham argues, from composing convincing, realistic descriptions, leading them to rely instead upon ready-made, traditional images of the land. Shoham contrasts this with what he considers the more "authentic" and realistic landscape poetry of Esther Raab, the first "Sabra" poet. While Shoham mounts a compelling argument about the ways in which the immigrant experience informed the writing of these poets, he fails to acknowledge that for a symbolist poet such as Bat-Miriam, abstract, metaphysical description represents a deliberate aesthetic stance and a preferred poetic practice. See Reuven Shoham, "Bat ha'arets," *Shedemot* 56 (winter 1975): 84–86.
132. Kartun-Blum, *Bamerhak hane'elam,* pp. 23, 62, 70.
133. From Renato Poggioli, *The Poets of Russia* (Cambridge: Harvard University Press, 1960), p. 118.
134. Ibid., p. 195.
135. Ibid., pp. 202–3.
136. Yokheved Bat-Miriam, *Merahok.* All citations to this work will be indicated within the body of the text by page number. All translations are mine.
137. Yokheved Bat-Miriam, "Yerushalayim," *Musaf davar* 12:1 (15 Sivan 5696 / June 1936). Reprinted in Yokheved Bat-Miriam, *Shirim* (Tel Aviv: Sifriyat Poalim, 1972), pp. 175–76. All citations from *Shirim* will be indicated within the body of the text by page number (and, in the case of *Erets Yisra'el,* by line number as well). For a useful and comprehensive bibliography of Bat-Miriam's collected and uncollected published works, see Kartun- Blum, *Bamerhak hane'elam,* pp. 165–75.
138. Bat-Miriam's constant use of *at* in this poem cycle as well as in others such as

'Agurim mehasaf is especially interesting in light of the fact that in life, rather than poetry, Bat-Miriam tended to address people in the third person, reserving the second-person address for such personified objects or concepts as land or love. See Kartun-Blum, "Immi Yokheved Bat-Miriam," p. 23.

139. Hélène Cixous, "Castration or Decapitation?" trans. Annette Kuhn, *Signs* 7:1 (fall 1981): 53.

140. Irigaray, *This Sex Which Is Not One,* pp. 28–29.

141. For a consideration of the common features of the landscape poetry produced by Second and Third Aliyah poets, see Reuven Shoham, "Bat ha'arets," *Shedemot* 56 (winter 1975): 74–93.

142. For a consideration of the images of the wing and flight in Bat-Miriam's work as a whole, see Dan Miron, "Kanfot ha'arets," *Gazit* 16 (1958–1959): 7–8.

143. Cixous, "Sorties," p. 96.

144. Fuss, *Essentially Speaking,* p. 69.

145. Ibid., p. 64.

146. Indeed, the Hebrew verb "m.s. kh," meaning to draw or pull, which figures in this verse from the Song of Songs *(meshakheini ahareckha-)* recurs throughout Bat-Miriam's poem cycle. The land draws the poet after her, is drawn into itself or drawn after the poet, and so on.

147. Kartun-Blum, *Bamerhak hane'elam,* p. 27.

148. See Phyllis Trible, *God and the Rhetoric of Sexuality,* p. 145.

149. Pardes, *Countertraditions in the Bible,* p. 126.

150. Hikllel Barzel and, later, Ruth Kartun-Blum, argue that Bat-Miriam's use of the color blue is deliberate. According to Barzel, in his article *"Besod haremez vehanirmaz"* (*Haboker* 9, September 1964), in Bat-Miriam's poetry the association of blue with the heavens, the ocean, and the horizon represents longing and yearning toward transcendence.

151. Song of Songs 8:14.

152. Alterman, "Kamah devarim besha'ah gedolah leshirateinu," p. 83.

CHAPTER 4

The epigraph is from Deborah L. Madsen, *Rereading Allegory: A Narrative Approach to Genre* (New York: St. Martin's Press, 1994), p. 13.

1. For an extensive treatment of the barrenness theme in biblical and midrashic sources, see Judith R. Baskin, "Rabbinic Reflections on the Barren Wife," *Harvard Theological Review* 82:1 (1989):101–14. See also Yael Levine Katz, "Ha'akarut ba'aggadah," *Te'udah* 13 (1997): 79–134.

2. Tikva Frymer-Kensky, *In the Wake of the Goddesses,* p. 98.

3. Exum, *Fragmented Women,* p. 120.

4. Mary Callaway, "Sing O Barren One: A Study in Comparative Midrash," Ph.D. diss., Columbia University, 1979, p. 87.

5. Ibid., p. 91. See Isaiah 49:19–21, 51:1–3, and 54:1–3.

6. This analogy is made even more explicit in *Aggadat Bereishit* 53:3, where the rabbis proclaim that there "are seven barren women, corresponding to the seven days of the week."

7. See S. Y. Agnon, "Aggadat hasofer," *Eilu ve'eilu* (Jerusalem and Tel Aviv: Schocken, 1959), p. 133.

8. Anne Golomb Hoffman, *Between Exile and Return: S. Y. Agnon and the Drama of Writing* (Albany: State University of New York Press, 1991), p. 34.

9. Agnon, "Aggadat hasofer," p. 136. Translation adapted from "A Tale of the Scribe," trans. Isaac Franck, in S. Y. Agnon, *Twenty-One Stories* (New York: Schocken Books, 1970), p. 14.

10. Cordelia Chavez Candelaria, "The 'Wild Zone' Thesis as a Gloss in Chicana Literary Study," in *Feminisms: An Anthology of Literary Theory and Criticism,* ed. Robin R. Warhol and Diane Price Herndl (New Brunswick, N.J.: Rutgers University Press, 1997), p. 250.

11. The idea of de-allegorization in relation to the fiction of Devorah Baron was first brought to my attention by Mark Bernstein in a paper delivered at the 1992 conference of the National Association of Professors of Hebrew titled "Midrash and Marginality: The ''Agunot' of Devorah Baron and S. Y. Agnon." Bernstein's paper has recently been published in expanded form in *Hebrew Studies* 42 (2001): 7–58.

12. Zilla Goodman notes that despite his name, "Shelomo the elder is anything but wise." See Zilla Jane Goodman, "Traced in Ink: Women's Lives in 'Qotzo shel Yud' by Yalag and 'Mishpacha'" by D. Baron, in *Gender and Judaism,* p. 202.

13. Translation quoted from *"The First Day" and Other Stories,* trans. Naomi Seidman and Chana Kronfeld (Berkeley: University of California Press, 2001), p. 60. For the Hebrew original, see Devorah Baron, *Parshiyyot* (Jerusalem: Mossad Bialik, 1968), p. 2.

14. Naomi Seidman, "Baron in the Closet," *A Marriage Made in Heaven,* p. 82.

15. According to Mishnah Yevamot 6:6, "If a man took a wife and lived with her for ten years and she bore no child, he may not abstain [any longer from the duty of propagation]. If he divorced her, she is permitted to marry another, and the second husband may also live with her for [no more than] ten years."

16. Bernstein, "Midrash and Marginality," p. 35.

17. For discussions of the relationship in the Bible between *rahamim* (pity or mercy) and *rehem* (womb), see Phyllis Trible, *God and the Rhetoric of Sexuality,* pp. 34–71. For an article that builds on and responds to Trible's insights, see Andrea Weiss, "Female Imagery in the Book of Isaiah," *CCAR Journal* (winter 1994): 65–77.

18. Gordon's poem decries the plight of women under Jewish law. It tells the story of a beautiful young woman named Bat-Shua whose father marries her off to a brilliant Yeshiva student, Hillel, who has no means of supporting a family. He eventually deserts her and their children, rendering her an *'agunah.* Bat-Shua's only hope is to be granted a *get* that will enable her to marry Feibe, a local railway supervisor who has fallen in love with her. But when the bill of divorce is finally procured from Hillel, it is cruelly invalidated by the chief judge of the local rabbinical court because Hillel signed his name "incompletely," without a "yud." For more on the relationship be°tween Gordon's poem and Baron's "Mishpahah," see Z. J. Goodman, "Traced in Ink," pp. 191–205. See also Seidman, *A Marriage Made in Heaven,* pp. 83–84.

19. Bernstein, "Midrash and Marginality," p. 34.

20. Ibid., pp. 32–58.

21. Agnon, "Aggadat hasofer," p. 15. *Twenty-One Stories,* pp. 15–16.

22. Baron, *Parshiyyot,* pp. 15–16; translation from *"The First Day" and Other Stories,* p. 64.

23. In her discussion of the impact of female readers on the nineteenth-century Jewish community, Iris Parush notes that many more Jewish women than Jewish men read novels, which furnished them with information about male and female relationships, matured them, and made them better prepared for married life. She cites, for example, A. B. Gottlober's account of a young bridegroom on his wedding night who was embarrassed because he "did not know how to read novels, had never heard any love songs . . . , and everything connected to love was like a closed book to him" (See Iris Parush, "Women Readers as Agents of Social Change among Eastern European Jews in the Late Nineteenth Century," *Gender and History* 9:1 [April 1997]: 70). We do not see Dinah reading in this story, but we do see her singing various songs of love and yearning (p. 18). The perspective of female readers is also evident in the voice of the educated female narrator of the story.

24. Baron, *Parshiyyot,* p. 18; translation slightly adapted from *"The First Day" and Other Stories,* p. 69. Seidman and Kronfeld translated the word *harhatsah* as ritual bath, which I have changed to "washing," given that immersion in the ritual bath is usually referred to as *tevilah* not *harhatsah.*

25. Arnold Band, *Nostalgia and Nightmare* (Berkeley: University of California Press, 1968), p. 110. For other interpretations of "Aggadat hasofer," see Judith Halevi-Zwick, *Agnon in Context* [Hebrew] (Tel Aviv: Papyrus, 1989), pp. 9–32. See also Risa Domb, "Be'ikvot ha'aggadah vehasofer," in *Hekrei Agnon,* ed. Hillel Weiss and Hillel Barzel (Tel Aviv: Bar Ilan University Press, 1994), pp. 197–203.

26. According to Anne Golomb Hoffman, for example, Raphael's "breaking the ice to immerse himself in the river can be read as the moment of the narcissistic fall: Raphael goes back into the mirror, drowning himself in a moment of icy ecstasy" (Hoffman, *Between Exile and Return,* p. 34).

27. Agnon, "Aggadat hasofer," p. 139; *Twenty-One Stories,* pp. 17–18.

28. Another story by Baron that critiques the allegorical speech patterns of the *maggid meisharim* is "'Agunah." Note that the female protagonists of both stories are called Dinah, and in both cases the women stand outside the allegorical tradition. For a discussion of the motif of the *maggid meisharim* within the context of the Lithuanian *mussar* movement, see Miriam Weinberger, "Tashtiyot min hamasoret beyetsirat Devorah Baron," *Mabi'a* 25 (1993): 97–103. For a discussion of Baron's use of the *maggid meisharim* in "'Agunah," see Bernstein, "Midrash and Marginality," pp. 40–52. See also Seidman, *A Marriage Made in Heaven,* pp. 84–87.

29. Baron, *Parshiyyot,* p. 29. Translation from *"The First Day" and Other Stories,* p. 81.

30. Agnon, "Aggadat hasofer," p. 140; *Twenty-One Stories,* p. 19.

31. Baron, *Parshiyyot,* p. 31; *"The First Day,"* p. 84.

32. Baron, *Parshiyyot,* p. 34; *"The First Day,"* p. 87.

33. Z. J. Goodman, "Traced in Ink," pp. 203–4.

34. Shir Hashirim Rabbah I:4:2. This translation is informed by Maurice Simon's translation of *Song of Songs Rabbah* (London: Soncino Press, 1939), pp. 48–49. Another version of this midrash can be found in *Pesikta de-Rab Kahana* 22.2.

35. Baskin, "Rabbinic Reflections on the Barren Wife," p. 107.

36. An interesting counterpoint to "Mishpahah" in this regard is Baron's story "Bereishit"; the title alludes to the biblical book of Genesis, but the tale culminates with the birth of a daughter rather than a son. See Baron, *Parshiyyot*, pp. 225–35.
37. See Exodus 35:30 and 38:22. See also 1 Chronicles 2:20.
38. Robert Alter, *Genesis: Translation and Commentary* (New York: W. W. Norton, 1996), p. 158, n. 1.
39. "Tell All the Truth But Tell It Slant" (Poem 1129) in *The Complete Poems of Emily Dickinson*, ed. Thomas H. Johnson (Toronto: Little Brown, 1960), pp. 506–7.
40. For a perspective on how the barrenness theme is treated by an early twentieth-century Jewish American woman writer, see Mary Antin, "The Amulet," *Atlantic Monthly* (January 1913): 31–41.
41. See Rachel (Bluwstein), "Yamim dovevim," originally published in *Davar*, 11 Tammuz 5689 / July 19, 1929. Reprinted in *Anda: Kovets ma'amarim, reshimot, vedivrei sifrut aherim im nisfah bibliographi*, pp. 9–10.
42. See "Hirgatani, Elohim / betitkha bi yeled," in *Yamim dovevim: Shirim* (Tel Aviv: Hotsa'at Zohar, 1929), p. 64.
43. For more on Pinkerfeld-Amir as an underacknowledged Hebrew (modernist) poet, se Michael Gluzman, The Politics of Canonicity: Lines of Resistance in Modernist Hebrew Poetry (Stanford: Stanford University Press, 2003), pp. 132–36.
44. Bentsion Benshalom, "Shirat Anda Pinkerfeld," in *Anda: kovets ma'amarim*, pp. 14–20; the quotation is from p. 15.
45. Benshalom, "Shirat Anda Pinkerfeld," p. 17.
46. Anda Pinkerfeld, "'Akarah," from *Yamim Dovevim* (Tel Aviv: Zohar, 1929), pp. 50–53. My translation.
47. See, for example, Ezra 9:5.
48. See, for example, Genesis 35: 11 ("I am El Shaddai, be fertile and increase"); Genesis 48:3 ("And Jacob said to Joseph, 'El Shaddai appeared to me in Luz in the Land of Canaan, and He blessed me and said to me, 'I will make you fertile and numerous'"); and Genesis 49: 25 ("The God of your father who helps you, and Shaddai who blesses you. . . . Blessings of the breast and the womb.")
49. Nehama Puhachevsky, " Asonah shel Afyah," first published in *Hashiloah* 43 (Tishrei-Adar 5685): 227–33. All citations from the Hebrew version of the story will be from *Hakol ha-aher: sipporet nashim 'Ivrit*, ed. Lily Rattok (Tel Aviv: Hakibbutz Hameuchad, 1994), pp. 89–99; they will be noted in parentheses in the body of the text.
50. According to a translator's footnote, Adyah and her husband Juku lived in the basement of Nehama Puhachevsky's home. Adyah was a child bride who had many miscarriages until she finally had a son. Juku was a true scholar, whom Puhachevsky often consulted on matters of Jewish tradition. See "Aphia's Plight," trans. Sonia F. Grober and Ida (Ayala) Myers, in *Ribcage*, p. 40, n. 13.
51. See Nurit Govrin, "Nefesh meRishon LeTsiyyon homiyah," in *Devash miselah* (Tel Aviv: Misrad Habitahon, 1989), p. 142.
52. Translation quoted from "Aphia's Plight," p. 39.
53. For more on this see Michelle Klein, *A Time to Be Born: Customs and Folkore of Jewish Birth* (Philadelphia: Jewish Publication Society, 1998), pp. 28–39. See also Antin, "The Amulet."

CHAPTER 5

1. Elaine Showalter, *A Literature of Their Own,* p. 7

2. Sarah Feige Foner, "From My Childhood Memories," in *Shaharut* (Youth) 4:16 (September 1919): 91–93, 109–10.

3. Information provided from correspondence with Foner's great-grandson, Morris Rosenthal.

4. Foner, "From My Childhood Memories," p. 92. Translation by Morris Rosenthal, in "A Girl Can't Become a Gaon?" *Women's League Outlook* 70:2 (winter 1999, Kislev 5760): 29–30. Reprinted in *A Woman's Voice,* p. 76.

5. Ibid., p. 92. Translation adapted from *A Woman's Voice,* p. 76.

6. Sara Feige Foner, "From My Childhood Memories" (part II), *Shaharut* 7 (October 1919): 109.

7. Ibid., p. 110.   .

8. *A Woman's Voice,* p. 30.

9. See Mary Antin, *The Promised Land* (Boston: Houghton Mifflin, 1969), pp. 32–34. See also the discussion of Hava Shapiro's "Kidush levanah" later in this chapter.

10. Foner, "Childhood Memories," p. 110.

11. Sarah Feige Meinkin Foner, *Ahavat yesharim o hamishpahot hamurdafot,* p. 10. Translations are by Morris Rosenthal in *A Woman's Voice* unless otherwise noted.

12. Foner, *Ahavat yesharim,* p. 11.

13. Sarah Feige Meinkin Foner, *Beged bogdim* (Warsaw: Alexander Ginz, 1891), p. 21. The translation is adapted from Morris Rosenthal's translation in *A Woman's Voice,* p. 126. All future citations from Hebrew text will be noted in parentheses within the body of the text. My thanks to Morris Rosenthal for pointing out the importance of Helen as a strong female figure in the novella.

14. My translation.

15. A similar pattern can be detected in the fiction of Shapiro's contemporary, Nehamah Puhachevsky, whose fiction I do not analyze in this chapter. According to critic Nurit Govrin, many of the stories in Puhachevsky two collections, *BiY'hudah hahadashah* and *Bakefar uba'avodah* were based in some way on actual events that occurred in Puhachevsky's own community, which Puhachevsky then recast in a more tragic, pessimistic form. Scant critical attention was accorded this volume by contemporary critics, with the exception of two reviewers who raise objections to the recurrent calamities depicted therein. "Where the reader hopes to encounter much life," writes Y. Zerubavel, "he trips, at every step over dead bodies."(See Yaakov Zerubavel in *Ha'ahdut* 26 Heshvan 1912, p. 1.) Gershon Shaked echoed this criticism in an article titled "Hagenre ve'avizreihu: iyyunim beyetsiratam shel Moshe Smilansky veNehamah Puhachevsky," in *'Al shirah vesipporet: mehkarim bisifrut ha'Ivrit,* ed. Tsvi Malakhi (Tel Aviv: Tel Aviv University Press, 1977), pp. 133–46. More recent critics have also puzzled over the question of why a productive feminist writer and activist such as Puhachevsky chose to write stories about women who suffer endless tragedy and failure, highlighting the ways in which the stories use tragedy or thwarted mobility to protest the status of Jewish women. See Yaffa Berlovitz, Nurit Govrin, "Nefesh miRishon leTsiyyon homiyah: Nehamah Puhachevsky" in *Devash min haselah: mehkarim besifrut Erets Yisra'el* (Tel Aviv: Misrad Habitahon, 1989), pp. 114–71.

16. Dr. Hava Shapiro, "Demut ha'isha besifruteinu," *Hatekufah* 26–27 (1930): 633.

17. Eim Kol Hai [pseudonym for Hava Shapiro], *Kovets tsiyyurim* (Warsaw: Y. Edelstein, 1909), p. 15. All future citations from this book will be noted within the body of the text by page number.

18. Adrienne Rich, "The Anti-Feminist Woman," in *Adrienne Rich's Poetry*, ed. Barbara Charlesworth Gelpi and Albert Gelpi (New York: W. W. Norton, 1975), pp. 99–104.

19. Naomi Caruso, "Chava Shapiro: A Woman Before Her Time," M.A. thesis, McGill University, 1991, pp. 37–38.

20. Carole Balin, *To Reveal Our Hearts*, p. 72.

21. See B. T. Sanhedrin 42a.

22. Hava Shapiro, "Yemei Hanukah," *Ha'olam* 12:52 (December 26, 1924), 1046–48.

23. Ibid.

24. Eli Schweid writes that "Devorah Baron is anchored in a stable spiritual realm that has never been overturned . . . as though, the *beit midrash* [study house] still stands, full of students, in its place, and the synagogue is still packed with worshipers, and weekdays are still strung next to Sabbaths next to holidays in an unsevered chain. . . . How did she manage to escape the destruction which hovers over all the literature of her generation? A riddle this is, and a riddle it will remain." Eli Schweid, "Hidat haretsifut," in *Devorah Baron: mivhar ma'amarim al yetsiratah*, ed. Ada Pagis (Tel Aviv: 'Am 'Oved, 1974) p. 116. Dan Miron makes a similar argument in his contribution to this volume. Highlighting Baron's emphasis in her fiction on themes of continuity rather than rupture or disjuncture, Miron contends that Baron responded superficially and misleadingly to the two central issues of her generation. See Miron, "Perakim 'al yetsiratah shel Devorah Baron," in *Devorah Baron*, pp. 117–30. Also in *Devorah Baron* see Hillel Barzel, "Mif'alah hasifruti shel Devorah Baron," pp. 102–9. As for Baron's treatment of the reality of life in Palestine, Nurit Govrin asserts that "Erets Yisra'el is hardly ever reflected in [Devorah Baron's] stories, and scarcely serves as a background to the stories, the events, and the heroes. All the gigantic changes that took place in Erets Yisra'el, in which she took part and continued to witness throughout her life, barely leave an impression on her literary work. One could even argue that someone who only reads her stories will hardly guess that the author had lived in Israel." See Nurit Govrin, "Devorah Baron— Ignoring the Reality of Erets Yisra'el: Back to the Shtetl," in *Alienation and Regeneration*, trans. John Glucker (Tel Aviv: Mod Books, 1989), p. 130.

25. Naomi Seidman, "Baron in the Closet: An Epistemology of the Women's Section," in *A Marriage Made in Heaven*, pp. 67–101.

26. Amia Lieblikh, *Rikmot* (Tel Aviv: Schocken, 1991). Translated as *Conversations with Dvora: An Experimental Biography of the First Modern Hebrew Woman Writer*, trans. Naomi Seidman (Berkeley: University of California Press, 1997).

27. Schweid, "Hidat haretsifut," p. 116.

28. Seidman, *A Marriage Made in Heaven*, p. 71.

29. Baron's skepticism about the relative merits and achievements of the Zionist pioneers is captured in this quotation from the posthumously published *Agav orhah* (Merhaviah: Sifriyat Po'alim, 1961): "People tend to speak about the moral person in

lukewarm terms: So-and-so is a good man, just like so-and-so has pretty eyes. When they speak about the pioneer who has come to build up the homeland, to carry large stones up a mountain on a path sown with obstacles, they express themselves with enthusiasm and sing songs of praise in his honor. Don't they know and understand that to be good and fair is seven times as hard as carrying heavy rocks up a mountain? To be a good person is to struggle constantly, ceaselessly, with endless obstacles and impediments" (p. 106).

30. As with all generalizations, there are always exceptions. In Baron's story "Gilgulim" (Vicissitudes), a young woman and her boyfriend elope and immigrate to Palestine, where they live happily ever after. In this story we do see a woman fulfilling her dream in the Promised Land. Significantly, however, this is not the real dramatic focus; the main issue explored here is that of the vicissitudes of fortune experienced by the woman's father, a wealthy businessman in Russia who loses his fortune and suffers great torment, until he immigrates to Palestine as well. See Devorah Baron, *Parshiyyot*, pp. 383–411.

31. Quoted in Baruch Kurzweil, "*Shekhol vekishalon:* hatahanah ha'ahronah shel kiyyum Yehudi absurdi," afterword to Y. H. Brenner, *Shekhol vekishalon* (Tel Aviv: 'Am 'Oved, 1972), pp. 251–52.

32. Gilbert and Gubar, *The Madwoman in the Attic*, p. 73.

33. Woolf, *A Room of One's Own*, p. 24.

34. Nurit Govrin, *Hamahatsit harishonah: Devorah Baron, hayehah veyetsiratah*, p. 16.

35. This volume includes all of Baron's early stories. edited by Avner Holtzman and titled *Parshiyyot mukdamot, sippurim 1902–1921* (Jerusalem: Mossad Bialik, 1988). All citations from this volume will be noted within the body of the text by page number. The same volume includes a long critical-biographical section by Nurit Govrin on the first half of Baron's career from which I have already cited: *Hamahatsit harishonah: Devorah Baron, hayeha veyetsiratah.*

36. It is worth noting that Tzipporah Aharonovitz self-selects herself out of *Agav orhah* (Incidentally). Nowhere does she attribute to herself any role in compiling the volume. Her editorship of this collection of her mother's writings is rendered entirely incidental. The title page of the book simply says, "Devorah Baron, *Agav orhah*, collected from her estate and her surroundings." Aharonovitz does not even sign her name to the biographical introduction to the volume.

37. Baron, *Agav orhah*, pp. 9–10.

38. Baron published another story by the same title in 1922; in this later story, however, the feminist anger over the marginalization of the female text characteristic of the first "Genizah" story is itself marginalized in favor of an omniscient, more detached perspective.

39. For a discussion of stories by Baron that specifically address the exclusion of women from study and ritual, see Seidman, *A Marriage Made in Heaven*, pp. 95–101.

40. Govrin, *Hamahatsit harishonah*, pp. 125–30.

41. Rattok, afterword to *Hakol ha'aher*, p. 282.

42. Seidman, *A Marriage Made in Heaven*, p. 92.

43. Govrin, *Hamahatsit harishonah*, p. 143.

44. Baron also published a Yiddish version of this story in 1912. See *Parshiyyot mukdamot,* pp. 678–85.

45. See 1 Samuel 9:2.

46. Bruno Bettelheim, *The Uses of Enchantment: The Meaning and Importance of Fairy Tales* (Harmondsworth UK: Penguin Books, 1978) p. 17.

47. Govrin, *Hamahatsit harishonah,* p. 204.

48. Devorah Baron, *Parshiyyot,* p. 549. All future citations from this volume will be noted by page number within the body of the text.

49. Rudolph Meyer, *The Wisdom of Fairy Tales,* trans. Polly Lawson (Edinburgh: Anthroposophic Press, 1988), p. 144–45.

50. In contrast, Baron's story "America" offers a more positive picture of women's experience of immigrating to America. In this story, the women who are left behind are actually sent for by their husbands. Though the parting scene featuring the immigrant and her family/neighbors is extremely heart-rending, according to a straight reading of the story the act of leaving Europe seems to be an essentially positive one. I would argue, however, that there is an ironic side to this story as well.

51. Sometimes, as in the case of Mina in "Mah shehayah," women immigrate vicariously and enjoy the Zionist dream through their brave and idealistic sons. In other cases, like the story of Ita Bloch—as told in Le'eit 'atah and continued in the posthumously published *Me'emesh*—the mother is survived (and perhaps compensated for) by a daughter.

52. The rabbi's wife's first name in "Masa" is never provided; her identity is established only as it relates to her husband and his profession.

53. "The day before the wedding, the girl walked out to the fields with her friends and there, among the hills of the countess' estate, she wept—as Jephthah's daughter had done—for the passing of her youth." See *The Thorny Path,* trans. Joseph Schachter (Jerusalem: Israel Universities Press, 1969), p. 43, or *Parshiyyot,* p. 39.

54. The intertextual relationship between Baron's stories and Flaubert's *Madame Bovary* is itself worthy of exploration, since Baron translated Flaubert's novel into Hebrew.

55. I quote here from *The Jerusalem Bible* (Jerusalem: Koren, 1988). The JPS translation renders this first part of the verse as consoling, yet in the context of Baron's story it seems unlikely she was interpreting the verse in this fashion. Baron quotes the same verse from Isaiah in an earlier story, titled "'Agunah," in the context of a sermon of consolation delivered by an itinerant preacher or *maggid.* See *Parshiyyot,* pp. 300–306. For readings of this story see Seidman, *A Marriage Made in Heaven,* pp. 84–87, and Lieblikh, *Conversations with Dvora,* pp. 71–72.

56. Translation from *The Thorny Path,* p. 47. Future citations from this volume will be by page number within the body of the text.

57. Baron's choice of names for the female characters in her stories seems to follow a principle of conservation: the same names appear over and over in her stories. The name Hannah-Gittel, for example, which Baron chose for Elka-Sarah's eldest daughter, is an amalgam of two names that recur in Baron's fiction. Hannah is the name frequently given to the young female narrator or principal female protagonist in her shtetl stories. Gittel is the name given to Hannah's close childhood friend in such stories as "Gilgulim";

it is also the name of the female town idiot in "Keritut," who protests the sufferings of the divorced woman in the story. Other names also recur, such as Dinah ("Mishpahah" and the early version of "'Agunah") and Mina ("Mah shehayah" and *Me'emesh*).

58. Nina Auerbach, *Communities of Women: An Idea in Fiction* (Cambridge: Harvard University Press, 1978), p. 5.

CHAPTER 6

1. Shoshana Verel, "Beveitah shel Devora Baron," *Ha'arets,* August 6, 1954.

2. bell hooks, "Choosing the Margin as a Site of Radical Openness," in *Gender Space Architecture: An Interdisciplinary Introduction,* ed. Jane Rendell, Barbara Penner, and Iain Borden (New York: Routledge, 2000), p. 206.

3. Carole M. Counihan, *The Anthropology of Food and the Body: Gender, Meaning and Power* (New York: Routledge, 1999), p. 46. For a fascinating collection of essays on feminism, food, and the symbolism of the kitchen, see *Through the Kitchen Window: Women Explore the Intimate Meanings of Food and Cooking,* ed. Arlene Voski Avakian (Boston: Beacon Press, 1997), especially Doris Friedensohn's essay, "A Kitchen of One's Own," pp. 238–45.

4. For a perspective that compares Hebrew texts on this theme with American writer Anzia Yezierska's novel *Breadgivers* (1925), see my article "The Rabbi's Daughter in and out of the Kitchen: Feminist Literary Negotiations" *Nashim* 5 (fall 2002): 83–104.

5. Gloria Anzaldúa, *Borderlands/La Frontera: The New Mestiza,* 2d ed. (San Francisco: Aunt Lute Books, 1999), p. 3.

6. See my discussion of this point in chapter 1. See also the introduction to *The Defiant Muse* which also provides a history of Hebrew women's writing before the modern period. In a personal response to my "The Rabbi's Daughter," Haskalah literary historian Tova Cohen pointed out to me that while in the premodern period the women of rabbinic families had exceptional access to the masculine tradition of Jewish learning, this picture changed considerably in the nineteenth century, when male *maskilim* began to play a major role in promoting Hebrew education for their daughters. In the nineteenth century most of the women who wrote in Hebrew (letters, essays, and the like), were actually the daughters of *maskilim* rather than rabbis. On this point, see Shmuel Feiner, "Ha'ishah haYehudiyah hamodernit: mikreh-mivhan beyahasei haHaskalah vehaModernah," in *Eros erusin ve'issurim,* p. 288.

7. Rabbinic literature offers a record of both the breadth and depth of Beruriah's Jewish legal knowledge. In B. T. Tractate Pesahim 62b, Beruriah is depicted as having achieved the formidable intellectual task of learning "three hundred laws from three hundred teachers in one day." In some cases she is even portrayed as ruling or interpreting more correctly than her male counterparts. See *Tosefta Kelim,* B. T. Bava Kamma 4:17, B. T. Berakhot 10a. Other sources refer to the extraordinary piety and self-control of the (unnamed) wife of R. Meir. In *Midrash Mishlei* 31:10, we read that when her two sons died from the plague on the Sabbath, the wife of R. Meir did not inform her husband of their deaths until his return from the *beit midrash* after Sabbath, for it is forbidden to mourn on the Sabbath.

8. The episode referred to here can be found in B. T. Kiddushin 80b, in the con-

text of a law which states that two men are permitted to sit in a room with one woman but not two women with one man, because "women are light-headed" or frivolous. The term light-headedness as used here yokes together female intellectual and moral weakness, a notion that Beruriah, from her standpoint of learned piety, must have found hard to bear. See also B. T. Shabbat 33b for another intriguing occurrence of this term.

9. Rashi, "Ma'aseh deBeruriyah," B. T. Avodah Zara 18b. For an extensive analysis of the Beruriah legends, see Daniel Boyarin, *Carnal Israel,* pp. 181–96. See also Rachel Adler, "The Virgin in the Brothel and Other Anomalies: Characters and Context in the Legend of Beruriah," *Tikkun* 3:6 (1988): 23–32, 102–5.

10. Ruth Almog, "On Being a Writer," in *Gender and Text in Modern Hebrew and Yiddish Literature,* p. 230.

11. See Jacob Steinberg, "Bat haRav," *Kitvei Ya'akov Steinberg,* vol. 2: *Sippurim* (Tel Aviv: 'Am 'Oved, 1937), pp. 44–64.

12. For two other modern Hebrew literary representations of the Rabbi's daughter, see S. Tchernihowsky, "Bat haRav" and "Bat haRav ve'immah," in *Shirim* (Tel Aviv: Dvir, 1966), pp. 285 and 486, respectively. Both poems are about rabbi's daughters who are sexually defiled by Gentile persecutors. The Rabbi's daughter here symbolizes Jewish purity and vulnerability. For an American variation on the theme see Hortense Calisher, "The Rabbi's Daughter," in *Jewish American Literature: A Norton Anthology.* ed. Jules Chametzky, John Felstiner, Hilene Flanzbaum, and Kathryn Hellerstein (New York: W. W. Norton, 2001), pp. 513–21.

13. Iris Parush, "Women Readers as Agents of Social Change among Eastern European Jews in the Late Nineteenth Century," *Gender and History* 9:1 (April 1997), p. 68. See also her "Readers in Cameo: Women Readers in Jewish Society of Nineteenth-Century Eastern Europe," *Prooftexts* 14 (1994): 1–23. For an expanded treatment of these issues, see Parush's recently published book, *Nashim kor'ot* (Tel Aviv: 'Am 'Oved, 2001).

14. It is important to clarify here that Morpurgo was not the daughter or wife of a rabbi. In speaking of her under the rubric of "the Rabbi's daughter," I use the term somewhat figuratively, referring to the fact that she descended from a long line of rabbis, scholars, and poets; had exceptional, high-level access to learning and canonical Hebrew texts, and had extended family members (especially her cousin S. D. Luzzatto) who were scholars of Hebrew literature and with whom she carried on lively study and conversation.

15. Alternative translation: "Even in dance / I shall surely renounce"

16. *'Ugav Rachel* (Tel Aviv: Hapo'el Hatsa'ir, 1943), p. 60. My translation. For another translation, by Peter Cole, see *Defiant Muse,* pp. 80–81.

17. Morpurgo includes a similar opposition between "*sir*" and "*shir*" in a verse letter written to Mendel Stern, the editor of *Kokhavei Yitshak,* which was published in *Kokhavei Yitshak* 18 (1853): 41, and reprinted in *'Ugav Rachel,* p. 77. In this letter Morpurgo expresses her misgivings about writing poetry, admonishing herself to return to her "pot *[lekhi etsel hasir]* / and prepare [her] provisions. / For the entire community / will prepare for themselves / to carry with them / *mitsvot* and good deeds / with which to approach God." What is so interesting about this letter is that it begins by associating women with the kitchen work of the pot, then undercuts it by construing the pot metaphorically. Instead of food, what is being cooked up here is a spiritual menu of

mitsvot and *ma'asim*. Thus whereas her letter seems at first to reject poetry on the ground that it is not proper women's work, it concludes with a concern for the religious implications of writing poetry and philosophy over and against the performance of traditional, religiously sanctioned good deeds.

18. Yaffa Berlovitz, "Rachel Morpurgo: Hateshukah el hamaret, hateshukah el hashir," *Sadan* 2 (1996): 34. My translation.

19. Caroline Walker Bynum, *Holy Feast and Holy Fast: The Religious Significance of Food to Medieval Women* (Berkeley: University of California Press, 1987), p. 191

20. Ibid., p. 35.

21. Translation from Ecclesiastes adapted from *The Writings* (Philadelphia; Jewish Publication Society, 1982), pp. 392–93.

22. See Feiner, "Ha'ishah hayehudiyah hamodernit," p. 261. As part of his discussion in this article, Feiner investigates the tendency on the part of Haskalah writers— including Morpurgo's relative, Rabbi Moses Hayim Luzzatto—to speak of feminine physicality and desire as threatening to male intellectualism and spiritual aspiration, an issue very pertinent to Morpurgo's poem (see p. 263).

23. For another work dealing with images of food, the kitchen, female community, and their role in the construction of an "alternative feminine national history," see Orly Lubin, "Zutot memitbaha shel nehamah: le'umiyut alternativit be*Hagolim* shel Devorah Baron," *Te'oriah uvikkoret* 7 (winter 1995): 159–76.

24. See Moshe Gitlin's reminiscence of Baron titled "Bine'urehah: mizkhronot ben-'ir" in *Agav Orhah*, p. 208.

25. Naomi Seidman, "Baron in the Closet," in *A Marriage Made in Heaven*, p. 73.

26. Devorah Baron, "Mah shehayah," in *Parshiyyot*, p. 126. Translation from Devorah Baron, *The Thorny Path*, p. 77. All other citations will be noted within the body of the text by title and page number.

27. Quoted in Renée Hirschon, "Essential Objects and the Sacred: Interior and Exterior Space in an Urban Greek Locality," in *Women and Space: Ground Rules and Social Maps,* ed. Shirley Ardener (London: Croom Helm, 1981), p. 78.

28. Ibid.

29. In her biography of Baron's early years, Nurit Govrin notes that Baron's tendency to remain confined to her living quarters, was symptomatic not only of her later years, but also of her youth. In her book, Govrin quotes a reminiscence by Dr. Barukh Ben-Yehudah, a member of youth group led by Baron, who mentions that when he and the other group members visited her, they would typically find her sitting or lying fully clothed in bed, "not sick, not fettered, not silenced; on the contrary, always alert, attentive, active." See Nurit Govrin, *Hamahatsit harishonah: Devorah Baron, hayehah veyetsiratah,* p. 40.

30. Amia Lieblikh, *Conversations with Dvora.*

31. Lily Rattok, afterword to *Hakol ha'aher: sipporet nashim 'Ivrit,* p. 276. My translation.

32. Counihan, *Anthropology of Food,* p. 49.

33. For another contemporary Israeli poem on femininity and the kitchen, see Dahlia Ravikovitch, "Cinderella bamitbah," in *Ahavah amitit* (Tel Aviv: Hakibbutz Hameuchad, 1987), pp. 38–39.

34. For more biographical information on Zelda, see Hamutal Bar Yosef, *'Al shirat Zelda* (Tel Aviv: Hakibbutz Hameuchad, 1988).

35. For more on the relationship between Zelda and Yona Wallach, see Lily Rattok, "Mal'akh ha'esh: al hakesher ben Yona Vollakh vezelda," *'Alei siah* 37 (summer 1996): 75–84.

36. Quoted in Bar Yosef, *'Al shirat Zelda,* p. 133.

37. Zelda (Mishkovsky), *Shirei Zelda* (Tel Aviv: Hakibbutz Hameuchad, 1985), pp. 10–11. My translation. Thanks to Stanley Nash and Bill Cutter for their comments on this translation.

38. See my discussion of this poem in chapter 2.

AFTERWORD

1. Amos Oz, *Oto hayam* (Jerusalem: Keter, 1999), p. 109. Translation from *The Same Sea,* trans. Nicholas de Lange (New York: Harcourt, 2001), p. 111. For the poem that Oz quotes from Zelda, see "Bekomah sheniyah" in *Shirei Zelda,* p. 164.

2. Lily Rattok, afterword to *Hakol ha'aher: sipporet nashim 'Ivrit,* p. 264. For similar observations, see Ruth Almog, "On Being a Writer," in *Gender and Text in Modern Hebrew and Yiddish Literature,* p. 229. Also see Amalia Kahana-Carmon's essay in the same anthology, "The Song of the Bats in Flight," pp. 235–45.

3. Many of these same women poets also wrote poetic tributes to male poets and writers. Leah Goldberg dedicated a poem cycle to Avraham Ben-Yitzhak; Rachel Bluwstein dedicated poems to A. D. Gordon, Zalman Shazar, and others; Anda Pinkerfeld-Amir dedicated poems to David Fogel, U. Z. Greenberg, and Sh. Shalom; Esther Raab wrote a moving poetic tribute to David Ben-Gurion and other male contemporaries, as well as her famous poem "La'av" (To the father). Rarely, though, do these women writers attempt to cast their own images or accomplishments in the image of their male compatriots. In contrast, the poems dedicated to women poets directly address or depict the woman poet, demonstrating an intimate connection, admiration, and common set of concerns.

4. Rachel, "Yamim Dovevim," in *Anda: Kovets ma'amarim, reshimot, vedivrei sifrut aherim im nisfah bibliographi,* pp. 9–10.

5. Elisheva, "Shireha shel Anda Pinkerfeld," in *Anda: Kovets ma'amarim,* pp. 29–33.

6. See Leah Goldberg, "Parshiyyot leDevorah Baron," *Devorah Baron: mivhar ma'amarei bikoret al yetsiratah,* pp. 93–101.

7. See Anda Pinkerfeld, "Kamu bi ga'agu'im 'alai," in *Yuval: Shirim,* p. 33 and Rachel, "'Ivriah," in *Rachel: Shirim, mikhtavim, reshimot, Korot hayehah,* p. 233. Rachel also wrote a number of letters that record her feelings about her female contemporaries. See *Rachel,* pp. 78 and 90. I translate and analyze these passages in my Princeton University doctoral dissertation (1995), "Border Crossings: The Emergence of Jewish Women's Writing in Israel and America and the Immigrant Experience," pp. 104–5.

8. See Yokheved Bat-Miriam, "Ve'at einekh," *Shirim,* p. 155.

9. See Anda Pinkerfeld, "LeRachel," *Davar,* May 10, 1940. The poem is dated April 30, 1931, which means that it was written shortly after Rachel's death. Gitl

(Mishkovsky) and Fania Bergstein also wrote poems in her honor, and Shulamit Kalugai contributed a prose remembrance, which included a humorous poem that Rachel wrote to Kalugai to apologize for coming late to a dinner party. See *Rachel veshiratah,* pp. 51–53. Yet there is a personal urgency and relevance to some of the women's poems and reminiscences. Several male poets and critics also wrote poems and reminiscences (see the selections in *Rachel veshiratah*).

10. See Esther Raab, "LeLeah Goldberg," *Kol hashirim,* p. 233. See my translations of "'Ivriah," "Ve'at einekh," and "LeLeah Goldberg," in my doctoral dissertation, "Border Crossings," pp. 106–7, 110–11, and 113.

11. Dahlia Ravikovitch, "Hakarpodim," in *Kol mishbarayikh vegalayikh* (Tel Aviv: Hakibbutz Hameuchad, 1980), pp. 79–82. Ravikovitch also wrote a poem dedicated to Yona Wallach, "Ha'ahavah ha'amitit einah kefi shehi nir'eit," in *Ahavah amitit,* pp. 53–54.

12. For a discussion of the various factors leading to the explosion of contemporary Hebrew novels by women, see Rochelle Furstenberg's "Dreaming of Flying: Women's Prose of the Last Decade," *Modern Hebrew Literature* 6 (spring/summer 1991): 5–7. See also Yaffa Berlovitz, "Ha'omnam feminizatsiah shel hasifrut ha'Ivrit?" *Moznayim* 10:9 (1992):45–48.

13. See Berlovitz, "Ha'omnam feminizatsiah."

14. Ariel Hirschfeld, "The Man Who Does Not Love Has Upset the Equilibrium," *Modern Hebrew Literature* 6 (spring/summer 1991): 20. For evidence of this abundance, see *The Defiant Muse* and *Dreaming the Actual.*

15. Hirschfeld, p. 20.

16. Between 1984 and 1988, Kahana-Carmon published a series of feminist essays that helped bring feminist literary theory to the forefront of Hebrew literary discussions. See Amalia Kahana-Carmon, "Lihyot isha soferet" [To be a woman writer], *Yedi'ot ahronot* (April 4, 1984): 20–21; "Lehitbazbez 'al hatsedadi" [To be wasted on the peripheral], *Yedi'ot ahronot* (September 15, 1985): 22–23; "Ishto shel Brenner rokhevet shuv" [Brenner's wife rides again], *Moznayim* 59:4 (1985): 13; "Hi kotevet dei nehmad aval 'al shebiyarkhatayim," *Yediot ahronot* (May 2, 1988): 20, 25. Yael Feldman gives considerable attention to Kahana- Carmon's feminist essays in *No Room of Their Own.*

17. See Yosef Oren, *Hakol hanashi besifrut haYisra'elit* (Rishon Letziyyon: Yahad, 2001).

18. See, for example, selections by Rivka Miriam, Miriam Oren, Galit Hazan-Rokem, Hava Pinchas Cohen, Nurit Zarhi, Yehudit Kafri, Shin Shifra, and others in *Bat-kol,* pp. 18–33.

19. See, for example, Amia Lieblikh's fictionalized postmodern biographies of Devorah Baron and Leah Goldberg (*Rikmot* (Tel Aviv: Schocken, 1991) and *El Leah.* See also Nurit Zarhi's story about Devorah Baron titled "Madame Bovary beNeve Tsedek," in *Oman hamasekhot* (Tel Aviv: Zemorah Bitan, 1993).

20. Feldman, *No Room of Their Own,* p. 40.

21. Quoted in Oren, *Hakol hanashi,* p. 13.

BIOGRAPHIES OF
POETS AND WRITERS

Devorah Baron (1887–1956) was born in Ouzdah, Belorussia, and studied and taught in Minsk, Kovno, Vilna, and Mariampol, where she attended a Russian *gymnasia*, worked as a tutor, and wrote fiction in Hebrew and Yiddish. In 1911 she moved to Palestine, where she worked as literary editor of *Hapoʻel hatsaʻir* and married its editor, Yosef Aharonovitz. She and Aharonovitz had a daughter, Tsipporah. In 1923 both Baron and Aharonovitz left their posts at *Hapoʻel hatsaʻir*. From that point until her death, Baron remained confined in her Tel Aviv home and adhered to a strict diet, due to an unspecified illness. A writer of Hebrew as well as Yiddish prose fiction, Baron's first short story was published in 1903. In her lifetime, she published several books of fiction, including *Sippurim* (1927), *Ketanot* (1933), *Mah shehayah* (1929), *Leʻeit ʻAtah* (1943), *Misham* (1946), *Halaban* (1947), *Shavririm* (1949), and *Meʻemesh* (1955), as well as an expansive collection of short stories entitled *Parshiyyot* (1951). Baron purposely left out many of her earliest stories in this collection, an omission that was rectified with the publication of *Parshiyyot mukdamot,* edited by Avner Holtzman, (Mossad Bialik, 1988), which accompanies Nurit Govrin's masterful biography of Baron's early years, *Hamahatsit harishonah.* Her translation of Flaubert's *Madame Bovary* was published in 1957. *Agav Orhah,* a compendium of letters and reminiscences, edited by her daughter, Tsipporah, appeared in 1960. Joseph Schachter's translations of selected stories, titled *The Thorny Path and Other Stories,* appeared in 1969 (Institute for the Translation of Hebrew Literature). Chana Kronfeld and Naomi Seidman's more recent *The First Day and Other Stories* (2001) includes several previously untranslated works, such as selections from Baron's earlier stories.

Yokheved (Zhelzniak) Bat-Miriam (1901–1980) was born in the village of Keplitz in White Russia. When she was seventeen years old she changed her name to Yokheved Bat-Miriam as a means of identifying with her mother (whose name was Miriam) and with the biblical Miriam. She studied at the Universities of Odessa and Moscow. In Russia she participated (together with another Hebrew woman poet, Malka Schechtman, who wrote under the pen name Bat-Hamah), in the literary activities of a Hebrew Communist group known as the "Hebrew Octoberists," which published an anthology titled *Bereishit* (1926). Bat-Miriam never married but had two children with two different men. While in Moscow, she had a daughter (Mariassa Bat-Miriam Katzenelson) with fellow Hebrew Octoberist Shimon (Tarbukov) HaBoneh. Later in Paris, with writer Haim Hazaz, she had a son, Nahum (Zuzik) Hazaz, who was killed in the 1948 War of Independence. In the wake of Zuzik's death, Bat-Miriam ceased writing and publishing new poetry. Her first Hebrew poems were published in 1923 in *Hatekufah*. *Merahok*, her first published collection of poetry, was published in 1932, four years after she settled in Palestine. Her other published works include *Erets Yisra'el* (1937), *Re'ayon* (1949), *Demuyot meofek* (1942), *Mishirei Russyah* (1942), and *Shirim laGhetto* (1946). In 1963 a collection of her poetry was published under the title *Shirim* (1963). Bat-Miriam received the Bialik Prize in 1968 and the Israel Prize in 1972.

RACHEL (BLUWSTEIN) (1890–1931) was born in Saratov, Russia, and grew up in Poltova, Ukraine. She began writing poetry in Russian at age fifteen. After completing her studies at the *gymnasia* in Poltova, she studied art in Kiev. With her sister, Shoshana, she immigrated to Palestine in 1909, where she engaged in agricultural work at Hannah Meisel's farming school near the Kinneret, studied Hebrew, and met A. D. Gordon, the spiritual father of the Second Aliyah. In 1913 she left Palestine to study agriculture in France and found herself stranded in Europe as a result of the outbreak of World War I. Rachel completed her agronomic studies and then returned to Russia, where she taught refugee children and fell sick from tuberculosis. In 1919 she returned to Palestine and settled in Deganiah, but poor health prevented her from resuming her agricultural work and necessitated a city life, primarily in Tel Aviv, where she died in 1931. During World War I, Rachel began publishing essays and translations in Russian. Her first Hebrew poem was published in *Hashiloah* in 1920; later, most of her work was published in *Davar*. Her poetry was published in three volumes: *Safiah* (1927), *Minneged* (1930), and *Nevo* (1932). These volumes were later collected in *Shirat Rachel* (1935). In 1988 her grandnephew, Uri Millstein, published *Rachel: Shirim, mikhtavim, reshimot, korot hayehah*, which includes all her poetry, translations, essays, and letters, as well as biographical material. Robert Friend's English translation of selected poems by Rachel (*Flowers of Perhaps*) was published by Menard Press in 1995.

SARAH FEIGE MEINKIN FONER (1854–1936) was the first modern Hebrew woman novelist and short-story writer. As a child she studied Hebrew with her father; she was given further Jewish education in a coed *heder*. When her parents moved to Dvinsk, she learned German and became exposed to the literature and philosophy of the Haskalah. Her first novel, *Ahavat yesharim o hamishpahot hamurdafot*, was published in Vilna in 1882 when she was twenty-six. David Frischmann wrote a scathing review of the work. Despite rejection by the critics, Foner persisted. In 1886 she published *Derekh yeladim*, a historical novel for children. In 1891, she published *Beged bogdim*, an historical novel based on personalities and events from the Hasmonean period. And in 1893 she published a memoir titled *Mizikhronot yemei yalduti*. She eventually immigrated to the United States, where she continued to write Hebrew sketches and supported the cause of Hebrew education. She died in Pittsburgh, Pennsylvania, in 1936. A volume of English translations of her work, *A Woman's Voice: Sarah Foner, Hebrew Author of the Haskalah*, was recently published by her great-grandson, Morris Rosenthal.

LEAH GOLDBERG (1911–1970) was born in Königsberg, Prussia. As a child, she lived in Russia and Kovno, Lithuania. She attended the Universities of Kovno, Berlin, and Bonn, where she received a Ph.D. in Semitic Languages in 1933 and moved to Palestine in 1935. After a brief period as a teacher, she joined the editorial staff of *Davar* and then *Mishmar*. In 1952, she founded the Department of Comparative Literature at the Hebrew University, where she worked until her death. Goldberg began writing Hebrew poems at a very young age and published eight volumes of poetry in her lifetime. Her primary poetic mentor was the modernist poet Avraham Shlonsky. Goldberg's first book of Hebrew poems, *Taba'ot 'ashan*, was published in 1935. Other books include *Mibeiti hayashan* (1944), *'Al haperihah* (1948), *Barak baboker* (1956), *Mukdam ume'uhar* (1959), and *Im halaila hazeh* (1964). She wrote three plays, including *Ba'alat ha'armon* (1955), and three works of prose fiction, among them the novel *Vehu ha'or* (1946). Goldberg was a prolific literary critic, publishing studies on poetry, short fiction, drama, and Russian literature. She was a noted children's writer and served as children's literary editor for the Sifriyat Po'alim publishing house. Her celebrated translations encompass works by Ibsen, Tolstoy, Shakespeare, and Petrarch. She was also an accomplished painter, providing illustrations for several of her own works.

SHULAMIT KALUGAI (1891–1972) was born in Poltova, Ukraine, and was a good friend of Rachel (Bluwstein), also from Poltova. Sister of Yitzhak Ben-Tzvi (Israel's second president) and the novelist Aharon Reuveni, she studied at the Sorbonne and in Pittsburgh, Pennsylavania. In 1910 she immigrated to Palestine, where she taught at the Hebrew Gymnasia in Jerusalem. With her husband Yitzhak Kalugai, a professor at the Technion, she lived in Haifa and taught at the Re'ali School. Her first published book was a prose work, *Gymnasistit* (1938). Her later books included *Nashim* (1941), a volume of poetry that includes several portraits of biblical women, *Shirim umanginot* (1951), *Le'an tso'ed hayom, 'Oded?* (children's verse, 1960), and *Aderet Shelomo* (1963).

RACHEL (LUZZATTO) MORPURGO (1790–1871) was born in Trieste, Italy, and was a descendant of an eminent line of rabbis and Hebrew poets (among them Rabbi Moses Haim Luzzatto (RaMHaL) and Samuel David Luzzatto (ShaDal). At home, Morpurgo received a rich education in Jewish/Hebrew sources, including the Talmud and the Zohar. At a young age she fell in love with the merchant Jacob Morpurgo, and though her family disapproved of the match, Morpurgo refused to consider any other marriage prospects. Eventually her parents relented; Rachel and Jacob were married when she was twenty-nine. After her wedding, Rachel Morpurgo dedicated herself to her domestic duties as wife and mother, giving birth to three sons and a daughter. Only at night, when all her other work was completed, did she have time to study and write poetry, a situation that resulted in a measure of frustration and bitterness, evident in some of her poems. These limitations notwithstanding, Morpurgo wrote more than fifty Hebrew poems, many of which were initially published in the Haskalah journal *Kokhavei Yitshak.* Her collected poetry, titled *Ugav Rahel,* was published posthumously in 1890, then republished in Palestine in 1943.

ANDA PINKERFELD-AMIR (1902–1981) was born in Rzesza in Western Galicia on June 26, 1902. Her parents were assimilated Polish Jews. A former officer in the Polish army, her father designed train stations for the Austro-Hungarian government. As a child, Anda began writing poetry in Polish. Her first poem, written when she was seven, was a patriotic prayer for the liberation of Poland. Her first volume of Polish poetry (*Pieśni Życia*, 1921) was published when she was eighteen. Later an ardent Zionist, she immigrated to Palestine in 1920, but due to illness she was compelled to return to Europe, where she studied microbiology at the Universities of Leipzig and Lvov. In 1924 she returned to Palestine, this time with her husband, the agronomist A. Krampner-Amir. Under the influence of the poet Uri Tsvi Greenberg, Anda abandoned her native Polish and began to write Hebrew poetry, publishing her first Hebrew collection in 1929 under the title *Yamim dovevim*. After World War II she was sent by the Jewish agency to work in the Displaced Persons camps in Germany. She later worked in the archives of the Ministry of Defense, assembling records of those who were lost in the 1948 War of Independence. Pinkerfeld-Amir's early Hebrew poetry consists mainly of love poems and imaginative reworkings of the stories of biblical women, written in free verse form without set meter or rhyme. The outbreak of World War II compelled her to shift her subject matter to those who were perishing in the war, resulting in some of the first Hebrew poetry on the Holocaust, most notably her epic poem *Ahat* (1952). Other published volumes of poetry include *Yuval* (1932), *Geisha Lian Tang Sharah* (1935), *Gitit* (1937), *Dudaʾim* (1943), *Gadish* (1949), *Kokhavim bideli* (Children's poems, 1957), and *Tehiyot: Shirim* (1967), and *Uvekhol zot* (1980). Best known in Israel as a children's writer, Pinkerfeld-Amir received the Bialik Award for children's literature in 1936 and the Israel Prize in 1978. For her poetry, she received the prestigious Haim Greenberg Prize in 1971. Chaya Cohen's 1999 doctoral dissertation (Bar Ilan), titled, "Anda Pinkerfeld-Amir: Monographyah," is an excellent resource on all aspects of Pinkerfeld-Amir's work.

NEHAMAH (FEINSTEIN) PUHACHEVSKY (1869–1934) was born in Brisk, Lithuania. As a child, she began her studies at a Russian *gymnasia* but was later removed by her parents, who elected to give her private tutoring at home, including instruction in Hebrew language and Bible. From an early age, she began carrying on a Hebrew correspondence with Y. L. Gordon and contributing articles to *Hamelitz*, a journal under Gordon's editorship. In 1886 she became involved in the *Hibat Tsiyyon* movement and began to consider aliyah to the Land of Israel. Her Zionist dream was fulfilled when she married M. Puhachevsky, a Zionist activist who was among those chosen by Baron Rothschild to study farming in Palestine. The couple moved to Rishon LeTsiyyon in 1899. In Rishon, Puhachevsky farmed, wrote, and served as a member of the municipal and cultural councils and the writers association. As chairperson of the women's association, she worked on behalf of women's rights in her community. Under the pen name "Nefesh," she wrote Hebrew essays and stories. Her stories were collected into two volumes, *BiY'hudah hahadashah* (1921) and *Bakfar uba'avodah* (1930).

ESTHER RAAB (1894–1981), the first "native" modern Hebrew poet, was born in Petah Tikvah, an agricultural settlement her parents helped found. As a teenager, Raab lived for a while in the farming collective Deganiah. From 1920–1925 she lived in Cairo, and married her cousin, Isaac Green, who died in 1930. From 1925 she lived in Tel Aviv, and thereafter in Petah Tikvah. Raab's poetry has been celebrated for its representation of the landscape of the Land of Israel. Her first book of poems, *Kimshonim,* was published in 1930, the year of her husband's death. Following this loss, Raab withdrew from the literary scene, writing no poetry for eleven years. The reprinting of *Kimshonim* in 1963 led to enthusiastic reviews by contemporary poets and the reinvigoration of her poetic career. In 1972 Raab published *Tefilah ahronah,* which was followed by *Hemyat shorashim* in 1976. A collection of her prose writings, *Gan Sheharav,* was published in 1983 by her nephew Ehud Ben Ezer, who also published a volume of her collected poetry, *Kol hashirim* (1988), and a biography of Raab entitled *Yamim shel le'anah udevash* (1998); he has also been responsible for collecting and preserving her notebooks and other writings. Scholar Zvi Luz published a monograph on Raab's poetry, *Shirat Esther Raab,* in 1998. *Thistles: Selected Poems by Esther Raab,* a volume of English translations by Harold Schimmel, was published in 2003 from Ibis Press.

HAVA SHAPIRO (1878–1943) was born in Slavuta, Volhynia, to a family of printers. In 1895 she married Limel Rosenbaum and moved to Warsaw. She and Rosenbaum had a son in 1897. Although Shapiro initially enjoyed the cultural and intellectual life of Warsaw, hers was an ill-fated marriage. In 1899, while on vacation with her mother and son in Francisbad, Shapiro met and fell in love with the older Hebrew writer, Reuven Brainin. The relationship had a profound influence on Shapiro's life but ultimately proved to be a great disappointment. Eager to write and gain an education, Shapiro left her husband in 1904 (they divorced in 1907) and moved first to Vienna and then to Berne, Switzerland, where she earned a Doctorate in Philosophy in 1910. Around the same time, Shapiro began to publish Hebrew literary criticism and fiction, which culminated in the publication of *Kovets tsiyyurim* in 1909, published under the pen name *"Eim kol hai."* Subsequently she contributed articles to Hebrew journals, such as *Hatoren, Ha'olam,* and *Hado'ar.* In 1930 she married Dr. J. Winternitz of Prague, another misbegotten alliance. In 1941 she was deported to Teresienstadt, where she perished in 1943.

Reference Sources

Balin, Carole, *To Reveal Our Hearts: Jewish Women Writers in Tsarist Russia* (New York: Hebrew Union College Press, 2000).

Encyclopedia Judaica (Jersualem: Keter, 1971).

Harari, Yehudit, *Ishah ve'em beYisra'el* (Tel Aviv: Masada, 1959).

Kressel, Getzel, ed., *Leksikon Sifrut ha'Ivrit badorot ha'ahronim* (2 vols.) (Mehaviyah: Sifriyat Po'alim, 1965–1967).

Rokem, Galit Hasan, Shirley Kaufman, and Tamar S. Hess, eds., *The Defiant Muse: Hebrew Feminist Poems* (New York: Feminist Press, 1999).

Rosenthal, Morris, *A Woman's Voice: Sarah Foner, Hebrew Author of the Haskalah* (Wilbraham, Mass.: Daily International, 2001).

Zierler, Wendy, "Anda Pinkerfeld-Amir," in *Literature of the Holocaust,* ed. S. Lillian Kremer (New York: Routledge, 2002).

INDEX

INDEX